Proper Words in Proper Places

Dialectical Explication and English Literature

By the same author:

Daniel Defoe's Moral and Rhetorical Ideas
Presenting the Past: Philosophical Irony and the Rhetoric of Double Vision
from Bishop Butler to T. S. Eliot
Daniel Defoe: Contrarian
Imperial Paradoxes: Training the Senses and Tasting the Eighteenth Century

Proper Words in Proper Places

Dialectical Explication and English Literature

Robert James Merrett

 FriesenPress

One Printers Way
Altona, MB R0G 0B0
Canada

www.friesenpress.com

ISBN
978-1-03-918754-2 (Hardcover)
978-1-03-918753-5 (Paperback)
978-1-03-918755-9 (eBook)

1. LITERARY CRITICISM, MODERN, 18TH CENTURY

Distributed to the trade by The Ingram Book Company

Testimonials for
Proper Words in Proper Places

JOHN BAIRD, UNIVERSITY OF TORONTO: "'Proper words in proper places' may sound obvious, even trite, as a definition of style, but there is little that is obvious and nothing that is trite about this book, which analyses works from the 17th to the 20th century to demonstrate the protean nature of language, written or spoken, straightforward or oblique, always essential to the public sphere but ultimately and essentially private."

FRANS DE BRUYN, UNIVERSITY OF OTTAWA: "Robert Merrett offers in *Proper Words in Proper Places* a clearly argued and powerfully engaged meditation on reading, arguing for a renewed conception of literary history and genre to serve present-day readers and students of literature."

APRIL LONDON, UNIVERSITY OF OTTAWA: "*Proper Words in Proper Places* offers a bracing interdisciplinary examination of the dialectical thinking that reanimates the principles of Renaissance humanism in diverse works from the long eighteenth to the early twentieth century".

KATHERINE FAIRPLAY QUINSEY, UNIVERSITY OF WINDSOR: "IN this era where 'proper words in proper places' have more importance than ever, Rob Merrett has given us a valuable reminder of the present power of language as it still shapes thought and society, redefining and reawakening humanist perspectives and showing their crucial applicability in today's world of instant and explosive communication—and miscommunication. This is a delightful and probing book reawakening critical sensibilities much needed."

In Memoriam

Paul Kent Alkon
(1935–2020)

Mysteriously, we continue to read without a satisfactory definition of what it is we are doing.

Alberto Manguel, *A History of Reading*

Literary history differs from history because the works it considers are felt to have a value quite different from and often far transcending their significance as a part of history. In other words, literary history is also literary criticism.... It seeks to explain how and why a work acquired its form and themes and, thus, to help readers orient themselves. It subserves the appreciation of literature. The function of literary history lies partly in its impact on reading. We write literary history because we want to explain, understand, and enjoy literary works.

David Perkins, *Is Literary History Possible?*

Table of Contents

Acknowledgments

Alberto Manguel tells of the many forms of writing and reading in world cultures. Peoples have written on the walls of caves and temples, on rock cliffs and burial plinths as well as on papyrus, cloth, and diverse kinds of paper. There are so many forms of inscribed mediations that it is impossible to arrive at a singular definition of what humans do when we read, its multiplicity dissolving into mystery. David Perkins holds that chronologies cannot apply to the history of reading. In orienting readers to formal themes of texts, literary criticism, since its goals are cyclical and evolving, resists the objective principles of historical writing. *Proper Words in Proper Places: Dialectical Explication and English Literature* confronts, in practical criticism, Perkins's paradox that literary history is theoretically impossible but pedagogically necessary.

His dialectic of the impossibility and necessity of literary history has led me to probe the coexistence of classical and Christian allusions in major and minor texts published between 1670 and 1920, one result being to examine the perpetuity of Renaissance humanism in English literature. Analyses of traditional and experimental rhetoric in my texts confirm how *the long eighteenth century* offers, according to Neil Postman, a bridge to later times; the double vision of the humanities shows how the liberal arts enlighten contemporary moral issues. In diverse models of reading, my chapters convey how mixed literary genres invite us to create unique textual memories as our readings unfold.

Forty-five years of teaching at the University of Alberta have led me to illustrate methods that may serve students and faculty to develop pedagogical styles. I was early inspired by the dialectic practised by Paul Fussell, Wayne Booth, and Irwin Ehrenpreis. In Fussell's *The Rhetorical World of Augustan Humanism: Ethics and Imagery from Swift to Burke* (1965), literary humanism entails arguing in images; in Booth's *The Rhetoric of Fiction* (1961), prose structures clarify the humanities' investment in complex techniques that map readers' relations with implied authors and unreliable narrators; in Ehrenpreis's *Literary Meaning and Augustan Values* (1974) and *Acts of Implication: Suggestion and Covert Meaning in the Works of Dryden, Swift, Pope, and Austen* (1981), imagination exercises allusive, analogical, symbolic, and inferential thinking. Augustan humanism conveys how readers may celebrate oblique and properly unresolved argumentation.

In adopting this view, I have learned from many scholars: I owe much to Michel Baridon, Tom Cleary, Mark Davies, Milan Dimić, Susanne Hagemann, Robert Hopkins, Haydn Mason, François Moureau, Bill New, Serge Soupel, and Joseph Schwartz. R.D. McMaster explained the influence of eighteenth-century authors on nineteenth-century culture, while Evelyn Hinz taught me how to voice interdisciplinary insights in plain language. The following colleagues have improved this volume with comments: John Baird, Frans de Bruyn, Isobel Grundy, April London, Don Nichol, David Oakleaf, Tiffany Potter, Katherine Quinsey, and Peter Sabor. I much appreciate Lu Ziola's skills in managing computer files.

R. J. M.
Edmonton, Alberta
Spring 2024

Introduction

My title, *Proper Words in Proper Places*, comes from "A Letter to a Young Gentleman Lately Enter'd into Holy Orders," written with pedagogical acuity by Jonathan Swift (1667–1745) on 9 January 1719/20.[1] In challenging ecclesiastical and theological obfuscation, Swift addresses a young cleric about speech and writing ineffectually voiced from pulpits. He exposes lexical and syntactical affectations that fail congregations who need to be persuaded to apply moral truths to daily life. The rush for preferment that stunts clerics' "Improvement of their Minds" leads them to forget sound oratory, grammatical rules, and elocution crucial to memorable delivery of sermons. To Swift, many preachers display "a certain ungratious Manner, or an unhappy Tone of Voice" and, lacking "the least Conception of a Style, ... run on in a flat kind of Phraseology, often mingled with barbarous Terms and Expressions, peculiar to the Nation." Since they evade their "Wants upon this Head," he urges that "Proper Words in proper Places, makes the true Definitions of a Style." While orality should address "*common Men*" in terms of "*common Life*," he feels that "Professors in most Arts and Sciences, are generally the worst qualified to explain their Meanings to those ... not of their Tribe." Thus, he spurns the jargon of law, pharmacy, surgery, and theology. Since "a Divine has nothing to say to the wisest Congregation of any Parish in this Kingdom, which he may not express in a manner to be understood by the meanest among them," he need not discuss "*Omniscience, Omnipresence, Ubiquity*." To Swift, "many Terms used in Holy Writ, particularly by St. *Paul*, might with more Discretion be changed into plainer Speech, except when they are introduced as part of a Quotation." Oddly, the clergy are habituated to the opposite of technical jargon: "young Divines" in "fear of being thought Pedants" adopt "*Polite Conversation*" involving "a quaint, terse, florid Style, rounded into Periods and Cadencies, commonly without either Propriety or Meaning."

If Swift's linguistic sense has been faulted for upholding the seventeenth-century wish to standardise the English language as an institution based on prescribed rules in orthography, pronunciation, and syntax, this view is overstated, judging by what he tells his clerical addressee:[2]

> our *English* Tongue is too little cultivated in this Kingdom; yet the Faults are nine in ten owing to Affectation, and not to the Want of Understanding. When a Man's Thoughts are clear, the properest Words will generally offer

themselves first, and his own Judgment will direct him in what Order to place them, so as they may be best understood. Where Men err against this Method, it is usually on purpose and to show their Learning, their Oratory, their Politeness, or their Knowledge of the World. In short, that Simplicity without which no human Performance can arrive to any great Perfection, is no where more eminently useful than in this.[3]

To Swift, expressive voicing is natural, not dependent on formal learning or social conformity. A humanist who decries clerical abuse of "heathen philosophers," he finds Plato (428–348 B.C.) and Aristotle (384–322 B.C.) finer commentators on the gospels and Christian ethics than Demosthenes (384–322 B.C.) and Cicero (106–43 B.C.), orators whose passionate eloquence is often mistaken for models of pulpit oratory. A clue to Swift's humanist resistance to fine rhetoric is found in his preference for natural reason over rationalism and in his promotion of combined pathos and reasonableness in preaching. In treating language as an institution with relatively stable grammatical and lexical rules that resist fashionable idioms and casual slang, he upholds the Anglican middle way, his dialectic of heart and head belittling the intellectualism of atheists, free-thinkers, and enthusiasts. Granting that standards of learning and communication ebb and flow, he says of the changing relations between lay and clerical learning that

> whoever knows any Thing of three or four Centuries before the Reformation, will find the little Learning then stirring was more equally divided between the English Clergy and Laity than it is at present. There were several famous Lawyers in that *Period*, whose Writings are still in the highest Repute, and some *Historians* and *Poets* who were not of the *Church*. Whereas now a days our Education is so corrupted, that you will hardly find a young Person of Quality with the least Tincture of Knowledge, at the same time that the Clergy were never more learned, or so scurvily treated.[4]

Since philosophers are no better teachers than laymen, Swift boasts he has been "better entertained, and more informed by a Chapter in the *Pilgrim's Progress*, than by a long Discourse upon the *Will* and the *Intellect*, and *simple* or *complex Idea's*." Promoting literary texts as models of humane learning, he advises clergymen to speak sermons "from the heart without witty conceits." One of his humanist tenets is that, since knowledge and probability are mutually reciprocal, clergymen should value the dialectic of certainty and mystery as well as that of head and heart. In discussing the origins of Renaissance humanism and the paradoxes inherent in dialectic, he tells clergy not to presume on their interpretive powers:

> I do not find that you are any where directed in the Canons or Articles, to attempt explaining the Mysteries of the Christian Religion. And indeed since Providence intended there should be Mysteries, I do not see how it can be agreeable to *Piety, Orthodoxy* or good *Sense*, to go about such a Work.

> For, to me there seems to be a manifest Dilemma in the Case: If you explain them, they are Mysteries no longer; if you fail, you have laboured to no Purpose ... neither is it strange that there should be Mysteries in Divinity as well as in the commonest Operations of Nature.[5]

Murray Cohen explains how Swift's dialectical sense of mystery and fallibility affects readers of *A Tale of a Tub* (1704), *Gulliver's Travels* (1726), and *A Modest Proposal* (1729). To Cohen, Swift, in these texts, targets people who "completely and literally" claim omniscience, using "language efficiently, as if it consisted of objects ... or consisted of objective propositions. The reader's alternative to being implied and totally mirrored by the satire is to read differently, to recognize the mental habits that lead, miserably, to literalization." Swift offers "us the maddening experience of translating likeness into identity, metaphor into fact, possibility into idealized actuality. His literary language, even when not antagonistically satirical, works by deidealizing, by undressing illusions. He would have us deny a self-sufficient definition of man as *animal rationale* for one that designates and values process and possibility, *animal rationis capax*."[6]

Swift valued the Renaissance double vision of Desiderius Erasmus (1466–1536), the Dutch Catholic priest and scholar; of John Colet (1467–1519), the English educational pioneer who inspired followers to make scripture their guide; of François Rabelais (c. 1494–1553), the monk and Greek scholar whose satire employed bawdy jokes and grotesquerie; and of Miguel de Cervantes Saavedra (c. 1547–1616) who mocked chivalric romances and depicted life in everyday speech. As John Hale says, fifteenth-century humanism addressed the secular human condition through classical texts: grammar effectively mastered exemplary texts and made speech and writing "adaptable to different themes and audiences"; history was thought to yield "examples of behaviour to shun or follow"; and poetry induced desires "to imitate the virtues of the heroes of epic literature." Above all, moral philosophy was appreciated for stressing "the high standards of personal behavior that were expected of the responsible citizen." To humanists, the purpose of education was to facilitate contact with the past, which would enrich life in the present; they linked education to conduct, saw "authors in the round rather than as providing snippets for discussion," and tracked the sources of secular literature and Christianity. Colet's exegesis of the *Epistles to the Corinthians* is a model; it tells how their form and language were conditioned by St Paul's view of those to whom they were sent. Colet sets Paul in the context of Roman civilisation in the early years of Christianity, so he speaks "almost as directly to the students of Oxford as he had spoken to the Corinthians - to bear witness from the beginnings of the church and to encourage personal reflection instead of being used as the excuse for a display of erudition." Thus, Colet displaces "scholasticism, the matter and manner of medieval university teaching," that was restricted to "training the mind without affecting the heart."[7]

Like Swift, Edmund Burke (1729–1797) thought "No sound ought to be heard in the church but the healing voice of Christian charity." He despised spectacular sermonizing, since sympathy naturally arises from

> the unstable condition of mortal prosperity, and the tremendous uncertainty
> of human greatness; because in those natural feelings we learn great lessons;
> because in events like these our passions instruct our reason; because when
> kings are hurl'd from their thrones by the Supreme Director of this great
> drama, and become the objects of insult to the base, and of pity to the good,
> we behold such disasters in the moral, as we should behold a miracle in
> the physical order of things. We are also alarmed into reflexion; our minds
> … are purified by terror and pity, our weak unthinking pride is humbled,
> under the dispensations of a mysterious wisdom.

To Burke, religious and aesthetic evolution equally inform moral sentiments. Proud "to know, that man is by his constitution a religious animal," he upholds Renaissance humanism: "the generosity and dignity of thinking of the fourteenth century … We know that we have made no discoveries; and we think no discoveries are to be made, in morality; nor many in the great principles of government, nor in the ideas of liberty, which were understood long before we were born." Society is a partnership in science, art, and ethics: "As the ends of such a partnership cannot be obtained in many generations, it becomes a partnership not only between those who are living, but between those who are living, those who are dead, and those who are to be born." Revolutionaries would secure the citizen and the state *tout d'un coup*, evading and slipping aside from difficult problems. But Burke upholds a dialectic common to most authors studied in this book:

> [Difficulty] has been the glory of the great masters in all the arts to confront,
> and to overcome; and when they had overcome the first difficulty, to turn
> it into an instrument for conquests over difficulties; thus to enable them to
> extend the empire of their science; and even to push forward beyond the
> reach of their original thoughts, the land marks of the human understanding
> itself. Difficulty is a severe instructor set over us by the supreme ordinance
> of a parental guardian, who knows us better than we know ourselves, as
> he loves us better too. *Pater ipse colendi haud facilrm esse viant voluit.* He
> that wrestles with us strengthens our nerves, and sharpens our skill. Our
> antagonist is our helper. This amicable conflict with difficulty obliges us to
> an intimate acquaintance with our object, and compels us to consider it in
> all its relations. It will not suffer us to be superficial.

The Latin sentence from Virgil's *Georgics*, together with allusions to Horace, Juvenal, Erasmus, and Cervantes, confirm Burke's Christian reliance on classical texts.

Among modern commentators who adapt the humanism of Swift and Burke to criticism of professional and technological education are Martha Nussbaum, the philosopher, and Neil Postman, the cultural critic. The former sees radical changes "in what democratic societies teach the young, and these changes have not been well thought through." Bent on "national profit, nations, and their systems of education, are heedlessly discarding skills that are needed to keep democracies alive." The liberal arts model is "relatively strong" in élite institutions but severely limited "in this time of economic hardship" because champions of economic growth "more than ignore the arts"; they fear them since "a cultivated and developed sympathy is a particularly dangerous enemy of obtuseness, and moral obtuseness is necessary to carry out programs of economic development that ignore inequality." To Nussbaum, "political struggle for freedom and equality must first of all be a struggle within each person, as compassion and respect contend against fear, greed, and narcissistic aggression." Society needs critical voices to create a culture that values individuality and collective accountability. Without "the skills of imagining and independent thinking" that liberal arts foster, society will not renew itself through innovation.[8]

Postman claims that eighteenth-century literary culture forms a bridge to the present, repeating the humanistic tenet that progress is "the business of the heart, not the intellect." To Postman, reason, "when unaided and untempered by poetic insight and humane feeling, turns ugly and dangerous." He repeats the warning of Matthew Arnold (1822–1888) that "faith in machinery" is our "greatest menace." Postman cannot think of a "single technology that did not generate new problems as a result of its having solved an *old* problem." New technologies alter "the structure of discourse." The Internet and social media are changing the function of conversation and community. While "the relationship of language to thought and reality" is "a preoccupation of postmodernism," it forms no "break with the past" since enlightenment thinkers were not naive. While they held that "non-words could be represented with approximate verisimilitude by words," they knew that the "process of making meaning from a text involves as much withholding meanings as adding them" and saw that "the rules that govern when it is appropriate to do either is at the core of reasonable interpretation."[9]

Swift's pulpit oratory conveys how personal and public reading might facilitate pedagogy and learning. His satires exploit the complexities of reading; they ask readers to undertake mental rewriting and to see why a heightened awareness of the multiple operations of language is required in that process. To Alberto Manguel, "Mysteriously, we continue to read without a satisfactory definition of what it is we are doing."[10] So, readers must be humble before reading's dialectical paradoxes: individual readers are provoked to belong to an imaginary community and to realise that authored narratives give and withhold, reveal and hide. They must more than accept the dialectic of reason and uncertainty; they must enjoy it. To Wolfgang Iser, literary works entail reading artistic and aesthetic poles; artistic poles are made by authors, aesthetic ones are "the realization accomplished by the reader." Polarity means that literary works are identical neither with texts, nor with their realisation. It is the "convergence of text and reader" that "brings the literary work into existence, and this convergence can never be precisely pinpointed, but must always remain virtual, as it is not to be identified either with the reality of the text or with the individual disposition of the reader." Iser trusts that reading endows literary works with a dynamic character, tracing his reader-response theory back to Laurence Sterne (1713–1768) and *Tristram Shandy* (1759–1766). Sterne's Menippean fiction engages readers' imaginations so that they will experience reading as pleasurable only when active and creative. To stimulate this participatory experience, *Proper Words in Proper Places* studies how sentences interact in a range of literary texts to deepen discursive implications.[11]

Explicated texts contribute diversely to readers' awareness of the dialectical complexities of language. Geoffrey Harpham contextualises this sense when telling how, in the past two centuries, philosophy has dominated philology and modified traditional humanism. As he says, when "we look closely at language, we see not simplicity but a warren of interlaced elements, codes and levels, and mysterious horizons beyond which it cannot venture." His humanist stance on language is validated in my chapters: to Harpham, tradition holds that language is the "defining achievement or attribute of the human species, an inborn capacity that enables human beings to exercise legitimate dominion over the rest of creation, and defines them as distinct from brutes." Yet, influential thinkers presume language may be treated as a rational science apart from humans. Hence, the absolute statements of Martin Heidegger (1889–1976): we neither possess the language we speak nor initiate discourse. Language speaks itself; speakers are spoken by language: postmodernism refutes the self-mastering subject, calling it "an illusion, an aftereffect, a mirage generated by language."[12]

If linguistic humanism has been unsettled, literary history has similarly been challenged. Robert Darnton shares Manguel's sense of mystery. To Darnton, there is no "strategy for understanding the inner process by which readers make sense of words. We do not even understand the way we read ourselves despite the efforts of psychologists and neurologists to trace eye movement and to map the hemispheres of the brain." Critics, Darnton says, whether seeking deep structures or analysing systems of signs, "increasingly treat literature as an activity rather than an established body of texts." Since "a book's meaning is not fixed on its pages" but "construed by its readers," their response is the basis of literary analysis. By contrast, the methods applied to defining and illustrating the history of reading have proved futile, given incomplete data about readership, libraries, and the book trade along with indeterminate contexts regarding literacy, generic history, and bookshops.[13] Yet, literary history helps teachers develop students' aesthetic pleasure. As David Perkins says, it treats works "felt to have a value quite different from and often far transcending their significance as a part of history. In other words, literary history is also literary criticism.... It seeks to explain how and why a work acquired its form and themes and, thus, [helps] readers orient themselves. It subserves the appreciation of literature. The function of literary history lies partly in its impact on reading. We write literary history because we want to explain, understand, and enjoy literary works."[14]

Challenges in promoting humanism and liberal arts education are illustrated by the disagreements of two major apologists for the humanities, George Grant (1918–1988) and Northrop Frye (1912–1999). They were preoccupied with changing definitions of liberalism. Grant asserted that society does not debate what it concerns a human being to know since mastery of nature by technology is assumed to be the purpose of education. So monolithic is society's assumption, so pervasive the ideology of liberalism which expresses that view, that the question about knowing cannot be raised seriously, the motive of wonder being ever more subsidiary to the motive of power. In "The University Curriculum" in *Technology and Empire*, Grant holds that, since positivism dominates life, institutions cannot examine themselves or be tested by moral ideals. Arnold's aesthetic philosophy of sweetness and light has been so corrupted by capitalism that universities merely aim to turn out personnel to run society, thereby devaluing liberal processes of learning. Since universities claim a utility that upholds private and public corporations, power displaces the wonder of science and learning: liberalism is no more than the propaganda of technology generated by *multiversities*. Agreeing with Arnold that humanist education in the antique world sought by free insight the essence of collective life, Grant stresses that this leisured education confronted dialectical tensions between human and non-human perspectives. But current debate about moral purpose yields to statistics and empiricism. Bitterly, Grant asserts that humanities teachers have vitiated their disciplines by professional scepticism. He blames historicism for not defying complacencies about progress, condemning non-evaluative analysis in the humanities, which he attributes to Frye. Grant says humanities professors evade social relevance by preaching the sufficiency of liberal knowledge and promoting antiquarianism. They have lost the authority to address immediate and ultimate meanings by adopting unassailable, opaque expertise. Claiming that liberalism legitimates technological society by subjecting human excellence to the dogma of the powerful in society, Grant foresees the humanities subsiding beneath the performing arts since the humanities are submitting to a curriculum that guarantees there can be no real criticism of the university or of the society it ought to serve.[15]

Frye's view of liberal education in *Divisions on a Ground* is optimistic: an idealist, he holds that cultural vision will reform society by universities which form counter-environments. True scholars are detached but not withdrawn from life so that they may advance classless society as culture's final embodiment. Frye concedes that advanced knowledge is unintelligible to citizens. What liberal arts education can do is to free them to the power of articulacy in confronting the confusion of modern life. Stressing the reciprocity of word and idea, he insists students be taught the instrumentality of language: the university's mission is to foster the conditions under which literature may be appreciated. Thus, he defends a phenomenon that cannot be thought of as progress and that requires leisure (scholarship's semantic root). Despite this aim, he presents liberal education in individualistic terms: leisure is less conduct than the self-conscious freedom to weigh conduct with personal goals. Freedom is less the privilege of not having to work than the choice to work in the light of a rational conception of self and society. Opposing Arnold's middle-class ideology, he denies that education is preparation for work. Education to real life does not adjust students to social illusions. Frye approaches Grant's institutional criticism when alleging that faculty have adopted leisure-class norms. He despises the professional autonomy that lets them think upper-level teaching preferable to service instruction: research-minded professors who think teaching a burden betray the dialectic of participation and detachment that is vital to encouraging society to criticise itself.[16]

Proper Words in Proper Places promotes traditional literary studies while conceding that disputes in the humanities have eroded rhetoric, grammar, semantics, etymology, speech-act theory, and discourse analysis. Yet the latter are vital to aesthetic experience. What pedagogy may have lost is awareness of dialectical tension between spoken and written words and understanding that expression operates differently when vocalised and printed. Thus, I highlight diverse kinds of literary learning that derive from cultural pluralism, recalling the range of philological criticism open to students. I promote figures of speech such as hyperbole and bathos while showing that metaphor is a natural principle of speech. I also illustrate the lexical differentiation in loan words taken from Latin, French, and other tongues at various and multiple occasions; the structure of the vocabulary and cognate terms; the influence of science and technology on the lexicon; archaisms from scriptural and canonical texts that evade contemporary signification; the coexistence of inflected and uninflected syntax in normal word order and grammatical inversions; and the broadening and narrowing of reference in allusiveness.

Proper Words in Proper Places avoids the elitism of *Englishness* by upholding dialectic in liberal arts education, which includes the training of leaders and the provision of disinterested learning to the general public. A foundation of professions, liberal education is supposed to renew common sense in the organisation of daily life. If opposing otherworldliness, it regulates society by ultimate questions and tests sectarianism by wider perspectives. Informing national identity, it demands cross-cultural ideas. This complexity shapes what individuals pursuing liberal arts education learn: they study the rules of artistic expression in different media; the conventions governing effective speech, writing, and thinking; the history of institutional, literary, and metaphysical discourse; the principles guiding the moral and spiritual development of individuals and society; the political structure of countries, nations, and empires; and the reasons why learning requires continuous rediscovery of the past. Such claims may well make us wonder how institutions that function as corporate multiversities could integrate the fine arts, humanities, and social sciences pedagogically. Still, critics aver that disciplinary fragmentation and professionalism belittle holistic education.

Proper Words in Proper Places crosses boundaries since texts adopt the sister arts of painting and music among other genres. Their diversity is unified by exploiting verbal, situational, and dramatic ironies, arising from the pluralism with which words operated in the long eighteenth century. Committed to paradoxical sense development and scriptural, pictorial, musical, and theatrical allusions, the texts powerfully radiate personal and social issues. My eight chapters qualify the nature of discourse and explication by showing how deliberative, judicial, and ceremonial rhetoric enter the realm of narrative rhetoric, no matter the literary form.

The first chapter presents the fusion of epic and mock-heroic modes in Augustan narrative poems by poets whose theological sensibilities lent them authority to write as political and social critics. Poet Laureate and Historiographer Royal, John Dryden (1631–1700) upholds the Divine Right in *Absalom and Achitophel* in witty sequences of sacramental terms that mix comedy, invective, biblical allegory, church history, and political ideology. In *Eloisa to*

Abelard, Alexander Pope (1688–1744), a marginalised Catholic, fashions a monologue that moves between erotic confession, rationalising self-exploration, and spiritual autobiography. In *The Rape of the Lock*, he uses classical epic and Catholic rites to mirror and distort society's death denial and to expose playfully its obsessive consumerism and narcissism.

The second chapter further details narrative hybridity. Emerging as a genre in the face of the greater production of religious and non-fictional secular texts, novels slowly won identity and respectability by appropriating such established forms as sermon, travelogue, letter, and essay. Henry Fielding (1707–1754) justifies his narratives by imitating legal and philosophical discourse as well as the picaresque of Cervantes. Other proto-novelists, such as Tobias Smollett (1721–1771) and Oliver Goldsmith (1728–1774), adopt modes of natural history and natural philosophy to depict urban and rural scenes and to challenge the market economy with communitarian and ecological perspectives that question society's institutional hierarchies.

Tensions between words and pictorial imagery and the mixed aesthetics of the sister arts occupy the third chapter. After surveying leading prose writers and major and minor poets, such as William Cowper (1731–1800) and Anna Seward (1742–1809), who debate the sensuous and spiritual appeal of George Frideric Handel (1685–1759), questions emerge as to the precedence of sense and sound: do words govern sound, does sound shape sense, or are both true? German-born Handel was lauded but not universally; he was denigrated and praised for contrary reasons. Conflicting views also arose in debates about the status of pictorial artists and about whether paintings are merely visual illusions or may be said to narrate, to speak, and to exploit synaesthesia. Since Samuel Richardson (1689–1761) and Fielding hold opposing views of pictorial history, they commission portraits on diverse principles and employ visual allusions to different effects, confirming that the novel's growth was far from simply progressive.

The fourth chapter relates theatre history to pedagogy. It treats *The Beggar's Opera* by John Gay (1685–1732) as self-reflexive meta-theatre, applying teaching contexts to this most performed play. Fusing high and popular culture, Gay farcically links politics, business, and high society, pretending to dignify criminal life in hilarious forms of bathos that demand intellectual flexibility from readers. The chapter then surveys tragedies and comedies between the times of William Wycherley (1641–1716) and Richard Brinsley Sheridan (1751–1816). Their treatment of libertinism and sentimental gentility exposes a growing reliance on narrative tropes. While Gay honours and ridicules Handel in his mock-opera, earlier and later playwrights, seeking to reform the stage or re-establish Restoration modes, weakened dramatic power by not satirising modish consumerism and imperial wealth with the energy of Dryden, Swift, and Pope.

The fifth chapter advances interdisciplinary methods by contrasting the biculturalism of an English and a French author. While the former, imitating Pope and Richardson, applies propaganda to support colonial pretensions in North America, the latter, who imitated the first-person narratives of Daniel Defoe (c. 1660–1731), developed experiments later adopted by English authors. The romantic epistolary novel of Frances Brooke (1724–1789) about settlers in Quebec dubiously celebrates the Conquest of New France, while Pierre Carlet de Chamblain Marivaux (1688–1763), who imitated the essays of Joseph Addison (1672–1719), creates autobiographies that treat narrative whimsically to amuse readers by unsettling mediation. Brooke's characters' narrating selves are inconsistent, their refined sentiments undoing their wish to plant English institutions in Canada. By contrast, Marivaux's picaresque mode advances the inward turn of narrative, his tropes of evasive self-awareness admired by English authors. Sterne learned from Marivaux how compellingly identity may dissolve in the act of narration.

The nineteenth-century novelists in chapter six follow predecessors' double vision about institutional reform and self-discovery. In presenting abusive and abused characters, they employ dialectic: class and educational and ecclesiastical hierarchies do not displace legal equality; civility balances callous self-centredness, yet economic power degrades humble people. The novels ask readers to identify with arrogant, anti-social, and unworldly weak characters. In *Emma*, the heroine presumes to direct society and Harriet Smith's future but is discomfited by a vainer woman and a dashing poseur who tortures his affianced. George Knightley, a landowning mentor, brings Emma to awareness modestly and humanely. While Jane Austen (1775–1817) suavely reveals the mixed motivation of sympathetic characters, Charlotte Brontë (1816–1855) writes passionately from the stance of Jane Eyre, an orphan victimised by male and female superiors. Subjected to dishonest, dogmatic, and snobbish individuals, her self-examination rarely achieves true spiritual insight. The Barchester novels focus on professionalism and politics in the established church. This institution is, as Anthony Trollope (1815–1882) thinks, infected by class. Paying lip-service to missionary welfare, it is distracted by the media. Still, Trollope defends ecclesiastical functions innovatively through the symbolic infusing of wine consumption.

The dialectic of E.M. Forster (1879–1970), whose novels are discussed in reverse chronology in chapter seven, covers tensions between religious sensibility and multiculturalism, desire for and brevity of spiritual vision, and hopes and frustrations of adventure. Nonetheless, *A Passage to India*, *Howards End*, and *The Longest Journey* follow Fielding, Austen, and Trollope in showing how idealism problematizes humanism. Sexual repression, recoil from materialism, and disgust with imperialism are sentiments assigned to sympathetic but disillusioned creatures. In dissecting faith and identity, Forster is a modernist who defined agendas for later novelists; seeing past acculturated individuality and gender hierarchies is necessary for personal growth that also requires defiance of cultural myths and renewal of humanism.

The final chapter, a coda, builds a biography from the difficult-to-trace bibliography of an educated cleric who sought to imitate the poets, novelists, and critics discussed earlier. He tried to forge an identity through publishing but failed to gain credentials for authorship because the reviewing system and publishing cartels divided along lines opaque to outsiders. The genres to which the tireless Alexander Bicknell (d. 1796) was obliged, by economic necessity, to put his hand —biographies, novels, histories, biblical commentaries, essays, poems, treatises, a play, and analyses of the sister arts—illustrate the book trade's hunger for materials. If a conservative and conventional thinker, Bicknell was alert to social trends by writing as a feminist sympathetic to forlorn actresses, critics sensationalising and degrading this sensitivity.

Thus, *Proper Words in Proper Places* presents texts diversely, ranging from the study of lexical items, semantic ironies, conceptual dialectic, and aesthetic allusiveness. Since language and literariness are institutions, the volume poses reflexive questions about them. One question involves reviewing the cooperation of spoken and written discourse. While speakers and writers are born into linguistic communities to which they cannot dictate, they may somewhat control how they speak and write since speech and culture are not monolingual: speakers employ more than one idiolect, and writers mix registers, idioms, and loan words from many languages. The linguistic tension between continuity and change is a major aspect of literary creativity since, while language may be viewed as a single institution, it entails others, such as government, law, and religion. Moreover, lexical archaism is a semantic principle that enables purposeful narrowing and broadening of meanings. Without the inherited formalities of public discourse, it would not be possible for authors to exploit the colloquialisms of daily speech. What further makes meta-language key to definitions of literary and pedagogical methods is that daily speech is illocutionary and metaphorical. Hence, we may ask *is daily speech poetic* and *is there a distinctive literary style*, questions Swift would have found both necessary and provocative.

In its critical pluralism, this volume explains many forms of discovery and knowing open to students of literature. These include explication of texts, histories of genres, analysis of mixed genres, comparative and interdisciplinary surveys, and historical contextualisation of the book trade. While literary theories have become increasingly contested, especially as regards political and aesthetic ideologies, eighteenth-century emerging genres reveal how engaging imaginatively critical experience may be. Most writers of the period opposed systematic or utopian thinking, making words work as fully as possible through various kinds of sense transference and dialectic. The chapters dealing with nineteenth- and twentieth-century texts describe the lasting effects of earlier satiric, ironic, and comic modes that collapsed distinctions between tradition and progress and low and high culture and that challenged colonial and nationalistic thinking. This is not to claim that the literary canon was never an institution closed to writers. Still, one set of motifs running through this book concerns theological and imaginative transcendence. The motifs raise such questions as who creates political, religious, and aesthetic laws and who, in applying them, claims to be above them. My explications touch on spiritual pride and authority to interest readers in the issue of how English literature is preoccupied with cultural pretensions. In sum, *Proper Words in Proper Places* unsettles notions of literary periods and renews pedagogy by promoting dialectical stances on narrative, irony and satire, the sister arts, natural history, and social norms. Far from upholding nationalism and periodicity, it offers literary history that is cross-cultural, interdisciplinary, and encyclopedic. Ultimately, it shows how eighteenth-century double vision was creatively adopted by writers of later times.

CHAPTER ONE
Poetry

Restoration and eighteenth-century poets often shared Swift's and Burke's humanist concept of the common sense of conversation. Like them, Dryden and Pope saw humanism not as a formal philosophy but as a method for presenting texts by joining scholarship on classical authors and the Church fathers. When they invite readers to enjoy lexical precision in the comic intricacies of the heroic couplet, they call for spiritual renewal and institutional reform of Christian society. They offer readers linguistic and rhetorical schemes that give diction cumulative powers that are both dark and light, sombre and humorous. To Dryden and Pope, words are phenomena with complex semantic histories; lexical items are instrumental to emotionally moving yet ironic discourse, their provenance arising from sacred and classical texts and from vernacular speech. They mix verbal registers to heighten and diversify tone. By employing ritual and secular terms and by mocking learned words, their highly inventive discourses inspire dialectical analysis. Their cumulative power of diction quickens textual memories with double vision; wordplay with Christian and classical allusions mixes archaic and contemporary expressions about politics and religion, generating comic implications and provocative ironies. The three poems explicated here deepen their implications by mingling genres: distinct kinds of narrative, they involve parody, mock-epic forms, and dramatic monologues which move between comedy and high seriousness, yielding curious yet startling analogies. Dryden's *Absalom and Achitophel* creates a dialectic of divine and secular rights, which performs heavenly transcendence and worldly justice. Pope's *Eloisa to Abelard* sets monastic commitment in conflict with romantic retreat, and his *Rape of the Lock*, introducing classical and theological models, exposes individual and social idolatry by means of moral sense.

Diction in *Absalom and Achitophel* (1681)

Operating analogy and typology, Dryden makes these tropes embody a dialectic of secular and religious ideas. But the schemes embodying those ideas have not met agreement. Emphasising "conventional seventeenth-century typology," one critic claims the poem gains nothing from "exhaustive analysis" since Dryden simply revised "biblical data to suit the circumstances of the Popish Plot and Exclusion Crisis."[17] To another, ties between devotional and political typology are real: "David's transformation from christic mildness to Jehovic authority" reflects the "divinity" of kingship, which guides the dialectic created between Judaic and Christian hermeneutical ways of giving history coherence through narrative foreshadowing and figural types.[18] Despite holding that Dryden integrated political and religious ideas, critics often subordinate one set to the other. One says Dryden was inspired not by "politics and hopes for scientific and secular progress" but by the "realm of the spirit," arguing that his poem radiates a distrust of the world as arena for "redemption and salvation."[19] Yet another critic claims that King Charles II (1630–1685) was the immediate audience of the poem, since its closing speech is a "very human performance, free of pretensions to divinity or even human reverence." To this critic, Dryden instructs the king while presenting him as a worldly hero.[20]

But lexical sequences bind politics and religion in poetic processes. In *Absalom and Achitophel*, abuses of political and religious ideas are complementary, as are implications from satire of the two orders. Diction clarifies how these orders are integrated in dialectical tensions, displaying the typological reconciliation of historical fact and spiritual truth. To K.G. Hamilton, Dryden's belief in poetry as plain discourse led him to insert into his verse "a rather unobtrusive word or phrase that is yet charged with structural significance."[21]

Dryden widens the gap between biblical and non-biblical words in his exordium. Word choice and collocations in the eighty-four lines introducing David, Absalom, and the Jews reveal that politics and religion are unintegrated. Not one alliterated word, namely, "pious," "Polygamy," "Priest-craft," "Promiscuous," or "prompted" is biblical. Far from conveying the Old Testament era, these plosives convey a modern, secular viewpoint. David's procreative habits are couched in non-biblical words such as "Succession" and "Progeny": their anachronism renders the Old Testament setting comically dubious. To Absalom, Dryden applies "Conscious destiny," "Imperiall sway," and "Foreign fields," phrases which, reminiscent of classical epic, imply that biblical allegory is no easy vehicle for politics. By applying non-biblical words, such as "Headstrong," "Moody," "pamper'd," and "debauch'd," to the Jews, Dryden turns allegory to bathos. The pejorative epithets suggest that, if Judaic typology is to apply to politics, it needs renewal. By exordium's end, when circumstances leading to the plot opposing David have been put in biblical and non-biblical words, "manag'd" set against "randome," "contemplation" against "Pimps," and "mildness" against "byast," connotations induce readers to study the allegory's comic mode for juxtaposing political and religious meanings.[22]

The exordium's conflicting verbal registers and ironic antitheses confirm that Dryden at first applies comic modes to typology. Since, David, "Israel's Monarch," procreates "after Heaven's own heart," the seeming harmony between king and God is undone by the clash between the non-biblical "Monarch" and biblical words, which suggests that the king has ignoble views of kingship, preferring to justify sexual appetite in biblical jokes rather than consider the figural basis of kingship. Because Absalom fights for "Kings and States ally'd to Israel's Crown," the non-biblical "States" implies his political and religious goals are discordant. The collocation of biblical and non-biblical diction in the phrases "Idoll Monarch" and "that Golden Calf, a State" reveals the Jews' discrepant political and religious values. The phrases imply that the English, far from viewing Charles and the constitution in orthodox terms, treat monarch and state as idolatrous Old Testament types. The verbal ironies mock society's poor sense of typology, anticipating the political and religious reconstruction the poem finally articulates.

Semantic playfulness is the ground on which Dryden erects lexical series that ultimately confirm typological relations between politics and religion, an effort evident in the word *grace*, which, appearing nine times as a noun and once as a verb, gains a climactic sense in David's speech. Its first denotation is secular. At line 29, it signals Absalom's elegant deportment. Yet the restriction of "*Paradise*" to a bodily denotation in the next line suggests that physical displaces spiritual grace. The second use occurs in the first of three couplets that emphasise the Jews' spiritual ingratitude: in the phrase "th' extent and stretch of grace," line 46 imports a physicality, stressing the English do everything *not* to deserve grace. That this religious grossness has political aspects appears in the ironic parallelism of line 48: "No King could govern, nor no God could please" them. Abusing grace is equivalent to despising monarchy. The involvement of politics with religion is as clear at line 526 where Dryden attacks the priesthood, "Aaron's Race," for pretending to "Reign" and base "Dominion" on "Grace." Chiding dissenting ministers for making grace a mask for clerical self-interest, he refuses to link grace to political theory. The next occurrence entails a permitted sense of the involvement of political and religious values. At line 580, he will not name the rabble who advanced the Popish Plot, those "Whom Kings no Titles gave, and God no Grace." The inversion in the first and the ellipsis in the second clause parallel kingly and divine favour without equating secular and divine benefits: by placing dissenters outside the pale of grace, Dryden theologically justifies withholding political honours from them.

Two uses of *grace* in the portrait of Corah, indicating the false doctrine and political unreliability of Titus Oates (1649–1705), further define the typological connection of political and religious values, showing it to be dialectical. At line 643, feigning that Oates's ignoble upbringing does not discredit his witness, Dryden recalls that the genealogy of St. Stephen's accusers was irrelevant because they were but the means of gracing the first Christian martyr.[23] This ironically secular use of *to grace* proposes that Oates's victims will receive grace despite his false witness. The second instance also effects political satire through biblical allusion. Line 648 says Corah has a "Saintlike Grace" since his face is the colour of church vermillion, shining as brightly as Moses's on receiving the ten commandments. This hyperbole reveals Oates has but the appearance of grace. The mock application of scriptural analogy, in exposing his debasement of political and religious truth, implies grace has a constitutional meaning since religious principle ideally underlies political conduct.

The primary meaning of the next instance, at line 831, in the elegy to Thomas Butler, 6th Earl of Ossory (1634–1680), stresses his achievements. But the poet's declaration he will for ever mourn the Earl, since ordained to do so, suggests that religious are close to secular denotations. For the elegy holds that the Earl's achievements were divinely inspired. There is no sense of the displacement of religion as in the earlier application of the word to Absalom. An ideal son and loyal subject, Ossory is eulogised for having been a military hero inspired by divine power. Absolom—James Scott (1649–1685), 1st Duke of Monmouth—deserves criticism because his military capacities imply filial and social ideals, but Ossory is praiseworthy given his actual political and religious commitments; the secular use of grace implies the doctrinal concept.

A like extension of secular meaning occurs on its eighth appearance, at line 865, in the portrait of Zadoc. Unlike sectarians who hide political guile under religious zeal, William Sancroft (1617–1693), Archbishop of Canterbury, scorns power and place. Yet religious ideals have advanced him to "*David*'s Grace"—to royal favour. The phrase implies harmony between church and crown; in bestowing favour, the king has a spiritual acuity not unlike God's. Since David respects political and religious integrity, the grace the archbishop receives, if primarily secular, implies spiritual purity. David's dialectical sense of grace explains why, at line 972, he denies that Achitophel—Anthony Ashley Cooper, 1st Earl of Shaftesbury (1621–1683)—owns any and judges gullible his natural son's belief that Achitophel does possess it. Given Monmouth's delusion that Shaftesbury, rather than his father, is truly concerned with "Religion and the Laws," Charles's insistence that Shaftesbury lacks grace affirms his own divinely charged responsibility for political and religious values. David's grace is ultimately defined by the word's appearance at line 1007 where it conveys his resolve to mete out law to rebels. In this, grace and law are equivalent. David recognises that, not having seen him operate the law, rebels do not believe he has the grace to do so. He also knows that, because they evade the implicit grace of the law, they will have to be blinded by it. He counts himself, like Moses, the mediator of grace unharmed by it, while he knows that, when rebels see the grace of the law in him, they will be destroyed by this divine emanation. David trusts that grace blesses him with divine power: leader of men, he likens himself to Moses and exponent of divine law to God. This double analogy testifies that David harmonises political and religious values while revealing Dryden's wish to oblige Charles to own up to his responsibilities and the spiritual imperatives of monarchy.

Key to defending King Charles are Dryden's covenantal terms, the "language of sacred anointment" essential to royalist typology.[24] Anointment gains force on four occasions. The first, "God's Anointed" at line 130, applies to anti-royalist clergy hypocritically anxious that Catholics may kill Charles with long-since invented guns, anachronism comically exposing dissenters' abuse of biblical covenant. Distracted by arms technology and obsessed by politics, they discard the figural rite of anointing. Line 265 reveals Achitophel's scorn for "Anointing Oyle." It appears in his contention that, had David not dared to respond to fortune's call at the Restoration, "heavens Anointing Oyle had been in vain." Using the rite to get Absalom to replace the king, Achitophel views anointment contingently. Similar irony stems from the third reference. At line 430, Achitophel, granting that God loved David since He anointed him king, glibly says David should do for Absalom what God did for David. Achitophel's false analogy subverts the rite by shunning the covenantal relation of political and religious values. The fourth reference, at line 584, conveys Dryden's stance. The positioning of "Heavens Anointed" between "wretch" and "dar'd to Curse" signals disgust at Shimei's sacrilegious contempt for the king. By announcing that Slingsby Bethel (1617–1697) curses what God hallows, Dryden implies the blasphemy of debasing the rite, thereby upholding the typology of monarchy and celebrating its sacramental significance.

The sequence in the biblical words, "ark" and "pillar," clarifies Dryden's covenantal stance. These words relate political and religious values to criticise excessively materialistic or spiritual use of scriptural reference. When Achitophel talks of "the Mouldy Rolls of *Noah's* Ark" (l. 302) in arguing that kings should be elected, he refers to one material ark for, in stripping its symbolism, he can mock the covenantal view of kingship. By contrast, Dryden refers to the Ark of the Covenant (l. 520) in his typological defence of national religion. Upholding the separation of the Levites from the ark recalls the 1662 Act of Uniformity's banishment of dissenting ministers. Besides countering Achitophel's debasement of biblical reference, this second use undermines the narrow spiritual hypocrisy of dissenters. Figuralism informs the third occurrence. At the end of his political essay, when he promotes reform rather than innovation, *ark* symbolises the holiness that gives the constitution eternal value. His urging that "our Ark" (l. 804) must not be touched stems from conviction that it conjoins "Divine and Humane Laws." This conjunction in the symbol of the ark advances a dialectical typology against the opposite relation of politics and religion upheld by Shaftesbury and the dissenters.

Dryden links political and religious imperatives by making *pillar* first signal false typology. Achitophel shakes "the Pillars of the publick Safety" (l. 176). His wish to rule or ruin the state opposes him to Samson, who heroically pulled them down. Lacking self-sacrifice, Achitophel is a false Samson. This implication is fortified by the false typology that lures Absalom. Besides addressing Absalom as a "second *Moses*" and "*Saviour*," Achitophel proclaims him the Jews' "cloudy Pillar" and "guardian Fire" (l. 233), alluding to the signs by which God led the ark and tabernacle out of Egypt and by which He appeared to Moses in the tabernacle. Achitophel identifies Absalom with pillars to render him divine. Against this blasphemy, Dryden, referring to loyal judges as "Pillars of the Laws" (l. 874), employs the word metaphorically, not typologically, to emphasise human aspects of the constitution. For the same purpose, he has David regard kings as the "publick Pillars of the State" (l. 953). The metaphor in David's use of pillar is stronger when he calls Absalom his "Young *Samson*" (l. 955), since he lacks political and religious integrity: as Dryden refuses to make Achitophel a type of Samson, so David denies Absalom this status. David's choice of architectural metaphor over typology condemns the inchoate spiritualising of hypocritical politicians and outlines the scope for legitimate typology. That his defence of ark and pillar symbolism relies on displacing the Samson typology illustrates the brilliant verbal intricacy with which Dryden integrates political and religious imperatives.

Repetitions of *godlike* confirm his application of typology; the analogy between David and God in this epithet affords scope to unify Old Testament and New Testament figuralism. At first, David is "Godlike" in siring "several Sons" (l. 14). The parallel between divine and royal fatherhood is strategically comic; it exculpates Charles yet conveys the simultaneity of all history. Absalom's justification of political ambition as "Godlike Sin" is less strategic and comic (l. 372); he misconceives divine nature to evade political sins. Loyalists view the king as a "Godlike Prince" (l. 823), Dryden calling him "God-like *David*" (l. 937), the monarch being God's vicegerent. Insisting David's followers "their Maker in their Master hear" (l. 938), Dryden applies the analogy cautiously: despite contrary claims, he never identifies David with God.[25] David's ethical appeal inheres in exercising typological caution. When rejecting parliamentary threats to established power and justice, he claims that "Gods, and Godlike Kings" inevitably protect loyal subjects (l. 997). While Absalom ignores this distinction, David preserves it in the parallel between godhead and kingship. With David's subtle application of the analogy, Dryden reiterates that the king is "Godlike" (l. 1030) since God has spiritually restored Charles. Far from betraying typological identification to give the king "Godlike powers in his own person," Dryden repeats *godlike*, implying that a true conception of God's covenant with humanity is inseparable from political tradition through similes, not through figural identification.[26]

Dryden's repetition of *god* offers crowning evidence that he renews typology by integrating politics and religion. As cited earlier, "No King could govern, nor no God could please" the Jews (l. 48). This line parallels faithlessness and unruliness. But Achitophel's use of the word marks an unwillingness to accommodate political to religious values. Persuading Absalom that God has endowed him with "Prodigious Gifts" to fit him for a wondrous reign (l. 377), he urges him to rely on the people since "God was their King, and God they durst Depose" (l. 418). His ideas are contingent not principled, anarchic not figural: he models politics on the Jews' rejection of the covenant, promoting faithlessness as a political rule. He repeats this speciousness when saying David cannot deserve to be called "Godly" if he deprives Absalom of the throne since "'Tis after God's own heart to Cheat his Heir" (l. 436). The warped view of covenant and false analogy between David and Absalom show Achitophel negating typology. The implications of Shimei's hypocrisy are similar: he pretends zeal for God to express hatred for the king (l. 586). Shimei's false worship and subversive politics arise from a refusal to relate divinity and monarchy. Dryden's condemnation of pragmatism in terms of the distorted relation of godhead and monarchy reappears in his criticism of the Jews for subordinating spiritual truth to contingency when they make "Heirs for Monarks" and decree "for God" (l. 758). To David, the debasement of God is inseparable from the abuse of monarchy: he knows that, if the Jews will not be satisfied with God, they will not be content with him (l. 988). His view of hierarchy inspires him to defend monarchical authority; his subordination to God leads him to safeguard political values with transcendent justice. His typological sense of God's covenant with the Jews protects David's regal power with divine ideas while cultivating spiritual humility.

His speech is climactic not because it embodies a contradiction between the king as "unprincipled politician" and as "image of God on earth" but because it addresses political and religious ideas from typological and personal standpoints and because verbal repetitions fuse satire and moral prescription, the king lessoning himself as well as the nation.[27] For evidence, David is as self-conscious in repeating political as religious words: consider *patriot*, which occurs thrice in his speech. He insists the name has degenerated, and its vulgar designation—a person who seeks by law to supplant the prince—has deceived Absalom into rebelling (l. 965). David understands the danger of verbal abuse to the state; he knows that patriot with its perverted, anti-figural sense has been rendered politically harmful by vulgar repetition. He redefines it by indicating its degeneration and reviling common usage: he classifies a patriot as a dupe, a fool, and a tool of politicians and the people (l. 968). He is clear that factional narrowing of the word's meaning involves religious hypocrisy: factions call patriots, who are but rebels, saints (l. 973). In reiterating patriot, David stresses that verbal repetition erodes the state and figural sense: his verbal repetition supports typology by attacking common usage. His reaction to the deceit entailed by patriot has positive implications by confirming the earlier claim that Achitophel had "Usurp'd a Patriott's All-attoning Name" (l. 179). Thus, Dryden clarifies the illicit conversion of the word into a slogan by linking it to religious affectation. While verbal sequence heightens the complementarity of his political and religious satire and shows that political words are abused on religious grounds, just as religious words are abused on political grounds, it proves he defends typology by making verbal repetition a theme in its own right.

The three most repeated political words to receive a typological defence are *right*, *government*, and *law*. Describing how Jews persecute the Jebusites, Dryden stresses that the more the English overlook the "Native right" of Catholics, the more they think them "God's enemies" (l. 91), probing why religious prejudice attaches to political inequity. A similar confusion is elicited by Absalom's changing ideas of rights. Resisting Achitophel's initial appeal, Absalom grants David's "unquestion'd Right" to govern (l. 317); he accepts his father as the "Faith's Defender." He grants that James, Charles's brother, is "Secure of Native Right" (l. 354) and that "Heavens Decree" gives himself no "Pretence to Royalty." Yet he alters his mind on hearing Achitophel will either force David to sell his "Right" (l. 405) or appeal to the people's "Right Supreme" to make kings (l. 409). Seduced by this false distinction between monarchical and popular rights and by Achitophel's anti-typological view that the Jews may depose their king since they have dared to depose God, Absalom agrees to be the popular candidate for the Crown, half-heartedly disavowing his non-existent right while agreeing that David has betrayed his own and the people's right (ll. 713–14). Absalom betrays political tradition since he is not enough committed to religious typology. This betrayal explains why, in his disquisition, Dryden holds that the law must be superior to kings and people if political rights are to be upheld (l. 764) and proposes that "private Right" exists only if sovereign sway does (l. 779). This cause makes him apply original sin to attack the "resuming Cov'nant" and its anti-traditional tenet that society may opt for natural rights. He applies the entail of Adam to argue that kings are images of God and that a reversion to natural rights undoes government. David's speech extends these religious attitudes to politics. Firstly, he justifies his own "Forgiving Right" (l. 944); secondly, he rejects parliament's right to depose the monarch (l. 980), insisting that the king's consent is integral to government; and thirdly, he announces his determination to exert regal authority and his conviction that this will lead the rebels to do him "Right" (l. 1017). Behind each instance of *right*, including this last adverbial usage, there lies a religious sense of political rights. When David says that rights are inseparable from divine dispensation, the poet remotivates the word by completing its interconnection of political and religious implications.

The repetition of *government* strengthens these implications. Firstly, Dryden claims that the Jews, while spurning its authority, force the Jebusites to submit to David's government (l. 93): political power masks religious intolerance. The satire is compounded since all factions debase the Eucharist: political differences, disjoined from sacramental doctrines, are matched, ironically, by uniform material self-interest. Sustaining this irony is the insistence that rebels undo government because "Impious Arts" seduce them into disloyalty (l. 498). The presentation of Shimei conveys how envy of the government induces Christian hypocrisy. As we saw, Shimei, a zealot, never curses except against the government (l. 590). He is a false disciple since he wields a "pious Hate" (l. 590) for "his Master" (l. 594) and loves only his wicked "Neighbour as himself" (l. 600). A false type of the Holy Ghost, he is found in the midst of those who gather together to decry monarchy. David's speech realises the typological implications of widespread hostility to government. Besides defending his governmental role (l. 977), he criticises "Pious Subjects" who sap his power while affecting to pray for his safety. He sees that, in presenting a Jacob instead of an Esau as heir to the throne, his subjects view him as an Isaac. Concern for true government makes him reject the restrictive Old Testament typology that irresponsible politicians exploit.[28]

Law and its cognates affirm Dryden's renewal of typology. Its occurrences in the exordium hint that David is above law: there are no bounds to his promiscuity (l. 5), and he prevents the law from punishing Absalom's excesses (l. 37). Still, his lawlessness is personal and domestic: it has few political repercussions. But Achitophel's lawlessness threatens the state. Formerly an exemplary judge, he dangerously wishes to pass Absalom's "doubtfull Title into Law" (l. 408). His counsel that Absalom rely on natural law and self-defence to excuse taking up arms to protect the "Sacred Life" of David (ll. 458–65) proves that he will abandon constitutional law and its covenantal foundation. The danger in his stance is explicit in Jonas's eagerness to make "Treason Law" and read statutes as validating rebellion (l. 582).[29] Against such legal abuse, David pledges to defend monarchy by committing himself to law. He resolves to make it force obedience on rebels (l. 991). Once reluctant to employ the "Sword of Justice," he sees that man's fallen nature renders law necessary (l. 1003) and that it rightly decrees the death of rebels. Accepting this necessity, he has his "Lawfull Pow'r" renewed (l. 1024); becoming the "Lawfull Lord" (l. 1031), he has his Crown blessed apocalyptically. His service to law entails typological confirmation of himself and his kingdom.

His speech fittingly ends *Absalom and Achitophel* since, in defining constitutional law, he obeys divine imperatives. His speech fulfils the poem's complementary political and religious implications by completing verbal sequences—dispatching negative and amplifying positive usages. Through the culmination of lexical sequences, Dryden defies resistance to the conjunction of political and religious values, embodying David's renewed typology. Confirming the speech as an index of David's typological sense is the balance between first- and third-person pronouns and possessive adjectives. This balance renders him assertive and modest in examining the rebels and himself: he is newly alert to his political power, but religious insight sensitises him to spiritual values. This balance adds to the rhetorical appeal of his speech, to its combination of judicial, deliberative, and ceremonial oratory: he judges opponents, defines political action, and specifies how the nation and he must exhort themselves to maintain their moral identity.

Given the rebels' abuse of names and praise, David enacts the constructive function of praise. Achitophel devalues it (l. 247), thinking it "barren" compared to power (l. 297). Yet he uses it to debauch Absalom (l. 312). While consigning lesser rebels to oblivion by not naming them (l. 569 ff.), Dryden praises loyalists by name. The rhetoric of David's speech creates and performs its own meaning. By completing verbal sequences and enhancing verbal repetition, the speech conjoins political and religious values, proving that David is concerned for "Church and State" (l. 930), for "Religion and the Laws" (l. 969). It is surely correct to see the poet deriving topics and ideals from rhetoric, if it is unhelpful to assign a "waning faith" in panegyric as a "serious kind" of poetry to Dryden.[30] Nor does it capture the poetic processes Dryden brings to a climax in David's speech to say they constitute "rhetorical bluff" and "sleight of hand."[31] Far from simply distancing Charles from blame, Dryden displays the king in a process of personal and spiritual self-criticism. Bruce King concludes that Dryden's "cultural and moral values emerge from the verse rather than being imposed on it," judging that *Absalom and Achitophel* places its subject in a "cosmic as well as a cultural dimension." Indeed, Dryden's lexical, semantic, and rhetorical processes join Old and New Testament typology to uphold a sense of "the simultaneity of all history."[32] Besides defending typology, his speech reveals the king to be turning himself via its articulation into a type of the prophetic king. By so presenting the king, Dryden implies his faith in the historical reality of the Messiah and Holy Spirit and in the apocalyptic future of The Revelation of St John. The "new time" (l. 1028) brought on by David's speech not only verifies Dryden's inclusive sense of typology but also realises his belief in the power of rhetoric and poetry to harmonise political and religious values and to confirm that typology.[33]

Emotional Dialectic in
Eloisa to Abelard (1717)

In *Eloisa to Abelard*, Pope humanely explores extreme forms of feeling and thinking in Eloisa's religious misconceptions and erotic narcissism. Her attempts to reconcile self, society, and God obliquely promote Catholicism. That she degrades theology by distorting the relation of time to eternity and of immanence to transcendence creates, despite her, positive implications about doctrine and liturgy. *Eloisa to Abelard* explores unorthodox thinking about divinity, laying out the abuse of sacramental rites with an intensity that draws on well-tested convictions.[34] This view of *Eloisa to Abelard* may seem unjust since it opposes Samuel Johnson (1709-1784), the formidable Christian critic who thinks the poem finally harmonises divine and worldly ideas.[35] However, setting aside Hoyt Trowbridge's study of Ovidian elements, which insists on the harmony of religion and eroticism in Eloisa's love, most commentators hold that the poem's tensions are not relaxed in Pope's argument.[36] In presenting a lively "picture of the struggles of grace and nature, virtue and passion," he does not say Eloisa's epistle reaches a state of religious resignation.[37] Its ending suggests that the poet's theology obliged him to make Eloisa an unreliable meditator.[38]

The final verses do not present her cogitations as religious; her imaginings are secular. She voices a gratifying sense of pathos rather than tests herself spiritually. Her claim that Abelard and she deserve sympathy from posterity suggests she is unmoved by faith. She is not contrite; she does not find herself or Abelard blameworthy. Since she is intent on self-exculpation, the former lovers are merely "hapless" (l. 343). Her sense that her love for Abelard is as "immortal" as his "fame" (l. 344) conveys a profane view of the afterlife. Her concession that future lovers will not imitate their love (l. 352) implies the unique pathos of their passion. Her final imaginings set aside immortal love since she directs mental energy at winning indulgence from mankind. Unable to pretend that Abelard and she will be models of erotic love, she is content to live in the imagination of later generations as an object of pity. She justifies indulging her passion by maintaining that it deserves heavenly indulgence too.

> From the full quire when loud Hosanna's rise
> And swell the pomp of dreadful sacrifice,
> Amid that scene, if some relenting eye
> Glance on the stone where our cold reliques lie,
> Devotion's self shall steal a thought from heav'n,
> One human tear shall drop, and be forgiv'n. (ll. 353–58)

Eloisa imagines a pious person, distracted in the Eucharist by pity for Abelard and herself, being forgiven. Her trust that pity wins heavenly favour sets aside divine love and the sacramental covenant between God and man. Yet Pope implies more than a sacrilegious comparison of human and divine love; Eloisa is complacent that God will justify the displacement of His love for mankind in His sympathy for Abelard and herself. If disregard for spiritual truth is evident in the pagan notion that her "pensive ghost" will be soothed to hear the rehearsal of her sad story (l. 365), the major irony of the paragraph is that she converts religious indulgence and sacramental truth to dignify her mortal memory in her own imagination. This is at one with her exploitation of dogma earlier: urging Abelard to write, she justifies this self-deceived plea by maintaining that

> Heav'n first taught letters for some wretch's aid,
> Some banish'd lover, or some captive maid. (ll. 51–52)

Displacement of scriptures and the religious primacy of writing rationalises unrealistic wishes for herself and Abelard. The repeated partitive *some* hides specificity as she tries to sustain the illusion of there being a divine sanction for erotic love. That she applies religious terms to her apology for love letters entails a reliance on divine authority and simultaneous wish to evade religious imperatives: by justifying love letters in terms of inspiration and faith—

> They live, they speak, they breathe what love inspires,
> Warm from the soul, and faithful to its fires, (ll. 53–54)—

she undermines spiritual values with sentimentality. Far from seeing erotic love on its own terms, she explains it by appealing to heavenly authority and rejecting that authority. Behind this inconsistency lies an assumption of omniscience and infallibility. Pretending to speak from a divine perspective, she evades her fallibility. When she insists Abelard's priestly words were so moving that, besides persuading her, they obliged heaven to listen (l. 65), her claim that God was moved by Abelard's rhetoric evades self-reflection. Unjustified omniscience is further shown by her claim that "truths divine" were "mended" by Abelard's tongue (l. 66). Confusing transcendent and immanent truth, she sets man over God. By subordinating praise of God to that of Abelard, she heightens her romantic sensibility. Yet supposition of heaven's fallibility reveals how prophane her worship of Abelard is: she dignifies passion and evades self-knowledge by inverting as well as displacing theology. She nearly acknowledges the blasphemy of her presumed superiority to divine truth when recalling the ceremony in which she took her vows as a nun. But rather than consider its spirituality, she stresses physical agency:

> As with cold lips I kiss'd the sacred veil,
> The shrines all trembled, and the lamps grew pale:
> Heav'n scarce believ'd the conquest it survey'd,
> And Saints with wonder heard the vows I made.
> Yet then, to those dread altars as I drew,

Not on the Cross my eyes were fix'd, but you. (ll. 111–16)

Obeisance to the veil exposes her pride in causing portentous signs and becoming heaven's cynosure. Confessing that eros, not grace, motivated her, she abuses divine omniscience: she says heaven doubted its conquest over her to degrade spiritual obedience and feel doubly superior in imagination. In telling how she approached the "dread altars" without religious awe, studied Abelard, and ignored the Cross, she reveals her need to set divine knowledge and monasticism below erotic love. Her reliance on institutional religion is perverse to the extent she wilfully displaces, inverts, and secularises religious ideas.

Pope draws ironies from Eloisa's discrepant affirmations and denials of orthodoxy. He heightens the discrepancies by making her an object of pathos. Her unreflective blurring of Christianity and Eros blinds her to the depth of her confusion; ultimately, she regards claims of faith and passion in total self-deception. On first reading Abelard's letter, she reacts profanely. It is as if the letter is an anti-Bible: she kisses Abelard's name, cherishes it though it is "fatal" (1.9), wishing it "ever unreveal'd." Worshipping it, she travesties the church's celebration of gospel revelation. If, like a priest, she reveres the Word, unlike one, she celebrates what is mortal and private. She manifests a gnostic impulse when, after pledging to exploit "holy silence" for the benefit of her heart's "close disguise," after claiming to adapt monasticism to secret purposes, she admits to letting ideas of God and Abelard exist "mix'd" in her heart (l. 12).

Ironies aggravate this mixture. Bent on equating God and Abelard, Eloisa sustains her intention only by abusing religious forms. Hoping for renewed correspondence with Abelard, she would transform religious lamentation to erotic sympathy:

> Tears still are mine, and those I need not spare,
> Love but demands what else were shed in pray'r. (ll. 45–46)

She trusts religious tears can be sexually tender. Despite this trust, she regrets the intrusion of amatory images into religious life. She laments that Abelard haunts her so much that acts of worship, symbolic rites, and meditation are no longer real (ll. 263–70). She bewails mingled divinity and eros she earlier cherished because of perceptual and conceptual disorientation. She glimpses but cannot defeat this self-induced confusion. The tears that drop as she tells her rosary are sensuous, not contemplative, conveying fallibility rather than meditation (l. 270). Her complaint that incense, music, and ceremony have lost ritual power through her obsession with Abelard tacitly admits that she has depended on liturgical forms beyond her blurring of faith and passion. The pathos of her confusion is deepened by the irony that, when sense assures her that worship reaches transcendence, images of Abelard signal damnation (ll. 275–76). Adding to this irony, Pope makes Eloisa confess in deep meditation—when faith, spiritual humility, and grace are operative—that she would appeal to Abelard to assist devils in taking her from God (l. 288). The irony more than shows she has shut herself off from reality by equating divine and erotic love: it proves she makes herself vulnerable to faithlessness. She calls for Abelard's "deluding eyes" to help blot out "each bright Idea of the skies" (1. 284); she exacerbates the gap between grace and guilt. Fruitless penitence and prayers (1. 286), far from alerting her to spiritual danger, are converted into a perverse laziness about disentangling religion and eros.

When trying to renounce Abelard, she continues in self-deception. She thinks separation from him will place her on the path to heaven; her prayer for "Divine oblivion of low-thoughted care" (1. 298) assumes she need not examine herself. Her notion of heaven, like her sense of love, is shallow. She shuns spiritual exercise by imagining heaven and love in pictures. That she does not test religion and eroticism against one another is clear when, in the midst of picturing her own death, she imagines Abelard making love to her when her soul passes to heaven (1. 324) and when, despite knowing death reduces us to dust, she remains obsessed with his beauty and hopes the saints in effecting his transfiguration will wrap him with a love like hers (1. 342). Eloisa is sadly naive about the afterlife since she entertains religious and secular ideas mindlessly. Her illusion that she is a paradigm of spiritual dying to Abelard and of love to saints in heaven inverts the relation of immanence and transcendence.

Dull to tensions between religious and secular love, Eloisa suffers them histrionically. Her abuse of theology stops her weighing religious and secular ideas. Hence, her attitudes to love and marriage (ll. 73 ff.). Owning the laws of secular love, she scorns marital convention: it is no divine institution. Granting affectedly that married women may possess *sacred* fame and social eminence, she evades relating religion and secularism by asserting that passion spurns worldly advantage. Ironically, this passion is monastic. She disclaims institutional standards of love by insisting that love is the sole reward of love (1. 84), but her view that love is a "jealous God," punishing those who *profane* him by visiting them with restless passion is also ironic. Not only does she seek fame through love only to be overtaken by restless passions, but her views of free love and a jealous god are incompatible: promoting secular love, she brings religious implications into her argument. She is unaware that hostility to worldly mores involves her in a paradoxical championing of free love: her contempt of the world stems from confusing religious and secular ideas. Her sense of mutual love as the state in which the soul is the chief agent in which nature is law (1. 92) appropriates religious conceptions. Her claim that erotic love can be fully satisfied, that there can be a perfect balance between possessing and being possessed, and that spiritual intuition precludes direct communication owes less to her feelings for Abelard than to her rejection of heaven. Her major inconsistency is that in promoting secular love she demeans society and covertly relies on monastic retreat. Erratic ideas undo her further. In begging Abelard to return to administer the convent (1. 129), she masks private feelings in public expressions of institutional concern. She calls Abelard to pastoral care by rehearsing the convent's origin. She praises its holiness, lauds Abelard's turning wilderness into "Paradise" (1. 134), and, despite earlier calling its walls "Relentless" (1. 17), thinks them "Hallow'd" (1. 133). She finds the building uncorrupted by the "false world" (1. 132); no fathers orphaned children by funding its decoration, and no misers donated "silver saints" to bribe heaven to ignore their irreligion (ll. 134–38). To this point, she faults religious hypocrisy, expressing concern for social welfare that harmonises with monastic integrity and devotional simplicity. Yet this balanced perspective is sustained only so long as she cares to mask her feelings. In asserting that without Abelard the convent is ineffectual, she is concealing personal motives. Insisting that Abelard alone reconciled everyone to religious seclusion (l. 145) and that he diffused a glory that brightened the convent's gloom, her celebration of him saps the grounds on which she praises the foundation. Saying that no one in the convent enjoys "divine contentment" and that all wear a "blank sadness" (ll. 147–48) counters remarks that "heav'nly-pensive, contemplation" (l. 2) and true vestals (l. 207) dwell there. The inconsistency proves that she deceptively gives public form to private feelings and reduces dialectic between religious and secular ideas for emotional reasons. If she becomes impatient with her deceit, accusing herself of the "pious fraud of am'rous charity" (l. 150), she does not connect public and private ideas. Denying the convent is a community, she luxuriates in imaginary relations with Abelard. Rioting in anti-spiritual fancies, she discredits meditation and retreat; obsession precludes a dialectic of public and personal values.

From the start, her inconsistencies convey a minimal sense of fallibility. In "tumult," she exclaims against the convent's dark walls. If she heightens its elemental horror as a strategy of self-exculpation, her remark that the convent emits "Repentant sighs, and voluntary pains" (l. 18) implies spiritual conduct governs material reality. The clash between emotion and self-justification is as evident when, after lamenting the rugged rocks out of which the monastery has been hewn, she notes that "holy knees" have worn them down (l. 19). After heightening the convent's elemental inhospitality, she conveys the dominance of spirit over matter.[39] Again, that saints' statues weep for nuns conflicts with her assertion that she has not become as unfeeling as stone (l. 24), since, in her words, stone need not symbolise insensitivity. Inconsistency about the convent's setting reflects her desire to rejoice in humanity uninhibited by spirituality. But, ironically, her sense of humanity is not as free of religion as she supposes. In describing her first encounter with Abelard, she cannot suppress an inevitable tension between religious and secular values; she insists on her guiltlessness yet reveals moral evasiveness. Recounting how she initially imagined him to be an angel, an "emanation of th' all-beauteous Mind" (l. 62), she reports that, once she enjoyed him as a man, she discarded angelic notions satisfied by "pleasing sense" alone (l. 70). That her reactions are excessive shows how fallibility affects her sense of the spiritual and sensual. Single-minded reactions confirm her avoidance of self-knowledge.

Admitting fallibility, Eloisa probes her outlook in a limited way. Saying she is "the slave of love and man" rather than "the spouse of God" (ll. 177–78), she does not admit the gap between knowing and willing. Telling that her prayer for divine help may be motivated as much by despair as piety (l. 180), she does not test her duplicity, being too easily contented with a paradox: she indirectly concedes that "frozen chastity" can harbour "forbidden fires" (1.182). Knowing what she ought to do, she does not will to do her duty: the antithetical way in which she explores her dilemma blurs spiritual and emotional values. She mourns the lover but does not regret the fault (l. 184); she repents former pleasures but is eager for more (l. 186); at one moment, she is mortified by her offence against heaven; at the next, she curses her innocence (l. 188). Her self-examination is specious because her terms of innocence are equivocal and because she luxuriates in her inconsistencies. She takes delight in confusing the grounds of self-examination. At one moment, she regrets the fact of her lover but is glad to have experienced erotic love. Next, she is sorry for this experience yet is excited by repentance to wish for illicit love. Again, her responsiveness to heaven leads her to decry enforced chastity and to expose her original sin. Her self-examination is implausible since she utters religious ideas and sustains erotic fancies without measuring the one against the other. That she can wish to be freed from sin while valuing it and that she can desire to love Abelard while rejecting the sinful experience of that love—

> How shall I lose the sin, yet keep the sense,
> And love th' offender, yet detest th' offence? (ll. 191–92)—

evidences a contrariness which, in addition to betokening little spiritual awareness of conduct and forgiveness, illustrates evasion of moral dialectic. Her view that "the hardest science" is "to forget" (l. 190) and her struggles to forget (l. 200) manifest a refusal to connect spiritual and physical life. Her pathetic contention that her heart is so deeply affected by love that her soul will not surrender its passion for Abelard unless enraptured by grace (l. 202) is exposed when she begs Abelard to be the agent of that grace. Her position that God is the only possible rival to Abelard (ll. 205–06) confirms that her awareness of tension between erotic and divine love is superficial. Her equation of Abelard and God proves that she has little sense of grace and that her appreciation of priestly mediation debases the priesthood.

Eloisa's notion of heaven is lost in her confusion of erotic and divine love. When contrasting her ghastly dreams to the visions of vestals, she betrays a pictorial and emblematic impression of heaven that avoids spiritual doubt. She conceives naively that the vestal who has visions totally forgets, and is forgotten by, the world (l. 208), and she holds, again naively, that a "spotless mind" enjoys "Eternal sunshine" in this life. Such notions permit her to heighten the pathos of her dilemma rather than connect it to immanence and transcendence. Her images of heaven are physical, given her weak sense of fallibility. She pictures grace and heaven in "golden dreams," "th' unfading rose of Eden," "divine perfumes," "heav'nly harps," and "visions of eternal day." These sensuous images do guide her conscience; they do not block her infatuation with "soft illusions" and "dear deceits" (l. 240). When she evokes the "roseate bow'rs, / Celestial palms, and ever-blooming flow'rs" (ll. 317–18), these emblems of heaven import no new spiritual insight, nor do they reflect a theological awareness. Matching inferior wishes, they do not represent the shape of spiritual experience since her sense of religious and secular ideas is feeble. Eloisa confuses herself in the struggle between grace and nature. Pope's consistent irony, while unsympathetic to her, invites readers to question her thinking and feeling and to examine her posturing with religious and secular ideas from a dialectical sense keener than hers.[40]

Death Denial in
The Rape of the Lock (1717)

What man is he that liveth, and shall not see death? shall he deliver his soul
from the hand of the grave? (Psalms 89: 48)

Having, at age twelve, contracted tuberculosis, Pope was afflicted all his life with spinal
curvature and ill health. When the second version of *The Rape of the Lock* came out in March
1714, near his twenty-sixth birthday, he had suffered three major illnesses: each had threatened
to be fatal—the second described as "a living, dead Condition." No wonder *The Rape of the
Lock* touches comically on social and ethical aspects of death denial. To Erich Frank, "Death
is the final touchstone of the sincerity of our moral actions"; it "makes us feel that we are not
centered in ourselves, but that we are dependent upon something beyond ourselves."[41]

That motifs of death inform Pope's early works supports the notion that he sustained the
wish to contextualise mortality in his mock-heroic poem. Between its first two versions, he
wrote two essays on death. They appeared in *The Guardian* following his first major illness
in 1710.[42] The first, "On Sickness," holds that illness inspires us to think about life beyond
death and to distrust the "Earthly State." In chronic ill-health, Pope says "the Attractions
of the World" do not remove his certainty about the "unsatisfactory Nature of all human
Pleasures." Consoled about dying early, he says "the best time to die [is] when one is in the
best Humour." He does not envy those whose prospects for pleasure are sure: he accepts death
resolutely, clear that his passing will not alter the world and human conduct: "The Morning
after my *Exit*, the Sun will rise as bright as ever, the Flowers smell as sweet, the Plants spring
as green, the World will proceed in its old Course, People will laugh as heartily, and Marry as
fast, as they were used to do." This outlook renders him content at "the Prospect of Death."
The second essay, "On Nature and Death," differs markedly. It reconciles him to death's
inevitability by translating pleasure: the world is "an ample Theatre" in which men displeased
by the "Wisdom and Power of their Creator" are impious. "Drama" on the "Stage of Nature"
distracts men from "Human Grandeur." Far from arousing human fancy, nature creates "a
distaste of the World" that makes the mind "impatient to see the Curtain drawn and [to]
behold new Scenes disclosed." Death "is no more than passing from one Entertainment
to another." Theatre images heighten dialectic; transitory pleasures inevitably create eternal
ones; the "very Imperfections of our Nature" are "Occasions of Comfort and Joy." Despite
diverse strategies, both essays argue that death fulfils earthly life and that religious imagination
naturally transmutes it into a stage of spiritual growth.

In poems about women, Pope develops literary roles on death. In *Epistle to Miss Blount.
With the Works of Voiture* (1710), he speaks of cultivating "wisely careless" attitudes like
the French poet. He would treat life as "an innocent gay Farce" (1.25) and write poems
that evade traditional preaching since Voiture's light-hearted verse won him immortality,

inducing callous people to mourn him. Since living a "strict Life" (1. 21) does not win this desirable fate, he will imitate Voiture. Adopting the role of libertine, he advises Miss Blount to ignore the social form of marriage. To dissuade her further, he anticipates Clarissa's advice to Belinda in *The Rape of the Lock*: he tells Miss Blount that "Good Humour" (l. 61) is the sole means of counteracting age and sickness should she marry.[43] Yet, if she remains single and faithful to him, she will win poetic immortality. He desires a lasting relationship with her, aware he cannot be a marriage candidate given his ill health. Here, poetic immortality functions rhetorically to secure Miss Blount's love. Emotion sets aside physical death to view the afterlife in literary rather than spiritual terms.[44]

Less traditional is his treatment of suicide and funeral rites in *Elegy to the Memory of an Unfortunate Lady* (1717). She whom he mourns killed herself to avoid a marriage arranged by a guardian. Treating her death as divinely inspired heroism, he berates the worldly guardian by foretelling wretched deaths for his family. Lamenting the inadequacy of the lady's foreign funeral rites, he thinks her well-off since conventional mourning constitutes a "mockery of woe" (l. 57). Ambivalence reflects his bitter desire to defy social norms. This is true of concern for her remains. Upset her grave is unsanctified, he seeks consolation; her "reliques" will make it "sacred" (l. 68). Valuing funeral rites, he is appalled by complacency about ritual. Melancholy underlies identification with the lady: "Ev'n he, whose soul now melts in mournful lays / Shall shortly want the gen'rous tear he pays" (ll. 78–79). The sole one to mourn her, he cannot himself expect to be mourned. Social disgust makes him distrust the efficacy of poetic immortality: he dignifies the lady's suicide, disenchanted with social and literary attitudes to death.

While unhappiness and discontent led Pope to question orthodox ideas about mortality, he continued efforts to give imaginative integrity to traditional ways of contemplating death, as clear in *Epistle to Dr Arbuthnot* (1735). Here, he self-consciously postures with death, turning self-consciousness into a means of satirising society's debasement of literature.[45] At the start, his allusions to sickness and closeness to death excuse his evasion of would-be poets who pester him for help. He heightens the vulnerability of his private life to sharpen his attack on the alliance between society, immorality, and bad poetry. His efforts to withdraw reveal that he is the centre of attention, the causes of which he condemns. By describing hyperbolically how deathly he finds the attention lavished on him by the public (l. 32), he dramatises the inhumanity of society's obsession with verse. Similar irony arises when he deflates the gross flattery he is paid. With ironic detachment, he reports that people compare him to classical poets. Painfully aware of physical handicaps and chronic ill-health, he finds such flattery self-interested and inhuman: it aggravates, rather than alleviates, the prospect of death (ll. 121–24). Alluding to Dryden's poverty, Pope decries the neglect in the misplaced expenditures of aristocrats at his funeral. John Gay (1685–1732), neglected by a society that patronises poetry while ignoring poets, he reveres as a model of ethical independence, just as his elegy for his father not only proposes a congruence between life and death but contains a prayer that, in this respect, son may be like father: "His death was instant, and without a groan. / Oh grant me thus to live, and thus to die!" (ll. 403–04). In the end, he makes acceptance of death and heaven's will the chief action of life. His initial posturing with death is doubly transformed: first, it is integrated into the satire of society and poetry, and second, it is converted into an exercise in spiritual integrity.

What *Epistle to Dr Arbuthnot* confirms is that illness inspired Pope to turn literary satire towards Christian humanism. This knowledge helps advance criticism of *The Rape of the Lock*. Ever since Thomas Campbell (1777–1844) argued that the "standard of [Pope's] ridicule and morality, is for ever connected with fashion and polite life" and William Hazlitt (1778–1830) insisted that "the fashion of the day bore sway in [Pope's] mind over the immutable laws of nature," ethical dimensions have rarely been attributed to *The Rape of the Lock*: that this mock-heroic satire has for its target religious hypocrisy and death denial has long been minimised.[46]

In her cave, Spleen vindictively hides behind false piety, "Ill-nature" taking the form of modish hypochondria: "With store of Pray'rs, for Morning, Nights, and Noons, / Her hand is fill'd; her Bosom with Lampoons" (IV, ll. 29–30).[47] "Affectation," feigning illness, invents maladies "for Show," Umbriel reports that Spleen sends "the Godly in a Pett, to pray" (IV, ll. 36 and 64). That from a religious stance Pope mocks society's posturing with illness is clear when he describes the imaginings of those under Spleen's influence. At one moment, these are as dreadful as the "Hermit's Dreams in haunted Shades"; they involve "glaring Fiends, and Snakes on rolling Spires, / Pale Spectres, gaping Tombs, and Purple Fire." At the next, they are as bright as "the Visions of expiring Maids"; they contain "Elysian Scenes, / And Crystal Domes, and Angels in Machines" (IV, ll. 41–46). Since images of death, hell, and heaven are transmuted theatrical properties, Pope implies that contemporary sensibility, erratic and self-dramatising, attains shallow meditations on the afterlife.[48] Hermit and virgin betoken gross secular imagination, which, affecting religious insight, shuns the dialectical reality of death. The parody of Ariosto's notion of the "Lunar Sphere" also debases ideas of heaven (V, ll. 113ff.).[49] The lost things that belong there comprise items that expose trivial anthropocentrism and an absurd sense of permanence. The "Sick Man's Prayers" and "Death-bed Alms" convey materialistic notions of heaven that arise from religious self-deception and hypocritical attitudes toward sickness and death.

The parody of sacramental ritual in the *toilet* scene is clear, if less so its hypocrisy about death and resurrection.[50] Belinda degrades the Mass, the transubstantiation rite that transmutes what is dead (the elements of the Eucharist) into what is spiritually alive (the body and blood of Christ). The cross she wears is more than a religious ornament; it symbolises the triumph of life over death.[51] Yet Pope turns the lock, his chief symbol, into a memento mori. While comically making the lock a sign of human glory, his mythopoeic vision is religious.[52] To counter her vanity, Belinda is told the lock will make her name immortal. As mythic symbol, the lock stops Belinda from enhancing her physical beauty and heightens her duty to confront mortality. His insistence that her "fair Suns shall sett" and that her "Tresses shall be laid in Dust" (V, ll. 147–48) asserts that literary and natural symbols do not displace religious ones: Belinda must contemplate death from a traditional Catholic perspective.

Such advice is needed since her society demeans death and evades spiritual meditation. To Ariel, death is but "a soft Transition" (I, l. 49); there is no discontinuity between eternity and human life; heaven is wish-fulfilment. Since social vanities, such as playing cards and riding in coaches, "after Death survive" (l. 56), Ariel embodies the impulse to belittle death. Emblem of Rosicrucian machinery, he is a gnostic; he supposes death does not lead to a different realm. Heaven is best conceived of in secular terms, and the soul is material. When he details the bickering about the raped lock, Pope suggests that death denial stems from literary posturing and Gnosticism. His characters inflate trivial quarrels into heroic struggles; thinking they are gods, they fight and do "not dread a mortal Wound" (V, l. 44). Since their fighting is neither real nor heroic, their imitation of gods heightens death denial. What heed they pay death is but literary. When Thalestris "scatters Deaths around from both her eyes" (l. 58) and "A Beau and Witling" perish, the one in metaphor, the other in song, the image of "living Death" and the song about Thalestris's "killing" eyes (ll. 61 and 64) stress that people posture with literary ideas rather than confront death. When Sir Plume takes Clarissa down and is killed by Chloe's disapproving frown, only to revive when the latter smiles, and when the Baron, whose mind is too lofty to be dejected by death, at one moment wants "no more than on his Foe to die" (l.178) and at the next wishes to burn alive "in Cupid's Flames" (l.102), death and mortality have become disguised terms for vicarious erotic desires.[53]

Reasons why society demeans death's spirituality relate to lost appreciation of heaven, hell, and judgment. When Ariel informs Belinda in a dream that she is favoured by heaven, he parodies the Annunciation while upholding trivial superstitions (I, ll. 29–46). His agency is limited to concern for a "Flounce" and a "Furbelo," and his sense of "Vengeance" for "Sins" is restricted to being "stopt in Vials. or transfixt with Pins" (II, ll. 100 and 125–26). In Ariel's trivialisation of heaven and hell, they are reduced by vain anthropocentricism. Umbriel's visit to the "Central Earth" affords another occasion to dramatise debased ideas of hell. This underworld is no abode of spirits but of social and psychological fantasies. Humans in this parodic hell are not changed by death and judgment but by society's vulgar obsessions:

> Unnumber'd Throngs on ev'ry side are seen
> Of Bodies chang'd to various Forms by *Spleen*.
> Here living *Teapots* stand, one Arm held out,
> One bent: the Handle this, and that the Spout:
> A pipkin there like *Homer's Tripod* walks;
> Here sighs a Jar, and there a Goose-pye talks;
> Men prove with Child, as pow'rful Fancy works,
> And Maids turn'd Bottels, call aloud for Corks. (IV, ll. 47–54)

These transformations depict a hell in trite modish and sexual images.[54] Pope similarly presents the debasement of judgment. Ariel, the embodiment of social conformity, thinks it appropriate that heaven might doom Belinda's lapdog (II, l. 119); Belinda would like to doom her partners at cards (III, l. 27); statesmen foredoom tyrants and nymphs (III, l. 6); and Partridge, the crazy star-gazer, is likely to foredoom the fall of France and Rome after viewing the translated lock (V, ll. 139–40). Thus, judgment is displaced by pretensions to foreknowledge; divinity and omniscience are displaced by banal presumption and self-deception. Pope's view of such displacements is explicit when, in rejecting the possibility of gaining Belinda's lock, he says, "With such a Prize no Mortal must be blest, / So Heav'n decrees! with Heav'n who can contest?" (V, ll. 111–12). Chastening presumption by mortality and absolute judgment, poetic omniscience serves the doctrine of divine revelation and omnipotence.

The relation between satire of death denial as an essential spiritual issue is striking in Pope's handling of time when he lowers the idea of eternity to emotional affectation. The meadows at Hampton Court are purportedly "for ever crown'd with Flow'rs" (III, l. 1), but this emblem of permanent courtly dignity is countered by temporal modifiers when Pope leads up the card game and the declaration of trumps with its parodic divine fiat.[55] A narrowing of time stresses the momentary and arbitrary—as distinct from eternal—value of courtly behaviour:

> Here Britain's Statesmen oft the Fall foredoom
> Of Foreign Tyrants, and of Nymphs at home;
> Here Thou, Great *Anna*! whom three Realms obey,
> Dost sometimes Counsel take - and sometimes *Tea*. (III, ll. 5–8)

The descent from "for ever" to "oft" and then "sometimes" is remarkable. The next lines sustain this descent in the "awhile" of courtiers' pleasures, the "hours" of their conversation, the "at ev'ry Word" of their scandal-mongering. Before the "now" of the card game, Pope suggests that judges obey natural, not moral, principles because the "soon" of their judgments reacts to the "mean while" of an afternoon. Incongruous human behaviours relate this episode to instances in which he draws a connection between the lack of religious perspective and the dejection that follows from a change in fashion. Temporal reactions to the rape exemplify the incongruities. Pope himself emphasises the finality with which the "sacred Hair" is cut; it has been dissevered "for ever and for ever!" (III, l. 154). This liturgical phrase, ironically acknowledging eternity, is comically inappropriate to the cutting of a lock. Belinda, the Baron, and Thalestris are, however, earnest about this rape. Belinda wants the day on which it happened to be "for ever curs'd" (IV, l. 147); the Baron solemnly claims he will wear the "sacred Lock ... for ever" (IV, ll. 133–38); Thalestris agrees that he will wear the lock "for ever" unless something is done to recapture it (IV, l. 116). Misplaced religion induces these three to feel there are eternal consequences to the rape: their notions of holiness are secular and selfish ideas are in masquerade. The analogies by which the Baron and Thalestris convey the permanence of their respective glory and dishonour confuse temporal and eternal values. The Baron believes his capture of the lock will redound to his honour as long as

"Birds delight in Air," "*Atlantis* shall be read," and "Nymphs take Treats, or Assignations give" (III, ll. 161–70). He thinks his fame immortal because he does not distinguish between elemental reality, cultural whimsies, and human fallibility. For her part, since she thinks honour a "Shrine" at which "Ease, Pleasure, Virtue" and all should be sacrificed, Thalestris, to stop the Baron wearing the emblem of Belinda's dishonour, is willing to give up driving round "*Hide*-Park Circus" and to have the globe collapse into chaos (IV, ll. 117–20). Neither considers orders of duration or secular values under the aspect of eternity.

Pope's most subtly compelling displacement of a religious perspective on death is found in Clarissa's address to Belinda. This speech, added to the poem in 1717, parodies lines twenty-seven to fifty-two of *The Episode of Sarpedon* (1707), where Pope explores the relation between heroic concepts of endeavour and death. Sarpedon urges Glaucus on to heroism by arguing that, since the two of them are "Admir'd as Heroes, and as Gods obey'd," their deeds must excel those of their troops. Sarpedon insists they must deserve the authority, wealth, and dignity given by the gods. He concedes that concern for fame would be unnecessary were death avoidable: "But since, alas, ignoble Age must come, / Disease, and Death's inexorable Doom," their sole route to heroism is to yield their lives freely to fame rather than pay them unheroically as a debt to nature. Speaking about how beautiful women may justify being honoured by men, Clarissa proposes that, since beauty is transitory, women will deserve admiring attention only by possessing good sense and virtue. She grants that cultivation of those traits would be unnecessary if ordinary conduct could charm "the Small-pox" or chase "old Age away":

> But since, alas! frail Beauty must decay,
> Curl'd or uncurl'd, since Locks will turn to grey,
> Since painted, or not painted, all shall fade,
> And she who scorns a Man, must die a Maid (V, ll. 25–28),

Belinda must accept the loss of her lock as an occasion to exercise "good Humour" and to earn a principled social eminence.

While Clarissa's address voices a worldly morality, it is not motivated only by secular imperatives.[56] Her rhetoric promotes a Christian attitude towards death.[57] She begins by accepting Belinda's superficial values, initially speaking as if it were desirable for "Beauties" to be "The wise Man's Passion, and the vain Man's Toast."[58] She seems willing to admit the value in women being called "Angels" and "Angel-like ador'd." As her speech unfolds, the illogicality of these premises becomes manifest, and she discounts beauty, maintaining that physical decline, sickness, and death are inevitable. She decries women who assume the cosmetic arts can render them saints and implies that it is "a Sin" for a woman to feel she can avoid the effects of time by painting herself. Ultimately, her insistence upon the acceptance of old age, sickness, and death anticipates Pope's address to Belinda at poem's end, when he heightens the theme that, whereas death destroys, the idea of death can save. As such, *The Rape of the Lock* foretells what social science says about death and dying. Like C.W.

Wahl, Pope explores how people defend themselves against death by turning it into a "fictive experience," and like Elisabeth Kübler-Ross, he dramatises the way in which the denial of death leads to social disorder.[59]

CHAPTER TWO
Philosophy and Narrative

The developing novel favoured no one narrative mode; it exploited plural discourses–empirical, historical, journalistic, epistolary, legal, constitutional, and theological–and tested intellectual systems with humanistic stances. It arose from detailing the problems of challenging society's trust in moral progress. The fictions of Henry Fielding, in upholding the liberal arts, debate legal and moral imperatives, unfolding issues about judicial and political privilege. His voices are facetious and philosophical, while his comic and satiric talents mock self-interested professionalism like Swift. *Tom Jones* links romance and empiricism dialectically.[60] *Joseph Andrews* assails "metaphysical rubbish" and philosophers' obsessions with "some favourite hypothesis," bringing liberal education to bear on epistemology.[61] In *Tom Jones*, romance and philosophy are reciprocal; romance mediates philosophy and philosophy mediates romance. Scott Black describes this dialectic: not taking romance "as a naive epistemology or a dated ideology against which modernity is articulated but rather as an answer to conceptions of the modern as sharply opposed to the past," he calls it "a self-consciously secondary genre that takes old forms ... as still forceful but not fully defining and reuses them but not simply instrumentally." Situated between story and truth, myth and history, tradition and modernity, epic and novel, long time and local time, romance doesn't resolve into one or another of these poles but rather hovers halfway between them, exploring and indeed enabling their interactions.[62]

To promote benevolence and active virtue, Fielding applies empirical tenets to conditions of learning and, in defence of Christian ethics, disparages systematic rationalism. That the eighteenth-century novel could not claim the status of a single genre is clarified by its varying dependence on another multifarious literary kind: natural history. This form of writing features discourses evolving from natural science, global exploration, the agrarian revolution, and political economy. Using traditional emblems and fables as well as classical texts to represent creation, the novel was informed by encyclopaedic knowledge of animals, plants, and geology, which enabled its humanism to comment profoundly on themes of ecology and conservation.

Henry Fielding and Justice

Experience with legal administration and courtroom procedures led Fielding to feature the law in his romances. Certain that litigiousness does more harm than good, he voices positive legal commentary in his fiction and non-fiction to review professional and constitutional aims and to voice a conscientious desire as magistrate to uphold the Hanoverian settlement.[63] He personally respected the legal profession as a body with defined political responsibilities and as a set of judicial ideals validated by Christian imperatives. To him, lawyers were obliged to implement the law and effect constitutional and social reform based on religious ideals.[64]

This outlook informs *Joseph Andrews* (1742). Thus, Fielding faults the lawyer who wishes his travelling companions "had passed by without taking any notice" of the injured Joseph. No good Samaritan, this man has no conscience; his concern for Joseph is legalistic since he is aware that to leave the scene of a crime is an indictable offence. When this lawyer threatens the coachman with legal action unless he takes up Joseph, Fielding focusses on the poor postilion who, a criminal since given to swearing and eventually transported for robbing a hen-roost, pities Joseph. The lawyer is more to blame than the postilion: the latter practises religion, but the lawyer merely obeys the letter of the law.[65] High expectations of the profession govern Fielding's view of Lawyer Scout. A pettifogger, Scout degrades the law in the heads of "weak persons" who bear it "ill-will." He makes the law harm those critical of the profession since he acts "in defiance of an act of Parliament" intended to regulate attorneys and solicitors and exclude them from practice. Ready "to prevent the law's taking effect" and to maintain that the "laws of this land are not so vulgar" as to grant poor men rights, Scout uses knowledge of legal administration to subvert the law and to equate legal rights with social privilege. His calling for "an act to hang or transport half" the poor and antipathy to justices who scruple about sending them to prison where they starve to death betray a reactionary separation of law and social reform. His callous proposals show that Scout's sense of the law is unprofessional, unconstitutional, and inhumane.[66]

That Fielding views the legal profession as a society with political ideals validated by religion shows in his anti-clerical satire. Take the parson who, in a "state of civil war, or, which is perhaps as bad, of civil law" with Sir Thomas Booby and his tenants, impoverishes himself in litigation to have his stipend returned to the tithing system, yet he congratulates himself that his suits have "utterly undone many of the poor tenants." This parson, whose self-interest is undone in court, dabbles in law to avoid pastoral duties and aggravate communal harm. Parson Barnabas behaves similarly. While not loving the public since he never delivers a sermon without payment, he pretends zeal for "publick justice" and theorises about evidence. Without professional interest, he exploits legal ideas to parade in his parish, his posturing creating dissension. His dabbling in law exposes anti-social worldliness and gross clericalism while suggesting how open to corruption the law is. That the clergy abuse the law is clear when Mrs Trulliber tells her husband to "show himself a true Christian, and take the law" of Parson Adams. The latter's belief that using the law vengefully is a villainous betrayal of the clerical order accents the view that the clergy, if not upholding the law's ideals, distort its practice.[67]

Idealism about the law shapes Fielding's satire of arbitrary magistrates. That they evade religion is clear when Adams decides that Joseph answers his catechism "better than Sir Thomas, or two other neighbouring justices of the peace could probably have done." Hypocrisy governs Lady Booby. Shocked when Joseph defends his chastity, she protests that "magistrates who punish lewdness" do not scruple to commit it themselves. Their hypocrisy is stressed when Fanny and Adams come before one. At first, the justice reviles them; thinking them poor, he rages about making them deterrents to highway robbery. On learning Adams is a clergyman, he reverses himself without process; he does not cross-examine Adams but accepts "every syllable of his story on his bare affirmation, notwithstanding the depositions on oath to the contrary." Bias against committing gentlemen shows that this justice mindlessly debases the law.[68]

In Fielding's texts, lawyers, clergymen, and magistrates betray the law and its mores since they do not question the acquisitive callousness of the rich. They defer to Peter Pounce whose greed assails Christian charity to claim that "the greatest fault in our constitution is the provision made for the poor." To Pounce, their distresses are illusory; it is foolish to relieve them. His desire to ignore Christian doctrine and to abolish the Poor Laws stems from his reluctance to pay taxes and to recognise that the distresses of the poor are aggravated by his amassing of country estates. Lady Booby's avidity evades her duty to redistribute wealth. She is acclaimed by the poor when she returns to her country estate—ironically since she is ruining it by having rents drafted to London "without a shilling being spent among them." She could remedy their plight at little cost to herself. But avarice makes her rail at the parish poor whose hardship she has caused and induces her to try to strip them of legal settlement. Pounce and Lady Booby embody the economic and social power to which lawyers, clergymen, and magistrates succumb.[69]

Allusions in *Tom Jones* (1749) confirm Fielding's intent to integrate legal and parochial systems as well as professional and social benevolence: he continues weighing gross against ideal standards. After Partridge works for a lawyer who is "an Honour to his Profession" because he does "good and charitable Acts" and spurns "paultry and oppressive" business, the ex-schoolteacher discovers another side of the profession when his pig trespasses on the property of a neighbour who hires a lawyer to get revenge. This lawyer aggravates the case against Partridge by bringing his own action so that Partridge is ruined financially and spends seven years in prison. In a note saying this incident is factual, Fielding condemns such inhumanity. Yet, to counter prejudice against the profession, he insists, when he suggests that Lawyer Dowling has not shed his "Humanity by being an Attorney," that "Nature works in Men of all Professions alike," they are being more humane at home than at work. If it is unjust "to carry our Prejudices against a Profession into private Life," Fielding insists there should be no gap between the professional and domestic values of those who administer the law.[70]

Much satire in *Tom Jones* stems from Fielding's criticism of this gap. Squire Western, whose legal administration evades differences between public and private values, exposes the need to integrate them. He almost gets his way in having Tom committed for possessing Sophia's muff since he would take advantage of a justice who is ignorant of statutes and processes. As a justice, Western confuses values. He is the only one in his parish to swear with impunity, for he puts "the Laws very severely in Execution against others" but ignores his own infringements. He typifies justices of the peace who presume they have "a large discretionary Power" in executing the laws. They operate the Game Laws partially; they "often commit Trespasses, and sometimes Felony" in making those laws serve self-interest. Western's constitutional disrespect furthers his hypocritical subversion of law. Opposed to the Hanoverians and not the Stuarts, he rants about being a "free-born Englishman," constitutional dislike making him believe he is above the law. For Fielding, the gap between values in the legal system is attributable to constitutional errors. This is substantiated by the episode in which a legal clerk affects being a lawyer in the debate about whether Tom is mad and should be returned to Allworthy. At first, he is legalistically cautious. When the debate touches on rights and law, he scorns the priority of rights; as he says, "Who hath any Right but what the Law gives them?" But his stance on Jacobite rebels inconsistently wants to have "Right take Place." His view that the state's laws are secondary to natural rights and that the law alone establishes rights reveals a subversive sense of public and private values which refuses to consider the law from a constitutional perspective.[71]

Fielding's conviction that dialectical values are essential to social reform is substantiated by embedding legal satire into characterisation and literary commentary. When Sophia mistakes Mr Fitzpatrick for her father, her timidity is likened to "the common Fault of a Justice of Peace" who is "apt to conclude too hastily from every slight Circumstance, without examining the Evidence on both Sides." When Tom cannot jilt Molly, his heart pleads her cause not like "a cold venal Advocate; but as one interested in the Event." So, too, when she would betray Sophia, Mrs Honour is contrasted to one who is "too upright a Judge to decree on one Side." Her shallow plan serves calculating selfishness. That he builds such analogies into characterisation evidences Fielding's determination that, if the law is to be guided by moral imperatives, it must be based on a proper relation of public and private values. Legal satire in his literary commentary makes this point. By comparing classical critics to sound legal clerks who responsibly "transcribe the Rules and Laws laid down" by judges and contemporary critics to judges who "adhere to the lifeless Letter of Law, and reject the Spirit," he parallels the decline of legal values and aesthetic taste. His allusion to the biblical text that "the letter killeth, but the spirit giveth life" shows he views the reciprocity of public and private values from a religious perspective. Similarly, when he objects that theatrical criticism is practised by unsuccessful lawyers for whom judgment means condemnation "without Mercy," his objection is not only to the confusion of legal and aesthetic values but to the immorality that debases these values and blocks social reform.[72]

Fielding's humanistic beliefs that legal administration must be guided by religious imperatives, that justice must be tempered with mercy, and that social reform must be grounded on more than casual benevolence inform his attitude to characters. He distinguishes between them on the basis of whether they are legalistic or grasp the relation of public and private values. Consider the aftermath of Tom's striking Blifil when the latter has called the former a "*Beggarly Bastard.*" An "indictment of Assault, Battery, and Wounding" is "instantly preferred against Tom" by Thwackum. Tom defends himself "against all Form of Law," and Allworthy refuses to "sign the Warrant for the Execution of *Jones*": Thwackum and Blifil think of justice apart from mercy; Allworthy and Tom do not since they temper justice with mercy. When Thwackum covets Allworthy's sister, he hides his hypocrisy by seeing "Divine Law" only in terms of civil law, and when lustful Blifil passes "Sentence against *Sophia,*" he acts like an inhuman judge. By contrast, Allworthy is merciful to Tom while visiting an "inflexible Severity" on Black George, and Tom balances justice with benevolence since he views the law from the perspective of conscience. Tom resists Partridge's urging to take Sophia's money since "*in Foro Conscientiae*" such a crime warrants capital punishment. Balancing this principled severity is Tom's compassion for Anderson, the highwayman. While Partridge wants him to kill Anderson, Tom feels for those whose "unavoidable Distress" leads to "illegal Courses" and "shameful Death." Partridge's callous opinion that the law should hang all robbers heightens Tom's distinction between robbery and robbery with violence. His visit to Anderson's house proves Tom right not to listen to "the Voice of strict Justice." Another example of his refusal to be litigious occurs when Tom is imprisoned for alleged murder. Certain he is not guilty in "the Eye of the Law," he feels culpable for having shed Fitzpatrick's blood. Aware that false evidence may bring "the Severity of the Law" upon him, he is untroubled since he respects a "Throne still greatly superior" to that of the court. Religion helps him balance values and temper justice with mercy.[73]

Like Tom, Allworthy balances rigour and clemency. Lenient to Jenny Jones, regardless of knowing compassion will bring calumny on him, he desires her reform. By "tempering Justice with Mercy" in his treatment of her, he rejects the mob's desire to have her sacrificed to justice so as to exercise pity. He resists their crude relation of severity to benevolence. His treatment of Partridge, if fallible, manifests the same resistance to debased legal concepts. The evidence on which he convicts Partridge is greater than "would have satisfied a Bench of Justices." In judgment, Allworthy is neither reactionary nor arbitrary. On the one hand, he opposes the view "that Mercy consists only in punishing Offenders"; on the other, he will not "pardon great Criminals wantonly" or "because the Offender himself, or his Friends [are] unwilling that he should be punished." His sense of deterrence is neither legalistic nor subject to social pressure. Fielding emphasises Allworthy's just principles by comparing how the squire tempers judgment of Partridge and anonymously relieves his distress to how the populace compassionates him hypocritically yet forgets charity. He similarly justifies the "Rigour" of Allworthy's dismissal of Tom. Since those who originally censored the squire's adoption of Tom condemn Allworthy for the dismissal, the squire's severity and benevolence as a magistrate are beyond challenge. Allworthy balances concern for legislation with concern for conscience. When he criticises "the Laws of our Country" for failing to proscribe forced marriages, he does not hold legislators solely accountable since "a good Conscience is never lawless in the worst-regulated State, and will provide those Laws for itself, which the Neglect of Legislators hath forgotten to supply." His legal authority stems from his balancing of values. His authority is assured because unjustified mercy is as harmful to society as severe or arbitrary administration of justice. Shocked there is no penalty for Black George's fraud, he rejects Tom's "forgiving Temper" as "mistaken Mercy" and as "pernicious to Society." Granting that dishonesty is forgivable, he convinces Tom that, when it is compounded with ingratitude, as in Black George's case, it is unforgivable. This severity illustrates Allworthy's belief that justice and mercy must be mutual and that knowing when compassion is appropriate is part of judging how to uphold the deterrent effect of the law.[74]

The narrative upholds Allworthy's legal authority. Alert to society's need for compassion, Fielding concedes the harm done by inappropriate benevolence. About Northerton's fear of the gallows, he refers to "a certain wooden Edifice" in mock conformity to society's euphemistic evasiveness about capital punishment. But he avers that the gallows are "of more Benefit to Society than almost any other public Erection." He does not scruple to condemn Northerton; he attributes the ensign's bad conscience to an awareness that he had "forfeited his Life to the Law." Certain the law cannot deter offenders like Northerton, he argues that its capital powers should be retained. While his narrative stance insists society not discount capital punishment, he often addresses readers in legal terms to get them to see the right relation of severity and benevolence.[75] When Mrs Partridge falsely accuses her husband and her neighbours, acting as a court, judge his astonished silence to be a "Confession of the Charge," Fielding asks readers to "bear Witness" for Partridge. When Square ineptly defends Tom, Fielding trusts his "Readers will be much abler Advocates for poor *Jones*." Speaking as a barrister, he approaches the reader as if the latter is a judge or member of a jury. When pretending it is hard to acquit Tom of the charge of backwardness to Sophia, he leaves judgment to "the Reader's Determination," sure they will accept the mitigating evidence, and, when asking the reader to agree that Tom's supposition about Molly's love for him is natural, he feels sure "the Reader will allow" the evidence which he has given. By thrusting legal roles on readers, he invites respect for benevolent administration of the law that does not exclude moral and theoretical consideration of its deterrent effects.[76]

An Enquiry into the Causes of the Late Increase of Robbers (1751), in concern for reform, broadens Fielding's view of the constitution. If it covers "the original and fundamental law of the kingdom," all "legislative and executive authority," and all "municipal provisions commonly called the laws," it also includes "the customs, manners, and habits of the people." Not "uniform and permanent," the law varies according to the "order and disposition" of its elements. This organic and evolutionary definition implies the insufficiency of mere litigiousness. While "a competent knowledge of the laws" yields "a just notion" of the constitution, Fielding feels that a lawyer who ignores "the genius, manners, and habits of the people" sees but its "exterior form." Legal knowledge must involve historical and social insights; it must see that "the disposition of the several parts" of the constitution "can never be altered without producing a proportional change" in the whole. To Fielding, detaching the law from evolutionary changes in the populace causes a decline in civic power and allows the people to laugh at magistrates and pettifoggers. Alert to the growing power of the lower orders, Fielding castigates lethargic politicians and magistrates whose inaction lets a "wild" notion of liberty destroy "true liberty." Convinced increasing commercial activity in the lower orders exposes them to luxury and crime, he urges civil authorities to control more fully the lives of the working poor.[77]

This severe tract is hard on those who administer law. In proposing that masquerades be closed to the poor and that proper licensing and inspection of inns reduce gin-drinking, Fielding urges legislators, magistrates, and parish officers to be more conscientious: he accuses parish officers of viewing their work merely in terms of private emolument and blames tradesmen for failing to donate to charity. Denying that statutes requiring the poor to work and magistrates to legislate wages are repressive, he thinks it better to control wages than to allow the poor to set their own rates of pay. For if the poor do not get what they demand, they stop working and draw on public charity. He thus castigates magistrates who reprimand the lazy rather than sending them to prison: magistrates should respect the Poor Laws by obliging parishes to construct workhouses and enforce legal settlement. He tells conscientious magistrates to make society more cohesive and increase legal deterrence. He grants, however, that, if society does not adopt every conceivable way of using the constitution to prevent crime and poverty, his proposals for regulating the poor are unjustifiable. While he treats the poor as objects of a stringent legal system, he dwells on the greater moral responsibility of higher levels of society.[78]

The perspective on reform in *An Enquiry into the Causes of the Late Increase of Robbers* obtains in his last novel, *Amelia* (1751), which unsettles political and legal complacency. Fielding finds "defects of polity even [in] this well-regulated nation"; these "imperfections" exist in "the laws themselves" as well as in their ill execution. Since good "laws should execute themselves in a well-regulated state," he holds that the legislature which "provides the laws" must provide for their execution. That the watch cannot safeguard property and magistrates, like Justice Thrasher, know nothing of "the laws of England" while having a gross sense of "the laws of nature" reflect, in Fielding's eyes, the deficiencies of the legislature.[79]

Passion for reform leads him to make Captain Booth, the protagonist, aware of legal deficiencies. While he is not "deeply learned in religious matters" and disbelieves in providence, Booth upholds "the necessity of human actions." Still, he is shocked the law treats perjury as a bailable misdemeanour and stealing a loaf from hunger as a non-bailable felony. This sense of inequity belies his mechanistic ideas of human nature and impels him to decry corrupt legal administration. Knowing little of statutes, he recognises that Lawyer Murphy misrepresents the charge against Miss Matthews to get her to spend more than necessary; greed makes Murphy disparage legal knowledge and rules of evidence. Booth learns from Bondum the bailiff that legal corruption saps society; he sees that Bondum seizes victims for gain and that his pretended constitutional interest in liberty is absurd. At one moment, Bondum insists everyone should be coerced into paying debts; at the next, he vaguely equates "the constitution of England" with liberty. The contradiction between severity and vagueness shows that imprisonment for debt undoes constitutional tradition and that the bailiff's notion of liberty subverts society.[80]

Through his protagonist's intuitions, Fielding assails arbitrary legal penalties, Booth becoming a spokesman for equity. After trying to prosecute Betty, his servant, for stealing his wife's clothes, Booth is angry. His vengeance is not tempered by Amelia's tenderness. At first, he spurns Betty as "an object of mercy"; he holds it a "charity to the public" to remove such people from society, adopting the view that they should suffer capital punishment for their eternal good. But when he discovers that Betty has pawned the stolen shifts for five shillings while they are worth thirty and has spent the five shillings on a silk-gown scarcely worth a farthing, he states that severe laws must also apply to pawnbrokers and shopkeepers. Outraged that Betty may not be charged with a "felonious breach of trust," he is angrier that shortcomings prevent the arraignment of the pawnbroker, a receiver of stolen goods. That the laws should be stricter is reinforced by the justice before whom he brings Betty; the latter thinks them made rather for "the protection of rogues than for the punishment of them."[81]

While voicing the need for reform through Booth, Fielding shows that irreligion limits his protagonist's outlook. Settling in Dr Harrison's parish, a Christian community free from profanity, beggars, and lawsuits, Booth disrupts it with an ostentation that rouses neighbours to trespass against him and entangle him in lawsuits. He brings litigation on himself. By contrast, Harrison promotes ties between legal and social reform and between justice and mercy. Criticising the custom of remunerating bailiffs for "not acting in an unchristian and inhuman manner," Harrison is appalled such negative virtue is rewarded and proposes laws to punish bailiffs since their office concerns "those poor creatures who cannot do themselves justice." His reformist sense also condemns duelling as "a direct and audacious defiance of the Christian law." Since adultery is "protected by law and countenanced by custom," he insists the "governors of the world" and the clergy are failing to make England a true "Christian society."[82]

Harrison's reformist stance is confirmed in discussions with a clergyman who, holding there would be "an end of all law and justice" if a man were obliged to love his enemies, evades the biblical injunction, wanting to be free to prosecute "his enemy in a court of justice." Shocked by this impiety, Harrison avers that legal prosecution is public duty, not personal revenge. When the priest says the "utmost severity" of the law should be visited on critics of clergy and claims that "Fines and imprisonments and corporal punishments operate more forcibly on the human mind than all the fears of damnation," desire for prestige induces him to subordinate religious to legalistic imperatives. But Harrison will not excuse the priesthood; its "grosser crimes" must be proscribed, and it must be modelled anew on the ten commandments. He is convinced reform will transpire only if clergymen shun worldly ambition.[83]

Harrison spurns political customs when seeking a place from a nobleman for Booth. This aristocrat, for whom patronage entails bargaining, cares nothing for Booth's qualities; to him, it is utopian to base preferment on merit since corruption is inevitable and since neither classical nor Christian virtues matter to the constitution. But Harrison thinks unethical preferment a "manifest act of injustice." This "kind of injustice" harms society by inhibiting moral incentives to the arts, sciences, and professions. That he defies the political pressures which the nobleman cynically accepts is seen when he searches Murphy's house and arrests the corrupt attorney. Sure "the law of England" lets anyone "arrest a felon without any warrant whatever," Harrison shows that no man acts below himself who protects an innocent person or brings a rogue to the gallows.[84]

Harrison's faith that humanistic reform aids Christian fellowship obliges him to temper justice with mercy and to relate public to private values. This faith guides his insistence that the well-to-do and powerful do not enjoy superior legal rights. Congratulating the Booths for holding that all men are brothers and refusing to view the poor "as a species of beings of an inferior order of creation," Harrison's voice gains influence since it reflects Fielding's belief that people are equal before the law and that moral imagination is vital to reform. Like Harrison, the Booths grasp that one barrier to reform is that "great men" think of themselves as "a distinct species," having "no perfect idea of those common distresses of mankind which are far removed from their own sphere." Amelia sees herself as a "partaker of one common nature" with "the wife of the honest labourer," and Booth feels that upper-class life is complemented "with too much injustice" at the expense of the lower since "greatness of mind" is found in beggars as well as in princes. This equality gathers rhetorical power, for, at the beginning in presenting Justice Thrasher, Fielding suggests that a major cause of legal corruption is the prevalent assumption that truth is not the property of the poor. While Thrasher never sullies "his sublime notions" of truth "by uniting them with the mean ideas of poverty and distress," Fielding employs the motif to defy legal prejudice and to insist that reform must be based on Christianity.[85]

Fielding's humanistic and constitutional perspective on reform and on the deterrence of capital punishment marks his final work, *The Journal of a Voyage to Lisbon* (1755). Imminent death made him neither callous nor self-sympathetic. His tone ranges between the judicial and the compassionate, between the severe and the benevolent. Proud of having curtailed "street-robberies," he laments the difficulty of convicting known criminals, blaming this on faulty rules of evidence and the inflexible aloofness of "courts of justice." He is proud his legal severity has been conscientious and his arbitration of disputes among the poor charitable, not mercenary. He holds all ranks responsible for the need for reform; he blames the barbarous conduct of the lower orders on "an uncontroul'd licentiousness mistaken for liberty" and accuses the higher orders who ignore social evils of indifference to "the regulation of the mob." While he reiterates his long-held view that vagrancy laws should be imposed on the poor and that the price of labour should be fixed by legislation to oblige the poor to work regularly, he defends their interests by denouncing "monopolizing fishmongers." These men overfish the Thames to satisfy luxurious tables with small fish and fail their duty to supply the London market with cheap, large fish. To promote inexpensive nutrition, he judges fishmongers' conduct felonious, their subversion of the market and public charity a capital offence.[86]

Fielding's views on the law resist two views of his legal references: they defy opinions that he deals with legal and social problems in his fiction sentimentally and that he is increasingly reactionary in his non-fiction. A balanced concern for justice and mercy shows that his fiction argues for legal severity as much as his non-fiction does for benevolence. He expresses ideas about law, reform, and religion consistently. He respected the legal profession even as he presented its degradation, and he constantly related legal to social reform. His reciprocal sense of justice and mercy allowed him to argue that divine judgment is the ultimate imperative for law, and his attacks upon immoral ideas of justice and mercy in all his works demonstrate a humanistic awareness of how legal, social, and religious values should be integrated.[87]

Humanism in *Tom Jones*

Mixed comedy and philosophy in *Tom Jones* make its humanism entertaining, Fielding treating empirical ideas dialectically since he realised problems of knowledge are prior to understanding and judgment, a realisation causing him to base comedy on the many ways in which knowledge springs from experience. *Tom Jones* manifests an epistemological impulse which informs readers that the novel is "about judgment, and the understanding necessary for good judgment," the plot revealing "how we acquire knowledge of human experience."[88] Dialectical empiricism shows how Fielding wanted readers to respond. This claim may seem odd since he is usually said to embrace the benevolence and optimism of Latitudinarian churchmen and the Earl of Shaftesbury (1671–1713).[89] The sparse attention paid to his empiricism depends on his supposed reaction to John Locke (1632–1704).[90] Yet affinities make the two thinkers comparable. Locke's educational views make it apt for Fielding to exploit empiricism for comic and serious purposes.

Locke and Fielding agree about contexts of learning. In *Some Thoughts concerning Education* (1693), Locke defends physical and scholarly discipline but opposes mindless corporal punishment and abstract studies. Since pain coarsens children, he argues that, when reproving misbehaviour, adults should claim to be amazed by ill-conduct so that children will benefit from being assumed to be responsible.[91] In *Tom Jones*, Thwackum, whose name and meditations are "full of Birch," goads Tom to rebel. While Thwackum is deflated because of his coarse pedagogy, Allworthy is an ideal teacher who will not preach to Jenny Jones about her sins but trusts her sense of responsibility: "A Hint therefore, to awaken your Sense of this Matter, shall suffice; for I would inspire you with Repentance, and not drive you to Desperation." To Locke and Fielding, learning must be humane: Locke celebrates example for reaching children, and Fielding holds that a narrative incident is more enlightening than "the longest Dissertation."[92]

Since both hold that conditions of learning involve religious values, they distinguish between education and learning. Locke scorns traditional education, valuing conduct more than learning, and Fielding delights in revealing how vulnerable traditional education is to doctrine. Locke's demand that education fit disposition and individuals be trained to social affections insists that learning depends on temperament and habit more than on step-by-step mental processing. To Locke, an individual's acquisition of proper conduct becomes second nature: it requires no thought or reflection.[93] When Fielding wittily refers to Tom's conscience, he substitutes a practical integrity of conscience for nominal categories and rational absolutes:

> Mr. *Jones* had Somewhat about him, which, though I think Writers are not thoroughly agreed in its Name, doth certainly inhabit some human Breasts; whose Use is not so properly to distinguish Right from Wrong, as to prompt and incite them to the former, and to restrain and with-hold them from the latter.

With mock deference to critics, Fielding does not discriminate between the guiding and judging aspects of conscience; he stresses that Tom's conscience is an "active Principle" which "doth not content itself with Knowledge or Belief only" since virtue is not the object of reason or the effect of education.[94] Locke and Fielding limit the scope of education and advance practical virtue given their Christian beliefs in human nature. Locke thinks innate dispositions temper educational ambition: "God has stamp'd certain Characters upon Men's Minds, which like their Shapes, may perhaps be a little mended, but can hardly be totally alter'd and transform'd into the contrary."[95] Similarly, Fielding contends that "Men of true Wisdom and Goodness are contented to take Persons and Things as they are," there being "perhaps, no surer Mark of Folly, than an Attempt to correct the natural Infirmities of those we love." The impossibility of perfectibility means that men must learn to possess an "overlooking Disposition" in friendship. A religious sense of forgiveness together with awareness of requisite social conduct is Fielding's goal for learning.[96]

To Locke, the worst effect of traditional education is affectation, which he attributes to lazy teachers who promulgate rules with theoretical examples. True learning avoids affectation by enhancing God-given dispositions to unite thought and conduct: "The Actions which naturally flow from such a well-form'd Mind, please us also, as the genuine Mark of it; and being as it were natural Emanations from the Spirit and Disposition within, cannot but be easy and unconstrain'd."[97] This implication about affectation as pretence to a good disposition and disguise of a bad one recalls Fielding's sense of affectation in the preface to *Joseph Andrews*. In distinguishing between the ostentation of vanity and the deceit of hypocrisy, Fielding holds that the discrepancy between thinking and action merits ridicule. An example of this concern in *Tom Jones* is the amusing generalisation about Square's failure to practise what he preaches:

> For though such great Beings think much better and more wisely, they always act exactly like other Men. They know very well how to subdue all Appetites and Passions, and to despise both Pain and Pleasure; and this Knowledge affords much delightful Contemplation, and is easily acquired; but the Practice would be vexatious and troublesome; and, therefore, the same Wisdom which teaches them to know this, teaches them to avoid carrying it into Execution.

Here, Fielding deflates self-contained thinking by granting achievements to mind that make little sense without commitment to social conduct.[98]

Related to the dialectic of thinking and action is prudence which joins the secular and the religious. If Locke's educational emphasis is secular because teaching should help men live in society without excessive suspicion or confidence and develop mutual understanding, he insists that sociable thinking ultimately serves faith. The "Enlargement of our Minds towards a truer and fuller Comprehension of the intellectual World," and the "Works of Nature" not reducible to "a Science," call for revelation and reason. Deficiencies in natural philosophy and systematic spiritual knowledge require education to be tempered by prudence which entails understanding religious principles through faithful practice. For Locke, prudence is second only to faith: "A man may be, perhaps, a good man (who lives in truth and sincerity of heart towards God) with a small portion of prudence, but he will never be very happy in himself, nor useful to others."[99] Fielding voices a similar tenet in *Tom Jones* when, in a crucial yet playful paragraph that moves from speculating about future readers to magisterially addressing "worthy Disciples," he says that the individual cannot generate interior goodness: "Prudence and Circumspection are necessary even to the best of Men."[100] Indeed, "no Man can be good enough to enable him to neglect the Rules of Prudence." To a generous temper, Tom must add prudence and religion. For Fielding and Locke, prudence is no mere consideration of circumstance: it is "the Duty which we owe to ourselves" to protect virtue and win a constructive relation with society. They both value prudence because it imposes on learning an accommodation of religious and secular ideas and obliges it to be connected to action and social commitment.[101]

Fielding's narrative modes recall Locke's notions of learning, reading, and the writer's role in *Of the Conduct of the Understanding* (1706), which details the idolatry men pay to their own ideas and maintains that conversation alone remedies such prejudice. Locke also relates fallibility to reading, suggesting that training in moral theory offsets readers' tendencies to lose themselves in textual facts and to generalise too easily from particulars. To Locke, the writer must dutifully provoke connected thinking in readers and assume that reading leads to proto-thought rather than actual thinking: he who grants he cannot transfuse knowledge into readers accepts the priority of truth and ensures that literary devices convey this priority.[102]

Fielding derides those who idolise their own ideas. The landlord who deceives himself into believing that Sophia is Jenny Cameron likes to be thought to see "farther and deeper into Things than any Man in the Parish." Exposed by political prejudice and self-interest, he loses authority by posturing in conversation. Claiming tentative reasonableness, he is simply vague: he lets auditors understand more than he says. His reputation for wisdom is valueless since "Men are strangely inclined to worship what they do not understand." Both Squire and Mrs Western are mocked for pretending to authoritative ideas. Fielding gives their mental perversities comical complementarity. While the Squire never bothers to look ahead but concerns himself only with the present, Mrs Western, ignoring the actual, views everything from a distance. Their excesses are self-defeating: "For as the Sister often foresaw what never came to pass, so the Brother often saw much more than was actually the Truth." They disjoin perception and reflection; the Squire over-particularises and Mrs Western over-generalises, but illusion is the common result.[103]

His awareness of readers' tendency to be absorbed by details leads Fielding to comment slyly on the writer's role in leading audiences to self-consciousness and critical intelligence. He stresses the facticity of story to show that reading provides material for thought rather than thinking itself. When he says "it is our Province to relate Facts, and we shall leave Causes to Persons of much higher Genius," he warns of the irrelevance of philosophical causation and makes his dictatorial tone the object of laughter. If, by emphasising facts, he illustrates the empirical basis of reading, he does not limit himself to them. Admitting that he suppresses detail, he tells what is minimally necessary: "it is not our Custom to unfold at any Time more than is necessary for the Occasion." Yet, he does not always provide what is necessary; this prerogative obliges readers to think under restricted conditions. He limits their scope for induction and deduction while permitting them an amused reaction. Because Fielding comically reveals and conceals, readers enjoy connecting the particular and general, the fact and idea.[104]

Like Locke, Fielding confronts superficial reading because people often "read Books with no other View than to say they have read them." He obliges readers to make moral inferences: he provides occasions for controlled conjectures but announces the occasions with suspiciously ironical inductiveness.[105] He teasingly pretends that to speculate about unrecorded events is more significant than to conjecture about unspecified mental conduct in a context which renders it imperative to judge characters in terms of general human nature. Holding that "every Book ought to be read with the same Spirit, and in the same Manner, as it is writ," he does not make his spirit obvious since he recognises the impossibility of transfusing knowledge into readers. His trust that his novel will mediate knowledge, however, explains why readers must recognise the need to keep story within the bounds of human agency and shun the imaginative surprises of mere fiction. He will not be accused of "falling into

Fiction": probability and truthfulness to history are criteria he applies to rhetoric, imagery, and plot. When he describes Mrs Wilkins's visit to the parish with the simile of a kite, he acts the proud, refined, and magisterial writer:

> The sagacious Reader will not, from this Simile, imagine these poor People had any Apprehension of the Design with which Mrs *Wilkins* was now coming towards them; but as the great Beauty of the Simile may possibly sleep these hundred Years, till some future Commentator shall take this Work in hand, I think proper to lend the Reader a little Assistance in this Place.

Intrusiveness, aestheticism, and doubt about posterity's response ironically stress that he is interested in the general significance and illustrative force of the simile rather than in its capacity as a token of psychological analysis. This is true of his skilful deployment of literary devices.[106]

The sense of learning he shares with Locke informs Fielding's disposition of narrative stance. Comic oscillation between affirmative and tentative expressions governs this stance, obliging readers to test the limits of knowledge, to see how knowledge comes from experience, and to realise what part causal explanations play in acquiring knowledge. When Fielding narrates Northerton's escape, he employs a sentence structure of a main clause and two subordinate but coordinate adverb clauses of condition. This structure seems to offer a categorical explanation of alternative causes: "But whether *Northerton* was carried away in Thunder or Fire, or in whatever other Manner he was gone; it was now certain, that his Body was no longer in Custody." Responding to the disappearance, readers cannot take it as a given since the clauses of condition are not equivalent: the first mockingly voices a superstitious explanation; the second is goadingly uncategorical since it simply makes us want to know the landlady's relation to Northerton which, while hinted at, is ironically claimed to be irrelevant. The alternatives are not alternate. Fielding has disclaimed narrative omniscience to induce readers to see facts as they are and as they require further explanation. Often, his pretence to unfold causal alternatives leads us to recognise the empirical reality of the event described and to ponder a finite judgment. When the sentinel fires his gun at ghostlike Tom, Fielding will not say "Whether Fear or Courage was the Occasion of his Firing, or whether he took Aim at the Object of his Terror." He flourishes his lack of omniscience. This alerts readers to deduce that the adverb clauses of condition are not equivalent and that "Courage" in the first is eclipsed by "Terror" in the second. Aided by Fielding's ironical avoidance of judgment and by Tom's sense of the sentinel's superstitious fear, we deduce the sentinel's mental state. Comic tensions between assertiveness and tentativeness forestall speculative generalisations and direct attention to proper understanding of evidence.[107]

Even when Fielding's speculation about causes is expressed in precise and equivalent categories, a humorous and thoughtful response is the outcome. The following disclaimer adds to the bathos of Square's being discovered in Molly's closet: "Now, whether *Molly* in the Agonies of her Rage, pushed this Rug with her Feet; or, Jones might touch it; or whether the Pin or Nail gave way of its own Accord, I am not certain." The descent into particulars and away from the likely human cause is amusingly gradual. The categories become more limited but, paradoxically, vaguer. We do not know whether the rug is attached by a pin or nail. Dissolving speculative and empirical categories, Fielding illustrates his story's human reality, inviting us to construct the fictional context supporting that reality. Through assertive and tentative narration, he asks us to expatiate responsibly with phenomenal and verbal possibilities: this is amusingly serious. He adopts the same stance towards mind, intent on inducing us to realise the difficulty of knowing the existence of ideas in the mind. So, he praises Sophia's modesty in her early relations with Tom but will not describe her emotional responsiveness theoretically:

> Though neither the young Man's Behaviour, nor indeed his Manner ... were such as could give her any just Cause of suspecting he intended to make Love to her; yet whether Nature whispered some-thing into her Ear, or from what Cause it arose I will not determine, certain it is, some Idea of that Kind must have intruded itself; for her Colour forsook her Cheeks, her Limbs trembled, and her Tongue would have faultered, had Tom stopped for an Answer.

He avoids causal justification of Sophia's idea of love. Yet, after denying the applicability of a systematic explanation, he records changes in her physical appearance as signs of her mental state. He is hypothetical about her behaviour but not about her ideas. He supposes the existence of a cause of her love but will not delimit it, pointing to the difficulty of knowing mind rationally and the need to know it empirically. He purposefully operates within restricted categories and is cheerfully cautious in describing the interior life.[108]

If avoidance of causation draws us to Sophia's interior and representative attractiveness, elsewhere, it compounds irony. In mock speculation about Mrs Blifil's reaction to her husband's death, tentative grammar and suggestive vocabulary expose the histrionic behaviour of the widow and the hypocritical greed of her physicians: "Whether, as the Lady had at first persuaded her Physicians to believe her ill, they had now, in return, persuaded her to believe herself so, I will not determine; but she continued a whole Month with all the Decorations of Sickness." Her illness is a sham, but there is a tacit contract of self-interest between her and the doctors. A similar double irony arises when Fielding pretends to be unable to judge Dr Blifil's faith: "Whether his Religion was real, or consisted only in Appearance, I shall not presume to say, as I am not possessed of any Touchstone, which can distinguish the true from the false." Not only does context make Dr Blifil's acquisitiveness and hypocrisy clear, but the peremptory and haughty tone of the disclaimer signals the narrator's unreliability. The disclaimer may be valid theoretically since there can be no a priori way of measuring inner integrity. But, if complacent, abstract judgment is condemned implicitly by the disclaimer, Dr Blifil is satirised firmly, implying Fielding's trust in a practical touchstone. While the ironical presentation of evidence and conclusion stems from an unsystematic attitude towards causation and from belief in the need for personal realisation of knowledge and judgment, Fielding's practical trust in knowledge of causation can be illuminated by the following passage in *Of the Conduct of the Understanding*:

> Every man carries about him a touchstone, if he will make use of it, to distinguish substantial gold from superficial glitterings, truth from appearances. And indeed the use and benefit of this touchstone, which is natural reason, is spoiled and lost only by assumed prejudices, over-weening presumption and narrowing our minds. The want of exercising it in the full extent of things intelligible is that which weakens and extinguishes this noble faculty in us.

Locke here insists that exercise of judgment is essential in the development of human potential, yet he stresses that it can operate properly only by being based on empirical assumptions about learning. Fielding's ironical narrative stance exercises readers' natural reason and induces them to think of judgment in terms of continuous effort and constant practice.[109]

That allusions to Locke in *Tom Jones* are not respectful does not negate the contention the novel's ideas of learning and judgment resemble the philosopher's, Fielding being amusingly indirect about sources of ideas. In a passage emphasising the accessibility of ancient ideas and the bankruptcy of modern ones, he insists with comic hyperbole that he will never "scruple to take to myself any Passage which I shall find in an antient Author to my Purpose, without setting down the Name of the Author from whence it is taken." His humanism leads him to mock truistic citations of writers and ideas: "It hath been observed by wise Men or Women, I forget which, that all Persons are doomed to be in Love once in their Lives"; "It hath been observed by some Man of much greater Reputation for Wisdom than myself, that Misfortunes seldom come single"; and "It was well-remarked by one, (and perhaps by more) that Misfortunes do not come single." Such formulae expose pedantry and pretension: vagueness about authorities and obviousness of saws wittily imply that ideas are common property in that they stem from the accumulated experience of mankind. However, Fielding wins comic effects from detailing the abuse of authorities. When Mrs Western defies Sophia to argue with her, she asserts that "The antient Philosophers, such as *Socrates, Alcibiades,* and others, did not use to argue with their Scholars"; her claim to follow Socrates's pedagogy exposes her ignorance of the philosopher's dialectic. Citing authorities may rationalise pride and laziness and fortify moral evasiveness. Although Square models himself on Plato and Aristotle, he does so with no eclectic capacity: "In Morals he was a profest *Platonist,* and in Religion he inclined to be an *Aristotelian.*" His academic sense of philosophy heightens his hypocrisy. Unsurprisingly, Fielding does not treat modern philosophy respectfully. With tongue in cheek, he praises Shaftesbury's great elegance but is derogatory when refusing to justify Sophia's deception of Lady Bellaston with that philosopher's sense of permissive prevarication and when deflating Square's enthusiasm for Shaftesbury's stoicism by cheerfully describing the disruptive effect which the divine's biting his tongue causes. Fielding is engagingly indirect in criticising Locke. Holding that invention and judgment are reciprocal as far as writers are concerned, Fielding rejects the well-known, if unspecified, Lockean position that memory and judgment operate apart. That Mrs Fitzpatrick has read *An Essay concerning Human Understanding* (1689) on Locke's explanation of cognitive weakness to excuse her incoherence implies that he models moral duplicity.[110]

Still, Fielding follows Locke's empiricism. Satirising dramatic rules, he cites Locke's blind man whose synaesthesia likened scarlet to the sound of a trumpet. The bombastic, archaic language of heroic plays justifies the blind man's likening the trumpet sound to that colour since both produce mere sensations. He cites the blind man again when he assumes readers have experienced love if he is to write about it; it would be as absurd to write without this assumption as it is for a blind man to talk of colours. The first allusion to the blind man asserts that simple ideas are important as touchstones and that ideas of sensation must be connected to ideas of reflection, and the second suggests that ideas of sensation may serve as a paradigm for ideas of reflection. His comic accounts of perception and comprehension are often empirical. He enjoys describing "the Operations of the Mind" when Mrs Partridge's jealousy fluctuates between certainty and doubt: he limits himself to the evidence she has about her husband's infidelity and, with cheerful equivocation, maintains she has enough to warrant suspicion about his deficiencies but not enough to doubt his sexual conduct. He similarly justifies Sophia's suspicion about Mrs Fitzpatrick: Sophia does not have a "Quicksightedness into Evil."[111] Slow to be provoked, she upholds "the Faculty of seeing what is before your Eyes, and of drawing Conclusions from what you see." Far from suspicious, Sophia is a model of judgment; she balances diffidence and perspicacity with empirical acuity. Ironical about Tom's diffident passion for Sophia, Fielding bases Tom's realisation of her love for him and awareness of his feelings for her on empirical processes. Alert to Sophia's bad piano playing, observant of her face, and recalling events, Tom detects her love and discovers his passion for her. Thus, observation, memory, reflection, and intuition wittily betoken a model of mental operations.[112]

Fielding obliges us to treat the activity of reading empirically. When he introduces Sophia, he claims to help us form an "exact Idea" of the heroine. But images which to him represent Sophia are to us mere allusions. Besides, each attempt to elucidate resemblance shows the impossibility of conveying an exact idea of her. Frustrated, the narrator finally links his image of his wife to that of Sophia, claiming this image gives us an "adequate Idea" of the heroine. The change from exact to adequate idea is as informative as the inaccessibility of the "adequate Idea." Readers see that simple ideas cannot be shared and that representational images are arbitrary and conventional: we are taught that fictional ideas can never be exact and that they are adequate only in contradistinction to ideas of sensation. Fielding invites a similar response when he toys with the solipsistic notion that we know only our own ideas. About a footman's resounding knock he says: "To attempt to describe this Noise to those who have heard it would be vain, and to aim at giving any Idea of it to those who have never heard the like, would still be more vain." He pretends to be trapped by the tenets that words cannot substitute for simple ideas and that experience alone validates the use of words. This ironically excessive commitment to theory prompts us to understand the extent to which fictional resist philosophical ideas and to respond to narrative conventions with pragmatic assumptions.[113]

However, Fielding does use empiricism to direct readers' judgment of characters. He justifies Tom's reverence for the gipsy king via the association of ideas. Although this leader has none of the accoutrements of kingship, Tom beholds him with "an Idea of Awe and Respect." To obviate the judgment that this idea is imaginary, Fielding claims that "such Ideas are incident to Power, and almost inseparable from it." He also employs empirical ideas to create sympathy for the hero when he humorously describes Tom's need for a shilling to go to the masquerade. Addressing readers who might regard Tom's petty wants as ridiculous, he asks them to reflect on their larger wants in order to have "a perfect Idea of what Mr. *Jones* felt." To Fielding, material need is not affected by scale. Tom's monetary requirements may be comically small, but they represent a modification of the idea shared by the audience: Lockean simple modes complement Fielding's preference for dealing in natural motives and rejecting supernatural ones. He often makes perceptual experience and empirical modes the measure of his characters' moral ideas.[114]

Irony and humour shape Fielding's education of readers' judgment with empirical ideas. His anticipation and redirection of audience response, at the expense of the narrator's standing, emphasise that understanding arises only along with a sense of fallibility. We are seldom allowed a total judgment: we must be satisfied with partial causes, the narrator comically pretending not to know whole causes. Thus, he is tentative about Jenny Jones's dismissal from the Partridge household: he neither explains her conduct nor analyses her state of mind but speculates about the violence she escapes by fleeing. Nor does he determine whether surprise or fear renders Partridge speechless before his wife but is sure about his sexual consolation of her, this certainty couched in mock tentativeness. Exercising our appreciation of ironic withholding of causal explanation, he invites us to think about sufficient and necessary empirical ideas independently of narrative stance.[115]

Fielding disclaims omniscience to get readers to trust conjectures about causation. So, he mocks himself and goads us when he pretends that he cannot describe Sophia's love for Tom: "Her Sensations, however, the Reader's Heart (if he or she have any) will better represent than I can." Similarly, he will not describe Sophia's reaction to the garrulous and coarse Mrs Honour since readers "may probably conjecture" soundly about the heroine's mind. In cases when he claims to find narrative commentary problematic, such as the deteriorating relationship of Mrs Blifil and Mrs Wilkins and Allworthy's complex idea of charity, Fielding serves as an ironical model for thinking about cause and effect: indirection provokes common-sense, causal thinking. He rouses awareness of imputing motives that respects empirical assumptions. While his manipulation of narrative stance implicitly reveals his concern to encourage readers to expatiate sensibly about causation, he also explicitly advises us to think according to a restricted model of causation. After surprisingly explaining Betty Seagrim's hatred of her sister, Molly, in terms of sexual jealousy, he announces that "we did not think it necessary to assign this Cause sooner, as Envy itself alone was adequate to all the Effects we have mentioned." To dispel easy notions of cause and effect, he occasionally demonstrates the undesirability of judging narrative events simply. Regarding Sophia's loving but fearful obedience to her bullying father, he argues that "it is no unusual Thing to ascribe those Actions entirely to Fear, which are in a great Measure produced by Love." At one time, then, he advises readers to regard causation in a serial manner, and at another, he counsels a balanced, unconventional judgment.[116]

To respect this view of causation, Fielding denies parallels between literary and actual causes. Thus, he saps the report that Sophia's charming voice made a horse stop:

> Perhaps, however, the Fact may be true, and less miraculous than it hath been represented; since the natural Cause seems adequate to the Effect: For as the Guide at that Moment desisted from constant Application of his armed Right Heel ... it is more than possible, that this Omission alone might occasion the Beast to stop, especially as this was very frequent with him at other Times.

He is tentative about the fact to stress the relation of knowledge to experience. The amusingly indirect style describing material functions heightens the gap between narration and reality. To this effect, he declares, about the Lieutenant's anxiety to capture Northerton rather than aid the injured Tom, that "We mention this Observation, not with any View of pretending to account for so odd a Behaviour, but lest some Critic should hereafter plume himself on discovering it." By pretending to eschew causal analysis, he saps literary observation. He differentiates between actual and literary causation to heighten judgmental tensions. He tenaciously maintains that viewpoints afforded by fiction do not obtain in life: he constantly justifies Allworthy's actions and judgments, while charging readers to remember their fallibility and to look beyond fictional knowledge. But, while he variously and unsteadily rouses readers to judgment founded on the distinctness of fiction and life, he trusts that affective literary devices will absorb readers and lead them to real learning. Despite the playfully rhetorical styles which introduce Sophia, he grants us a "perfect Intimacy" with his heroine. She is "really a Copy from Nature": the "Idea of Female Perfection" she embodies is true of "many of our fair Country-women." Fielding's mediation often leads readers to this sort of knowledge. As he says, "it is a kind of tacit Affront to our Reader's Understanding, and may also rob him of that Pleasure which he will receive in forming his own Judgment of her Character," if he is always told how to react.[117]

Tom Jones improves our humane judgment: Fielding induces us to understand causation and knowledge practically. Although he neither composes a "System" nor feels "obliged to reconcile every Matter to the received Notions concerning Truth and Nature," his playfulness elicits empirical awareness of learning and judgment. Humour prevents the novel from fortifying the predispositions of wise and silly people: it lets him avoid voicing precepts. Glad not to be "an ordinary Parson [who] fills his Sermon by repeating his Text at the End of every Paragraph," he is adamant about "the great, useful and uncommon Doctrine" of prudence. The comic ways in which he connects empiricism and judgment show that, besides being aware of the dangers of didacticism, he celebrates how humanism informs literature and life.[118]

Natural History and the Novel

In 1800, natural history more than rivalled the novel. Longer established and published in greater numbers, it affected the English language more.[119] Still, its empirical and literary diction shaped its rival in a curious dialectic: scientific words influenced fictional procedures as poetic diction induced authors of natural history to employ "genteel vocabulary" and imagery to personify phenomena. This reciprocity challenges literary history's equation of science with the plain style and the novel with realism.[120] Natural history, being both a literary genre and scientific pursuit, extends narrative processes. Its influence on fiction's diversity upsets the claim that by the 1740s, the novel was a stable "conceptual category."[121]

From the time of Daniel Defoe, narrative artists developed techniques in the face of natural history, tensions between admiration for and rejection of natural history continuing well past 1740. When *The Natural History of Selbourne* appeared in 1788, Gilbert White had digested twenty years of field-work and epistolary correspondence with naturalists. But his text embodies more than empirical observation; it is the acme of a genre whose dialectic involves social hierarchy, economic progress, and spiritual meditation.[122] Despite contributing to the Royal Society in appreciation of Carl Linnaeus (1707–1778) and Count Buffon (1707–1788), White draws on theological views in John Ray's *Wisdom of God Manifested in the Works of the Creation* (1691) and William Derham's *Physico-Theology, or a Demonstration of the Being and Attributes of God from His Works of Creation* (1713). No less than Ray (1627–1705) and Derham (1657–1735), White inspects plants and animals to defend providential order and the reciprocity of fact and meditation. Tensions between materialism and spirituality in *The Natural History of Selbourne* confirm the dialectic Keith Thomas traces in natural history.[123] He shows that, while this genre permeated society, it was inherently aristocratic. Since aristocratic ideals informed seventeenth-century bourgeois ideology, he indicates that social and theological themes in the genre instantiate aristocratic values more enduringly than literary history has admitted.

If physico-theology defies simple-minded progress, its tracing of providential design and spiritual order upholds stable hierarchies. Apologies for natural history opposing aristocratic ideology clarify its dialectic. Take Joseph Priestley (1733–1804), the radical Unitarian, and

Frances Brooke, the orthodox Anglican. In 1769, shortly after White began his journals, these authors, in defending physico-theology, treated relations between tradition and progress in bourgeois thinking somewhat slackly. To Priestley, "Natural history exhibits a boundless variety of scenes" that are "infinitely analogous to one another." Yet he limits its meditative dialectic, its "contemplation of uniformity and variety," to material evolution: the "new plants, new animals, and new fossils" found by naturalists testify to the "unbounded power, wisdom, and goodness of God," proving that "every object in Nature" is "rising in due degree to its maturity and perfection."[124] Brooke approaches natural history with sentimental gentility. The heroine of *The History of Emily Montague* (1769) is a "little natural philosopher" who reads "Ray, Derham, and fifty other strange old fellows that one never heard of" and "eternally" pores "through a microscope to discover the wonders of creation," physico-theology being for her a feminine pursuit that disdains economic and aristocratic power.[125]

Since her novel promotes imperialism, Brooke's view of physico-theology evades natural history's dialectic, as does Priestley's. Their belittlement of it implies that middle-class ideology, far from joining intellectual and social tensions, is unstable. However, White's trust in aristocratic ideology allows him to bring the genre's dialectic to its acme in *The Natural History of Selbourne*. Its formal eclecticism and social philosophy evince the creative flexibility of aristocratic ideology. His methods and attitudes clarify the rivalry between natural history and the novel as well as that between earlier and later fictional models. He links linguistic and literary invention to science and reconciles social hierarchy to economic progress, showing how well fictional images of plants and animals embody dialectic. Given its reliance on the taxonomies of physico-theology, the novel could not avoid aristocratic ideology. That it was not governed by a stable, progressive bourgeois ideology is clear from how fiction of the 1740s anticipates White. Analogies, fables, and hierarchical motifs reveal figurative modes, illustrating how the novel tried to imitate its rival.

The Natural History of Selbourne epitomises natural history's literary and scientific methods.[126] Its epistolary mode and digest of journals that advance observation and classification testify to White's acceptance of collaborative study, social discourse, and humanist letters. His allusions to Virgil embody an equal esteem for poetry and science: they show that natural history uses deduction as well as induction and that lexical and empirical style is reciprocal.[127] Whether Virgil describes a dove haunting a cave, a swallow nesting among rafters, or frozen Italian rivers, White treats the Roman poet's diction as phenomenal evidence. Granting that Virgil and the "ancients" did not "attend to specific differences" like "modern naturalists," he comfortably deduces information from classical texts. He reads epithets in Virgil about birdsong, plumage, and nests as specifying swallows rather than martins, confirming that philology and classical poetry sustain natural history. Besides addressing the "classic reader," he cites vernacular poetry to validate eclecticism and illustrate dialectic: the black-cap's "wild sweetness" recalls the song in *As You Like It* about the merry human voice tuning itself to the "*wild* bird's throat." He contrasts the ecological and theological views of John Milton (1608–1674) and James Thomson (1700–1748); he belittles Milton's vagueness about how birds migrate and mocks his refusal to admit "mutual fellowship" between birds and animals but upholds Thomson as a "nice observer of natural occurrences." If Milton's similes describe the world, White rejects the epic poet's scorn for converse between species, preferring Thomson's natural systems. When Thomson explains how cows bedung the water they drink and introduce to streams and lakes the insects that fish eat, White lauds this creaturely interdependence, showing that literary associations and judgment should deter a single-minded view of human uniqueness.[128]

White's biblical allusions tie analogical bonds between species like Derham's *Physico-Theology*. For both men, providential design comprehends all species. So, White applies Isaiah's verse about the gratitude of ox and ass to their keeper to the tortoise: that this "torpid" and "abject" reptile is grateful to man emblematises God's ordering of nature. He extends Job's image of the ostrich's callousness to the cuckoo and adapts Psalm 78:19 to affirm that winter insects "furnish" the wheat-ear and win-chat "with a plentiful table in the wilderness." In physico-theology's fusion of empiricism and meditation, White's respectful adaptation of biblical words fits his paradoxical view of the theological distinctiveness and comparability of animals and humans. His allusive self-consciousness cannot be gauged until his aim for developing tensions between empiricism and spirituality is measured. In his mind, natural history must uphold social hierarchy. Scornful of the "want of a liberal education" in the "lower people," he accepts that natural history has placed him in a "circle of gentlemen." Hierarchy lies behind his trust that the agrarian revolution has reached a "pitch of perfection" and that enclosure is enlightened. He naturalises hierarchy by attacking the press for blaming grain shortages on "combinations" of landowners: rabid journalism forgets that improvements in husbandry have reduced hunger. He sees himself as the equal of those he defends: he, too, owns "extensive shrubberies," his retainers protecting ornamental plants from killing frosts. He regards aristocratic advancement of horticulture and landscape design as an ultimate emblem of hierarchy: the gardens of aristocrats are major elements of natural geography for White.[129]

His commitment to hierarchy reconciles methodical doubt to ecological system. Stressing that "candour and openness" in undoing false analogies are the "life of natural history," he constructs analogies that figuratively embody tensions between the hierarchy of creation and the logos in all creatures.[130] If he dissects a cuckoo to refute the "idle notion" that this bird does not incubate, his wish to study the "life and conversation of animals" requires him to explain a cat's liking for a leveret, its natural enemy, by the myth of Romulus and Remus. His sense of the "chain of beings" sees him applying imperial myth to animals while treating them as scientific objects. When he compares the owl's voice to man's and cooing doves to moaning lovers, his perception of birds' "ancient" and "elliptical" language links them to humans. His fusion of empiricism and emblems climaxes in his account of barnyard fowl: hens warn chicks about birds of prey, chicks twitter when fed flies, and, giving a "favourite concubine" food, "gallant chanticleer" chooses "amorous phrases" from a "considerable

vocabulary." Humanising and objectifying animals, White accommodates hierarchy to creaturely interdependence.[131]

Conceptual and political tensions between observation and meditation and between tradition and progress lead White to heighten the applicability of linguistic analogy to natural history. Aware of the limitations of scientific classification and the need to name plants and animals severally, he makes polysemy and metaphor instrumental to designation. Spurning "bare descriptions" and "few synonyms," he uses correlative terms: the beech has "smooth rind or bark" and "glossy foliage, or graceful pendulous boughs." Polysemy serves naming: hence, "greater brambling, or snow fleck"; "house-swallow" or "chimney-swallow"; "heath-cock, black-game, or grouse." Giving "common birds" English names, he adds metaphors. He replaces Pliny the Elder's term for the long-legged plover, *Himantopus*, finding the image of a leather thong inapt, with Mathurin Brisson's *l'echasse*, which he adapts to "stilt-plover." While complaining the "bane" of "our science is the comparing one animal to the other from memory," he insists on analogies in the belief that naming creatures entails deductive similes. Thus, stone-curlews run from the egg like partridges, have manners "analogous to the bustard," and take flight like herons; bats drink, like swallows, on the wing; and the brown owl regurgitates fur and feathers like hawks while hiding food like dogs. Analogical observations merge into mental association: the snipe's "ventriloquous hum" is like the turkey's if made by its wings; the red-start wags its tail like fawning dogs; and the wagtail moves its tail like a jaded horse. The fusion of empirical and figurative terms is complete in human analogies. Saying that sparrow-hawks living in a crow's nest keep a "good house" and ample "larder"; that a snake in a "good humour" is "sweet" in its "person"; that a field-mouse nest, "the size of a cricket ball," is a "wonderful procreant cradle"; that corn-ricks are their "grand rendezvous"; and that a tortoise hates rain like a lady in "her best attire," he transfers humanity into natural observation. In claiming *Œdicnemus*, the curlew's Latin name, is expressive since the bird's legs seem "swoln like those of a gouty man," he admits anthropocentrism into scientific classification.[132] His fusion of empiricism and analogies shows that he stresses physico-theology's pluralism by adopting contrary stances to creation. If a bat is a "wonderful quadraped," its movement on the ground is "ridiculous and grotesque"; if a frog's limbs wonderfully exemplify providential economy, it remains "so vile a reptile"; if instinct drives birds to nest wisely but forces martins to build stupidly, it is "above" and "below" reason. The biblical, political, and rhetorical forces thwarting single-minded empiricism are epitomised when, urging botanists to advance study of grasses, he insists that "to raise a thick turf on naked soil would be worth volumes of systematic knowledge," validating natural science with the King of Brobdingnag's humanism voiced by Swift.[133]

Tensions between empiricism and meditation arising from natural history's debt to physico-theology show that White's middle-class contemporaries upheld hierarchy. Thomas Turner (1729-1793), a grocer, and James Woodforde (1740-1803), a parson, enjoyed natural history's speculative and economic benefits. Visiting exhibits of a raccoon, chameleon, and salamander, Turner also read Tournefort on coral, sponges, sea mushrooms, and lithophytes.[134] Interest in the latter's vegetative life of stones matches admiration of Derham's *Physico-Theology*: like White, Turner searches the world for signs of the "all-wise creator." While he explores economic and social bases of natural history, the need for food makes him study the viability of vegetable seeds. To produce cider from apples and perry from pears, he studies new methods in arboriculture. He values sharing game, fish, and produce: the fruits of the earth tighten social bonds. Indebted to the Duke of Newcastle, Turner, on receiving pears and melons from the latter's estate, treats such gifts as a desirable form of communal benevolence.[135] With mixed curiosity and meditation, Woodforde views a Madagascan mongoose and a learned pig, praising God when a peacock fans its tail.[136] That he repairs his cat's broken ribs, keeps a spider as a pet, measures the growth of oaks and scotch firs long after planting them, and records bird-sightings manifests sensitive empiricism. Typically ambivalent about natural history, he is cruel and superstitious: he shoots an old woodpecker for pulling reeds from thatch, and to cure a swollen eye-lid, he rubs it with a black cat's tail. If, richer than the grocer, he farmed cash crops such as turnips, his diary, like Turner's, confirms natural history's ideology. Exchanging apple-trees, shrubs, and laurels with friends, he gives parishioners pears, while accepting trout and pike from his landlord. Hierarchy is firmly maintained.[137]

Natural history's promotion of hierarchy to the middle classes makes it a fit context for the novel, more so since it shaped travelogues as well as diaries, these genres informing the novel's evolution before and after 1740. White knows travelogues mediate natural history.[138] They evidence the growing reciprocity of natural history and novel, confirming the dialectic in this evolution. Travelogues by Defoe, Fielding, Johnson, and Tobias Smollett (1721–1771) prove them precursors of White, this influence again illustrating the novel's generic unfixity.

Tensions between hierarchy and progress in White, Turner, and Woodforde motivate *A Tour through the Whole Island of Great Britain* (1724–1726). To Defoe, animals and plants denote food, scientific knowledge, commerce, and rank: naturalists compete for specimens with investment-conscious landlords and poor peasants.[139] His view that animals are economic and social signs arises when pheasants in Norwich fields prove the city to have more tradesmen than hunting gentlemen and when, on the accidental killing of an eagle in a duckoy, he notes the landlord's anger at not being able to gain by displaying the rare bird or selling it to gentlemen "curious in such things." His lists of birds and fish sold at markets symbolise natural plenitude, national wealth, and local civility. Before White, Defoe is happy wheatear or "English ortolans" cost more at Tunbridge than nearby towns; consumer demand means the resort is economically healthy. Like White, he will not treat natural history in mere empirical terms: leaving naturalists to decide what migration says about avian intelligence, he insists, inspired by a flock of departing swallows, that our "summer friends" think. Narrative playfulness and social ideology govern his empiricism, as in his account of how duckoys operate. Fascinated that ducks lure foreign birds to slaughter, he enters the heads of the "naturalised" ducks, giving them sharp rhetoric: they fly abroad to betray their fellows, telling of easy living conditions in England and reaffirming the message when newcomers reach the duckoy. He then impersonates both sets of ducks, conveying the victims' terror and the well-rewarded cunning of the Englishmen's servants.[140]

Divided sympathy for the ducks—the clever ones are "traytors" and the "guests" willing victims—shows that Defoe's narrative is energised by contrary attitudes. He enjoys satirising naturalists' methods and anthropocentricism. He sneers at Charles Leigh (1662–1701), Charles Cotton (1630–1687), and Thomas Hobbes (1588–1679) for promoting the "wonderless wonders" of the Derbyshire peaks. His account of Soland geese, seasonal visitors to the Firth of Forth, illustrates his ambivalence. Mixing direct and reported evidence, he says the birds' migration is and is not explained by herring schools: the geese arrive with the herring but do not follow the fish. Disparaging causal analysis, he humorously creates analogies which link the geese, the fish the birds eat, and the locals who think the geese a "dainty." Since the birds have the "coarse, rank, ill-relish'd" taste of the fish, the locals' taste is compared to the Egyptians' notorious love of garlic and onions. He mocks the categories of natural history and stresses tensions between classification and analogy when characterising the Soland goose:

> It is a large fowl, rather bigger than an ordinary goose; 'tis duck-footed, and swims as a goose; but the bill is long, thick, and pointed like a crane, or heron, only much thicker, and not above five inches long. Their laying but one egg, which sticks to the rock, and will not fall off, unless pull'd off by force, and then not to be stuck on again; though we thought them fictions, yet, being there at the season, we found true; as also their hatching, by holding the egg fast in their foot. What Nature meant by giving these singularities to a creature, that has nothing else in it worth notice, we cannot determine.

Thus, he anticipates White's sense that natural science entails amplification and fanciful analogy and that tension between specific and generic names involves fact and imagination.[141]

While travel-writing taught Defoe that natural history lends itself to narrative invention and experimentation, Fielding's sensibility spurned travel-writing and natural history as aspects of the novel. *The Journal of a Voyage to Lisbon* will not harmonise physico-theology and empiricism since he rejects both genres. To him, natural historians lie "for the lying sake," telling "monstrous improbabilities and absurdities." Pliny offers "facts contrary to the honour of God, to the visible order of the creation, to the known laws of nature, to the histories of former ages, and to the experience of our own."[142] The exploitation of nature by empirical study and social ideology is pernicious. Unlike Defoe, he will not rejoice that some species are dainties: he refuses to see food in terms of status. He gibes that, were ortolans as big and cheap as "bustards," the rich would turn the common sparrow into a dainty. Angry that London markets sell expensive "john doree" and not whiting and sole the poor can afford, he is disgusted that the rich enjoy food less for intrinsic quality than for costly exclusivity. Outraged by the economic and social differentiation of animals, he holds himself aloof from travelogues and natural histories. About the capture of a shark, he describes the event briefly, not conforming "to the rules and practice of voyage-writing." Support of Derham's *Physico-Theology* clarifies his scorn for natural history. Citing Derham's views that wasps warn those they sting and that the rattlesnake "never meditates a human prey without giving warning of his approach" to the "most venomous" of "human insects," Fielding insists that animals serve humans by providential design and that natural analogies are valid only since they dignify providential power. He uses Derham's sense of vicious insects to subsume biological taxonomy under the religious trust that vicious humans are harmless since they wear their "dispositions in their countenances."[143]

Contrary reactions to natural history in the travelogues of Defoe and Fielding are mirrored by Johnson and Smollett: Johnson comes to natural history with intellectual curiosity, Smollett with dismissive scorn. In *A Journey to the Western Islands of Scotland*, which White admired, Johnson promotes empiricism for illuminating morality. Aware that natural science is upheld in Scotland and that naturalists tend to generalise instead of being "rigidly philosophical," he urges Scots to determine whether Loch Ness remains unfrozen in winter. His observations explore categorical problems for signs about dialectic. He finds Hebrides geese "to be of a middle race": domestic enough to "own a home" yet wild enough "to fly quite away." If an otter's foot is "formed" for swimming, it is like a spaniel. Natural problems spur his ecological ideas. Surprised no naturalist has proposed that the world must have once been as empty of animals as of men, he sees both that the absence of creatures explains the growth of forests and that men and beasts share the environment. He warns that, if species are vanishing, animals no match for guns, mankind too is at risk: no creature, certainly not humans, may live in barren regions.[144]

In *Travels through France and Italy* (1766), Smollett subjects the categorical and semantic aspects of natural problems to satire of French and English culture. He chides the Benedictines of Boulogne for calling the wild duck they eat a species of fish and mocks English prudery for translating *cul-blanc* as "wheatear" rather than "*white-a--e*." If visiting France lets him damn its culinary habits, he lauds its natural plenitude to demean England. Since the "*becca ficas, grieves, or thrushes*," served in French inns, are raw or overcooked, he offers a recipe for making them tender and crisp, opposing his culinary skill to French waste of natural resources. He esteems such resources: France has more varieties of fish; its partridges are bigger; its flowers have stronger scents than in England; standard fruit trees at Nice are unrivalled by English wall-fruit, producing peaches more "solid and tasty." His travelogue turns natural history into cultural ideology like Defoe but with an opposite sense of nationalism and without the latter's narrative playfulness. Nor does he regard humans ecologically like Johnson or promote physico-theology like Fielding. Unlike Defoe and Johnson but like Fielding, Smollett resists writing natural history on its own terms but differs from Fielding in making it serve political, not theological, aims.[145]

The stances on natural history adopted in travelogues confirm that the novel did not have a stable identity when *The Natural History of Selbourne* appeared. The stances clarify the variability of narrative ideologies, a variability the dialectic of which may be defined by analysing how novels both appropriate and resist natural history.

Classification generates problems for the adventurers who cross Africa in Defoe's *Captain Singleton* (1720). Flora and fauna have teasing contrariness, made strange and familiar in a dialectic of experience and imagination. In the "horrid Desart," they find a "moist and nourishing root" for their beasts of burden to eat, a root "not much unlike a Pasnip." The animals forage on a "kind of Herb like a Broad flat Thistle, tho' without any Prickle." The setting is fearful since unclassifiable creation sustains beast and man. The desert alienates and nurtures: seemingly endless, it is "pretty full of green Stuff, of one sort or another," the men feeding on "great Quantities of Roots" and "Things like Pumpkins." Verbal imprecision effects a dialectic proving nature trustworthy. When the men eat "a Root like Carrots, tho' of quite another Taste, but not unpleasant neither, and some *Guiney* Fowls whose Names we did not know," tensions between word and thing, between general and specific names, create and dissolve problems. Fusing analogy and classification, Defoe makes competing stances paradoxically reassuring. When Singleton compares "Wild-Fowl" to those "we have in *England*," namely "Duck, Teal, Widgeon," yet sees "kinds that we had not seen before," classification is disorienting yet comforting.[146]

African animals disturb the adventurers' world view but confirm creation's beneficence. Eating "a creature like a Goat," they enjoy its meat, but it is "no Goat." Natives give them "three living Creatures as big as Calves, but not of that Kind." Categorically puzzled, the Europeans invent analogies only to find them inapplicable: they trap hares "of a kind something different from ours in *England*, larger, and not so swift of Foot, but very good Meat." Baffled classification pushes them towards legend, as in the case of animals which are "between the Kind of a Buffloe and a Deer, but indeed resembled neither; for they had no Horns, and had great Legs like a Cow, with a fine Head, and the Neck like a Deer." Recalling Pliny, this passage muddles the boundary between empiricism and invention which Singleton crosses in anthropocentric complacency. Though Africa has a "Collection of fierce, ravenous, and devouring Creatures," his band grew to not "much mind them." Calling fearful events "pleasant Adventures with the wild Creatures" and ferocious beasts "Gentle-folks" at a "general Rendezvous," his posturing is suspect.[147] His failure to grasp dialectic is clear in his views of elephants: detailing their herbivorous habits, he sees them as terrifying yet compares them to a harmless "Drove of Cattel" raising dust on summer roads in England. Polarity confirms Defoe's irony: admitting and denying the elephant's specificity, Singleton evades physico-theology, prompting readers to meditate on it.[148]

Rather than dramatise natural history, Fielding belittles the rival genre. His observation and classification of animals usually serve as satirical devices. In *Joseph Andrews*, when Lady Booby calls her servant "a reptile of a lower order, a weed that grows in the common garden of creation," and Mrs Slipslop laments that her mistress thinks servants not "born of the Christian *specious*," natural history exposes aristocratic pomposity and lower-class illiteracy. Fielding's satiric typology reduces bad characters to animals and devalues empiricism.

Mock-epic similes call Slipslop a cow, tigress, and pike and Parson Trulliber a goose and pig, the animal analogies severing human dignity from vice by trivialising the latter. When a would-be ravisher of Fanny is presented as a game-cock toying amorously with a hen till it spies a rival, the simile offsets the sexual violence by degrading the rapist and creating the antithesis by which Parson Adams is called "no chicken." Good characters are not compared to animals. Birds and dogs revere Joseph because of his compatibility with Fanny: these two see animals as fellow creatures. But those who see humans as animals are evil. The squire who uses "dogs of his own species" to hunt men is a barbarian who sees Adams as "the largest jack-hare," and his view that the poor need clothes no more than a "horse or any other animal" damns Peter Pounce for lacking Christian charity; he grossly rationalises economic greed and social snobbery.[149]

In *Tom Jones*, animal concern signals hypocrisy. In freeing Sophia's caged bird and seeing her as a "human Ortolan," Blifil displays his envy of Tom and his prurience. Neither meditative nor scientific views of animals escape satire. The Man of the Hill's physico-theology is spurious; if all insects and vegetables are "honoured with bearing Marks of the Attributes of its Great Creator," he holds that man has lost His favour. Fielding mocks the Royal Society's "laws of Animal Œconomy." He jeers at its likely reaction to the "Bird with a Letter in his Maw," by which Tom writes to Sophia, to criticise the Society's confusing empiricism and scorn for common sense. Abuse of natural history explains why Fielding resorts to fables. In fitting Grimalkin to Mrs Partridge when she attacks her husband and to Squire Western when he stops tracking his daughter, he applies the fable's comic ambivalence to the motif of the interdependence of animals and mankind for moral aims: the jealous wife who is a ferocious tiger and ignoble cat and the obsessive hunter who is a driven mouser are bathetic images which convey that animal analogies applied to humans show that conscience divides the two orders of creation. Rejecting concern for the animal realm fortifies Fielding's humanistic tenet that mankind is paramount in creation.[150]

Samuel Richardson, translator of Aesop, draws analogies between animals and humans that stress his heroines' pathos by joining fables and biblical allusions.[151] In *Pamela* (1740), fear makes the heroine liken herself to weak animals. Mr B. forces her to see herself as a bird: he makes her heart flutter "like a Bird in a Cage new caught," causing her to think of living on hips, haws, pig-nuts, potatoes and turnips. Her victimisers are dangerous beasts: Mrs Jewkes is a "*Wolfkin*" and "inhuman Tygress." Charging herself with superstition when she thinks Mr B. and Mrs Jewkes turn the bull upon her, Pamela hardly doubts the validity of her observations and judgments of animals. She is sure that "Bulls, and Bears, and Lions, and Tygers," as well as wicked humans, are her enemies. The fables by which she tests herself uphold analogical sense: she judges her imprudence in terms of the grasshopper and ants, defines her timidity in terms of the town and country mice, and sees her vulnerability in terms of the sheep accused by the wolf and tried by the vulture. By coming to natural history through fables and the Bible, she gains coherence: she feels marriage will prove her a pliant willow, not a rigid oak, and, citing 1 Samuel 17:37, thanks God for delivering her from the "Paw of the Lion and the Bear." Her mixed typology is clarified by garden images. If the Lincolnshire garden flourishes, as its nectarines attest, Richardson, far from stressing the social implications of horticulture, emphasises Pamela's pretended ignorance about beans and sunflowers as an epistolary stratagem. Disgust with a "great nasty Worm" says less about her gardening than her self-dramatising faith in her belief that marriage renders her an undeservedly exalted worm. The typology by which Richardson frames natural history is apparent when Pamela leaves the Lincolnshire estate and likens her exodus to that of the Israelites longing for the onions and garlic of Egypt.[152]

Ritual aspects of natural history let Richardson infuse *Clarissa* (1748) with the dialectic of physico-theology to endue his epistolary writing with energy. The Harlowe estate's "rambling Dutch-taste garden"; its filbert-walk and yew-hedge; its plantations of oaks, elms, and limes; and its phyllirea hedge symbolise the Harlowes' belief in horticultural and political progress. Their belief heightens the allegory with which Clarissa clothes horticulture. Seeing herself as a fallen blossom, she lays on her coffin a lily along with a verse from Psalm 103 that values flowers as signs of transience. Imaging her seduction in terms of buds in spring, nipped by severe frost and blighted by the east wind, she makes Lovelace the epitome of garden pests: he is the caterpillar eating the fair leaf of virgin fame, the eastern blast, the mildew thwarting the husbandman, and the canker-worm turning the damask rose yellow. Her transcendent faith is revealed in her trust that her spiritual hopes, being better rooted than her earthly ones, will bring forth more fruit.[153]

Ornithology in *Clarissa* heightens secular and religious dialectic. Her bantams, pheasants, and pea-hens, a legacy from her grandfather, Clarissa visits twice a day: she enjoys watching their "inspiriting liveliness." They aid her sense of analogy. So, she challenges her brother's claim that sons, not daughters, are chickens produced for the home table by asking when their necks are wrung, yet she sees herself as a bird caught in her brother's snare. Her critical yet pathetic analogies are justified by Lovelace's narcissism. He stirs his fantasies by picturing her as a trapped bird. His knowledge of how birds come to accept entrapment feeds a wish for sexual power. To conquer her resistance in fantasy, he details the mating of poultry: he observes how the strutting cock invites his favourite mistress to take a barley-corn in an affectedly meek prelude to mounting her exultantly. While he imagines the cowering hen to dream of sexual control, Clarissa treats birds as social and religious symbols. Stating that parental wings must protect young girls from vultures, hawks, kites, and other birds of prey, she meditates her relation to the pelican, owl, and sparrow—scriptural emblems of spiritual exile. Her allegorising is validated by Lovelace's histrionic analogies. Thinking himself an eagle that preys, not on wrens, phil-tits, or wagtails, but on the noblest of quarries and imagining himself a strutting villain of a bird who imperially feathers lady after lady and abandons them to hatch the "genial product," he sees Clarissa as an innocent chicken whom he may capture with the aid of fellow rakes.[154]

The analogical inconsistency of his intention to sap Clarissa's physico-theology extends to animals. Granting her nobility by calling her lion-hearted, when opposed by her family, he sees himself as a lion like James II. Forgetting this monarch fled the throne, he reveals he is as vulnerable to Jacobite prejudices as to sexual fantasies: his images recoil on him since he lacks Clarissa's figurative discipline. Prospects of violating her make him compare himself precariously to a hungry but bashful hound with froth on its vermillion jaws, an elephant attempting to snuff up the moon, and a fly buzzing round a taper. To Clarissa, such analogies form part of his rattle: alluding to Derham, she claims Lovelace warns people that he is a snake. His histrionic abuse of natural history means he never joins ecology to spirituality. While he cites David's remorse about the lamb to flatter himself for not violating Rosebud, Clarissa, in the trauma of rape, applies to herself the fable of the wild animal becoming a dangerous lapdog. Such self-criticism makes her seem Johnsonian: like Richardson's friend, she fortifies her case against Lovelace by arguing that, having destroyed other species, man attacks the weaker of his own.[155]

Lovelace and Clarissa voice opposing views of natural history: secular libertinism is overmatched by ecology and spiritual transcendence. Illuminating the opposing ways in which natural history induced Defoe to build paradoxes into narrative and Fielding to endorse an outlook sympathetic to traditional tropes, the conflict between Lovelace and Clarissa helps define variable reactions to natural history in later novels. It clarifies the dialectic in *Rasselas* (1759), Johnson enlivening his fable by various stances to natural history. Rasselas defines his discontent in the Happy Valley by contrasting himself to birds and beasts, yet learning he needs a goal comes from observing lambs and kids. At first, failing to escape the valley, he finds plants and animals engrossing. If he criticises simple-minded analogies between animals and man, Johnson still promotes them dialectically. The artist who models wings on the bat's fails not because of the folly of the attempt but because he forgets his model, deluding himself that bat-wings will carry him beyond eagle and vulture. When the upward, oblique line of conies' burrows leads to escape, Johnson shows that reason and common-sense must acknowledge animal instinct: he implies the necessary coexistence of empirical observation and traditional fable.[156]

While Johnson depicts Rasselas's contrary reactions to the animal world, Sterne, in *A Sentimental Journey* (1768), makes Yorick's erratic reactions convey tensions between sensibility and satire. Yorick pretends to identify with myrtles, cypresses, and starling but avoids traditional ritual in his self-indulgence. Instead of heightening sensitivity by addressing the trees and the bird, Yorick converts them into rhetorical or heraldic emblems, exposing both his fine but coarse awareness and Sterne's double vision that empirical precision and subjective rationalisation are inextricable. The recoil of Yorick's wish to cultivate sensibility by eschewing common experiences of the Grand Tour is histrionic materialism like Lovelace's. Yorick's response to the dead ass is slow and mechanical unlike his pony's intuition, and his citation of Bevoriskius on copulating sparrows displays a prurience remote from scientific observation. Set on getting close to nature and his heart, he meets the contraries of life and writing with only momentary comprehension. If the dead ass creates anxiety one second, the next he falls asleep; if the starling's notes rouse him to the Bastille's horrors, he sells the bird to unfeeling lords, reducing it to heraldic prestige.[157]

That Yorick's declarations about natural history mask an uncritical acceptance of the status quo shows how Sterne applies his experimental satire to attack the complex of economic progress and social hierarchy noted in Defoe and fulfilled by White. Smollett, rejecting Sterne's experimentation, promotes this complex. Allusions to natural history in *Humphry Clinker* (1771) promote a dialectic of tradition and progress. Some allusions are comic, as when Matt sees himself and fellow old-timers at Bath as "Chinese gudgeons" in a punch bowl and Jery calls marriage partners widgeons about to find themselves in a duckoy. But most champion social hierarchy, ecology, and agricultural and financial innovation, Smollett reconciling diverse ideas systematically. When Matt calls lower-class women seeking rich husbands "shovel-nosed sharks" preying on the "blubber" of "uncouth whales of fortune," natural history defies change in social structure. A landowner, Matt upholds ecology to deflate London's economic centrality and to honour the rural gentry: while he boasts that his bread and poultry are products of natural soil and moderate cultivation, he mocks London's artificial soil and the diseases of its force-fed poultry. Like White, Matt promotes enclosure for boosting productively new modes of cultivating turnips, apricots, nectarines, pineapples, and grapes. He enthuses over the notion that the earth's fruits strengthen economic and political culture. At the end of the novel, he expounds the virtue of capitalising land: families become self-sufficient and finance their own mortgages. Following the restoration of one estate according to modern principles of enclosure, drainage, and shelter-belts, Matt renews a friend's estate by undoing its fashionable landscape: he turns a shrubbery and pleasure grounds into corn fields and pasture, planting clumps of firs, beech, and chestnut to make a windbreak that will yield fuel and make the fields more productive.[158]

Urban incursions into rural life appalled Oliver Goldsmith, Henry MacKenzie (1745–1831), and Thomas Day (1748–1789); they neither shared Smollett's trust in the agrarian revolution nor reconciled hierarchy to social progress. The names Thornhill, Primrose, and Burchell in *The Vicar of Wakefield* (1766) convey Goldsmith's feelings. When libertine Thornhill kills a stag on the Primroses' land, giving them the venison, and when his chaplain shoots a blackbird that her mother forces Sophia to accept, Goldsmith shows that *ownership* of wildlife means that gifts of food from the upper classes fortify privilege and compromise recipients. If the Primroses enjoy idyllic farm life, their insensitivity to natural history makes them vulnerable to the landlord who traps them in political and legal systems. The vicar sells "old Blackberry" cheaply, deceived into thinking his healthy horse diseased. Urban fashion ensnares the Primroses because they ignore the sense of nature in Burchell, the true landlord. His love of children, ballads, and folk ways as well as scorn of high life make him an ideal landowner.[159]

Harley, MacKenzie's hero in *The Man of Feeling* (1771), despises fashion. In disgust, he likens the profit a keeper of a London asylum makes from charging people to view his "fierce and unmanageable" inmates to that of those who display wild beasts. He spurns landscape gardening and the "sacrilege of the plough" since modern agriculture displaces the rural populace. An idealist, he works the soil by hand and houses a displaced tenant, giving him subsistence in a contemplative setting. To MacKenzie, the gap between landlord and tenant is closed by fellow feeling with trees, the tenant viewing those near his farm as family members and the master buried in the churchyard under the one he had long loved.[160] Such sentiment evades natural history's complex of scientific classification, agricultural innovation, and aristocratic power.[161]

In *The History of Sandford and Merton* (1783-1789), Day naturalises sentimental ecology dogmatically, insisting that bourgeois ideology cannot escape natural history's dialectic. Harry Merton, a middle-class boy, is innately sympathetic; he gives his supper to robins and avoids stepping on worms. Forgetting that robins eat worms, Day presents Harry eagerly learning the properties of plants and convinced the rich destroy hedges, poultry, dogs, and cattle. Tommy Sandford, an upper-class child, is cruel to animals. Since Harry upholds the utility of work, he lectures Tommy on reindeer and Laplanders and on the deadly nightshade. The dubiety of such lectures is matched by the inconsistency the boys' teacher manifests on animal rights. He urges that larks not be shot for eating farmers' turnips and that hares ought simply to be fenced out of gardens, yet he defends singeing cats that attack caged birds because this will change them permanently. Tension between adapting and accepting animal nature and between ecological and utilitarian stances to natural history is avoided by Day. He relies evasively on fables: in his work ethic, Harry compares himself to ants as against flies, citing the fable of the ass dressed in a lion's skin to mock aristocracy and rationalise ignorance of polite manners. Paradoxically, ancient fables justify scorn for cultural tradition and reactionary emblems match natural history to innate principle.[162]

By century's end, Maria Edgeworth (1768-1849) in *Castle Rackrent* (1800), after Fielding, equated aristocracy with ecological ignorance and argued that absentee landlords extorted money from estates and abused tenants.[163] Yet, the novel still drew on its rival, as the less doctrinaire Jane Austen shows. *Mansfield Park* (1814) deploys natural history more obliquely than the radical sentimentalists. Fanny Price is a natural historian: she collects plants, studies "inanimate nature," identifies with trees but shuns the design of Humphry Repton (1752-1818) for improving Sotherton. Reshaped landscapes convey her more radical physico-theological interest in nature's plenitude than Harley's or Harry Merton's. She deplores the regular pruning of larches, laurels, and beeches at Sotherton; plants' natural forms mediate knowledge; the thriving evergreens in Mrs Grant's shrubbery tell her the vicarage's soil is better than Mansfield Park's. Beautiful in themselves, trees are more so since they lead her to contemplate nature's variety. To Fanny, it is spiritually inspiring that the growth of evergreens varies from that of deciduous trees: the commonest species and botanical principles satisfy her "rambling fancy." Unlike the Man of the Hill, her love of nature is not solitary. At Portsmouth, she misses Mansfield Park's springtime vegetation but its people more: physico-theology improves her sociability. Austen stresses Fanny's maturity by contrasting her with pretenders to natural history. When Tom placates his father by noting pheasants in the woods, he masks filial callousness. On taking a specimen of heath and pheasants' eggs from the gardener at Sotherton, Mrs Norris says, in her avariciousness, that the birds will console her loneliness. Absurdly claiming to have improved the vicarage by planting one apricot tree, she dignifies Fanny's spiritual love of natural history.[164]

That Fanny links aesthetics and science, finding sociability in physico-theology, shows how the novel absorbed natural history to advance its modes. Natural history influenced its formal experiments and obliged it to face its rival's aristocratic codes. In facing natural history's dialectic of empiricism and spirituality, the novel could not ignore the latter's emphasis on social hierarchy. Natural history's eclecticism implies that its border with the novel was permeable and reveals the novel does not operate a uniform ideology: satire of aristocracy and economic progress does not mean it displays a middle-class outlook. In promoting hierarchy and progress and joining spiritual perspectives to empiricism, natural history made it impossible for the novel to avoid dialectic. Novelistic ideology is more variable than literary history might claim, given the novel's co-existence with natural history: the novel documents the emerging middle class in no straightforward way; it attacks as much as promotes social evolution. By the same token, fiction gains from natural history's empirical and social strategies: scientific classification with its dependence on philology and literary tropes together with the promotion of agrarian reform and new forms of capitalism enrich narrative procedures. By alluding to and appropriating natural history's forms, if but to subvert them, eighteenth-century novels realised the ideology of the landowning classes: in extending literacy and giving a wider readership cultural identity, the novel, in the face of natural history's popularity, informed itself with a genre that values theology and poetry and that welcomes social change by upholding political tradition. Natural history endowed the novel less with conceptual uniformity than with experimental diversity.[165]

CHAPTER THREE
The Sister Arts

Parallels between music, painting, and poetry confirm the humanism of the liberal arts in the long eighteenth century. Their distinct modes of mediation were often treated as equivalent in purpose, content, and basic nature. The saying of Quintus Horatius Flaccus (65–8 B.C.), "as is painting so is poetry," was adopted by Dryden, who lyrically imitated the Roman poet's odes, and by Pope, who trenchantly applied Horace's Augustan satires to court politics. To Lodovico Dolce (1508–1568), a Venetian humanist, all creations of learned men were paintings. Still, a dialectic of the one and the many was not valued by all musicians, painters, and poets; some differed about how the senses respond to mediation and operate in synaesthesia. If analogies of family structure, birth order, and sibling rivalry clarified the role of imagination and cognition in the arts for many, the dialectic of mutuality and competition involved psychological difficulties about mind–body relations and about how the sense of beauty draws on different mental operations and aesthetic memories. Related issues concern how humanist moral theories bear on secular and Christian values in narrative art. Thus, this chapter starts with the praise and dispraise Handel's music received during and after his life. Leading poets and narrative writers of the new sensibility laud him, but minor poets disparage his sound and sense to dignify their own art: they question whether sense controls sound or sound controls sense. The chapter next presents authors' relative applications of painting and narrative: novelists' visual thinking is copious; allusions to Renaissance pictures informs the humanism of their texts. Their preoccupation with such art confirms that the novel remained a proto-form in its generic experiments.

England's Orpheus: George Frideric Handel

Some authors spurned the idea that sound controls sense; to them, music was a branch of rhetoric. From the Middle Ages, music had been valued for imitating words and feelings denoted in texts. The Augustan view that music was valuable as it imitated tropes was subsumed under a theory of the sister arts which upheld poetry's superiority. In his fine words about Handel, Pope praises the composer's music for borrowing "aid from Sense," unlike Italian opera's empty sounds.[166] With declining rhetorical imperatives after Pope's death and Lockean psychology suggesting a poet's emotions are a fit subject of poetry, one might have expected the new emphasis on expression to lead to new ideas of music. But not so for poets who animated their poetry by saying Handel's music quelled bodily senses. However, those who belittled rationality thought that sound is sensible and that genuine human passions exist in powerful indeterminacy. They upheld the ancient creed that music conforms to spirit and that poetic concern with music reaches the soul. Faulting Pope for murdering Homer's "Musick," Edward Young (1683-1765) insists that "Harmony as well as Eloquence is essential to poesy," and in "The Passions, An Ode For Music," William Collins (1721-1759) criticizes his "laggard Age," wanting poetry renewed by the sublime, orphic power of ancient music.[167]

Narrative artists celebrated music, often attributing moral power to Handel. In *Tom Jones* and *Amelia*, Fielding joins music appreciation to sensibility. Sophia Western, the heroine of *Tom Jones*, is "a perfect Mistress of Music": she performs Handel's music admiringly. But her drunken father prefers "light and airy" music, making her play his favourite tunes on the harpsichord. Squire Western calls himself "a Lover of Music" but dislikes Handel.[168] This distaste makes him a "Connoisseur" in town. Fashionable dislike of Handel is a satire on English culture. Sophia's reforming sensibility makes her play, whenever she can, Handel's music to her father.[169] Amelia also admires Handel. Her early arrival at the oratorio contrasts her innocence with Mrs Ellison's hypocrisy. Indifferent to the oratorio, the latter exposes Amelia to seduction during the performance. That abuse of Handel reflects urban corruption is confirmed in the masquerade when town bucks in the opera house joke about having a matrimonial letter set by Handel as an oratorio. This confirms Fielding's view that Handel's music defies vicious urbanity.[170]

Richardson links music to mores in *Sir Charles Grandison* (1753-1754). In a debate between Sir Hargrave and Mr Greville, the former champions English music, the latter Italian. Both admire Handel yet disagree whether he is English and whether he is unique. Harriet Byron's skill on the harpsichord smooths their "rough" talk. Neither is well "grounded" in music: their words lead not to the harmony which love for music promotes but to the strife Harriet overcomes by playing "light pieces." Harriet and Sir Charles equally respect Handel: she eagerly performs songs from *L'Allegro* (1740) and the oratorios, and he admires *Alexander's Feast* (1736) as the "noblest composition," finding it "as finely set, as written." Harriet pleases Sir Charles by playing a "fine piece of accompanied recitative" from *Alexander's Feast*. She sings it since, without any "accompanying symphonies," it stands alone better than other airs. Sensitive to compositional form, she realises that an air taken out of context loses much while performing "proper transitions" between one strain and another adds to the beauty of songs.[171] Lauding her technique, Sir Charles approves its social value. Hence, he asks her to play the harpsichord to ease a tense situation. He does so, neither assuming music is women's work nor scorning performance, like Lord Chesterfield (1694–1773) who warned his son that

> As you are now in a musical country [Venice], where singing, fiddling, and piping are not only the common topics of conversation, but almost the principal objects of attention; I cannot help cautioning you against giving into those (I will call them illiberal) pleasures (though music is commonly reckoned one of the liberal arts), to the degree that most of your countrymen do when they travel in Italy. If you love music, hear it; go to operas, concerts, and pay fiddlers to play to you; but I insist upon your neither piping nor fiddling yourself. It puts a gentleman in a very frivolous, contemptible light; brings him a great deal of bad company; and takes up a great deal of time, which might be much better employed. Few things would mortify me more, than to see you bearing a part in a concert, with a fiddle under your chin, or a pipe in your mouth.[172]

Despite Chesterfield's advice, Sir Charles harmoniously plays his violin and takes a lesson on the harpsichord. On giving up his suit, Mr Greville fittingly blesses Harriet's marriage to Sir Charles by citing *Alexander's Feast*: "*Happy, happy, happy pair! – None but the brave deserve the fair.*"[173]

Allusions to Handel manifest social functions of instrumental and textual music as well as suggest that its technical, pedagogical, and expressive aspects were popular, if denigrated by some theorists. Relevant here are remarks by Defoe, Johnson, and James Boswell (1740–1795). In *Augusta Triumphans* (1728), Defoe, a "Lover of the Science" from infancy when he learned to play "the Viol and Lute," says music rounds out the individual, giving him a way of achieving mental relaxation and avoiding vicious pastimes. Music being one of the "liberal Sciences" and a "Branch of the Mathematicks," he insists on its cultural value; he believes imported Italian opera discourages native talent. Refusing to scorn Arcangelo Corelli (1653–1713), Giovanni Bononcini (1670–1747), Francesco Geminiani (1687–1762), and Handel, he says preference for them blocks English progress in the science. He asks: "Would it not be a glorious thing to have an *Opera* of our own, in our own most noble Tongue, in which the Composer, Singers, and Orchestra, should be of our own Growth?" Referring to Henry Purcell (1659–1695), he thinks an academy of music would found a national tradition and help England rival Rome. Academy musicians might well establish "Performance of Musick" and "Sacred Poesy" in churches "every Sunday after Divine Service." Upholding music's scientific integrity and educative value, Defoe expresses moral, cultural, and nationalistic values which Handel's music embodies.[174]

In the dedication to George III in Charles Burney's *Account of the Musical Performances in Commemoration of Handel* (1785), Johnson explains musical humanism.[175] Since native music will not develop without royal patronage, he stresses how fundamental music is to humans. Travel literature teaches him that love of "modulated sound" is universal. Music is civilising: it helps savage minds ward off evil and affords refined people elegant pleasures. Anthropology shows that music advances when knowledge aids natural inclination: "science and nature must assist each other." Since music is rational and instinctive, Handel deserves scientific praise. In *The Journal of a Tour to the Hebrides* (1785), Boswell links Handel and Johnson given music's growing cultural power. Defending his friend's loud, deliberate voice by arguing Johnson's articulation increased the worth of his talk, Boswell says that the "*Messiah*, played upon the *Canterbury organ*, is more sublime than when played upon an inferior instrument." This analogy makes the composer into a figure for honouring the period's great man of letters: conceding that Johnson's thoughts and style were occasionally mismatched, as when slight music employs a majestic medium, Boswell claims that, while Johnson "might be an ordinary composer at times, he was for the most part a Handel."[176] Since Defoe and Johnson mention mathematics and science in the context of music and since Boswell cites Handel to defend the reputation of the great literary arbiter, clearly not all authors were preoccupied with music in terms of single-minded literary concepts. Defoe, Richardson, Fielding, Johnson, and Boswell did not simply assume that music is a natural language of the passions. For them, music educates individuals, elucidates the process of writing, and informs culture, whereas minor poets' praise of Handel voices unresolved tensions between traditional and progressive, natural and scientific, ideas of music.

"An Ode to Mr Handel, on His Playing on the Organ" (1722) by Daniel Prat (1682/3–1723) is ambivalent but voices some progressive concepts. Prat initially subordinates poetry to music: he cannot praise Handel since unable to express thought in music. Whereas Handel reaches his audience's souls, Prat cannot command words for that purpose. Hearing Handel play the organ is a spiritual experience given differentiation of sounds. Swelling and lengthened notes along with pauses function distinctly; they inspire visionary, apocalyptic, or rapturous thoughts. For Prat, music has religious meaning. To him, people who zealously object to music are heathens: they typify the killers of Orpheus. Music's theological and cosmological aspects have psychological value: Handel's music, especially his fugal interweaving of notes, is healing; it banishes ill-humour and prepares the mind for religious faith. Music, "like the sacred Page," redeems human nature. Yet, if music is spiritually curative, Prat's celebration saps his poetry. Handel's "Notes provoke [him] to sing their Praise," but, having been inspired to feel poetry within himself, he belittles his own efforts. The relation between music and poetry, sound and sense, is not a happy one for him. That is why there are echoes of Dryden's "A Song for St. Cecilia's Day" (1687) throughout his poem. Prat's notions that no "Voice with equal Thought can reach / Thine and the sacred ORGAN's Praise" and that to unschooled listeners the organ's divinity allows it to "speak so sweet, so wond'rous well" are from Dryden. If bent on praising the uniqueness of Handel's music, Prat draws on Dryden's power. In citing the idea that the organ emblematises the heavenly "Harmony of Thought and Voice," Prat presents less of a gap between sound and sense than he intends; he cannot but imply that literary tradition condemns his poetry for failing its subject. Although music is the impulse and subject of Prat's poem, he concentrates reflexively on poetry. Despite claiming that music is psychologically beneficial, he cannot look inside himself to describe its effects. While it elicits a latent poetic impulse, music cannot give his poetry religious percipience. The functions Prat claims for music his poem shows do not work for him. His poem proves that, while he may have progressive ideas about music, he cannot embody them; nor can he balance traditional and progressive ideas like Dryden in "A Song for St. Cecilia's Day."[177]

Trying to judge Handel's music in new ways often recoils on poets; they fail to focus on music and musical analogies without resorting to clichéd notions. The anonymous "Epistel to Mr. Handel, upon His Operas of Flavius and Julius Caesar" (1724) stresses music's political function in metaphors that rely on Andrew Marvell (1621–1678) and Dryden.[178] In this poem, Handel is a king "Crown'd by the gen'ral Voice" of those who think music will overcome political strife; they are like sounds which agree only if governed by harmony. Handel's music instils collective identity, but those hostile to it are "Rebels" lacking poetic sense; they displace him from fashionable entertainment. Yet he has been restored and "Musick's Empire own[s] its lawful *Lord*." The analogy insisting that music unifies society draws on the myth in Marvell's poem, "Musicks Empire" (1681), about how the "Mosaique of the Air" rules the "Empire of the Ear," and on Dryden's typology in *Absalom and Achitophel* that fuses political and religious history.

The anonymous "To Mr Handel," published in *The Gentleman's Magazine* of May 1740, is similarly informed by analogy: the poem replaces orphic with political myth. Had the story of Orpheus been true, says the poet, British forests would have crowded to hear Handel. But his music addresses the soul, not nature, in order to control the passions. Handel is a sovereign to whom audiences submit. Here theological, psychological, and political claims converge: Handel's music, like that of the spheres, spiritually tunes subjects and gives nations coherence. Since he is "sovereign of the lyre," those who ignore music "rebel." Regal power joins *musica mundana* to *musica humana*, typology helping to resolve conflicts about musical performance and theory.[179]

But "An Ode, on Occasion of Mr. Handel's Great Te Deum, at the Feast of the Sons of the Clergy" (1733) by Aaron Hill (1685–1750) shows typology debasing musical integrity.[180] The musician in this ode is David, not Orpheus. David sung men's thoughts in godlike sounds; he tuned "mortal Lays" to "deathless Concords" and "with a Sound, like Heav'n's, gave Heav'n its Praise." For Hill and the former poet, music mediates between transcendence and immanence. The reciprocity of human sound and divine sense, far from precluding political aims, heightens them. Speculating about music since David's time and insisting this cosmological force inspired Handel, Hill counts on Handel's music to renew national prayer, reform religion, overcome psychological conflict, convert wanton hearts to spiritual happiness, and end factionalism. While others laud him for raising England's international reputation, Hill praises Handel for opposing international alliances. Thus, Hill's typology lends itself to propaganda.

His analogical sense is less balanced than Dryden's, other poets also using typology less precisely than Dryden. Henry Carey (1687–1743), in "To Mr. Handel, on His Admetus" (1727) praises the composer as the "unexhausted Source of Harmony," calling his songs eternal.[181] He imagines that, when the world ends in flame, Handel's music will rise to the skies, supersede angelic music, and fill heaven with endless harmony. Dryden's "A Song for St. Cecilia's Day" says that music will bring about the end of the world:

> So when the last and dreadful hour
> This crumbling Pageant shall devour,
> The TRUMPET shall be heard on high,
> The Dead shall live, the Living die,
> And MUSICK shall untune the Sky.[182]

Dryden holds that earthly anticipates heavenly music but does not, like Carey, equate the two. While Dryden balances psychological and cosmological aspects, Carey's enthusiasm raises Handel's music to a cosmological level. To Dryden, earthly music will end with the apocalypse by heralding the eternity of divine music; to Carey, Handel's divine music replaces angelic music.

An issue for literary history in eulogies of Handel is the mythical elevation they give to music and the degree of poetic imitation involved. In the anonymous "*To Mr. Handel*" (1733), the poet, like Daniel Prat, finds music inspiring. Handel's songs elicit his latent songs: "Tun'd by thy Art, my artless Muse may live."[183] But, as with Prat, the introspective influence of music does not inhibit poetic imitation; this poet alludes to Dryden's verses about the dead awaking and the living dying. Further, he describes the psychological effect of Handel in the present rather than looking to the apocalypse: he simply parallels rising music with rising passions and dying music with dying passions: "But when the full-mouth'd Chorus wounds the Sky, / The Dead with Fear awake, the Living die." This adaptation of Dryden to music's auditory and psychological impact borrows poetic diction while displacing mythical justification, upholding Richard Wendorf's sense that the century saw declining cosmological explanations of music and rising psychological ones.[184] Still dialectic between *musica mundana* and *musica humana* remained. Citing Dryden's diction, poets ask to be judged by the balance of myth and expression which he achieved.

Unwillingness to find meaning in sound and to consider its syntactical nature is strong in poets who discount *musica humana*. Elizabeth Tollet (1694–1754) resists the integrity of sound and musical affect in "To Mr. Handell" (1742).[185] To her, poetic inspiration comes, not from pure sound, but from music governed by "just Reason." She praises Handel because of the superiority of rational poetry to music: Handel is great by making music imitate great poetry. She ends by asking Handel to set Milton's *Samson Agonistes* (1671) to music, since great poetry must stem from religious principle. Another poem decrying pure music is the anonymous "An Ode, to Mr. Handel" (1745), which also binds imitation and religious doctrine.[186] After calling Handel's music seraphic and lamenting his own impotent verse, the poet lists Handel's compositions according to their imitative effects. Music for the flute in *Acis and Galatea* (1718) feigns a stream, being "tuneful to the tale" of Acis, she being turned into a stream. Music in *Alexander's Feast* imitates the voice of battle, its "successive sounds" enacting Timotheus's power over Alexander. About *The Messiah* (1741), the poet says the music fits the themes but gives no analysis, other than to say divine breath was somehow in the composer. Decrying secularism, he disparages "senseless glee," "empty trills," and "mimic'ry of sounds." Handel's faith alone justifies musical imitation.

Denial of music's autonomy seems odd in "To Mr. Handel" (1739) by Newburgh Hamilton (1691–1761) since he had adapted *Samson Agonistes* for the composer. [187] He praises the musical setting of *Alexander's Feast* but rejects the orphic myth, Handel's greatness affecting humans, not wild animals. Conservatively, Hamilton appreciates *Alexander's Feast* in terms of the sister arts: it is complete in sense and sound since Handel has "cloath'd [Dryden's] Numbers in so fit a Dress"; the latter's "majestick *Poetry*" has been crowned by "Magnificence of *Sound*." This view prevents acute analysis. Yet, touching on reflexivity, Hamilton is close to understanding musical meaning. He proposes that Handel's harmony rivals that of Greece and that, in celebrating the musician Timotheus's power over the warrior Alexander, Handel outdoes the ancient musician. Imagining that Dryden is happy to have his poem set by Handel, Hamilton treats the archetypal musicians, Orpheus and Timotheus, dismissively. Handel's music excels since, in setting poems about music and musicians, poetry allows him to surpass ancient performers. Far from seriously examining music by stressing music's dependence on poetry, this poem contains an important reflexive idea that heightens the meaning of performance and musical form.

Signs of music's autonomy appear in other poems, but, usually, technical ideas are comprehended by theology. Laurence Whyte (c. 1683–1753) wrote a poem on *The Messiah* for *The Dublin Journal* of 20 April 1742.[188] Having heard "various strains" in the oratorio "repeated and improv'd," Whyte senses differentiation in musical expression; this leads him to propose that sounds are "articulate." Having touched on meaningful sounds, he treats the content and inspiration of *The Messiah*: The Messiah must have inspired the oratorio. To Whyte, Christ disproved all fictitious myths and fulfilled or made redundant all serious ones. This Christian emphasis overwhelms the humanistic idea that music is a contrastive system of meaning.

Music's autonomy is vague in the anonymous "To Mr. Handel" printed in *The Daily Advertiser* of 21 January 1745. This poem, praising the "Musical Omnipotence" with which Handel added "solemn Sounds to Sense," complains the English do not respond to his harmony. Next, it parallels Orpheus and Handel in terms of hostile audiences: if malicious people had their way, Handel would suffer Orpheus's fate. Drawing on Ovid, the poem details Orpheus's musical power over animals and the Thracians' implacability. It then promises Handel a better fate, one of royal recognition and renewed popularity. This Orphic myth conveys less an ancient sense of music to dignify Handel than satirises the composer's opponents allegorically.

The myth in an anonymous poem in *The Daily Gazetteer* of 13 March 1745 also limits music's autonomy. "*After Hearing (last Spring) Mr.* Handel's *Oratorio of* Saul" suggests that, while Pythagoras' transmigration of souls has long been exploded, Handel's music convinces people to reconsider it, for what "*Orpheus* was, is *Handel* now."[189] But the poet moves on to Christian myth, viewing it as a nobler source of praise. He appeals to readers who anticipate the sound of angelic choirs in heaven: those who cannot wait for universal nature to celebrate divine goodness should listen to Handel since his music is the "Sweet Antepast of Harmony in Heaven." This poet uses diction reminiscent of Dryden but employs and then drops the orphic myth, just as Dryden does in "A Song for St. Cecilia's Day." Although several poets allude to Orpheus to maintain that Handel helped English culture rival classical times, they could not evade Dryden's restrictions on the myth. The orphic myth remained a witty resource but was not consistently integrated into Christian myths of the cosmological and psychological functions of music. The myth could not connect the two harmonies, the *musica mundana* and *musica humana*, if this was the humanistic wish of poets. The affects of harmony and the theory justifying affectiveness absorbed their attention more than did the orphic myth and music itself.

Efforts to define music's integrity appear in elegies for Handel. "An Attempt towards an EPITAPH" in *The Universal Chronicle* on 21 April 1759 calls his compositions a "Sentimental Language," not "mere Sounds."[190] Voicing human passions, they surpass the "Power of Words." If Handel's sound surpasses sense, it does so not by musical integrity but by *musica humana*; the elegist holds that music is a natural language, not a formal system of contrastive signs. Benjamin Martin (1704–1782) in "On the Death of Mr. Handel" (1759) values Handel's organ music for being autonomous, this idea then overwhelmed by convention.[191] Handel's numbers are "faithful to his fancy," his "echoing fugues" and "mingl'd sounds" expressing distinct emotions. In summary, Martin thinks words control Handel's music. Having first equated Handel and Orpheus, Martin ends by contrasting them: Orpheus's body was translated as Handel's soul is since the latter's more harmonious art matches heavenly singing.

"To The Memory of Mr. Handel" (1759) by John Langhorne (1735–1779) fails to reconcile traditional and progressive ideas.[192] He holds that poets cannot harmonise classical and Christian myths about music's integrity. Diffident about his own poetry, he cannot find "fit numbers" to praise Handel, the composer having created pure sound. His music is so great that it has restored mythical figures. Having heard *The Water Music* (1717), Echo could "melodise" her singing and mourn Narcissus. And the Naiads, listening to that work, felt what they had not since the great days of music in ancient Greece and Rome. Unhappily, Langhorne expects his elegy to yield to time, sensing his own death. More focused on dying than celebrating the composer's death, he does not work at expressing how Handel remakes the classical past and prefigures the Christian heaven. Pathetically, he claims he would praise Handel sublimely were he spared death. Despite morbidly subordinating his poetry to Handel's music, he imagines receiving the "sacred impulse" of "symphony divine," and, with the hope this music gives his verse, he pretends to mediate the Messiah's desire to have Handel "wake to higher strains [his] sacred lyre." Encouraging the composer to perform in the eternal realm, Langhorne claims experience of the "harmony of heaven" and describes the music of *Judas Maccabaeus* (1746) and *Samson* as matching that harmony. Inconsistency about his own verse and Handel's music is striking: unable to describe music since its graces are not conveyed by words, he describes it superficially. Transcribing his responses to *Samson* and *Jeptha* (1751), he explains himself overconfidently despite professions to the contrary. Far from analysing music in poetry, he uses music to hide poetic inadequacy.

Twenty-five years after Handel's death, when a series of commemorative concerts was held in Westminster Abbey, music's autonomy was more widely understood.[193] Yet, literary resistance was stronger. Among journalistic accounts of the concerts, *The London Magazine*, reporting on the fourth performance at the Abbey in June 1784, says that the "feelings of the auditory stirred to all the kindred emotions of the music, of which the character and articulation is every where as distinct as language."[194] This praise implies music has a syntax. A similar insight is found in "Ode Sacred to the Genius of Handel" (1784) by Thomas Maurice (1754–1824).[195] This poem claims Handel's music improves Dryden's poetry and realises Milton's conceptions:

> From his bright sphere astonish'd DRYDEN bends,
> Owns thy bold song his loftiest flight transcends,
> And learns to glow with more exalted fire.
> With all thy warm, energic fancy fraught,
> The mighty soul of MILTON smiles to see
> Its vast conceptions realiz'd in thee.

For Maurice, music transcends words; fulfilling them, it gives them fresh meaning. Music informs poetry with spirituality, sustaining the poetic past and inspiring modern poets.

But William Cowper spurned the commemorative concerts. For doctrinaire reasons, he would not grant that balance of musical, literary, and mythical ideas which Maurice upholds. In his letters and in the sixth book of *The Task*, he mocks the concerts by insisting on their profanity. He will not accept that a performance of *The Messiah* could honour Handel:

> ten thousand sit
> Patiently present at a sacred song
> Commemoration-mad; content to hear
> (O wonderful effect of music's power!)
> Messiah's eulogy for Handel's sake.

This sarcasm is illogical: Cowper equates *The Messiah* with The Messiah, assuming the former has no existence independent of the latter. Since man cannot praise man to the glory of God, he degrades the concerts by saying they merely gratified "an itching ear." His illogic is clarified by his concession that Handel was the "more than Homer of his age" and that his musical skills form a divine talent worthy of remembrance. Oddly, he honours Handel with a heroic image that belittles his musical stature: Handel was more than a Homer in his single talent. His scorn for the commemorations originates in Cowper's belief that music "destroys … spiritual discernment."[196]

Most poets disagreed with Cowper; to them, music served political and religious reform. They tried to dignify music's affective and mythical aspects. Anna Seward is a late example. In 1788, she wrote "Remonstrance," calling Cowper's view of the concerts "fanatic and illiberal." In "Briarean Handel," she finds the "harmonic strength of Europe," his music having many reforming and religious effects and he himself possessing, not one as Cowper meanly claimed, but ten divine talents. Admitting she is not as talented as Cowper—her lyre is "Less richly strung"—she insists that poetical praise of musical virtue is morally imperative. In her view, Handel's lyre was matchless; he attuned it to the English tongue, creating and applying a harmony that lifts the soul to heaven. She joins classical and Christian imagery in praise of Handel which recalls Pope's praise in *The Dunciad* (1743):

> Strong in new Arms, lo! Giant Handel stands,
> Like bold Briareus, with a hundred hands;
> To stir, to rouze, to shake the Soul he comes,
> And Jove's own Thunders follow Mars's Drums.

Seward asserts the superiority of music by using "lyre" to refer to poetry once she has established it as a symbol of Handel's genius. Like other admirers, she would have known the statue by Louis-François Roubiliac (1702–1762) which figures the composer as an eighteenth-century Orpheus playing the lyre. Her *lyre* conveys her trust that Handel's music can lead to an orphic regeneration of poetry. Like others, she does not put herself forward as the instrument of literary renewal. She is content to testify to the power of music that Handel symbolises. One imagines that, in her mind, Handel's music created hope for a poetry as excellent as Pope's.[197]

Turning to Handel for orphic renewal, poets did not display precise technical knowledge in their dependence on the sister arts. But, in praising Handel's music to animate their eulogies, they offer insights into the period's dialectical habits and aesthetic challenges. If their verse is poor and conceptions of poetry and music unsystematic, their poems do explore music's mythic importance. Ironically, praising Handel to discover poetic rules, they weaken their performances. Praising him calls for a respect for orphic myth that heightens their inadequacies: honouring him in mythical imagery meant that, to dignify their verse, they often were unhappy with their poetry: after relating Handel to Orpheus, they admit their relation is inept. Their orphic imagery makes the burden of the past heavier, rendering actuality unheroic. If they link Handel to Orpheus as a basis for creating the emotional dignity which might free them from reason and rhetoric, they finally see that Handel displaces rather than fulfils the myth of the Thracian poet. Some painfully realise that, if orphic myth helps them believe that Handel's ability to make sound comprehend sense benefits their sensibility, this same myth burdens them with the superiority of classical poetry. Not freed by humanism to create innovative poems, they sense Handel deserves transcendent praise yet cannot extend the musical dialectic voiced by Milton, Dryden, and Pope.

Pictorialism in Eighteenth-Century Fiction

The summit of excellence seems to be an assemblage of contrary qualities, but mixed, in such proportions, that no one part is found to counteract the other. How hard this is to be attained in every art, those only know, who have made the greatest progress in their respective professions.

Sir Joshua Reynolds (1723–1792) traces aesthetic excellence in dynamic tensions: mediation operates through "contrary qualities"; creating and sustaining conflicts is the duty of artists. Before defining this dialectic, he scorns connoisseurs who, "not being of the profession," are "liberal of absurd praises in their descriptions of favourite works": their "disquisitions" on "the cartoons and other pictures of Raffaelle" reflect "their own imaginations"; finding "what they are resolved to find," they laud "excellencies that can hardly exist together." They claim to see "with great exactness the expression of a mixed passion" that is "out of the reach of our art."[198]

Spurning psychological reflexivity since paintings resist discursive criticism, Reynolds implies that philosophical issues complicate dialectic in artistic expression. Despite denigration by Samuel Taylor Coleridge (1772–1834) of the Augustan imagination for lacking creative dialectic, post-Restoration authors valued Heraclitean contraries in nature and art, and, while William Blake (1757–1827) said Reynolds was "full of Self-Contradiction & Knavery" since he held that "Without Contraries is no progression," Reynolds's age appreciated irony, double vision, and paradox.[199] Dryden mixes mirth and gravity in tragedy since "contraries, when placed near, set off each other" and defines sub-plot in terms of the "contrary motions" of planets in the Ptolemaic system, voicing a dialectic that successors as well as contemporaries valued.[200] Robinson Crusoe's claim that "we never see the true State of our Condition, till it is illustrated to us by its Contraries" suggests dialectic mattered in narrative.[201] Johnson caught this sense of dialectic by defining a contrary as a "thing of opposite qualities," a sense validated by the Oxford English Dictionary's definition of contraries as "things the most different of their class." R.S. Crane's claim that "a just mixture" of "opposite qualities" informed the eighteenth century upholds W.J. Hipple's analysis of Reynolds:

The primary and ubiquitous principle of Reynolds's aesthetic system is the contrariety of universal and particular. Whether the discourse is of nature or of art, of invention or imitation, of subject or style, of taste or genius, the analysis proceeds in a dialectic of the one and the many, the changeless and the transient.[202]

Lawrence Lipking agrees: he holds that a "mixture of contraries" informs Reynolds's paintings and that he often promotes a stance involving more complex dialectical processes.[203] If the arts are equivalent in terms of aesthetic mediation, Reynolds's claim that Raphael's paintings defy verbal discourse shows that he rejects as well as affirms the sister arts: seeing contraries in all works of art, he subjects this primary dialectic to further contraries.

Reynolds explains meta-critical issues in pictorialism and helps to contextualise factors that enhance visual thinking in fiction. William Holtz's book on *Tristram Shandy* linked Sterne's uniqueness to his dialectical pictorialism. Not only, argues Holtz, did Sterne model his book on the opposing attitudes of William Hogarth (1697–1764) and Reynolds, but he mocked them equally.[204] Jean Hagstrum and Lipking, studying the prevalence of eighteenth-century visual thinking, question Sterne's uniqueness.[205] Not only did novelists allude to painters and paintings, perhaps they upheld and decried the sister arts as Reynolds did. The relevance to narrative history of pictorial allusions is many-faceted: it shows that visual ideas were integral to social and cultural life; it clarifies the dialectical mediation operated by novelists and the diversity of narrative styles; and it reveals how readers were expected to experience novels. Despite Wendy Steiner's claim that Renaissance realism ended pictorial narrative, eighteenth-century respect for Raphael (1483–1520) and portraiture reveals painting's temporal and spatial aspects.[206] That Defoe, no less than Jonathan Richardson (1667–1745), the precursor of Reynolds, could see in the cartoons of Raphael and the portraits of Anthony van Dyck (1599–1641) ideological and biographical stories is germane to the novel's history. To Defoe and Richardson, the novel's pictorial allusions bind it to a dialectic that entails cultural meaning and reflexive processes. W.J.T. Mitchell's view that the "dialectic of word and image" is a "struggle for dominance" which endlessly exposes the "fundamental contradictions of our culture" justifies studying how visual thinking about pictures helps define narration and how paintings share novelistic textuality.[207]

While Defoe and Richardson relate the sister arts to public virtue and the need for social change, their pictorialism adopts a civic humanism that values class hierarchy, courtliness, and aristocracy.[208] Their visual thinking implies that reading novels and paintings is a social activity. Readers were expected to have in mind palaces, churches, country houses, and repositories of art, besides recalling travelogues, prints, and engravings of renowned paintings. Dialectic in the visual thinking of Defoe and Richardson revises literary history and shows that Sterne's narratives are typical. This dialectic illustrates how novels stratify readership while generating political ideas. Defoe's and Richardson's visual thinking explains how pictorialism in fiction works. Since Defoe esteemed and belittled painting while Richardson praised and demeaned literary discourse, and since both analyse the "assemblage" of "contrary qualities" in Raphael's works, they testify to a dialectical sense of culture and relations between the media. Their contrary views elicit tensions between art and politics.[209] Their complementary sense of pictorial and narrative art defies histories of fiction that uphold single-minded progress:

visual thinking involved public, traditional, and aristocratic with private, innovative, and bourgeois values so that criticism must consider the novel's uniformity and diversity.

Aesthetic and political dialectic abounds in Defoe's *A Tour through the Whole Island of Great Britain* that describes mansions of the "British nobility and gentry" on the banks of the Thames. Upholding the Revolution of 1688, he views the mansions as symbols of the harmony of nature and art arising from the new political order; they impart a "character to the island of Great Britain in general"; close up, they are "pictures and paintings" and "all art" but, at a distance, they so fit the landscape they are "all nature." This dialectic between nature and art, the one and the many, leads him to dignify aristocracy by making one mansion, "justly call'd a picture of a house," symbolise the "luxuriant age" and "overflowing riches of the citizens." If visual ideas suggest that mercantile energy renews the aristocratic order by improving Britain's economic prosperity, his propaganda is resisted by the dialectic of continuity and change in art history. To promote the Revolution, he would displace Stuart patronage and make William III the ideal patron. But his claim that William created the English love of "fine paintings" and caused Europe to be "rumag'd" is weak since cultural history does not serve constitutional reform. William's example was harmful since Britain was "glutted with copies and frauds of the Dutch and Flemish painters" who "imposed grossly" on buyers. Further, its renown for art started with the Stuarts. Defoe celebrates not the Revolution of 1688 but the Restoration of 1660 as "that memorable event, to which England owes the felicity of all her happy days since that time."[210]

Seeing Stuart patronage as the basis of art collections redounding to the nation's glory, Defoe values aesthetic tradition that reaches back before the Restoration to Charles I's acumen. He records this tradition by visiting palaces and mansions whose galleries house works of artists patronised by that king and paintings glorifying the Stuart court. The "family pieces" by Van Dyck and Peter Lely (1618-1680) at Wilton House are a European cynosure, the best being modelled on a portrait of "King Charles I, with his queen, and children."[211] Wanting such collections to symbolise the Revolution, he actually views paintings that elevate the Stuarts. At Kinross, he admires portraits of Charles I and Henrietta Maria; at Duplin Castle, he is touched by one of Charles I handing a letter to the Duke of York. Offsetting import in the works of Van Dyck and Lely, he presents portraits of Oliver Cromwell and General Monk at Duplin as of a "contrary sort," distinguishing between cavalier models in the former and natural face-painting in the latter. If Cromwell's face is taken "from the life" while courtiers' portraits reflect royal models, Defoe cannot so distort history as to view Cromwell's face as a sign of progress. He may want to distinguish between natural and artificial modes, but he testifies to the pictorial dialectic of aesthetic and political values, since art and society are continuously transformed, not displaced. Denying Charles II's claim that Lely's portrait of the Duchess of Portsmouth is the "finest painting of the finest woman in Christendom" by declaring the "gallery of Beauties" done for Queen Mary by Godfrey Kneller (1646-1723) contains "as good faces and as good painting," Defoe opposes Stuart values in a voice muted by implications in his comparison. When he displaces Stuart art to promote the Revolution's Protestantism, irony recoils on him since he lauds the portrait of King William on horseback by Antonio Verrio: he ignores Verrio's Catholicism and the fact he took Van Dyck's cavalier portrait of Charles I as a model.[212] Yet Defoe's inconsistency heightens the pictorial and political dialectic: reading portraits as political signs was second nature to Defoe's contemporaries, but dialectic took them beyond conscious intention.[213]

Religious art confirms the dialectic in Defoe's visual thinking. Depending on his aims, he treats it as unrelated to or as defined by theology. *A Tour* views such art as forms that honour national glory. At Wilton House, a painting of "our Saviour washing his disciples' feet" is "admirable." At Yester, "Passion pieces" and "very fine altar pieces" he enjoys by ignoring their Catholic iconography. The Earl of Exeter's Tuscan paintings at Burleigh signify English nobility's prowess. Those religious images trumpet aristocracy: products naturalised by consumption, they remain metonyms of national economic power.[214] But *Religious Courtship* (1722), in prescribing Protestant harmony for marriage partners, attacks Catholic iconography: paintings extending the Bible to aid worship are disparaged. In its second part, a young woman who evades her late mother's injunction to wed a Protestant, marries a merchant who, like the Earl of Exeter, acquires, from residing in Leghorn, a "noble collection of very fine paintings, done by the best Masters in Italy." His paintings aid his observance of Catholic liturgy, but his sister-in-law argues that God's Word makes religious art idolatrous, and the father, who regrets having bartered his daughter for the "toys and fine things of Italy" by not examining the suitor's creed, declares that investing in pictures is more rational than praying to them. By idealising the merchant, Defoe heightens dialectic: the merchant is a gentle husband and loving father, but his iconophilia endangers his wife and children. His character shows that, if Defoe often attempts to displace or ignore iconography, at other times, he attacks it for sectarian goals. His dialectic is clear in his explication of two works by Raphael. If he adopts positive secular and negative doctrinal stances to religious art, he can welcome how art extends the import of the Bible.[215]

He views "St. Paul Preaching on Mars-Hill to the Self-Wise Athenians" (c. 1515) and "St. Peter Passing Sentence of Death on Ananias" (c. 1514) from a stance that anticipates Reynolds's dialectic: he identifies contrary qualities, tracing the reciprocity of visual and narrative ideas. If the stories of the cartoons are familiar, they "strike the mind with the utmost surprize"; art makes them seem original. The "terror and death in the face of Ananias; zeal and sacred fire in the eyes of the blessed apostle; fright and surprize upon the countenances of the beholders" are "so drawn to life" they "describe themselves so naturally." Impressions of spontaneity arise from systematic composition, tension between pictorial means and ends effecting involvement and inspiration in a viewer who "cannot but seem to discover something of the like passions, even in seeing them." Responses to Raphael's cartoons quicken Defoe's sense of formal and substantive dialectic: group portraits with diverse viewpoints, they are unified by strategic design, as his sense of facial reactions to Paul reveals. The saint confronts a "sett of men" whose faces contain:

anticipating pride and conceit in some, a smile or fleer of contempt in others, but a kind of sensible conviction, tho' crush'd in its beginning, on the faces of all the rest; and all together appear confounded, but have little to say, and know nothing at all of it, they gravely put him off to hear him another time; all these are seen here in the very dress of the face, that is, the very countenances which they hold while they listen to the new doctrine, which the apostle preached to a people at that time ignorant of it.

Paul's auditors signify collectively and individually, common and distinct motives being created by contrary mediation: the cartoon strikes Defoe's fancy "at first view" yet gradually induces the "dress of the faces." Spatial and temporal responsiveness ground exegetical interpretation. Antipathy to Catholic iconography is lost to a dialectic that treats Raphael's works less as scriptural illustrations than as pictorial texts with distinctive narratives.[216]

Jonathan Richardson, despite misgivings, promoted literature and painting as sister arts, like Defoe, exploring pictorial textuality. His views of the advantages to painting of its alliance with writing explain how this precursor of Reynolds advanced the pictorial contraries formulated by the later theorist. For Richardson, painting requires the conceptual approach of writing. In representativeness, pictorial detail addresses the mind like literature. In *An Essay on the Whole Art of Criticism* (1719), "Author" is a synonym for painter, and pictures express a painter's characteristic "Manner." Connoisseurs appreciate paintings only if informed about a painter's biography: all "the Parts of the Lives" and "all the Circumstances of the Masters" precede judgment of their works. This biographical imperative means a picture's "Intrinsic Qualities" matter less than the "Idea of the Painter, and the Beauties of the History, or Fable." Literariness dominates visual detail; a painting's intellectual appeal outweighs its "little Circumstantial Parts," its "Rich Hangings," and its "Representation of common Nature." Van Dyck's portrait of the Countess of Exeter is a "Picture of the Mind," not an "Insipid Representation of a Face, and Dress." Since they are "a sort of General History of the Life of a Person" and "answer the Ends of Historical Pictures," portraits not only conform to biographical and textual conceptions but serve narrative functions: they oblige owners to recount the memoirs of those portrayed, this fusion of pictorial and verbal mediation binding artist and owner. From this perspective, literary and social discourses are equally crucial to the conception and the reception of portraits.[217]

Dignifying portraits extrinsically, Richardson values painting's intrinsic expressivity. In *A Discourse on the Dignity ... of the Science of a Connoisseur* (1719), pictorial ideas are not what "we may receive otherwise, but Such as without this Art could not possibly be Communicated." Dialectic in art's imitative and original meanings is clarified by the following statement about the sister arts of painting and writing:

> Painting is another sort of Writing, and is subservient to the Same Ends as that of her younger Sister; That by Characters can communicate Some Ideas

which the Hieroglyphic kind cannot, As This in other respects supplies its Defects.

As sisters, they signify equally, their semiosis—unique and complementary. In sibling rivalry, painting has priority of age yet serves her younger sister. The more Richardson tightens the bonds between writing and painting, the more he stresses the bonds between pictorial and visual thinking. If painting finishes what words start and "perfects all that Humane Nature is capable of in the communication of Ideas," "Hieroglyphic Language" communicates in its own right, even in depicting biblical subjects. He grasps St. Paul's mission as much "by once walking through the Gallery of Rafaelle at Hampton Court, as by reading the whole Book of the Acts of the Apostles tho' written by Divine Inspiration." Painting does as much as "Discourse, and Books" and "in many Instances much more, as well as more Speedily, and more Delightfully." Insisting that viewing a "Picture aright is to Read," he heightens the analogy by referring to a third sister: "'tis not only to read a Book, and that finely Printed, and well Bound, but as if a Consort of Musick were heard at the same time." Synaesthesia treats intrinsic and extrinsic mediatory functions as dialectically as relations within them. That painting does and does not resemble script is clarified by Richardson's social attitudes.[218]

At times, he abstracts apologies for painting from daily life, at others from social hierarchy; at times, he dignifies art as ideally received; at others, connoisseurs operate a system of national development and moral reform. If Britain is so mature that Catholic iconography cannot harm church-goers who shun "Danger of Superstitious Abuses," the "vulgar" are so ignorant that their dullness is a "Sort of Illiterature, and Unpoliteness." Upper-class aestheticism is treated as contrary. Nobles should import foreign art and re-export inferior works since their "Haughty Impatience of Subjection" will make Britain dominant in Europe. Yet Richardson holds that foreign art will improve their taste and distract them from vice. Aristocrats are cultural leaders and moral reprobates: connoisseurs are economic imperialists. Tension between social disengagement and hierarchical status informs his definition of connoisseurship. He insists critics be "free from all kinds of Prejudice" and converse only with the "Better Sort of People." Such critics are credible since aesthetic experience gives nobles superior capacities: "conversing with the Works of the Best Masters," they acquire a "fine Collection of Mental Pictures" and a "Superinduc'd Sight," lifting them above the vulgar. The tension between pictorial intelligence and visual illiteracy in the lower classes is balanced by the sense that upper ranks are ideal patrons who transcend human nature and effect cultural progress. This tension between reform and connoisseurship recurs in prescriptions of a portraitist's authorial responsibilities.[219]

In *An Essay on the Theory of Painting* (1725), Richardson applies idealistic and political concepts to visual representation. True portraitists do not put on canvas what they see; "Proper Resemblances" draw on mind. Not taking other portraits as models, they adopt conceptual models: their primary object of imitation is the thought of sitters who are, as a rule, "People of Condition," that is, courtiers and aristocrats. Yet representing interior life does not produce "Refin'd Taste" in portraitists unless they idealise all classes: they must depict peasants and gentlemen as superior to themselves. Thus, portraitists develop paradigms in a dialectic of abstract idealisation and political hierarchy. This dialectic extends to rules for dress: a true portraitist makes dress both antique and modern. "Artificial Grace and Greatness" in portraits require classically abstract and contemporary actual styles. Like Reynolds, Richardson calls this rule the "Opposition" of "Contraries." Distinguishing true and false imitation, he applies dialectical representation to portraiture, criticizing it generally while revering Van Dyck. Portraitists who ignore the latter's paradigms are "mercenary Flatterers" who have "Prostituted a Noble Art," whereas Van Dyck's works permit England to be the "Best School of Face-Painting Now in the World" and confirm that Britain has the "finest Living Models." That his nation has the finest portraitists and subjects, along with meretricious painters, is based on trust that dynamic tensions in the intellectual and political worlds and between tradition and progress inform the best visual thinking of true artists.[220]

Richardson did not read paintings steadily for their "contrary qualities" if theory helped him unfold the Masters' textual meanings. His reactions to Raphael educe the limits of applying narrative processes to paintings. Finding disunity in *The Transfiguration* (1516–1520), he laments that its "Principal Action" is no more "conspicuous" than the "Incidental Action" in which the disciples cannot exorcise the possessed boy's devil: dull to its iconography, he ignores the spatial division in the action that sets divine transcendence above earthly agency. The deductions he draws from the cartoon of St. Paul are more astute; he treats its planar division as systematically significant. The unity of this group portrait he ascribes to its plural viewpoints. The "Back-Ground is not without its Meaning," for the faces of Paul's auditors expose the superstition that he disclaims. His "Figure" is more eloquent than oratory, its expressiveness contrasting with the background. Tension between the auditors' plurality and the apostle's singularity goes beyond oratory and history yet also involves them as his account shows:

> Some appear to be Angry, and Malicious, Others to be Attentive, and reasoning upon the Matter within themselves, or with one another; and One especially is apparently Convinc'd. These last are the Free-Thinkers of That time, and are placed Before the Apostle; the others are Behind him, not only as caring less for the Preacher, or the Doctrine, but to raise the Apostolick Character, which would lose something of its Dignity, if his Maligners were supposed to be able to look him in the Face.

Integration of historical context and pictorial construction illustrates how creative his view of the sister arts can be. Yet his reading of *The Transfiguration* reminds us that aesthetic contraries are problematic. If Richardson, Defoe, and Reynolds apply dialectic unsteadily, it is important to put visual thinking in a context that relates its challenges to its prevalence.[221]

Promoting the sister arts of painting and narrative as well as tensions between art and politics, Defoe and Richardson were innovators, but the ideas to which they gave dialectical expression were commonplaces. Derivative aspects of their visual thinking clarify its dialectic.

In *The Spectator*, Richard Steele (1672–1729) anticipates Richardson's apology for portraiture in averring that the populace does not abuse religious art, that love of portraits reflects "National Good-Nature," and that England has the "greatest Number of the best Masters in that kind" and "beautiful and noble Faces."[222] He also anticipates Richardson by affirming that painting is a "Poetry" more moral than writing and that a "real Life" portrait is as much an "instructive Lecture" as a "good History-Piece," justifying this by saying the cartoon of St. Paul conveys "all the different Tempers of Mankind" and conveys "Piety" better than the "most moving Eloquence."[223] Dignifying portraiture via the sister arts and history painting, Steele joins contemporaries in decrying pictorial meaning from prejudices Richardson tried to counteract. While, with Joseph Addison, he agreed to sit for Kneller in the new format and plain style the latter created for the Kit-Cat Club, Steele limits portraiture by denying it conceptual worth. Shaftesbury set the tone for such disparagement. Scorning the analogy of painting and poetry, he saw the "mere face-painter" and "mere historian" as tasteless copiers of minute detail since representation of nature could not improve painters.[224] Shaftesbury's scorn of pictorial discipline and reduction of painting to visual illusion are perpetuated by Addison in *The Spectator* when he relates the debate about the ancients and moderns to portraiture. He assails modern portraitists for bestowing a "certain smirking air" on sitters of "every Age and Degree of either Sex" but champions the convincing verisimilitude of the Masters: Titian (c.1488–1576), Raphael, Guido Reni (1575–1642), and Peter Paul Rubens (1577–1640).[225] Tracing the insipidity of modern portraitists to French influence, Addison degrades pictorial tradition in England. By praising the Masters for making subjects so "real and alive" they do not seem to be pictured, he devalues painterly representation: he disjoins resemblance and style, rendering illusion and technique opposites rather than contraries. Political and cultural nationalism explain why Addison relegates pictorial mediation to naive and overgeneralised realism.

Addison's willingness to sit for Kneller and satire on portraiture raise questions about how writers relied for self-images on painters and how prejudices offset this reliance. That authors belittled portraiture lets us probe issues arising from the novel's reliance on painterly allusion and visual thinking. Responding to Boswell's question as to whether he preferred "fine portraits" or ones "whose merit was resemblance," Johnson valued "likeness" more. Like Addison in severing pictorial realism from idealism, Johnson asserts that portraits are "valuable in families" for depicting dress of the times but discounts them as historical documents.[226] While Richardson requires that drapery be antique and contemporary to heighten narrative dialectic in portraits, Johnson discards this public function. Richardson's celebration of the English school of portraitists was rejected by Thomas Gray (1716–1771). Fond of Stuart portraits, Gray, in the presence of murals by Verrio and Louis Laguerre (1663–1721), scorned the idea of a national school. In 1763, he averred England had made no "advances hitherto in painting." Following Shaftesbury, he saw painters as "slaves and mercenaries" and "people without education." Disgust with political corruption and cultural decline led him to mock portraits in a letter to Horace Walpole (1717–1797) when his friend went home to Houghton, the prime minister's house. Gray imagines Horace ignoring Sir Robert and his gang, the "dead living," by keeping company with the "living dead"—the figures in family portraits.[227] The clash between flesh-and-blood and pictorial residents of the prime minister's house involves an oxymoron; Gray belittles painting as he endows it with comic reflexivity and satirical power.

Contradictions in Johnson's and Gray's resistance to aesthetic theory are clarified by the former's claim that the lesser known a sitter, the greater the need for an accurate portrait. If pictorial detail informs without serving recognition, portraits must perform documentary and domestic functions. Lord Chesterfield and William Shenstone (1714–1763), with reputations as patrons and connoisseurs, scorn aesthetic theory more contradictorily. Contempt for the Masters' idealism is Chesterfield's pose: disliking Rembrandt (1606–1669) and alleging the latter's ignorance of "*la belle nature*," he buys two portraits by Titian as "furniture." His painterly allusions are jocular because the man who studies art is a "frivolous virtuoso." Mockingly, he tells his son to acquire the "colouring of Titian, and the graces, the *morbidezza* of Guido" since his tutor, "*Raphael Harte*," has made a fine outline of his education.[228] Aesthetically refined, Chesterfield enjoyed demeaning the language of art appreciation. Shenstone, no less paradoxically, condescends to painting. In "Vanity," he insists that portraits, because they "gratify the vanity of the person who bespeaks them," bear no analogy to histories or biographies.[229] Opposing the sister arts like Edmund Burke (1729–1797), he insists that the "effects of the pencil are distinct and limited, whereas the descriptions of the pen leave the imagination room to expatiate." If his antagonism to painters claims portraits are valuable only for indicating sitters' rank, Shenstone's concern for his portrait done by Edward Alcock (d. 1782) goes beyond extrinsic value. He fusses over its draperies and trophies, ignoring their part in pictorial convention. But the Pan, Apollo, the water-nymph and urn, the Latin on the scroll spelling out his love for woods and streams, and his dog are emblems common to portraiture: he treats them as flattering decorations, but they belong to a typology that resists his superciliousness.[230] His pictorial arrogance is contradictory when he receives a portrait of Richard Graves (1715–1804) from this friend. He says a friend's likeness is worth more than a portrait by Raphael, thus rejecting the dialectic between personal and high art. Yet he faults the portrait for its smile, wanting it amended by an itinerant artist.[231] If he mocks pictorialism by giving portraiture private, exclusive roles, he upholds theory by making Graves's portrait obey the rule that the transitory succumb to the permanent—the smile to general character. Opposing visual dialectic, Shenstone realises it contradictorily, if not unwittingly.

As patrons and connoisseurs, Chesterfield and Shenstone so debase the sister arts that they ironically emphasise the values they scorn. Their trivial selfishness about acquiring portraits and disparagement of pictorialism heighten biographical and historical functions of portraiture. In this context, we may suggest how novelists' attitudes to the sister arts emanate from portraiture: narrative implications in their portraits offer scope to deductions about their visual thinking. How authors were depicted is a clue to the function of their pictorial dialectic.

While portraits of Samuel Richardson, Fielding, Smollett, and Sterne highlight various conventions of pictorial biography, this variety exemplifies a range of textual referentiality in pictorial mediation which, in turn, illuminates their diverse narrative procedures.[232]

The three-quarter-length portrait of Richardson done by Joseph Highmore (1692–1780) in 1747 stresses his rich red coat and bland gaze. The stolid figure resembles Hogarth's *Captain Coram* (1740), but its pose is more mannered, and the absence of maps or charts means tensions between Van Dyck's aristocratic emblems and bourgeois style are slack. Richardson, amid elegant, outdoor scenery with right hand in bosom and left holding a book, embodies social success without modifying pictorial rules. Highmore's 1750 full-length portrait emphasises the sombre luxury of dress too, but its writing-room with bare floorboards, worn quill-pen, bookshelves with massive tomes, and correspondence tell of hard work and professional dedication. While his face is as bland and the pose, with right hand in coat, as mannered as in the earlier portrait, letters on the desk and in his other hand depict commitment to epistolary narrative clarified in the inscription "Samuel Richardson Author of Clarissa." The picture within the picture—a country mansion with figures and deer in a park—links author to heroine: perhaps depicting Harlowe Place, it may be read as one of Clarissa's works. Given his claim that Highmore painted Clarissa and his detailing of her painting, the textual and painterly references in the second portrait suggest he was not averse to being depicted as an accomplished middle-class writer through a reciprocity of painting and narrative in courtly traditions.[233]

Hogarth's posthumous engraving for the frontispiece of Fielding's *Works* (1762) images a man more reserved about portraiture and the sister arts than Richardson. While Hogarth heightens etching conventions against those of portraiture, the engraving has "more truth than caricature."[234] In a frame within the picture, Fielding's sloping forehead, arched brows, long nose, and sharp chin give him a medal-like detachment. The painter's and writer's shared unconcern with scenic illusion and verisimilitude separates the bust from the emblems of Fielding's career: the ink-pot, worn quill, sword in sheath, and titled books and pamphlets rest on a mantel in a plane apart from the illumined bust. His name on the bust's frame and the emblems of his work as dramatist, novelist, lawyer, and social critic endorse verbal and allegorical reference more than spatial mediation. The transparent artificiality of the hatching accents the tension between heroic allusion and burlesque in the medal-like profile, confirming an ironic emphasis in this pictorial biography. Hogarth's portrait of himself and Fielding in *Characters and Caricaturas* (1743) further attests that the two friends celebrated the sister arts with satirical humour.

Unlike the portraits of Richardson and Fielding, the three-quarter-length one of Smollett by William Verelst (1704–1752) is derivative and pretentious. Rejecting scenic detail and professional emblem, it is pictorially allusive. Right hand in coat, Smollett holds his right glove in his gloved left hand in a pose recalling Rubens's self-portrait of 1638–1640. But, while Rubens's body minimises background, Smollett's small person lets the ambient space signify prissy refinement and aristocratic affectation. If this portrait's rich dress resembles

Richardson's, Smollett seems to value elegance in itself. Vanity is lesser in the Italianate half-length portrait from about 1770 in the National Portrait Gallery which, in graceful sadness, presents a luxurious jacket that sets personality above integrated signs of social conduct and narrative mediation.[235]

Reynolds's 1760 portrait of Sterne is unorthodox, this indicated by its being exhibited under the sitter's name in the Royal Exhibition of 1768. This portrait challengingly fuses professional with personal signs. Sterne's clothes image general drapery and a recognisable clerical habit, and his writing table with worn quill is given unique force by the highly lit face and what Holtz calls the "subversive play of the left hand against the right." Seated, leaning on the manuscript—not the first published volumes—of *Tristram Shandy*, with face on right hand, its index finger on forehead, and left arm akimbo, he poses with a mixture of weariness, nonchalance, and defiance. His provocative gaze and incipient smirk convey an equivocal interest in self and viewer. By endowing Sterne with such whimsicality, Reynolds heightens tensions between pictorial form and informality to reflect his sitter's view of aesthetic mediation.[236]

Portraits reveal that authors of prose fiction, often mediated by painters, viewed their calling diversely. Upholding no one model of representation, their portraits testify to a range of visual textuality: compositional, scenic, material, and facial signs as well as emblems and symbols diverge. This variability manifests changing relations between narrative and painting. Tensions between imitation and innovation in the self-portraits of Reynolds and Hogarth, the artists who most influenced authors, reveal why variable stances on the sister arts bear on the history of fiction. If Reynolds, in his humanism, relished psychological ambivalence and generic mixture, as in the Sterne portrait, so Hogarth, in debunking the Masters, imitated them. Both assemble contraries, their rival dialectics contexts for understanding the period's narrative mediation.

Reynolds and Hogarth differed theoretically about whether paintings should enhance or illustrate literariness, yet allusions in their self-portraits transcend debate: pictorial and literary dialectic brings them together. In his self-portrait as president of the Royal Academy (1773–1780), Reynolds mixes allusions: he leans on a bust of Michelangelo (1475–1564) in the style of Rembrandt. Contraries enliven his portrait of Jane Hamilton, Lady Cathcart, as a Madonna (1755) and his *English Connoisseurs in Rome* (1751), a parody of Raphael's *School of Athens* (c. 1510).[237] Reynolds cultivated both dignified and satirical imitation, as did Hogarth. In his *Self-Portrait with Pug* (1745), set in a frameless picture within the picture and his dog in the primary plane, Hogarth, as in his image of Fielding, seems to subordinate painterly to literary pride. In neither form nor function does the pug revere his master: he looks at the world with a complacency like his master's. His bust resting on tomes of William Shakespeare (1564–1616), Milton, and Swift, Hogarth directs his gaze in celebration of English literature rather than pictorial mediation. Yet the noble dog, the pile of books, and the drapery along with the picture in the picture belong to traditional iconic painting, showing that Hogarth's irreverent allusiveness imitates literary bathos.[238] He no more rejected the grand style of painting than Reynolds embraced it single-mindedly. Hogarth's boast that he would rather have painted *The Four Stages of Cruelty* (1751) than Raphael's cartoons is unconvincing; inclination led him to copy the Masters. The drapery and pillar in his portrait of Thomas Coram (1740) allude beyond French portraitists to Van Dyck. His linking of the Masters with immorality in *Marriage à la Mode* (1745) is positive: in symbolising corruption, the Masters thematise artistic indebtedness. The satire arising from the old Earl of Squanderfield's pictures of pagan gods and a portrait of himself as a "Jupiter furens" requires Hogarth to have the young squire die in the pose of a "descent from the cross" in the fifth plate. The imitation of *Jupiter and Io* by Antonio da Correggio (1489–1534) in plate four shows that Hogarth's narrative cites masterworks and traditional genres.[239]

Since tensions between imitation and displacement shape painterly allusions, reflexivity in the works of Hogarth and Reynolds invites viewers to join spatial and temporal meaning and to sense the juncture of pictorial and narrative mediation. Allusions to pictorial genres in series such as *Marriage à la Mode* also invite us to read continuous action and spatial meaning in plates in which discontinuities demand theatrical or narrative exegesis. Taking Highmore's *Twelve Scenes from Pamela* (1744) as an example, we see that our sense of mediation and the sister arts is fortified by a reflexive mode of illustration that is directly and obliquely allusive: besides translating Richardson's pictorial references, Highmore adds paintings to and deletes them from scenes to heighten religious themes. The complex allusiveness of his pictures within pictures derives from a double imitation of Hogarth and Richardson that proves the complementarity and uniqueness of their media. Highmore's first plate showing Mr B's first encounter with Pamela contains a "Good Samaritan" which pits Pamela's dead but motherly mistress against the new master's hypocrisy. The Van-Dyck-style portraits, partly discernible in the scene when her father visits Mr B (plate VIII), show that Highmore displaces cavalier and courtly modes to focus on Pamela's filial love, emblematised by the card-table she overturns in her enthusiasm to greet her father. Omitting the religious art of the chapel in which she marries to focus on her (plate IX), Highmore places a "Madonna" over the mantel in the final plate where she reads a nursery tale to a circle of children. Since it adapts Hogarth's and Richardson's styles of mediation, Highmore's series illustrates how the histories of painting and literature are involved in tensions between the sister arts. The influence on Highmore of pictorial satire and puritan idealisation that does not preclude Catholic iconography confirms that paintings and fictions share as well as question one another's boundaries: narrative extends pictorial reference as pictorial extends narrative references.[240] Since dialectical mediation is germane to pictures and novels, these sister arts may be seen to share concepts of textuality in ways that help revise the novel's history.

If authors belittled painting, their narratives employed visual thinking and painterly mediation. Samuel Richardson's pictorial scorn is reflected in Hill's prefatory letters to *Pamela*. He decries visual thinking: "any figur'd Pretence to Resemblance" detracts from the "inward idea of Pamela's Person." But he still applies pictorialism: he calls the word "naughty," applied by Pamela to Mr B, a "speaking Picture" of her struggle between respect and contempt, seeing in this a "picturesque glowing Likeness to *Life*." Like Hill, Richardson equivocally associates visual and moral ideas in satire. While Pamela's superiors demean her ideals by mockingly framing her in pictorial terms, she voices a keen Hogarthian sense of her moral inferiors. Mr B decries Pamela as a "speaking Picture," and Lady Towers mocks her "pretty image" with "speaking eyes," but Pamela paints a "Picture" of Mrs Jewkes, stressing her broad, flat face, crooked nose, grey, goggling eyes, and skin colour that looks to have been "pickled for a Month in Salt-petre." Her view of Colbrand's "blubber lips," "long yellow Teeth," and "Wen" of a neck is a keener pictorial satire than her betters: they abuse visual thinking but she embodies visually graphic realism.[241]

Aiming at transcendence, Richardson does not steadily use tensions between pictorial idealism and realism in Pamela's character. Like Hill, he does not want to objectify her. If her visual thinking symbolises moral superiority, she sets religious art below prayer, subordinating narrative to spiritual truth. In the chapel where she is to be married, she notices its "little pretty Altar-piece" but turns aside to pray, leaving Mr B and Parson Williams to study the "Communion-picture." In the Bedfordshire house when she thanks God for saving her from Mr B's assaults, she images piety better than Mr B's "charming Pictures." Since Mr B gives his "angel" these pictures, Richardson equates her spirituality to aestheticism: Pamela is a pure visual object, an icon mediating grace to Mr B. The contradictory ways in which Richardson disjoins and joins visual and spiritual ideas indicates the importance of the sister arts to narrative mediation: Pamela is and is not a visual object, but Richardson hardly confronts this dialectic.[242]

Rival and complementary ways in which characters visualise each other in *Clarissa* confirm that this fiction draws heavily on iconography. Producing his "faint sketch" of Clarissa, Lovelace depicts "every meandering vein" of her "wax-like flesh." His sketch is erotic and erratic: he images her body to demean her spirit and makes her beauty depend on his aestheticism. Bent on self-stimulation and sexual power, he claims she is beyond painterly imitation once he puts her on his mind's canvas. But his declaration that no pencil can do justice to the "mingled impatience which visibly informed every feature of the most meaning and most beautiful face in the world" arises from his self-deception in proposing marriage: he says her beauty transcends painting and poetry in an effort to hide his possessive fantasies from himself.[243] His licentious pictorialism is exposed by Belford's view that Clarissa's "different airs and attitudes" should inspire artists to have the "virtues and graces all drawn in one piece." This view of Clarissa as a model whose composite virtues demand pictorial allegory suggests that Richardson aimed to develop a systematic narrative appreciation of pictorial genre.[244]

This appreciation is key to Clarissa's image. To Anna Howe, a portrait of herself requires the "Shades and lights" that are "equally necessary in a fine picture" but one of Clarissa should emit a "flood of brightness," here distinguishing between conventional portraiture and religious art. If Clarissa's idealism deserves transcendent iconography, she does not despise secular art. Despite scorning connoisseurship, she approaches painting with a sense of its historical, social, and domestic purposes, not unlike Jonathan Richardson's dialectical sense of verisimilitude and idealisation. If self-criticism directs her "gaudy eye inward" to value death more than the cultural enrichment of the Grand Tour, she does not repent her love of painting. So, she faults Anna's "whimsical" verbal portrait of Hickman as unfair. Anna misrepresents her lover, making him "set and formal" like portraits from William III's reign, but Clarissa's antiquarian trust in that period's "cravat" and "chin-cushion" tells her she can produce a "much more amiable and just likeness" of Hickman. If her scorn of connoisseurship suits her design of coffin emblems celebrating the annihilation of fancy, she does not spurn the biographical and domestic worth of portraiture, as her will shows. Bequeathing family portraits inherited from her grandfather, she wills a portrait of herself to Anna, a full-length one in Van Dyck's style to her mother or aunt, and one of her own flower paintings to a cousin. A practised artist, she is, in Richardson's eyes, worthy of being depicted in an aristocratic mode. Moreover, when, close to death, she doffs the miniature of Anna, asking that it be sent to Hickman, she invokes it as friend, companion, sister, and lover, making it an icon. Rejecting simple differences between secular and religious art, she spiritualizes portraiture in a way likely inconceivable to a Shenstone.[245]

Richardson adds religious art to narrative, making Clarissa's transcendence draw on dying saints in Catholic iconography. Her "beatification" features the construction of death-bed scenes and assembles pictorial contraries. From Belford's perspective, Clarissa is "charming" and "heart-moving"; seeing her dressed in virgin white, sitting with Mrs Lovick's left arm round her neck, one cheek pale with the touch of death and the other warmed by the motherly bosom into a "faint but charming blush," he views her through a compositional dialectic which, opposing Lovelace's libertine imagery, translates white skin and meandering veins into a transcendent idiom. The death scene specifies the idiom: the grouped mourners in emotional and religious postures assume Clarissa's agony while reverencing her. Kneeling, Morden bows over and bathes with tears her right hand which he holds in his two. On the other side, Mrs Lovick lays her head on the bed's head while facing Belford with folded hands. Mrs Smith kneels at the foot of the bed with clasped fingers and uplifted eyes, praying tearfully. The nurse, used to death-bed scenes, kneels between these two women, her face swollen with weeping, while the maid, face on folded arms, leans weeping against the wainscot. This dialectic of scene and idea, emotion and spirit, is keener by contrast with Mrs Sinclair's throes, the brothel-keeper's death graphically hellish. Her "cursed daughters" circle her bed in "shocking dishabille": with streaked face-paint, wrinkled skin, and ragged hair, the strumpets travesty Clarissa's mourners. A "huge Quaggy carcase," Mrs Sinclair contrasts grotesquely with Clarissa: her goggling, flame-red eyes, livid, violently working lips, wide mouth splitting her face, and contracted forehead stress grossness: such stylistic contraries systematically base narrative mediation on painterly imitations.[246]

Appreciating dialectic in the sister arts—witness his claims that the writer has much to learn from the painter's "Contrast of ... Figures" and that the "Beauty and Excellence of any thing" is proven by "its Reverse,"—Fielding adopts pictorial stances less than Richardson since he shared Hogarth's distaste for the Masters. Yet gaps between his theory and practice of the sister arts exhibit narrative contraries. When, in *Tom Jones*, he applauds Hogarth for following "Nature herself" instead of painting humble folk in "a Rout or a Drum in the Dresses of *Titian* and of *Vandyke*," he decries the tenet that painting dignifies all subjects. Yet the artist is a narrative authority.[247] Praise of Hogarth champions narrative by limiting painting. In *Joseph Andrews*, he claims that "the inimitable Pencil of my Friend Hogarth" could not have depicted Lady Booby's surprise at hearing Joseph speak of his chastity. Yet, if painting's limits serve narrative realism, Fielding expands them. If Mrs Tow-wouse's face says more than any Hogarth work, he applies his friend's style of caricature to her physiognomy: her forehead, projecting in the middle, descends in a "Declivity to the Top" of her sharp, red nose; her lips are "two Bits of Skin" that draw to like a purse, her cheek bones almost hiding her small eyes. This sketch inverts pictorial inadequacy.[248] As allusions to Hogarth in *Tom Jones* show, Fielding invites awareness of pictorial styles and specific works. By saying Bridget Allworthy sat to Hogarth's portrait in *Winter Morning* (1736), he objectifies her hypocrisy and stipulates a fictional response to a given painting. When he insists that Mrs Partridge resembles the servant in the third plate of *The Harlot's Progress* (1732) and that Thwackum looks like the warder in the Bridewell plate, readers likely recall narrative features in Hogarth's works. How complex this recall may be is implied when, in arguing that wisdom is the moderate use—but not renunciation—of riches and pleasure, Fielding likens the hypocritical asceticism of divines to the ravings of Hogarth's poverty-stricken poet against riches. This allusion to *The Distrest Poet* (1740) recalls the print, links its emblems to the poet's hack work, and recovers its visual narrative in ironical parallels to priestly hypocrisy.[249] That such allusions enhance narrative is further epitomized in *The Journal of a Voyage to Lisbon*. About the "concord of sweet sounds" in the noisy streets of Wapping and Redriffe, Fielding ironically says those streets yield "a greater variety of harmony than Hogarth's imagination hath brought together in that print of his, which is enough to make a man deaf to look at."[250] Alluding to *The Enraged Musician* (1741), in which auditory ideas arise from scenic details to expose a musician falsely surprised by London's acoustic pollution, he stresses the limits imposed by life on aesthetic form. Yet, his synaesthesia, since it involves art dialectically with life, testifies to the harmonious power of Hogarth's work in ways Jonathan Richardson would have approved.

Theory of portraiture and dismissive allusions to portraits confirm that dialectic about the sister arts was a resource to Fielding. In *Joseph Andrews*, he echoes Jonathan Richardson on how portraits function; narrative imitates paintings since it offers "amiable Pictures" of virtuous people to readers open to "valuable Patterns" without knowing the "Originals." Approval of mental portraits is clear when Parson Adams's face is a "Portraiture of the Mind" and when Tom's manifests "Spirit and Sensibility."[251] In Joseph's bathetic allusions to "*Paul Varnish*" and "*Hannibal Scratchi*," Fielding denies ennoblement by Paolo Veronese (1528–1588) and Annibale Carracci (1560–1609). His images of Fanny and Sophia defy pictorial idealism. Fanny's "natural Gentility" cannot be depicted by the "finest *Italian* Paint."[252] The irony in which he pictures Sophia associates courtly portraits with prurience, not healthy sexuality. Saying Sophia is like none of the women in Kneller's gallery of beauties at Hampton Court, he likens her to Kneller's portrait of Lady Ranelaugh (1700) and then to Lely's portrait of the Duchess of Mazarine (1678). He finally displaces portraiture by likening her to his wife's "Image" in his breast and swearing that any "Idea of Female Perfection" created by his "Pencil" in depicting Sophia is matched by "many of our fair Country-women." Still, he faults middle-class painting, as reductive images of Captain Blifil and Mrs Western show. He first gives the captain an affable smile, good teeth, and a scar denoting honour, but the finished portrait has a beard covering his face, a figure like a ploughman, and limbs like a common chairman's. The gap between the generic title, "*A Picture of a Country Gentlewoman Taken from the Life*," and the affectation by which Mrs Western despises rural life shows that Fielding often links arrogance and hypocrisy to portraiture.[253]

Still, while disparaging portraiture, he exploits pictorialism. Certain that visual thinking is not valid when imposing painterly images on observed reality, he defines that thinking as moral discipline. In *Tom Jones*, he defends pictorial imagination against its dangers: he compares its moral worth with self-seduction, pornography, and superstition. When Tom, in love with Sophia, pictures Molly Seagrim from pity, he desires her. Sexual arousal stems from undisciplined visualisation; painting Sophia in "various ravishing Forms," he proceeds to the bushes with Molly. More calculated licence arises when Lady Bellaston incites her lust by advising Tom to sit for the "Picture of *Adonis*." To offset such vice, Fielding will not visualise her assignations with Tom, telling readers they do not need the "Help of Pictures" like Catholics or adepts of pornography. Equating praying to icons and staring at naked women, he distinguishes between visual thinking and gratifying illusion: Tom is educated to this distinction. Urging young Nightingale to be true to Nancy, Tom orders him to exercise pictorial imagination. He himself is chastised less for picturing Sophia than for retaining her "Image" no longer than a mirror. He must develop his imagination in conformity with Fielding's wish to engage readers in moral pictorial and narrative meaning.[254]

More than Fielding, Smollett relied on the Masters for his self-image. If he lauds them, cultural invective made him attack the idealism of Jonathan Richardson and Reynolds. In *Travels through France and Italy*, he equivocates in pictorial criticism, one moment deferring to the Masters, the next acting like a hypercritic. Having "neither capacity, nor inclination" to analyse art, he claims Titian's *Venus* has a "sweetness of expression and tenderness of colouring, not to be described," cheerfully adopting the stance of an uncritical viewer. But he chides the Masters for not idealising models: Raphael's *Madonna* (c. 1514) at the Pitti palace is "defective in dignity and sentiment"; its image is that of a "peasant rather than of the mother of God." Further, Michelangelo's "madonnas" lack grace and decorum, like figures from stables. Affectation gives way to critical understanding sometimes: like Richardson, he dispraises Raphael's "groupes" in *The Transfiguration* for being "independent of each other," yet avers that *The School of Athens* (1509–1511) makes Raphael "perhaps the best ethic painter." Similar contraries inform his view of Reni whose works express "tenderness and delicacy" while his figures are "affected and unnatural." Since his aesthetic serves polemic, he does not uphold Richardson's contraries: he scoffs at mixing antique and modern dress, is moved by Michelangelo's *Last Judgment* (1535-1541) to deny that a painting can unify a "multiplicity of groupes and figures," and likens absence of pictorial "subordination" to ugly orchestral sounds without theorising synaesthesia. His polemical ambivalence about religious art is comparable to Defoe's. Confidently reacting to a religious picture "merely as a portrait," Smollett loathes "religious fanaticism" in the "shocking subjects of the martyrology," which he judges "mischievous to community."[255]

But he so denounces politics and consumerism that his pictorial dialectic nearly always subsides into invective.[256] *Peregrine Pickle* (1751-1758), replete with art history, is yet motivated by satire of English aesthetics. Hogarth is named once when the narrator says the "inimitable" artist could not capture Commodore Trunion's "ludicrous expression." This sole allusion shows how Smollett marginalises English art appreciation. Far from making Hogarth an ally opposing the appropriation of foreign art, Smollett creates Pallett, a professional artist, as a surrogate for Hogarth and caricatured disciple of a national school of painting. Full of admiring jargon about Raphael and Rubens, Pallett knows no classical or modern languages and is mercenary to boot. He cannot judge the work of Charles Le Brun (1619-1690) or Eustache Le Sueur (1616-1655), totally ignorant of French art. He worships Rubens by taking imitations of him as originals and spurning the latter. A gross connoisseur, he reveres Rubens's birthplace with zeal while boasting a better "knack of trumping up an Apostle" than Raphael in the cartoon of St. Paul. His betrayal of the Masters is stressed when he judges Flemish realism equal to Rubens and views the latter's *Descent from the Cross* (1612-1614) and family portraits illiterately. When Peregrine visits a wealthy country squire, Smollett broadens his attack. The squire owns portraits by Van Dyck, each having been partly modernised: the subjects' heads are adorned with modern wigs, but their seventeenth-century footwear has not been updated since he would not pay the itinerant painter what he asked for re-doing the feet. As a patron, the squire is a "barbarous Goth," hiring a hack to alter a Master's work and tolerating half-finished adaptations in his miserliness. His debasement of classical portraiture lets Smollett apply pictorial contradictions to the myth of English cultural progress. Still, the question remains as to how he upholds the aesthetic standards, the debasement of which he constantly illustrates.[257]

In *Humphry Clinker*, Smollett endows Matthew Bramble, his spokesman, with pictorial acuity.[258] Disclaiming pictorial judgment, Bramble discusses the landscapes of William Taverner (1703-1772), praising the "warmth of his colouring," "spirit of his expression," and "execution" of *chiaro oscuro* and perspective with its progressive illusion of depth. Yet Bramble is pessimistic: the "dullness of the times" means no second Hogarth will arise, and the prevailing contempt for pictorial ingenuity shows the "degenerate age" sinking into "barbarism." In this less caustic work, Smollett's sense of social decadence still deplores abuses of painterly mediation: he will not exemplify visual thinking since society debases aesthetics. Tricking Lismahago about a fire, Sir Thomas Bullford voices contradictory allusions to enjoy his trickery: he sees Lismahago's flight as a "descent from the cross" and ascent to the gallows, noting the gap between the "expression above" and the "groupe below" and wishing for a Salvatore Rosa (1615–1673) or a Rembrandt to paint the scene. Sir Thomas makes nonsense of pictorial genre, compositional structure, and artistic uniqueness. Not probing such abuse, Smollett insists that social anarchy is advanced by religious fanaticism as much as by aristocratic decadence. So, he parodies disquisitions on Raphael's cartoons in the "strongly picturesque" scene where Humphry would convert prisoners to Methodism. Smollett fits the "variety of expression" in the "groupe" of felons to the cartoon of St Paul, creating a list of abstract, hard-to-picture responses: "In one, it denoted admiration; in another, doubt; in a third, disdain; in a fourth, contempt; in a fifth, terror; in a sixth, derision; and in a seventh, indignation." This parody confirms that generic allusions are governed by a satirical stance as critical of reform as decadence, by an outlook emphasising cultural decline and by a devaluation of visual thinking. If pictorialism does not matter to society, Smollett so often notices paintings, creating propaganda that enhances their value as cultural texts despite his intentions.[259]

By contrast, Sterne exploits aesthetic satire to explore narrative mediation. In *Tristram Shandy*, he mocks yet applies portrait rules to attach readers. At one moment, connoisseurs' "cant" being "most tormenting," he belittles the "*pyramid*" in the group, Titian's "colouring," Raphael's "grace," and Guido's "airs," stressing redundant jargon by inventing the "*corregiescity of Corregio*." At the next, likening Ernulphus's oaths to Michelangelo's works, he extends the jargon: the oaths, having that "*hardness*" and "want of *grace*" typical of the artist, have his "greatness of *gusto*" too. When following the portraitist's rule that the nose be placed a third of the way down the face, Tristram's aesthetic fussiness is fore-grounded. His protest about the innocent "nose" undoes itself: the "setting on of the hair" under which the nose is placed offers genital hints. Sterne here deflates single-minded applications of painterly analogies to invite readers to turn the narrator's inconsistency into a source of narrative dialectic. Addressed as connoisseurs, readers detect ironical tensions between pictorial and narrative ideas. Told that Raphael's image of Socrates in *The School of Athens* informs Walter Shandy's posture as he explains mental stamina to Toby, we are teased by the focus on gesticulation rather than on the painting's ethical meaning. Sterne teases us further by invoking David Garrick (1717–1779) to convey the scene's dramatic potential. The parallel between Raphael and Garrick complicates painting, narrative, and drama: that Tristram ludicrously bases his story on pictorial and spatial principles guides readers to an awareness of dialectic in narrative mediation. Take Tristram's claim that there is an "equipoise and balance" in his scenes and chapters, and his opinion that writing a book is like humming a tune. Gaps between form and informality and references to pictorial and musical composition stress the necessary dynamic between order and unruliness. Pictorial allusions lead us to reflexive compositional ironies in textual mediation. Saying Pope's authorial supremacy makes his portraits in the edition of William Warburton (1698–1779) trivial, Tristram undoes his divine pretensions. Undermining his pictorial analogies is the fact that, if he urges that his father deserves to be portrayed in Reynold's grand style, Sterne had Hogarth draw Tristam's baptism, depicting Walter Shandy barely able to keep his trousers from falling down.[260]

Jocular ambivalence about pictorialism in *A Sentimental Journey* shows Sterne making visual thinking integral to mediation, pictorial ironies stressing the cognitive appeal of textual reflexivity. If Yorick prefers "original drawings and loose sketches" in female bodies to Raphael's *The Transfiguration*, his placing of eros over art is undone by insensibility and prurience. In spurning the monk's appeal for charity, he pictures him in a Reni portrait. This view is as faulty as his disavowal of art: it conveys narrative unreliability. Open to the monk's face, he scorns the "rest of his outline," calling it "neither elegant nor otherwise" to cover his hardheartedness. But pictorial sense recoils on him for abusing the monk and illustrates the reciprocity of visual thinking and narrative. The scenes when Yorick portrays a woman at the Calais Inn and a prisoner in the Bastille unfold the dynamism of visual thinking, clarifying Sterne's tenet that visual images, if subject to whimsy, obey unwritten laws. Standing at the lady's side but avoiding her face, Yorick lets imagination paint her "whole head," as he condemns this faculty as a "seducing slut" to evade his concupiscence. Disjoining sight and invention while intent on pictorial models, he pretends imagination is simply autonomous and blinds himself to interacting visual ideas and words. This wilfulness about mediation wavers, however. Disappointed by her face and by not being found irresistible, he knows the scene conveys a "miserable picture" of his heart. His portrait of the prisoner heightens his sense of the reciprocity of visual and verbal mediation. The portrait is technically disciplined and personally involving. He paints an individual because "sad groups" cannot displace the "hard and deadly" colours his "sombre pencil" first applies to the Bastille. Placing the man in a dungeon and examining him through a grate, Yorick composes and narrates the picture. Framing this figment with imagery and words makes the prisoner seem autonomous yet renders Yorick as creator dependent on his creature. Mediation most moves him when he most asserts creative power: lowering light in the cell, he is torn by the prisoner's swift gesture of despair. Sensing the tension between images and words in narrative mediation, Yorick learns comprehensively about self, art, and political reality.[261]

The paradox that narrative experiments uphold the rhetorical rule that a writer must be moved by his images signals the revisionary impact of the sister arts on the developing novel. Sterne advances this revisionary force in *The Journal to Eliza* (1767), making visual and verbal images reciprocal, Eliza's portrait cited as icon and text: saying "matins and Vespers" to it, he gets it "*by heart.*" Detailing the reciprocity of representation and viewpoint, he links the portrait to the "Dearest Original" and wants it to depict the "Original" better. If the "Picture is Yourself" since it converses with him, his response to it conveys "the present Picture" of himself. Ekphrasis makes Sterne the subject of his own writing by giving him pictorial objectivity and letting him present that "same air and face" to the reader. That pictorial and narrative tensions sustain him obliges readers to trace unique expression inherent in traditional pictorial imitation.[262]

Variously promoting visual thinking, Richardson, Fielding, and Smollett shared Sterne's trust in a pictorially literate readership: they expected readers to value some painters more than others and to appreciate pictorial genres. Yet pictorial literacy stratified readers, as sentimental stories attest. Defying hierarchy and imperialism, *The Man of Feeling* deploys an aestheticism by which Harley puts Edwards, a former retainer, in a genteel Rosa landscape, and *The Vicar of Wakefield*'s hero, Burchell, a proponent of popular culture, places the "erroneous, but sublime animations of the Roman pencil" over the "tame correct paintings of the Flemish school," since he defends social hierarchy with traditional aesthetic discrimination.[263]

Elizabeth Bennet's learning in *Pride and Prejudice* (1813) involves a dialectic of visual thinking and artistic mediation, recapitulating what the sister arts reveal about readership. Standing before Darcy's portrait at Pemberley, she sees a picture that mediates unconventional and traditional values in ways she cannot grasp: knowing "nothing of the art of Painting," she finds it a "striking resemblance." Neither theoretically knowledgeable nor pictorially literate, she cannot tell that the smile on Darcy's face avoids Shenstone's modishness. Nor can she see how the political meaning of the portrait is heightened by Mrs Reynolds: since a servant, not an equal, sees Darcy's biography in the portrait, his nobility is verified unconventionally by a pictorial and social dialectic. Declaring him a perfect brother, master, and landlord, the house-keeper, intimate with the painting but not owning it, upholds hierarchy without being constricted by it. She guides Elizabeth towards Darcy's values. Studying the canvas, Elizabeth senses his gentle authority by becoming the object of his gaze; fixing his image on herself, she begins to understand how aesthetic and political values may be mutually reinforced.[264]

That Elizabeth reforms her attitudes to Darcy upon reading his portrait and subjecting herself to its mediation exemplifies the pictorial demands placed on readers by eighteenth-century authors. In reading Darcy's portrait, she sees that art mediates cultural and personal values. The portrait teaches her that art follows old and establishes new rules, that the depiction of faces may be challengingly ideological, and that looking at pictures is, like reading texts, a form of political and cultural conduct. Elizabeth helps us realise that paintings, such as the oft-cited Raphael cartoons, were cultural texts: objects of public reference, shared imaginative forms, and mediators of political and moral standards.[265] She confirms that writers alluded to paintings and imitated painterly modes, wanting readers to think visually. Stipulating pictorial responsiveness, they asked readers to experience the dialectic of word and image. If they scorned painting, scorn does not preclude pictorial affinities: tension between iconoclasm and iconophilia helped writers advance narrative invention, their awareness of what Reynolds called "contrary qualities" letting them move beyond single-minded models of representation and verisimilitude. That authors developed narrative forms in the face of pictorialism and the sister arts has major implications for literary history. For, if pictorialism led them to accept competing elements within the class of fictional narrative, it encouraged them to realise those qualities diversely. Then, despite distinct modes and styles, they were more or less obliged to work against court culture and aristocratic values embodied in portraiture. Demanding a complex cultural sense by embedding pictorial contraries into fiction, Richardson, Fielding,

Smollett, and Sterne sought a new class of readers. Their deployment of the sister arts engages us in aesthetic experiences that make sense to those who enjoy tensions between social realism and cultural tradition and who see that the history of fiction is traditional and progressive in ways as yet far from completely understood.

CHAPTER FOUR
Theatre History

D ramaturgy of the long eighteenth century reveals polymorphous influences. Since the late medieval theatre only gradually emerged from the authority of the church, its moral ideology remained rooted in the theological and educational ideals of Christian humanism. Plays written in the age of William Shakespeare (1564–1616) retained signs of mystery cycles and of miracle and morality plays. Thus, John Redford (c. 1500–1547), a distinguished composer of keyboard music, wrote *Wyt and Science*, a morality play about the need for education in the middle of the sixteenth century. His allegorical figure, Wyt, runs through a series of romance episodes, including the killing of Giant Tediousness, before subordinating himself to instructional guidance. Redford likely intended his play to be performed by the choir boys of St. Paul's Cathedral, where he was vicar-choral in the 1530s and 1540s and later choirmaster. As the theatre freed itself from church rituals, it became subject to royal ordinances and municipal regulations that restricted theatre managers, playwrights, actors, and playgoers in terms of licences, performance spaces, and other forms of censorship. Naturally, the public theatre creatively resisted the ways in which plays and actors were demeaned.

This chapter explains how the most performed play of the eighteenth century established a dramaturgical dialectic, making *The Beggar's Opera* a superbly provocative example of meta-theatre. A satirical pastiche, this polyvalent text challenges canonicity by mingling farce and opera, popular and classical music, and by dissolving social barriers between aristocrats, the middle classes, and the criminal underworld. Then it surveys plays from before the Restoration of Charles II until the end of the next century. Most plays were mixed forms too, drawing on fables, fairy stories, legends, chronicles, and classical and foreign plays, as well as on Elizabethan and Jacobean plots. The survey follows two major trends. The first is when, with new indoor theatres and their architectural and mechanical inventions such as the proscenium, stage and trap doors, there was a greater emphasis on spectacular action and grand declamation. The second is when the growing influence of narrative and mercantile sentimentality affected the nature of closure and denouements. By 1800, on-stage stories that were too easily resolved made upper-class decadence and commercial greed mere truisms.

Dynamic argumentation is more and more absent; stage tricks and secrets hidden from characters were transparent to the audience. The trend from political protest to display made thematic implications obvious and dialectically weak.

The Beggar's Opera (1728)

Mixed genres dominate this play, which is called a ballad opera or Newgate pastoral. Its topics deal with the new capitalism, the political system, the bourgeois family, the criminal underworld, the hypocrisies of gentility, and judicial corruption. Reflecting popular culture, it defies theatrical paradigms. Its structure refers to and prescribes its own reception, like *A Tale of a Tub* (1704) and *The Dunciad*. Its formal and ideological pluralism means it does not operate as a seamless work against a unified background; its reflexivity anticipates the recursive meta-criticism of postmodernism, the text resisting single-minded accounts of its functions. Since it is more than a transcript of its times, it validates plural forms of exegesis. By revealing how traditional and contemporary critical methods apply, the play shows how critical dialectic offers humanistic goals to readers who cannot avoid its contraries.[266] Unique in 1728, the play remains inimitable: if a ballad opera, it had no true imitator. Its uniqueness is paradoxical; in imitating plural theatrical forms, it probes many social practices. It borrows from opera, heroic tragedy, comedy of wit, the masque, the ballad, comedy of sensibility, farce, and criminal biography, satirising generic hierarchy. Its ironies defamiliarize the perspectives of habitual theatregoers.

When Max Goberman (1911–1962) recorded its songs with original instruments, he stressed *maestoso* and *allegro* styles in the overture by Johann Christoph Pepusch (1667–1752) as they alternate pathetic and comic modes. He then puts melodies by Purcell, Handel, and other composers into the throats of pickpockets, fences, and prostitutes. Grand arias clash with popular songs: bawdy tunes debase aristocratic pretensions of crooks, and ballads undercut their middle-class sensibilities.[267] Hearing bourgeois taste mocked, audiences enjoy tensions between arias, recitative, and duets, and grasp idioms in the original score.[268] Goberman validates historical recovery in comparison to the sweet orchestrations of Sir Frederic Austin (1872–1952) for the 1920 Hammersmith production and to the jazzy toughness of Kurt Weill (1900–1950) in *The Threepenny Opera*, the 1928 version by Berthold Brecht (1898–1956). Those versions question musical progress: that they separate high- and low-brow modes stirs us to revisit the original music to probe how first audiences might have responded to the complex social allusions which, in revealing tensions between aesthetics and politics, convey the paradox that Gay's exposure of abused dramatic illusion restores power to the theatre. Since audiences may be involved and unsettled, Gay questions the extent to which his audience was an established entity and the degree to which he used reflexive meanings to create it.

Augustan texts show that standard criticism deals stolidly with authors who valued anti-systematic systems: the texts foresaw problems in narrative realism and lamented lost mythopoeic vision. Gay's creativity is clear when he tests critical pluralism to advance historical dialectic. One test relates to whether scientific and literary progress are synchronous. To Thomas Kuhn, paradigms are necessary but limiting frameworks that must be broken if development is to happen. This is less germane to Gay than claims there is "no such thing as research without counter-instances" and that rivalry between research paradigms raises the question "Which problems is it more significant to have solved?"[269] Thus, we may ask if later paradigms invalidate earlier ones and if it is feasible to separate meaning that inheres in a text from significance that accretes to it in cultural reception. For E.D. Hirsch, texts have core meanings regardless of social history.[270] But hermeneutic recoverability is offset by Michel Foucault's view that evolving institutions like prisons are programmed by literary texts. Yet such linking of texts to political history subordinates aesthetics without showing how politics derives from aesthetic goals.[271]

Gay's text involves dialectical perspectives on politics and history. Conflating social groups to make the poor and the rich signify decadence, it upholds and derides hierarchy: while it debases opera through irony and parody, Gay's anti-form respects generic ideals.[272] Biography offers much in this regard, but its certitudes are not certainties. *The Beggar's Opera* neither supports traditional criticism nor privileges diachronic study. Gay follows the humanism of Pope and Swift, but it is unclear that his play is the acme of his opus and of Augustan ideology, as an editor claims. Gay neither portrayed the underworld simply to attack the Court nor stopped Handel composing Italian opera in the 1730s.[273] He used Italian operatic motifs in *Achilles* (1733) and cooperated with Handel in a production of *Acis and Galatea* (1732). While he was involved with political personalities and events, it is difficult, in considering influences on his play, to be exhaustive or to avoid being arbitrary about his life. Still, it is germane that he sought aristocratic patronage, having lost much in the South Sea Bubble. To appreciate *The Beggar's Opera*, it helps to trace its urban pastoralism and generic mixtures in his poetic career. But Edgar Roberts does not help in declaring that *The Beggar's Opera* is "above all a satire" because this discounts its reflexive ironies and European effects on the English stage.[274]

The Beggar's Opera's framing device mocks authorship and limits biographical criticism, showing how the dramatist appears obliquely on stage.[275] Since the frame levels the author with actors and audience, biography is subordinate to the text's material aspects. Plays exist to be performed; they are promptbooks offering cues to actors as well as plotted actions. As Gay's frame stresses, plays are produced by theatre managers for consumers and crucial to actors' welfare. Since a play-text does not primarily mirror its author, its functions require material study. The materiality of *The Beggar's Opera* necessitates exploring its debt to five-act dramatic and three-act operatic modes which entail distinct systems of mediation and commodification. Reconciling these systems must draw on the theatre's history as a public institution. Companies struggled for survival and patronage in the Restoration. Conflicts between the official companies affected *The Beggar's Opera*. Its rejection by Colley Cibber (1671–1757) and acceptance by John Rich (1692–1761), a rival theatre manager who demanded large returns, affected its production. Like Pope, Gay disliked the influence of Rich on theatrical practices. Gay's text does not simply defend drama against opera; he satirises musical effects on dramatic illusion while integrating music into the plot to resist the incursions of pantomime.[276]

With the return of Charles II, political forces aggravated the public theatre's problems. Their re-opening in 1660 led to twenty-five years of counter-revolutionary dramaturgy. The re-opening was so tied to anti-republicanism that plays were newly politicised: the reaction of Roger Boyle (1st Earl of Orrery, 1621–1679), Dryden, George Etherege (1636–1692), and William Wycherley to the ideology that had proscribed public theatres was deep. Yet their wish to deny the immediate past and recover Shakespeare, Ben Jonson (1572–1637), Francis Beaumont (1584–1616), and John Fletcher (1579–1625) was frustrated since the fabric torn by the Civil War was not mended by the Settlement; sequestrated properties of the lesser aristocracy and squirearchy were not all restored. Allusions to Shakespeare and Thomas Otway (1652–1685) in *The Beggar's Opera* expose unresolved strife between the politicisation of the theatre and playwrights' desire to unearth drama's roots. Further, Gay's folksongs are related to the carnival spirit of popular music that served as propaganda during and after the Civil War.[277]

If factionalism after 1660 affected dramatic codes, and if playwrights, theatre companies, and audiences divided along lines that grew sharper as rivalry between aristocratic, professional, and merchant classes intensified, these divisions led stage and social spaces to be extensions of one another. Arbitrariness in the Settlement gave playwrights a new sense of London that grew from tensions between the desire to recover the cultural past and the sense of its irretrievability. The plays of Wycherley and Etherege illustrate London's demographic changes since districts inside and outside the city became socially marked; their settings capture the wishes of the marginalised and transcribe London's remaking after the King's return, the Plague of 1665, and the Fire of 1666. Interacting social and dramatic settings appear in Gay's allusions that echo *The Country Wife* (1675) and *The Man of Mode* (1676); London is a set of social signs and an extension of the theatre. Gay's settings have characters displaced from social and economic hierarchies who treat urban landscape as a theatre to compensate for lost power and prestige.

To approach Gay's exploitation of literary history, one may contrast *The Beggar's Opera* with plays that are not counter-revolutionary and that do not create reflexive functions for setting. *The Squire of Alsatia* (1688) by Thomas Shadwell (1642–1692) anticipates Gay by depicting London's underworld and deploying its low-life idioms, but it upholds Whig patriarchalism. Without renewing drama, Shadwell sentimentally defends the status quo and debases theatrical processes. But Gay validates the stage by demeaning characters who belittle plays: like Wycherley and Etherege, he creates systems of representation with ambivalent relations to daily life. If Shadwell's play points up Gay's closeness to Restoration dramatists, it raises the question of whether conservatives tried to renew, while progressives tried to erode, theatrical history. This issue cannot be resolved by traditional views of setting. Editor Roberts identifies lanes, streets, parishes, and districts, connecting them to brothels, dens of thieves and gamblers, trade, medicine, and law, and to the routes between Newgate, the Old Bailey, and Tyburn as well as to the sites of theatres, but he does not link social and theatrical spaces. His place-names provide excellent geographical context, proving valuable familiarity with a historical atlas and London topography. But he ignores Gay's demography; we learn much by linking routes taken by condemned criminals to public spectacle and through the proximity of centres of lawlessness and legislation.

In proposing an equivalence of location and topicality in Gay's setting, Roberts does not see that its plurality is best approached by new historicisms. In mapping London's place-names, Gay treats the city in ways that oppose the sentimental line of plays from *The Squire of Alsatia* to *The Conscious Lovers* (1722) and *The London Merchant* (1731), plays which dignify the capital as the moral arena of merchants. Gay's place-names signal that crime defines London and that the underworld—less containable than Jeremy Collier (1650-1726), the non-juror bishop, hoped—flourished because of reformist platitudes. The social and dramatic contexts in which Gay's place-names challenge sentimental, mercantile values convey the plural functions of the names, expose the gaps between social principles and contingency and between linguistic rules and arbitrariness, and they show how setting involves characterisation. Gay's Newgate is an epitome of leading institutions: Peachum and Lockit make the prison stand for the Exchange, the High Court, the House of Commons, and the Cabinet Chamber. Their organised corruption of money, politics, and law means that Newgate displaces, as it represents, other institutions. The type of all institutions and the image of systematic evil, it shows all ills stemming from criminal practice.[278] Like the "double capacity" of Gay's characters, the prison has specific and general functions which, in heightening tensions between referential and systematic meaning, require the dialectical application of historicist and semiotic interpretations.[279]

Plurality of setting points up Gay's complex topicality and literary allusiveness in which historical figures are represented and displaced. If Peachum images Jonathan Wild, the thief-taker and gangster hanged in London in 1725, Wild is also enacted by Lockit, Peachum's partner and rival. In this field of reference, Macheath is Jack Sheppard, the famous prison breaker and creature of Wild's. Yet, each male part has one referent in the political world—Robert Walpole (1676-1745), the prime minister. Plurality of characterisation is underlined when Peachum and Lockit fight; they then convey the feud of Walpole with his brother-in-law, Charles Townshend, secretary of state (1674-1738). To heighten this intertextuality, Gay alludes to other plays and genres. When Peachum and Lockit fight, they recall Brutus and Cassius arguing in *Julius Caesar* (1599), and when they berate their betters, their words recall the discontented Jaffeir and Pierre in *Venice Preserved* (1682). When Macheath fears he is about to hang, he echoes the climax of Otway's play, this following his inability to choose between Polly and Lucy, a scene like the one in Dryden's *All for Love* (1677) when Antony faces the opposing demands of Octavia and Cleopatra. If *The Beggar's Opera* typifies Restoration comedy in burlesquing heroic plays, its allusions to Handel's *Floridante* (1721) and *Alessandro* (1726) draw on interchangeable roles and peripeteia of motivation and action in heroic tragedy and Italian opera to advance cultural and metatheatrical criticism. Given the longevity of heroic tragedies—witness Fielding's *The Tragedy of Tragedies* which travesties more than forty in 1731—we realise what light Gay's plural historical and literary allusions shed on the relationship of characterisation to genre.[280] The historicist phrase, "the novelization of culture," seems not to fit the complex intertextuality of *The Beggar's Opera*.[281] One reason is that Gay mixed so many generic modes. Another is that he exploits plural allusions and modes of characterisation to generate themes critical of sentimental reformers who subordinated drama to narrative. His text thematises drama's decline ironically: scorning Polly's playbooks, her mother apes the platitudes of bourgeois comedy, and the sentimentality of Polly and Filch springs from vulgar romance. The theatre and opera house are arenas for crime while the courts are stages on which illicit parts are performed with aplomb. Macheath's reprieve is the nadir of drama, Gay exposing the call for generic purity as a sign of popular surrender to narrative formulae and antidramatic dogma.[282]

Gay challenges traditional and contemporary criticism. Plural modes of allusion in his satire raze barriers between popular and high art, textual reflexivity defying generic history and truisms about literary progress. He defends drama by treating the marginalisation of theatre ironically and by heightening stage power with conflicting codes. Modern concepts of the rise of the middle classes and bourgeois progress, which he personally and textually opposed, are no more helpful than traditional exposition which, moving step-by-step from setting to characterisation to themes, cannot address the tensions he creates between presenting social change and registering cultural contradictions. Traditional exposition may establish that *The Beggar's Opera* deals with the growth of political parties, the role of the prime minister, the mores of court culture, and the problems of the financial revolution. But it deals less well with family and married life since Gay unsettles social and literary progress: he less faults social hierarchy than shows that, in aping the aristocracy, the lesser ranks betray reformist notions of companionate marriage to material and sexual vice. Further, themes created from contradictions in the reform of the penal code depreciate traditional exegesis. Shrewdly sensing that legislated increases in capital crimes defended property at the expense of individual rights, he assigns growth in the business of crime and thief-taking to legal reform. This reform commodifies the media: permitting newspapers to advertise stolen goods perpetuates robbery, and criminal biographies justify penal reform and reinforce the fantasies of the ruling class, as the hero-worship attributed to the audience in the denouement illustrates.

The performance history of *The Beggar's Opera* confirms that traditional explication must embrace scepticism. That audiences identified with characters while critics damned productions requires that its textual pluralism be seen in terms of cultural dialectic. Its record-breaking first season of sixty-two performances and more than one thousand before 1800 make it an acme of popularity. Its fame grew when Lavinia Fenton (1708–1760), the actress who played Polly, left the stage to marry Charles Powlett (1685–1764), 3rd Duke of Bolton, and when other actors were depicted on commemorative playing cards, fans, and screens. This context makes it hard to see why the text's irreverence was neutered as a result of attacks by Thomas Herring (1693–1757), the Archbishop of Canterbury, and Sir John Fielding (1721–1780), the police magistrate, yet celebrated in festive harmlessness when acted by children and by adults who reversed the dramatis personæ's genders. Such reactions—claims that *The Beggar's Opera* was nothing new and a dangerous novelty—illustrate the literary and social dialectic inherent in cultural history. Calling it an entertainment without serious intent but with incentives to crime, Johnson, if alert to its comic misrule, demeaned its satire. Defoe and Sir John Hawkins (1719–1789), Johnson's editor, also saw it as encouraging crime and envisaged criminals like Sheppard becoming folk heroes, but they ascribed crime to individuals and not to institutions.

The dialectic needed to explain the text's plurality and cultural reception makes efforts to reconcile traditional and new historicisms vital. Such efforts are rewarded when one determines the scope the text gives to critical methods that integrate literary and social history and that make sense of Gay's ambivalent literary and social conventions. Speech-act theory, semiotic analysis, and feminist perspectives renew literary history in the face of Gay's simultaneous criticism and promotion of literary and social hierarchies. *The Beggar's Opera* emphasises that spoken words change the world; they perform actions since language is an institution that resists abusive speakers. Speech-act theory is relevant to Gay since his characters depreciate words and linguistic contexts that render utterance significant and cohesive: they accept performative meaning in negative or inverted senses. Peachum holds that all "professions be-rogue one another." Since neighbours abuse one another, the lawyer necessarily "be-knaves the divine." To Macheath, a courtier is one who "professes everything and will do nothing," but neither fellow thieves nor gang-owners practise what they preach. All undermine the social basis of meaning, posturing with words anarchically.[283] The relevance of speech-act theory is clear when Gay treats conversation as mere formality and euphemism for robbery or sexual intercourse. To women, "spatter" and "chatter" are synonyms, while to men, what women "say or do goes for nothing." Male abuse of illocution shows how deeply misogyny is embedded in society. Macheath says a promise to a woman "signifies nothing" yet mouths the cliché that "his word is as good as his bond." Claiming to be above ceremony but subjecting it to their interests, characters abuse speech. When Mrs Peachum pronounces that Filch will be "a great man in history," she is personally and socially destructive. When Lockit says he "can forgive as well as resent," his substitution of *resent* for *forget* abuses words and degrades community.[284]

Performatives fortify satire by showing how semiotic concepts complement speech-act theory. Characters are puppets to society's codes; they speak erratically in mixed registers as they abuse linguistic and moral conventions. Aligning himself with other professions and classes, Peachum decries those alignments. He is proud to share the "honest employment" of lawyers by acting for and against rogues, yet admits that lawyers are "bitter enemies to those in our way." A gangster managing thieves' productivity, he poses like a judge who can "soften the evidence" or declare "death without reprieve" and like a rural squire whose wish to protect female partridges and breed "game" rules his sense of life and death. Obsessed with "industry," "stock," and "credit," Peachum also speaks like a moneylender. But greed and self-importance inhibit him from seeing conflicts among the codes he voices; conflicts arise from unintegrated professional and aesthetic pretensions. In saying he depends on female thieves since, in prostituting themselves, they breed thieves, harden men to crime, and spread disease, he falsely says surgeons and thief-takers are interdependent. Implausibly, he pretends to aesthetic superiority to dignify his profession. He exposes his taste when praising one thief's "engaging presence of mind" and "genius." The pun in *engaging* on highway robbery and personal grace and the notion that "Crook-fingered Jack" is a "mighty clean-handed fellow" show that, when he plans a "decent execution," aesthetic pretensions unmask his corruption and society's corruptibility.[285]

Pretension motivates the adoption of ecclesiastical, literary, and military idioms. Mrs Peachum thinks the Catechism useful for letting a man on trial make a good figure in court and the "Ordinary's paper," confirming Filch's view that "penitence" destroys a gentleman's spirit and a thief's commitment to crime. To Filch, Newgate's "favorite child-getter" has the "prowess of a knight errant" in saving "ladies in distress." Filch further perverts literary clichés, when, despite having been "pumped," he fears being cut off in the "flower of [his] youth." Polly's belief in the "great heroes" of the romances, lent to her by Macheath, perversely covers her wish to be seduced, while his attempt to dignify promiscuity by citing Orsino's talk of love and music in *Twelfth Night* (1602) rings hollow. Despite the gang's claim to fearless honour based on the "law of arms" and "right of conquest," Jemmy Twitcher's impeachment of Macheath shows they lack honour and are destined for the noose. In the condemned cell, Macheath's courage is coterminous with wine, his fanciful code signalling that "the world is all alike" in depravity.[286]

The Beggar's Opera exposes what abused codes say of discourse as society's instrument for sustaining itself; it dramatises abuses that sap relations between codes. Mrs Trapes, the bawd, is as familiar with the business world as Peachum and Lockit. Her women easily appropriate its codes, witness Mrs Coaxer's talk about "interlopers" and "industry." When Matt of the Mint says that Peachum is as necessary to the gang as "a bawd to a whore," abuse of codes appears to be as indiscriminate as widespread: the loss of systematic differentiation vital to their function implies that society is losing structural identity. Yet the ironical resistance of codes to abuse is clear when Macheath claims recruitment of prostitutes in Drury Lane depends on "gentlemen of the sword": equating highwaymen with professional soldiers, he adopts the implausible comparative logic that Peachum, his rival and employer, uses when he prides himself on being as indebted to the prostitutes of Drury Lane as surgeons are.

Interacting codes objectively ground Gay's irony, social history thereby informing the text and validating cultural criticism.[287]

Gay's systematic appreciation of codes involves characters in the ironies of class rivalry and rejection of hierarchy. The Peachums' erratic stances to Macheath's courtship of Polly are examples. Mrs Peachum thinks Macheath a worthy husband since he is a fine gentleman, but Peachum insists Macheath lacks a genteel education because he is always worsted at gambling by lords. Mrs Peachum would forgive Polly's affair since her daughter imitates fine ladies, but on confirming the marriage, she chides Polly for imitating the gentry and laments that Polly has not brought a distinguished person into the family. As erratic, Peachum wishes his daughter had a court lady's discretion, so he could better manipulate his gang, but he blames Polly for marrying since she will be as neglected as if married to a lord and since highwaymen abuse their wives. The Peachums' class views are consistently inconsistent, spurning and idolising the professions, the gentry, and the aristocracy. Their wide-ranging, reciprocal abuse of signs actualises drama's analytical power. By replicating as he defies ideologies, Gay invalidates interpretations based on single historical models: his text reproduces systems of signification, yet its pluralism is not determined by them. Unlike Brecht's systematic inversions, Gay's are reflexive and referential. While *The Threepenny Opera* presents monarchical and commercial motifs anachronistically and stridently, *The Beggar's Opera* privileges semiotic ambivalence to place itself outside and inside historical discourse, making this dialectical action a puzzling as well as polemical dramatic end.[288]

Contrasting Brecht's and Gay's semiosis reveals how *The Beggar's Opera* converts attacks on humanism into a radical defence. Brecht's explicit, monological reference is closer to the univocal, novelistic dialogue of *The London Merchant* (1731) by George Lillo (1691–1739) and *The Jealous Wife* (1761) by George Colman the Elder (1732–1794) than to the mixed modes in which Gay, Swift, and Pope treated the rising middle classes. Like his fellows, Gay defends humanism by eschewing an obvious programme and appropriating literary and social codes. Failure to grasp his radical conservatism heightens the need to revise literary history.[289] Semiotic analysis of *The Beggar's Opera* leads us to review the application of religious ideology, the growth of the aristocracy, increased differentiation in social hierarchy, the diminution of female power, and the decline of drama to the work of the Augustans in general.

Although Gay's satire is dramatic as well as social, *The Beggar's Opera* addresses feminist issues by tackling patriarchy and misogyny. While motifs of prostitution and widowhood qualify as themes of forced marriage that dominated comic plots after the Restoration, Gay satirises more than dramatic and social formulae. Aware that textual and sexual forms of gender may be reciprocal, he objects to social imitation of drama as much as to its self-perpetuating closedness to reality, this being evidence of how female characters objectify themselves when obsessed with death and sexual climax. Since they lay claim to affection and conscience while being aggressive and mercenary, their mixed motives clarify the harm done them by society as well as feminism's limits. While Mrs Peachum possesses an "overscrupulous conscience" that objects to murder, she urges Peachum to murder Macheath on account of "necessity." Holding that her "sex is frail," she believes the first time a woman is frail she can choose to be "somewhat nice." Her confusion presents what William Empson calls an "eerie insistence on the sex war."[290] To Mrs Peachum, men are handsome when facing death: the gallow's rope creates a "charming zone." Polly sustains her "bleeding heart" by picturing Macheath's ride in the "cart" to Tyburn. Her wish to save his neck undoes itself; she would "throttle" him with love. Declining to think of marriage in terms of widowhood, she enjoys that prospect when asking to stay with him "till death." The view that female desire depends on men's death is stressed by Mrs Trapes, the bawd, who announces, when trading for stolen clothes, that her girls are "very fond of mourning."[291]

Undermining the sentimental postures his women assume, Gay is as critical of male sexuality, intersecting codes revealing the hollowness of libertinism and the reciprocal structuring of society and gender. Calling himself a "lover of the sex," Macheath defames women by calling them "decoy ducks." Humorous self-exposure lies in the fact that, though betrayed by favourite prostitutes, he claims to be a gentleman hunter. Misogyny is stressed when he calls woman a "basilisk," the fatal mythical creature, and "treacle" in which flies drown, the clashing registers undoing his dissociated, self-entrapping images: misogyny stems from his baseless wish to pose as heroic victim. Peachum echoes this wish when consoling Macheath by saying the "greatest heroes" have been ruined by women—a "pretty sort of creature if we could trust them."[292]

Gay's delineation of female perversity further questions literary and social hierarchies. Speech-act theory, semiotics, and feminism are limited in this regard, pedagogical integrity requiring us to establish the reciprocity of traditional and historicist methods which test over-generalisations in biographical criticism, for instance. Patricia Spacks's book on Gay emphasises his temperamental weakness and personal ambivalence, claiming that he unwittingly inscribed these features into his texts and that his "ambiguities are valuable" only in *The Beggar's Opera*, the "logical culmination" of his dramatic works.[293] This generalisation needs qualification. The epistemology of Locke and George Berkeley (1685–1753) problematized identity. Their ideas of plural, discontinuous selves remind us that writers cannot simply inscribe themselves into their works. It is helpful to know that Gay was cheerful yet subject to despair, that he was careless about money though needy, and that he was an aesthete who cultivated plebian tastes.[294] But such ambivalence owes something to cultural ethos and the procedures of life-writing: Gay was probably no more ambivalent than his fellows, and biography inevitably stresses problematic traits. Far from being written single-handedly, *The Beggar's Opera* was composed by a member of a coterie: Gay was friend to Swift and John Arbuthnot (1667–1735), a translator for Pope, and secretary to the Scriblerus Club. That *The Beggar's Opera* appropriated well-known songs, that Gay's friends provided him with words and songs, and that he relied on subliterary texts which have not all been discovered or analysed form areas of indeterminacy within the field of biographical criticism that make further research excitingly necessary.[295]

Theatrical Genres

The re-opened public theatres heralded twenty-five years of counter-revolutionary dramaturgy. Plays mocked the Commonwealth (1649–1660) and led Goldsmith and Sheridan to close a chapter of stage history in the 1770s when they sought to reclaim Restoration models and to free the theatre from sentimental forces that were sapping drama. Yet, in these efforts, they upheld patriarchy and hierarchy: in their plays, imperial and commercial motifs confirm that England had replaced civil strife with international campaigns. Their comedies did not renew Restoration modes but conserved what they rejected; sentimental exposure of false delicacy highlights England's rise to imperialism and drama's fall from vital renewal.

To Restoration dramatists, re-opened theatres meant republicanism's end, playwriting inevitably chiding the ideologies that proscribed drama. To Etherege, Wycherley, Boyle, and Dryden, the stage had to reject the political past and recall the works of Jonson, Beaumont, and Fletcher from before the closure of theatres in 1642. Desiring political discontinuity and theatrical continuity is a crux in stage history; playwrights struggled with this dialectic. In their royalism, they confronted political continuity and defamed the court and the city. Theatrical continuity was as elusive as political discontinuity: stage tradition was as inaccessible to Shadwell and William Congreve (1670–1729) as to Goldsmith and Sheridan. New playhouses were unlike Shakespeare's Globe. Closed to the weather and daylight, they housed smaller audiences, relying more on costumes and machinery. Drama's roots were severed by more than architectural and technical progress. Production costs increased ticket prices. Theatres pleased coteries whose wish to see commerce, virtuosity, and radicalism debunked shaped styles of plotting that, if more responsive to Jonson than Shakespeare, drew on foreign drama: reaction to plays from abroad, underway before the Civil War, climaxed in the decades between 1660 and 1700.[296]

Efforts to recover the past adopted foreign rules, as versions of Shakespeare by Dryden and Nahum Tate (1652–1715) via French neoclassicism attest. Yet the English stage did not much respect Roman, Spanish, and French theatre: it mocked foreign cultures as much as the Commonwealth. Playwrights borrowed from Pedro Calderón (1600–1681), Pierre Corneille (1606–1684), and Jean Racine (1639–1699), but Spanish autocracy and French gallantry became mere clichés. Tensions between indebtedness to and debasement of continental drama form an important dialectic in English theatre, one related to European identity. If ambivalence towards the foreign renders dubious the internationalism of aristocratic neoclassicism, it also calls for revisions to domestic literary history. By proving that Etherege and Wycherley pleased audiences which liked the sentimental pathos of Steele and Lillo, Robert Hume (1983) shows theatrical taste to have been more heterogenous than supposed. Basing dramatic history on performance rather than composition, he insists that the social meaning of drama requires synchronic and diachronic studies, structuralist as well as developmental assumptions.

To Hume, theatrical decline is complex. That neoclassical and heroic modes ended with Charles II's reign and that the Revolution of 1688 created a taste for pathos that displaced aristocratic values are untenable. Formal and political evolution was as complex later as at the Restoration. While nationalism coarsened images of France, the success of *The Distressed Mother* (1712) by Ambrose Philips (1674–1749), a version of Racine's *Andromaque* (1667), and of Fielding's *The Miser* (1733), and an adaptation of *L'Avare* (1668) by Molière (Jean-Baptiste Poquelin, 1622–1673), shows that cross-cultural ties were tight. Lillo's impact on Jean-Jacques Rousseau (1712–1778) and Denis Diderot (1713–1784) and their sentimental influence on Richard Cumberland (1732–1811) indicate reciprocity in national theatres. If Garrick's recovery of Shakespeare resists the strictures of Voltaire (François-Marie Arouet, 1694–1778), plays of the 1760s and 1770s depend on modes from the French stage.

Polarities in domestic and foreign culture require a comparative approach to theatrical decline. If the Restoration distinguished between tragedy and comedy, it produced heroic plays that elicited laughter and comedies that parodied heroism: changes in generic awareness offset formal specialisation. In 1780, Restoration motifs obtained, but narrative dominated theatrical mediation. Drama became less public and more private, less political and more psychological, despite larger auditoria requiring grandiose declamation. The novel's rise saw relations between dramatic genres becoming less intense. The dominance of farce in *rehearsal* plays after *The Beggar's Opera* illustrates this slackening. But slacker tension is most evident in tragedies and comedies after 1750, satire and sentiment coexisting with little interaction. Faced by the novel, foreign models, and new social realities, drama spent more energy supporting patriarchal, nationalistic values than on renewing itself. The genres of the 1770s employ a narrative sense of conflict and a psychological view of identity, yet formal and ideological inconsistencies are as notable as in 1660. Indeed, the history of English drama is told best through dialectic: the volatile ways it appropriated and resisted foreign ideas while attacking and fortifying its own traditions.[297]

Heroic Plays, 1660–1677

The impact of French romance, with its imposing strains, on English drama is evident in Boyle's *Mustapha* (1665). Its hero's aristocratic sensibility transcends social chaos. His refinement defies pragmatism. Clerical and political characters are pragmatic, but he holds it worse to deserve death than to die. Yet, if Boyle debases commonwealth values by giving power to monarchy, his royalism holds that only aristocrats endure tragic conflict: he defends monarchy with the transcendence of nobles and their inevitable political failure. The heroism of Mustapha and his half-brother, Zanger, in reconciling friendship and rivalry entails self-destruction. Unmoved by Hobbesian self-interest, Boyle's heroes scorn religion and nationalism. His symmetrical characterisation conveys a rarefied identity. Facing political instability, his characters learn that shared sensibility limits unique agency and leads to oblivion. *Mustapha* promotes aristocratic magnanimity and internationalism but implies that scope for heroic idealism is minimal.

Dryden's heroic plays appeal to coteries eager for baroque elaboration of plot and motive in closed courts. The inventive dialectic within characterisation shows how the genre offers surprising implications for individualism and dramatic mediation: peripeteias defy received ideas of agency and narration. In *The Indian Emperor* (1665), Cortez, initially a spokesman for Christian imperialism, comes to defend Montezuma's absolutism. That his court collapses reflects colonial power's fragility. If Montezuma's absolutism bests Christian barbarity, courtly isolation fails its hierarchy. *Tyrannick Love* (1669) also shows how the politics of desire in an absolutist court erode aristocracy. Wildly in love with St Catharine who defies his apotheosis, Maximin disjoins classical and Christian creeds on whose union aristocratic myth depends. The irony is accented by a masque that predicts St Catharine's victory over the tyrant and mediates her divine rescue. Maximin's tyranny is deflated by his rant that is far from poised neoclassical rhetoric and by the irony that an aristocratic masque dignifies the Christian martyr.

In *The Rehearsal* (1671), George Villiers, Duke of Buckingham (1628–1687), attacks heroic plays, decrying their scorn for native drama. Parodying tropes that cloud plot and dialectic that debases closure, he sneers at Dryden's pretentious reliance on French romance. Villiers urges the genre's end, claiming it endangers peace: the theatre should oppose political plots. In *The Empress of Morocco* (1673), Elkanah Settle (1648–1724) defies calls for generic dissolution by linking theatrical and political plotting. Villains destroy innocent Muly Laby and Morena, making them act in a masque in which they kill each other. Spectacular violence conveys the fragility of aristocratic romance. Upholding absolutism, Settle, like Dryden, stresses political instability: the court is annihilated and the next king elected. The dubiety of heroic plays reaches an acme in Dryden's *Aureng-Zebe* (1675). Its court is afflicted by absurdly comical passion. Piously rejecting improper advances, the hero rashly suspects Indamora of infidelity. Jealousy being positive and negative, the play ends happily, its close having seemed doomed. Aureng-Zebe is gullible and noble: his misogyny is baseless, yet he is no sexual fool. The stress on sexual pathos is clarified in *The Rival Queens* (1677) by Nathaniel Lee (1653–1692). The power of female rivals for Alexander is dichotomous: his inability to control Statira and Roxana allows conspirators to undo him. An undignified tyrant, he is forced by love to sense his limits despite thinking himself favoured by the gods. His nobility rests not on autocracy but self-destructive passion. Stressing heroic plays' contempt for the Commonwealth in baroque images of carnival, *The Rival Queens* mirrors the genre's transgressions. Fostering aristocratic sensibility, the genre puts noble pain above real experience, yet not soberly. Lamenting heroism's fragility, playwrights enjoyed stage jokes, as when chaste roles in *Tyrannick Love* were played by the Court's notorious whores.

Early Comedies, 1660–1676

Revenge dominates comedy of the 1660s. *The Committee* (1662) by Robert Howard (1626–1698) and *The English Mounsieur* (1663) by James Howard (1640–1669) decry the Civil War. Set in the Commonwealth, *The Committee* faults "new gentry" for stealing estates. Dissenters' "pretended religion" and "open rebellion" are exposed for politicising marriage. Cheating guardians to restore the estates of cavaliers whom they marry, the heroines celebrate aristocratic sexuality: female dissimulation is a theatrical corrective to the puritan revolution. *The English Mounsieur* denies status to republicans. From merchant stock, Frenchlove mimics French modes; he thinks affected discontent with London a passport to Court. He is punished when Mrs Craft, mistress of a Cavalier, traps him in wedlock. Etherege develops marital typology in *The Comical Revenge* (1664) where carnivalesque Sir Frederick Frolick has marriage punish and reward several types. While penalising rogues and Sir Nicholas Cully, a base knight appointed by Cromwell, Frolick re-orders the lives of nobles ruined by heroic anxieties. His libertinism repairs society with class distinctions. Etherege's retaliation is not merely aristocratic: *She Would If She Could* (1668) assails rural gentry. The Cockwoods visit London, hoping sexual licence will not harm their name. Their wish to enjoy the urban pastoralism that town wits without estates cultivate is mocked. As *The Man of Mode* (1676) shows in the power Dorimant, the rake, holds over men and women, Etherege endorses the topography of the city held by displaced gentry. Dorimant's view of London as a stage for conquering Mrs Loveit and Bellinda and outclassing young Bellair signals a dramatic awareness that Etherege endorses: wits injured by the Civil War translate London into codes opaque to rural gentry. The keenest translator is Harriet's: thwarting Dorimant, she makes him act the role of Courtage and change his sexual stance. Affecting neither heroic passion like Mrs Loveit nor romantic intrigue like Bellinda, she resists Dorimant's courtship, signalling that women must develop a shrewd, pragmatic view of marriage if social progress is to unfold.

While Etherege explores stage illusions to reject the political past and envisage the social future, Dryden does so by exploiting the dualities of romance. The symmetries of *Secret Love* (1667) chasten Celadon's libertinism and deny the Queen's passionate regality. Stressing its dangers, the play upholds romance, a duality in *Sir Martin Mar-all* (1667), a work based on Molière. Unlike lecherous Dartmouth, Martin is admirable, but lacking the sense of agency found in romance, he undoes himself. A rural squire, he laughably applies bookish ideas to a resistant social context. The Spanish carnival setting of *An Evening's Love* (1668) lets Dryden turn romance upon England. The success of displaced cavaliers, Bellamy and Wildblood, with Spanish ladies undoes patriarchal autocracy. Yet the cavaliers' sexual appropriation of political, commercial, and rural diction recoils on English more than Spanish culture. The dualities of romance reach new heights in *Marriage A-la-Mode* (1672). For Palamede and Rhodophil, illicit sex offsets boring arranged marriages. Yet after chasing each other's partners and seeing that libertinism thwarts possession of female bodies, they form a compact against romance. Satire of those who model themselves on French romance is clearest in Melantha's case. Yet men behave "just like so many over-grown Puppets" so that libertine abuse of romance may be condemned. Resolution of the courtly plot—Leonidas's restoration which forgives the usurper—re-enacts 1660: here romance insists that legitimacy is needed by national life and that illicit passion destroys royalism.

Theatrical disputes clarify this ideology. In *The Reformation* (1673), Joseph Arrowsmith abuses Dryden, making him a stupid English tutor to decry imitation of French romance. *The Reformation's* gay couples parody *Marriage A-la-Mode*. Arrowsmith's foreign setting derides English modes in the name of lawful marital delights. Intent on mocking cultural analogies, he pretends that English carnival is perpetual, his Sicilian rakes diverting political slogans, such as the "good old cause," to libertinism. The topical transparency of *The Reformation* typifies Restoration farce. In *The Virtuoso* (1676), Shadwell's nationalism promotes it. Like Arrowsmith, he insists that talk of reform is cant. His leading hypocrite is Sir Nicholas Gimcrack: tyrannical father and cuckolded husband, he aims to undo the Restoration settlement and return church lands to the court. Imitating Jonson, Shadwell exaggerates social contradictions. In making satirist Snarl keen on flagellation and hostile to the theatre, Shadwell stresses that reformist pieties are corrupt but does not show how the stage might heal society by moral awareness; he prefers attacking the alliance of court, city, and science and decrying Dutch political reforms.

The dramatist most inventive with hypocrisy is Wycherley. His political retaliation binds polemic to dramatic awareness. In *Love in a Wood* (1671), he strikes as much at the romantic confusions of the urban gentry as at the mercenary lechery of Alderman Gripe. With provocative ambiguity, he decries and supports business and play. Dapperwit, who outsmarts the alderman, is overreached by Gripe's daughter, a better actor. Wycherley dramatises tensions between public and private illusions. *The Gentleman Dancing-Master* (1672) exposes two English merchants who copy Spanish and French modes. Father and intended son-in-law, blind to illusion since obsessed with the foreign, effect, against their interests, the marriage of Gerrard and Hippolita. Neither would-be autocrat nor stylish traveller penetrates the feeble acting of Gerrard, the dancing-master who cannot dance: they are manipulated by Hippolita whose self-awareness and sexual frankness show that facile cultural imitation breeds misogyny. Wycherley's satirical use of illusion is acute in *The Country Wife* (1675). Society credits Horner's impotency in its sexual hypocrisy and cliquishness. Characters devalue society by assuming they need not create and perform social rules. Pinchwife's claim to know the town leads him to hand his wife over to Horner: the cuckold's pretensions to control illusion recoil on him. Amusingly, Horner is victimised by group dishonesty: the deceit by which he is not exposed brilliantly integrates drama and illusion. The tenuous ending shows that identity is not the substance Alithea wants but the performance Harcourt enjoys, Wycherley proving his interest in illusory aspects of identity. He is exemplary of the Restoration and emblematic of modernity in his view that public govern private illusions and that identity is relative. This theme is clear in *The Plain Dealer* (1676), based on Molière's *Le*

Misanthrope. Manley, the protagonist, is ensnared by false idealism. His scorn for social forms makes him vulnerable to Vernish and Olivia, but his friends, Freeman and Fidelia, disarm his incivility by validating theatrical illusion. That Wycherley debunks Olivia's hypocritical scorn of *The Country Wife* shows his plays make drama correct ideology.

Sentimental Tragedy, 1677–1682

Wycherley's reciprocal social and theatrical ideas are rare; the Exclusion Crisis led dramatists to evade politics or to be partisans. Dryden's *All for Love* subordinates political action to pathetic renunciation. Antony's transcendence is emotional: love, not martial honour, leads him to fight. Political disgust drives him to surrender mythic fame. Such disgust informs Otway's *The Orphan* (1680) and *Venice Preserved*. In the first, Acasto, a royalist scornful of vice, raises his sons in rural retreat. Exiled from court, they suffer romantic agony, their mutual destruction symbolising the disharmony of public and private value and of royalist and courtly ideas. The second play demeans politics too. The reformers in *Venice Preserved* are as vicious as the senators: Renault's violation of Belvidera parallels Antonio's fetishism: sexual baseness signals political incoherence, as does the motif of insanity. Personal transcendence rather than political struggle accounts for the deaths of Jaffeir and Pierre. Belvidera's Ophelia-like madness forces her father to lament the evils of patriarchy, but his judgment cannot reconcile private and public values.

Forced into obliqueness by censorship, tragedians with political goals risked incoherence. Lee's hero in *Lucius Junius Brutus* (1680) berates Charles II's promiscuity in decrying Tarquin's "unlawful itch." Anachronistically, he assigns citizens commonwealth ideas of regal arbitrariness, blackening the nobles' plot against the popular revolt of Brutus. Incredulity mounts when Titus, his anti-republican son, accepts the death penalty from his father and endorses puritan standards in Rome. In Tate's *King Lear* (1681), propaganda also erodes sense. By removing the Fool and making Edgar and Cordelia lovers, Tate turns the king into a cipher. Lear is a tyrant, but his daughters are worse: the commons pine for the "re-installment of their good old king." Edmund's attempted rape of Cordelia is worse than Lear's paternalism. In Tate's royalism, Gloucester is a more active politician than in Shakespeare: a landlord adored by tenants, he rouses the nation in Lear's behalf. Edgar, scornful of politics, is a providential agent when he restores the king. As appointed king, Edgar testifies that monarchy is holy but not absolute. The deflation of divine right infects *Virtue Betrayed* (1682) by John Banks (c. 1650–1706). Anne Boleyn's marriage to Henry VIII and Cardinal Wolsey's plot against her oblige Banks to disjoin action and politics. His characters emote but do not confront hostile forces: righteous Anne is too easily deceived, and lust and Wolsey too simply victimise Henry. Finally, Henry pledges the absolutist scorn of the court, and Elizabeth, Anne's daughter, vows to banish Catholicism. Such propaganda exposes the damage pathos imposes on dramatic coherence: tragedy was set back by efforts to address the Exclusion Crisis yet to avoid it from a sense of political disenchantment.

Comedy and Politics, 1677–1688

Besides hampering tragedy, crises in Charles's reign incited comedy to expose sectarianism. *The Rover* (1677) by Aphra Behn (1640–1689) highlights feminism when not all her English men enjoy the Naples carnival. Willmore, an exiled cavalier, succeeds sexually, sleeping with the high-priced Angellica and winning Hellena in marriage. But Blunt, a squire who did not lose his estate, is duped by a whore who deposits him, naked, into the sewers. If Behn limits royalism with female equality, in *The Roundheads* (1681), her women uphold propaganda. Set before General Monk's arrival in London, this play depicts unfaithful wives of Commonwealth leaders who lust after cavaliers: puritans' marital failure reveals their hypocritical monarchism while cavalier libertinism coexists with reverence for the king. Loveless enjoys Lady Lambert but, at the sight of the "sacred Relicks," the crown jewels, in her chamber, he genuflects. The debasement of comedy by political retaliation is more farcical in *The London Cuckolds* (1681) by Edward Ravenscroft (1654–1707). About an attorney petitioning for a confiscated estate, Townly says "Cuckold the Rogue for [that] very reason." Lecherous town wits and impotent citizens are slogans. In *The Anatomist* (1697), Ravenscroft attacks urban professions: the domination of a virtuoso doctor by his wife and his feeble lust for a maidservant connect sexual dysfunction to Whig radicalism.

Powerful female characters are an index of comic energy in the Exclusion Crisis, royalist plays differing markedly in exposing sexual mores. Otway's *Friendship in Fashion* (1678) is reactionary in satirising Sir Noble Clumsey and Lady Squeamish, courtiers without birth or breeding. That his grandfather was a blacksmith and father an alderman says why Clumsey mouths heroic idioms and writes tragicomedy. Lady Squeamish compensates for her origin by pretending interest in French and Italian theatre and belittling native plays. If Tory scorn for new aristocrats makes him deride foreign drama, Otway embarrasses Goodvile, the rake-hero, by letting his wife control the plot. The relation of Toryism to women's rights is similar in Shadwell's *The Woman-Captain* (1679), where city values uphold misogyny. Hedonistic Sir Humphrey Scattergood is admirable unlike the tyrannical moneylender, Gripe. Freed from her husband's house by Humphrey's riotousness, Mrs Gripe gains a sense of carnival when she disguises herself as a soldier to mock military heroism. Her mockery shows her that Humphrey, the rural knight, is more humane than fellow cavaliers. Thus, she balances politics and personal action. This balance became harder to depict: *City Politiques* (1683) by John Crowne (1641–1712) and *The Squire of Alsatia* by Shadwell show that female characters were increasingly treated as stereotypes.

Satirical types govern Crowne's play: that courtiers, Florio and Artall, easily seduce citizens' wives signals political corruption; their success depends on Whig hypocrisy and disunity. Crowne lampoons Shaftesbury given the groundlessness of the Popish Plot, in the process, making women sex objects. Urging merchants to leave government to those with a traditional right to govern, Crowne endorses professional politicians rather than divine right, yet his traditionalism reduces women to farcical devices. If written from a Lockean, pro-revolutionary stance, Shadwell also limits female roles. His text attacks the authoritarian Sir William Belfond, whose son falls prey to the London underworld, and promotes the liberal Sir Edward Belfond, whose ward corrects his own vices. The indulgence meted out to Belfond Junior defies educational tradition but accepts female inferiority. Belfond Junior thinks that settling annuities on whores and being more sexually prudent than his brother, who stands for patriarchal absolutism, amends his misogyny. Refusing to drink wine between meals and seeking abolition of criminal sanctuaries, he upholds Shadwell's prejudice against female dramatic power.

Satire and Sentiment in Comedy, 1693–1728

The Revolution of 1688 effected legal and political reforms that comedy assimilated and resisted. To defend women's rights, Congreve opposed Collier's attack on the stage by upholding the reformative power of dramatic illusion. His first play, *The Old Bachelor* (1693), perpetuates types in Fondlewife, an impotent merchant, and Spintext, a fanatical dissenter, yet he freshly deflates military pride and national complacency. *The Double Dealer* (1694) links hypocritical courtiers and rural gentry: Maskwell, exploiting their hostility to theatre, discloses to victims the plots by which he gulls them. In *Love for Love* (1695), Congreve attacks hollow patriarchalism. The father, claiming the right to disinherit his son and marry his son's lover, is bested since the youngsters make legal and dramatic action complementary: surrendering his birthright, Valentine feigns madness, and to win legal power, Angellica dons a submissive mask with affected feminism. Defeat of litigiousness reappears in the control of legal instruments by self-conscious actors in *The Way of the World* (1700). Fainall, sure a deed of settlement will let him confiscate his wife's and Lady Wishfort's property, is thwarted by Mirabell, whose legal knowledge rests on trust in drama. When he and Millamant renew marital roles by enacting their limits, they challenge legal and political ideas to honour individual rights and social reform.

Cibber values legal custom: lacking reflexivity, his comedies harden sexual and national stereotypes in seeming to reform them. *Love's Last Shift* (1696) analyses male contempt of marriage from a female stance but does not embody feminist insight: Amanda sees that sexual excitement drives Loveless to abandon her, yet his vice seems merely modish. The paradox of Amanda becoming a virtuous prostitute to reform him is unexplored. Cibber's refusal to make moral ideas arise from action is plain in *Love Makes a Man* (1700): satire of France and Spain blocks credible motivation. The scholar's change to heroic lover and female rake's to self-effacing woman is mere sexist reversal. Imitation of Spanish intrigue in *She Wou'd and She Wou'd Not* (1702) limits the impact of Hypolita's feminism. Few implications arise in a plot so glibly based on sexual custom. Symmetry in *The Careless Husband* (1704) makes drama coarsen stereotypes too. Sir Easy's reform by a model spouse implies that men reform when tired of mistresses. Yet the taming of Lady Betty Modish holds that female libertinism must be castigated. *The Provok'd Husband* (1728), completing a work by John Vanbrugh

(1664–1726), reveals Cibber's conservatism as a homiletic comedian. The Wrongheads, bumpkin strangers to the parliamentary and social worlds of London, are standing jokes. The main plot concerning Lord Townly's marriage to a licentious woman ends with her submission, stressing again that Cibber's fame is based on a reactionary differentiation of gender and class.

Criticism of Cibber's ethic drives Vanbrugh's *The Relapse* (1696), a rewriting of *Love's Last Shift*. Vanbrugh endows his women with acute psychology and satire. With Sir Novelty Fashion, a Jacobite, buying Lord Foppington's title and with Loveless's relapse in spite of Amanda's ideas for theatrical reform, Vanbrugh queries the Revolution's effects. Worthy and Berinthia are reformed not by moral formulæ but by Amanda's ethics. While Cibber extends Foppington's part in *The Provok'd Husband* to give himself a virtuoso role, Vanbrugh, in *The Provok'd Wife* (1697), subordinates closure to integrating social detail, national types, and moral psychology. The linkage of the villains, Sir John and Lady Fancyfull, to French absolutism and the elaboration of women's painful legal status gather force from the Brutes' unresolved marital problems.

Vanbrugh's antagonism to Cibber exposes problems created by the reformist ethos. Farquhar's slide from satire and the unsteady feminism of Susanna Centlivre (1667–1723) accent sentimental closure over dramatic conflict. In the early *Love and a Bottle* (1698), Farquhar's militarism probes society: Roebuck's soldierly libertinism reveals hypocrisy. Farquhar, through Smuggler the corrupt merchant in *The Constant Couple* (1699), implies that the Revolution's ethos is low. Sir Harry Wildair, the anarchic military volunteer, is admirable by contrast. Yet, *The Recruiting Officer* (1706) faults army life for harming society: Silvia's soldierly disguise proves military heroism hollow. Still, Farquhar stresses women's dependence in *The Beaux' Stratagem* (1707). The heroism of Aimwell and Archer is sentimental; they are tired of London life, susceptible to women, and poor at hiding feeling. Mockery of French culture in Bellair and Foigard and the deflation of Sullen's boorishness lets Farquhar favour male superiority. That Aimwell becomes the man he acts means Sullen's brutality is displaced by male fantasy.

Centlivre avoids dramatic renewal; nationalism and sentimentality weaken her realism. Action and theme are cut in *The Busy-Body* (1709), a reworking of Molière and Dryden. Sir Jealous Traffick's affected Spanish autocracy assumes that mutuality is natural to decent married people and that town wits like Charles need no reforming. Miranda acts better than Marplot, given her legal acuity, but she parrots the idea that women have the right to choose spouses. Action and theme do not fuse in her success which denies the problem that is the play's ostensible foundation. The ease with which Fainwell wins Mrs Lovely from her guardians in *A Bold Stroke for a Wife* (1710) devalues drama in the face of reactionary nationalism. Mimicking a virtuoso, change-broker, old beau, and Quaker, Fainwell gulls those who idolise foreign culture. Besides rendering Mrs Lovely a sex object, Centlivre's nationalism treats social fragmentation so glibly that dramatic conflict is dissolved. *The Wonder* (1714) treats the friendship of Isabella and Violanta as heroic but spoils its theme by indulging Colonel Briton, the nationalist rake. If the Portuguese setting exposes the evils of patriarchy, it implies that women's lot in England is ideal, and the irony involved in applying foreign dramatic form to praise and blame society not tested.

Harmful reform appears in Steele's plays: promoting nationalism and patriarchy, they stereotype females to defend merchants. In *The Tender Husband* (1705), Clerimont Senior's wife, seduced by visiting France into fashionable vice and domestic unruliness, is humbled by a plot that relies on the agency of her husband's whore. Steele's anti-feminism leads to Clerimont Junior's duping of Biddy Tipkin, a banker's unruly daughter. Having fought in France, he postures with romance to conform to her prejudices while exploiting them. Insistence on gender differentiation and male superiority requires Steele to dissolve dramatic conflicts. Reformist ideology leads him to give narrative and religious answers to problems posed in *The Conscious Lovers* (1722). Conflicts between Bevil Junior, his father Bevil Senior, his friend Myrtle, and Sealand the merchant arise not because patriarchy is wrong but because it is not upheld. The plot, denigrating female rights, uses tearful Indiana as an object of providence's support of patriarchy and the gentility of merchants. Blaming the double standard in Sealand's tyrannical wife, the plot reconfirms it when its women worship fathers and lovers.

Homiletic Tragedy, 1690–1740

Propaganda harmed tragedy by replacing drama with tractate ideas. *The Fatal Marriage* (1694) and *Oronooko* (1696) by Thomas Southerne (1660–1746) decry patriarchy and imperialism, their translation from Behn's fiction highly doctrinaire. The first stresses the agony of a mother who, abandoned by husband and spurned by his family, remarries just before he returns. This *she-tragedy* isolates Isabella, unmerited pain deepening her victimisation: the pathos of her tortured fidelity is aggravated by mothering images, insanity, and suicide. That the father and brother of her first husband are patriarchal devils shows Whig reform controlling the play: coincidence and declamation rule plot and dialogue. *Oronooko* focusses on personal, not collective, experience. The African prince is so moral he is untouched by corruption in his homeland and the colony which enslaves him. A symbol of principled liberty, Oronooko is intellectually consistent so as to offset the vices of Christianity. Capable of heroic action in saving the colony from Indians, he commits suicide because he cannot tolerate the absence of ideal liberty.

Commitment to reform leads Nicholas Rowe (1674–1718) to subject tragedy to politics. *Tamerlane* (1701) allegorises William III's wars with Louis XIV: Tamerlane spurns absolutism and clerical power. His parliamentary interest in popular rights is inconsistent: he denies divine right but is regarded as a god; he champions pacifism yet is undefeated in battle. Indifference to fusing idea and conduct continues in *Jane Shore* (1714). An aside in Shakespeare's *Richard III* (c. 1592), Jane is central to Rowe: a victim of action, she neither analyses nor affects; she shows that court politics erode domesticity whereas Gloucester the usurper upholds Stuart absolutism. The crisis of succession at Queen Anne's death explains why Rowe lionises the protestant martyr in *Lady Jane Grey* (1715). A Hanoverian, he has her take the crown at King Edward's death to mock popish tyranny. Respecting the "voice of a consenting people," her nationalism transcends self and romance: devout anti-Catholicism makes her a willing sacrifice to political corruption.

Rowe's reformist scorn for political pragmatism and aloofness to dramatic mediation are matched by Addison and Lillo. In *Cato* (1713), Addison's hero defies Caesar's imperialism. Yet idealism not only frees Cato from domestic and erotic feeling but sets him above tragedy. His scorn for empire replaces Restoration dialectic with a code inimical to drama. Less neoclassical didacticism informs Lillo's *The London Merchant*, a conduct-book in disguise. Its historic setting boosts merchants' national pride, its characterisation warning that servants must not cheat masters. Its flaw is that Barnwell, the sinful servant, wins salvation while Millwood, the man-hating seductress, is punished for her feminism. His conversion into an angel and hers into a devil reveal the author's simple harmonisation of religion and politics. Bourgeois propaganda and melodrama dominate *The Fatal Curiosity* (1737). Its Shakespearean echoes stress mannered illogic. The Wilmots, opposing courtly vice, unwittingly murder their son. Proud of English civility, the son delays revealing himself to maximise everyone's pleasure! Pathos stops Lillo integrating action and word, his nationalistic and cultural propaganda proving mutually destructive.

Burlesque and Declining Dramatic Mediation, 1728–1780

Satire of propagandistic scorn for mediation drives the comedies of Gay, Fielding, and Sheridan. Yet their wit does not impede theatrical decline: reflexivity in *The Beggar's Opera*, *The Tragedy of Tragedies*, and *The Critic* (1779) equates literary and social discrimination. Since Peachum represents Walpole and Wild while the thieves imitate all classes and theatrical forms, Gay links society and literature severally. His deliberate inconsistencies show the theatre catering to audiences by vulgarising poetic justice and letting social injustice debase drama. By mixing ballads and arias, he mocks decadence, but satire does not prepare a future for the stage. Fielding also attacks high and low culture in *The Tragedy of Tragedies*, exploring why the ballad of Tom Thumb and heroic idiom do not fit. The pedantic allusions to forty-two heroic plays, the ridiculous closure which bumps off the characters, and the exposure of logical and rhetorical flaws in stage conventions proclaim the death of tragedy. The indecorous mixture of literary kinds and formulaic imitation implies that society has lost the capacity to mediate itself in drama. Assailing the thoughtless fusion of popular and aristocratic culture, Fielding, less than Gay, integrates society and drama. Sheridan widens the gap between theatrical and political worlds in the Dangles' contempt for the stage and its insulation from culture: Mrs Dangle hates the stage since it does not endorse her Francophobia, and Mr Dangle happily gives it an agency where lords hire fiddlers and opera teachers find jobs. Exposing the tasteless heterogeneity that prizes sentimental dramatization of the penal code like Congreve and Vanbrugh, Sheridan does not renew dramatic mediation. Puff's amusing analysis of the business of eulogy is journalistic, not theatrical. If Puff's play debunks nationalistic desires for spectacle, opera, and Handel, Sheridan still promotes a benevolism founded on imperial contempt of foreign culture.

Racine and Molière Translated: French Drama Appropriated, 1712–1733

Borrowings of Pierre Carlet de Chamblain Marivaux (1688–1763) from Congreve and Vanbrugh and English versions of Voltaire's plays evidence ties between the stages of France and England. But, as Philips's *The Distressed Mother* and Fielding's *The Miser* show, appropriation of Racine and Molière, if popular, did not stem declining mediation. Philips's text is verbally faithful to *Andromaque* (1667), if its blank verse lowers the original's intensity. Its major change is to add scenes to the end of the fourth and fifth acts with conflicting, rather than dialectical, images of the heroine. In the one, Andromache pledges to commit suicide after marrying Pyrrhus; in the other, she vows to avenge his murder. In the first, breaking her word to Pyrrhus heightens her love for the dead Hector; in the second, maternal love coexists with heroic commitment to the dead Pyrrhus. The radical disjuncture of her declamations is sentimental: emotionalism diffuses tragic conflict, rendering it contradictory. Sentimentality in Fielding prevents Molière from mediating Restoration comic modes. In *The Miser*, Lovegold is a true type of impotence and gullibility, but his children's sentimental passivity means servants direct the plot. Mariana's deception of Lovegold deceives his children too; there is no collective construction of illusion or semiotic codes in the urban scene. Fielding partly recovers Restoration typology, but contextual reference escapes him; he simply opposes illusions of materialism to pure good nature.

Comedy: Experimentation, Xenophobia, and the Novel, 1730–1765

In *The Modern Husband* (1732), Fielding realised that mediation required innovation. His attack on patriarchy's legal flaws is new: Mr Modern's plot to be compensated in court for his wife's adultery with Lord Richly reflects actuality. Exposure of Modern and analysis of how patriarchal materialism degrades sexual domesticity anticipate George Bernard Shaw (1856–1950). Yet the idealisation of Mrs Bellamant's contempt for opera, eagerness for social reform, and love of rural retirement indicates that Fielding heeds ideology more than mediation. Sentimental constraints on experimentation and the ethos of the 1737 Licensing

Act dominate *The Miller of Mansfield* (1737) by Robert Dodsley (1704–1764). Its historical vagueness, folktale satire of courtiers, praise of monarchy, and utopian justice are derivative and undramatic.

Topicality in farces by Samuel Foote (1720–1777) and Garrick that uphold gender binaries and Francophobia confirm the decline of mediation. Debunking citizens' pretensions to foreign art and travel, Foote's *Taste* (1752) mocks cultural exchange, showing that reactionary politics devalue drama. *The Englishman in Paris* (1753) and *The Englishman Return'd from Paris* (1756) exude Francophobia. In the first, Buck, a barbaric squire, views the modes of France as its revenge on Marlborough; in the second, Buck, now a gross Francophile, writes a play in imitation of Voltaire, only to be chidden by Crab, a satirist recalling Smollett's Crabtree in *Peregrine Pickle*. Bigoted Crab thinks patriotism is the first law of nature. Scorn for Methodism and merchants in *The Minor* (1760) accents the reactionary turning of George Wealthy from Francophile rake to preacher of the cliché that loveless marriage is legalised prostitution. Championing Shakespeare against Voltaire, like Foote, Garrick bends his farces even more to narrative. The serial, schematic satire of *Lethe* (1745) draws on Fielding's *A Journey from this World to the Next*. Like Foote, Garrick reduces dramatic coherence to social reaction. In *Miss in Her Teens* (1747), Biddy Bellair's victory over the effeminate Fribble and braggartly Flash celebrates her less than the masculine Loveit. Garrick's institutional validation of gender extends to class in *Neck or Nothing* (1766): Martin, a servant who would impersonate his master, lacks oral and acting skills and is denied social power. Trusting in political hierarchy, Garrick blames social wrongs on foreign countries. In *Bon Ton* (1775), Lord Minikin's rapacity is French, while Sir Trotley rescues his ward from the lord with unquestioning pride in the English legal system.

Unconcern for mediation leaps from the works of Arthur Murphy (1727–1805) which, if thematically close to Restoration comedy, are distanced by propaganda. *The Way to Keep Him* (1760) promotes marriage, yet wives preserve it from male licence: wives' sexism elevates domestic above stage acting. Distrust of drama informs *The Citizen* (1761); if Maria bests Old Philpot, the lecherous, avaricious citizen who defends forced marriages, her success leads to marriage with Beaufort whom luxury makes depend on city money. The Restoration typology that hides a new sexual and class differentiation is clear in Colman the Elder's plays. In *Polly Honeycombe* (1760), scorn for merchants is translated from the novel. Polly, fleeing an arranged marriage to Mr Ledger, guards herself with Richardsonian sentiment. Though her love for Scribble, the pretentious novelist, is absurd, Colman enlivens the plot with narrative allusions. Lack of dramatic invention is most notable in *The Jealous Wife* (1761), a bowdlerised version of *Tom Jones*. In the name of reform, Colman has Harriot (Sophia) correct Charles's (Tom's) drunkenness. Downplaying male promiscuity, he stresses the humiliation of Mrs Oakley, the matriarch, (Mrs Partridge). The audience has to admire Harriot's satire of the theatre and London society, but the plot demeans female intelligence. Social hierarchy and the double standard are maintained by *The Clandestine Marriage* (1766). Sterling, the merchant, is a laughingstock; his modish pretensions are undercut by his inability to control his matriarchal sister. Yet libertine aristocrats offset their absurdity with patriarchal sense: Lord and Sir John Ogelby protect Fanny and Lovewell.

Tragic Sentimentalism, 1750–1780

The erosion of drama by sentimentality reaches a nadir in *The Gamester* (1753) by Edward Moore (1712–1757). Its didactic characterisation derives from Fielding's *Jonathan Wild* (1743) as well as from *The London Merchant*. If the self-sacrificing and angelic Mrs Beverley is rewarded by her husband's reform, this providence is not mediated by plot: he is reformed less by love for his wife than by the unmasking of the villain. The dissolution of the tragic mood reveals the arbitrariness of Moore's dramatic conflict: a play with tragic features becomes a comedy because of its happy ending. In suggesting that Beverley's gambling addiction stems from fidelity to a supposed friend, Moore's stress on wifely pain is irrelevant to the reform. A similar treatment of female suffering informs *Douglas* (1756) by John Home (1722–1808). Promoting the 1707 Act of Union between Scotland and England, Home stresses the agonised memories and noble intuitions of Lady Randolph. Working from a medieval ballad, he creates an elegiac mood from a dialectic of secrecy and disclosure: the fragmented exposition in which Lady Randolph's second husband is jealous of her long-lost son recalls *The Tragedy of Tragedies*. If the action endorses narrative intuitions, the contingent death of all the characters means that cultivating these intuitions is personally and dramatically deadly.

More's reliance on French medieval legend and gothic topoi in *Percy* (1777) proves that attention to women's pains in forced marriages dulled tragic vision. Elwina's grief for Percy, her first husband, permits declamation against court, Catholicism, and patriarchy. But Percy's return and other narrative tricks, such as the false news of her second husband's death, that sustain the triangle serve only Elwina's Ophelia-like suicide; Shakespearean allusions do not aid social themes, but narrative fosters melodrama: offering pathos without purgation, story without logical action. Cumberland's unoriginal *The Carmelite* (1784) epitomises the end of tragedy. Contingently incomplete expositions cause the conflict: the long-lost husband, unable to disclose himself because of his wife's insanity, falls madly jealous of the son over whom she is so possessive. That the play ends happily exposes its illogic: Cumberland arbitrarily reduces action to psychological impressionism and surrenders dialectic between comedy and tragedy.

The Exhaustion of Comic Dialectic, 1765–1780

By the time of Goldsmith's and Sheridan's plays, comedy had been overtaken by ideologies about women, politics, and foreign cultures and by a divide between satire and sentiment: the best writers could not recover comedy's dialogic functions while the worst aggravated narrative intrusions on dramatic processes. In *The Brothers* (1769), through brief scenes, fragmentary exposition, and contrived motivation, Cumberland reduces comedy to novelistic dilemmas: he sustains cross-purposes and conceals narrative facts to heighten sentimental recognitions and story symmetries. His unwillingness to challenge social structure and to renew mediation limits characterisation: Belford Senior, a self-doubting villain, and Ironsides who, like Smollett's sailors, mocks parliament and boosts imperialism and patriarchy, radiate narrative psychology. The play's real action is the humiliation of Lady Dove for enjoying illicit sex and robbing her husband of heirs. *The West Indian* (1771) illustrates the conservatism and novelistic modes with which Cumberland saps drama. A naive colonial, Belcour, attacks London political customs but supports English imperialism, while his libertinism is excused as good-hearted since he prizes military sentimentality. His indulgence is contrasted by the punishment of Lady Rusport, a republican matriarch who defames the stage and charity. *The Fashionable Lover* (1772) ideologically excuses the Bridgemores for being money-grubbing citizens, Lord Abberville for abandoning French fashion, and Tyrrell, the professional lawyer, for being unchanged by error: their public actions and conscious behaviours matter far more than thoughtful and emotional expression.

Hugh Kelly (1739–1777) is disinterested in mediation and dramatic dialectic because he does not integrate satire and sentiment in *False Delicacy* (1768). Mrs Harley, his chief satirist, mocks sentimental refinement but lauds its self-abnegation. Kelly's theatrical confusion involves genre. When Miss Marchmount declares her "heart shall break before it shall be worthless," she evidences his comic reliance on heroic idiom. Yet his characters are uniformly passionless: their self-denial is not dialogic; it merely proclaims that marriage based on money is legal prostitution. Heroic idiom points up the characters' materialism and shallow unconventionality. The facile resolution of the artificial action leads a very sentimental Lord Winworth to affirm that the stage should "be a school of morality." Far from curbing excessive "false delicacy," Kelly's unrelieved pathos prescribes moral sense but does not embed it in action. Popular on the continent for its seeming revolutionary sentiment, this play is deeply reactionary and anti-theatrical. Kelly's ideological rigidity governs *The School for Wives* (1773), enforcing the double standard by having Mrs Belville rejoice in self-abnegation as the means to reform her husband's philandering. Without disguise and wit, she waits for him to exhaust himself. Preaching against adultery and illegitimacy, Belville returns to his wife after duelling with the brother of a girl he has tried to seduce. Evading his promiscuity, he decries duelling, patriarchy's most serious sin.

Critics of theatrical solecisms perpetrated by Cumberland and Kelly, Goldsmith and Sheridan do not rise above sentimental and patriotic ideology. In *The Good Natur'd Man* (1768), Goldsmith values characterisation more than plot and endorses the moral truisms he ostensibly satirises. Lofty, a political villain, lacks real autonomy, while gullibility and an inclination for citizenship render benevolent Honeywood heroic. If Lofty's acting is transparent, Honeygood's ineptness signals admirable humanity. Despite the skill with which he analyses the rival codes of the generations, sexes, and town and country in *She Stoops to Conquer*, Goldsmith limits mediation by virtuoso construction of scenes based on cross-purposes and by characters who feign from defensible self-interest. Kate's acting aims to capture Marlow: far from probing social convention and the double standard, her acting strengthens the "union of families." Miss Neville's refusal to elope to France strengthens the patriarchal authority of Mr Hardcastle, who, admiring Marlborough and hostile to France, relishes the humiliation of his matriarchal, absurdly modish wife. Sheridan's satire in *The Rivals* (1775) is keener. While he exposes Lydia Languish's novelistic sensibility, he treats forced marriage sentimentally by coercing Absolute to marry the woman he has chosen: farce belittles problems and the stage's ability to deal with them. Absolute's failure to act typifies Sheridan's insistence that characters be exposed in the name of, not collective action, narrative symmetry. That an extraneous duel corrects the unworldly sentimentalism of Lydia and Falkland is ironical; patriarchy is imported abstractly, not mediated by action. Satire of manners in *The School for Scandal* (1777) is not integral to plot: the latter is shaped by asides and off-stage facts more than staged action. Unconcern with mediating ideas formally is clear in Sheridan's virtuoso creation of the screen scene: when scenes are not satirical frames, they are beautifully self-contained. In wit, Sheridan is either formulaic or contradictory. When he associates Joseph Surface's platitudes and refined posturing with French culture, he employs the stalest of dramatic clichés. By contrast, when Charles Surface, who mocks commerce, is rescued from debt by his sentimental uncle's colonial wealth, indulgence of the hero is politically dubious. This ideological complacency is heightened when Charles ends up mouthing the sort of sentiments for which Joseph is punished. That Charles resists social norms only on the surface reveals that imperial ideology overcomes Sheridan's dialectical sense. If Goldsmith's and Sheridan's plays conform to European enlightenment, they pamper, but do not provoke, their audiences, proving that the nationalistic reforms spearheaded by Collier finally robbed the English stage of mediatorial power. Thus, Restoration drama was not trite and formulaic, as moral critics claim: despite counter-revolution, it was generically self-conscious and theatrically inventive. While politicisation of the stage by supposedly revolutionary sentimentality gradually reduced its ability to face political reality, anti-doctrinaire reactions to counter-revolution in the Restoration endowed its best drama with polemical reflexivity.[298]

CHAPTER FIVE
Canada, England, and France

Literary relations between England and France grew increasingly complex as the eighteenth century unfolded, to an extent matching political, military, and economic rivalries between the two countries and their colonies before and after the Seven Years War. Nationalism and imperialism embodied in texts strained traditional humanistic dialectic that lingered in limited ways in educational and pedagogical themes. Frances Brooke's English characters in *The History of Emily Montague* translate classical and French topoi to Canadian scenes, even as they would displace the French empire from North America. Hence, English literature exploits cross-cultural motifs that ironically problematize its nationalism; triangularity linking Canada, England, and France informs her work, Brooke voicing, not always consciously, colonial and imperial ideology. An epistolary text in the mode of Richardson, her story is imperial in aim and romantic in sentiment. It appropriates French wit and manners while proposing that legal and cultural institutions of France be displaced from New France.

A comparative relevance of geographical and national boundaries to literary history is clarified by impressions of Marivaux in English reactions to his translated works. Not only did he draw on Joseph Addison's periodical and essayistic styles but also, more generally, imitated the mannerisms of Spanish and English picaresque writings. His advanced first-person experiments were later re-adopted in Britain because he was less occupied with plot development than with curious oppositions between identities and characters to which he applied appealing techniques that dissolved narrative logic into self-conscious reflexes crucial to fictional autobiography.

Frances Brooke: Romance and Politics

Mary Jane Edwards's claim in her edition of *The History of Emily Montague* (1769) that Brooke expresses an "essentially positive view of the potential of the new British colony" is problematic for contextual and textual reasons. While Brooke dedicated her book on 22 March 1769 to Guy Carleton (1724–1808), governor of Canada, and heralded his governance, her optimism was frustrated by affirming the Conquest of Quebec. Lauding Carleton's "enlightened attention" in creating a "spirit of loyalty and attachment to our excellent Sovereign" and a "chearful obedience" to British law, her novel, plotting a retreat from Canada, embodies a less positive attitude than announced by the dedication.[299] When Mr Brooke returned to his wife and England in the autumn of 1768, his petition for a land grant had met with no more success than their campaign to establish the Anglican Church in Quebec.[300] The Brookes opposed social and political forces they understood only partly and could resist hardly at all. In the years following Carleton's arrival in Quebec and before Mr Brooke rejoined his wife, they should have had an inkling that the new governor would continue the policies of James Murray (1721–1794), the former governor, who, at first their benefactor, saw them at last as hostile to his strategic sympathies for the *habitants*: allusions to Carleton warn him not to continue Murray's appeasement of Quebec's English populace. Having written her book in Canada near the end of Murray's term and revising it in England in the summer of 1768, Brooke had time to see why the British government was abandoning the 1763 Royal Proclamation and ceasing to trumpet the Conquest of Quebec.[301]

The History of Emily Montague supports the Proclamation without foreseeing the 1774 Quebec Act. Depicting causes that reversed British policy, it does not sense the reversal. Instead, it aggravates political contraries that question Brooke's optimism. She resists political and economic change at home more than promotes Canada's future. She defends the Crown and attacks the Court by favouring military, Anglican, and rural over commercial, dissenting, and urban values.[302] Her bourgeois reaction to aristocracy's growing power emphasises freedom of choice for marriage partners: lovers' rights to choose mates without parental consent delivers a rear-guard attack on Lord Hardwicke's Bill of 1753, which forbade clandestine marriages and required ecclesiastical, legal, and familial consent. This Bill, drafted in the House of Lords, increased the power of the upper chamber over the House of Commons, limiting the mobility of the middle class. Brooke's attacks on arranged marriages signal an important yet ultimately contradictory relation of politics and romance in *The History of Emily Montague*. Taking her bearings from the Royal Proclamation, Brooke hoped to limit aristocratic power in church, army, and society, a power epitomised by arranged marriages in the English upper classes.[303]

Narrative logic requires Brooke to detail Canadian politics, but she does so with vague, self-exposing propaganda. Colonel Edward Rivers, her hero, hopes a "new golden age" will follow the "interregnum of government" with Carleton as governor. But hopes for British rule are not realised. When William Fermor, a military patriarch and her most astute commentator, leaves the colony, he sees the governor's "personal character" diffusing a "spirit of urbanity" in this "small community." But he will not judge the governor's politics, Brooke eulogising Carleton's personality and evading his French values: evasiveness leads her to bury conquest motifs and subsume politics to romance. When Indian women tell Arabella Fermor, the patriarch's coquettish daughter, that the English conquerors of Quebec are their "brethren," the theme that Aboriginal people want the British military system of land grants to operate is implausibly reinforced. Fermor finds the "politics of Canada" to be "complex" and "difficult," but Brooke, setting aside complexity, turns political evasion into female power. Arabella's pre-eminence at the governor's assembly matters, since "we new comers have nothing to do with" the "dregs of old disputes." Her amusingly proud diversion of politics to the "little commonwealth of woman" alerts readers to contradictions in Brooke's propaganda.[304] When Arabella says our "little coterie is the object of great envy; we live just as we like, without thinking of other people," she exposes contradictions in a community that sees itself as exiled yet exploits English patronage. It feels superior to the habitants while appropriating French *bons mots*. Aloof to Quebec society, it would impose itself on the conquered. Claiming isolation from the larger community, the English seek to dominate it yet rely on it unconsciously. When Arabella's courtship of Captain Fitzgerald is interrupted by French women at the governor's assembly who fail to follow English dancing codes, her protest that the "whole province" knows of her courtship is strikingly inconsistent: it involves more than unintegrated geographical and cultural values; it stems from Brooke's evasiveness. Since Arabella likens Quebec to a "third or fourth rate country town in England" but, on leaving, prefers living there than in "any town in England, except London," colonial progress bears neither contextual nor textual scrutiny: suppressing views of the habitants and governors, Brooke encodes politics with neither historical accuracy nor compelling narrative.[305]

Historians clarify what William Fermor finds complex and help assess Brooke's ideology of romance: their dialectical sense of the period from 1763 to 1774 uncovers propaganda in *The History of Emily Montague*. To Kenneth McNaught, the Treaty of Paris was "an unqualified British victory" over French imperialism, but the Royal Proclamation effected the "most perilous conditions imaginable" for controlling North America by a "substantial minority nation" and exacerbated mercantile and military tensions.[306] While the Proclamation counted on an influx of Protestants, the six hundred merchants who came to live among the sixty-five thousand Canadians did not weaken their identity. If the merchants wanted the Proclamation upheld by a legislative assembly, the establishment of English common law, and exclusion of Catholics from public office, hope for "assimilation was soon replaced by a quite exceptional tolerance" of the Canadians.[307] The Crown's sense that it needed military resources against the turbulent New England colonies led governors Murray and Carleton to oppose the merchants by tolerating the seigneurial system and Catholic institutions. The Quebec Act let the Canadian church collect tithes, enabled Catholics to hold public office, and endorsed French civil law, ending hope for assimilation. To W.L. Morton, the church remained strong given the "sheer inapplicability, in reason and humanity" of the Proclamation to the "circumstances of Quebec."[308] Shortly after 1763, Catholics served on juries and in the Court of Common Pleas. Five years after Brooke's novel appeared, the British government decided Quebec's future was to be more French than English, a reversal Brooke might have foreseen. Yet she discounted trends which, exposing flaws in colonialism, erode her narrative authority. While she and her husband sided with mercantile interests, her book does not support them. Wanting Catholic institutions assumed by Anglicans and reserved for seigneurs, she sees her gentry appropriating seigneurial landholding. To Morton, displaced seigneurs is the Proclamation's most irreparable effect, but Brooke believes French nobility can be preserved by an aristocratic order founded on English militarism.[309]

If nationalism dulled Brooke's contemporaries to political tensions in the colony, imperial enthusiasm likely blinded her to that clash. Scorn of "seigneurs" and "military tenure" in the French landholding system, along with Rivers' fantasies of owning a seigneury, show that her wishes to demean and appropriate French cultural forms prevent her from delving into the interaction of the European legal and political systems. Her hero's dreams of being "lord of a principality," acting "*en prince*," and building a "rustic palace" for Emily so he can see them "the first pair in paradise" and his spouse "the mother of mankind" combine sexual, religious, and royalist dreams that offset the wish for trebling the value of his land in a country which, without these fantasies, is but a "place of exile." Imperialism motivates Brooke's refusal to describe the habitants' well-known complaints about the British legal system.[310] Their anger at imprisonment for debt, at jail fees, at the expense and infrequency of court hearings, and at trial-by-jury in the face of numerous capital offences is neither presented nor allowed to generate implications. The gap between constitutional theory and political fact, brought in when the Test Act was abandoned to allow Catholics to do jury service as early as 1764, is also suppressed by Brooke's colonial ideology. Not admitting the implausibility of the 1763 Proclamation, she ignored that Carleton "utilisa au maximum l'élasticité des textes officiels pour redéfinir la politique anglaise."[311]

Brooke's politics are equivocal, her colonialism fused with class hierarchy: evasion of the alliance between governors and populace effects contradictory reactions to long-time residents of Quebec and newly arrived merchants. If ambivalence towards habitants and merchants values Augustan gentility, her novel contains unacknowledged tensions, her narrative letting political, social, and cultural contradictions coexist. Although commitment to the Royal Proclamation and the Conquest of Quebec degrades French culture and appreciates the merchant class, this is not simply the case. While she advanced Anglicanism in Quebec by siding with mercantile interests, her view of Sir George Clayton, the newly knighted baronet with ties to the city of London, is harsh. While Fermor criticizes the economic and political restraints imposed on American colonies, his sense they are "naturally inferior" implies that Brooke spurned settlers who were supposed to outnumber habitants. Since her stance on habitants is sympathetic and authoritarian, it recoils on British policy. If Rivers mocks consciousness of rank among the "noblesse" and laughs at the deference to "title in America," Fermor's creed that the noblesse should exchange their "croix de St. Louis" for a new "order" of honours binding them to English militarism is not self-evident. His view of French culture opposes British policy. If his claim that French officers have been "adopted into the savage tribes" stresses the hollowness of French culture and defies the habitants' sense of being "the flower of the French nation," he weakens his claim by arguing that convents in Quebec should be limited to "the daughters of the seigneurs" to preserve French hierarchy. This inconsistency is clear in light of repeated criticism of convents as agents of celibacy and depopulation. It is made more striking by his attacks on English economic and agricultural policies which, he fears, will so depopulate the English countryside that it will become an "uncultivated desart." His admiration of Rousseau and rejection of this philosopher's primitivism—belief in the virtues of "uncultivated nations"—shows that, while assailing British political dullness, he thinks his nation's culture more enlightened than that of France. But this pretension is unravelled: despite the running debate about the worth of French manners, characters proclaim their refinement in terms of French gallantry. Arabella may protest by proposing to marry "a savage," but she employs the phrase "British belles" earnestly. An ultimate sign of appropriated French modes is the closing masquerade at which Emily appears as a "French *paisanne*."[312]

Before analysing her ambivalence about mercantile wealth, we note how Brooke applies Augustan sensibility to a humanist mode that appropriates and bests French culture: classical allusion, Horatian ideas of retirement, and religious latitudinarianism coalesce into a myth of Anglican gentility. While her characters are displaced from England by economic and political change, their familiarity with Greek and Roman letters signifies Englishness. Rivers' knowledge of Virgil's *Georgics* and of Sophocles proves his gentility, and if Arabella says that Canadian scenery renews her familiarity with Greek and Roman "mythology," her allusions profess a sensibility that invalidates ideologies other than her own. She cites Horace to create an image of female grace applicable to "the church of England" but not to Presbyterianism or Catholicism. Far from steadily implying that Canadian settings uphold classical mythology, Brooke makes characters carry mythology with them as an aesthetic code for disguising and validating Augustan patriotism. This strategy uncovers the ideology in romance. If deities reside in Canada, they do so because of Emily. In her presence, Canada is "the habitation of the Graces," for she is "Venus amongst the Graces": Rivers sees her as "led" by them. Such hyperbole is not restricted to Canada or Emily; in England, Temple pictures his wife Lucy as attended by "the Graces," and, since England, supposedly alone among nations, permits marital choice to women, the country is personified as Venus "led" by the Graces. Arabella projects "Nereids," "naiads," and "tutelary deities" onto Canada, her mythic sense involving a nexus of political, class, and patriotic codes. In addressing a poem to his "household Gods" and esteeming his "native Dryads" more than an "imperial palace," Rivers affects humanism to defend a beleaguered, rural, Anglican gentry.[313]

While Brooke's gentrified characters disparage and imitate French culture, they are unclear about mercantile wealth. Inflation rates of twenty-five percent in the 1760s partly explain their distinction between the wealth of India and North America, between the wealth of imperial trade and colonial expansion.[314] Although Canada holds out to Rivers the prospect of landed wealth, the plot's resolution elevates Oriental riches. Yet, characters are unsure about Indian wealth since it is associated with city business. Spurning "the wealth of a Nabob," Rivers wishes his sister to spend her portion of two thousand pounds on jewels when marrying Temple to "be on a footing" with a "nabobess." Despite the insistence that love and friendship are richer than "an oriental monarch," and Lucy's claim that the return of Emily and Rivers from Canada is worth more than "argosies," Colonel Willmott, the patriarch who blesses Emily's marriage and endows her with his wealth, is a "nabob." While Rivers' house, Bellfield, is no "imperial palace," Willmott finances a new wing to complete its design. As evidence of the unsteady displacement of imperial wealth, take Arabella's contention that "no nabobess" could be as happy as Emily and herself in marrying the poor men, Rivers and Fitzgerald: she underrates their wealth which, if insufficient for peerages, is far larger at narrative's end than at its beginning.[315]

Ambivalence about mercantile wealth comes to the fore when Clayton is belittled, but in their scornful superiority, the gentry are no less mercenary. Rivers calls Clayton a "gentleman usher" whose dull sensibility fits him for a "rich, sober, sedate, presbyterian citizen's daughter." His "splendid income" leads Emily to mock his "parade of affluence," "false glitter of life," and "romantic parade of fidelity." Arabella disparages his prospective marriage to a rich citizen's daughter whose dowry is "fifty thousand pounds" and who brings with her "the promise of an Irish title." Her contempt arises from hatred of the "spirit of enterprise" that drives men to keep acquiring money and land. But, if she derides the peerage by claiming she would not give up the man she loves to be the "first dutchess in Christendom," her man is the son of "an Irish baronet" with "five hundred pounds a year" plus a military salary which he increases through the patronage system to become *Monsieur le Majeur.*" The gap between renouncing wealth and mercenary calculation is clear in Emily and Rivers who promote the myth of rural independence. Emily has "the genuine spirit of an independent Englishwoman" since she resists patriarchal hierarchy, and Rivers believes that "we country gentlemen, whilst we have the spirit to keep ourselves independent, are the best citizens, as well as subjects, in the world." Their romance, no simple matter of companionate individualism, entails an ironical debasement of mercantile and aristocratic interests, as shown by their financial attitudes and circumstances.[316]

To Rivers, love is "more essential, more real" than riches. He admits a "narrow fortune" is inconvenient but sees mutual love as a "treasure" that cancels fortune's power over Emily and him. Yet, familiarity with the "finest company in England" reminds him of a gap between his "birth" and "fortune." Far from endorsing the heroines' view that "our whole felicity depends on our choice in marriage" and treating riches metaphorically, Rivers is motivated by money and profit. Acquisitively, he accepts his sister's trust that "the future will pay us for the past." His desire for affluence appears in his wish to "treble the value" of his lands in Quebec by clearing and settling them. His attitude to his English estate is no less mercenary, despite his claims to the contrary. His definition of rural gentlemen as "best citizens" stresses the reciprocity of private and national profit: when he counts on "raising oaks, which may hereafter bear the British thunder to distant lands," he focusses on personal and public gain that stems from country gentry supplying materials for imperial war. His conformist ties to the crown and constitution are reflected by references to investment in the funds: he wants a larger income to entertain friends and to give to charity, this masquerade indicating his unacknowledged wish to imitate London fashion and urban luxury. The underlying acquisitiveness of Brooke's characters is elicited by references to River's income, Emily's dowry, and other financial prospects. With his "four thousand pounds in the funds," probably yielding five percent, and his military half-pay, Rivers is said to have an income of four hundred pounds per annum at one time and five hundred at another. Wish-fulfilment in these erratic figures motivates Brooke's endowment of Emily with a settlement of "twenty thousand pounds" which, setting aside her prospects and Willmott's improvements to the estate, trebles Rivers' income. Doubtless, an income of fifteen hundred pounds per annum does not lift Rivers up to the "finest company in England" but moves him from landed gentry to a class that gained from the financial revolution. Certainly, his ultimate income depends far less on Canada than on imperial wealth from India.[317]

Renunciation of and reliance on money confirms that Brooke's characterisation says less about Canada than the plight of British gentry. Mercenary calculation elicits themes of middle-class displacement and compensatory dreams of a class hierarchy responsive to romance and sensibility. If cultural flexibility is an illusion that reveals her characters' loss of social and economic power, it also applies to their progressive attitudes to gender, love, and marriage. As their myths about Canada subside, their fantasy of progressive romance strengthens forces they supposedly combat. Their romantic strategies, far from compensating for relative poverty, simply disguise their wealth and imperial resources. The closure so totally resolves the conflict between romance and money that, besides undoing the plot's motivation, it emphasises that Canada in the 1760s was neither a fiscal nor a social haven for English gentry. The boom foretold by the Proclamation did not materialise; a decade of recession followed, with business failures and fiscal muddle because of the colony's three currencies.[318] Paper money was overvalued, coins were scarce, and speculation in French bills led émigrés to export huge sums of specie and British traders to absorb losses that stunted capital growth. The Quebec economy did badly because of falling agricultural prices, caused by overproduction and barriers to international markets. While Brooke links Quebec to the wider scene, she regards its place in the world with utopian eyes. Quebec's problems convey themselves in transferred and covert ways: if her characters pretend that romance transcends economic power, their sexual and cultural codes prove otherwise. Their letters are uniformly imperialistic: illusory plural viewpoints and radical stances to gender mask values that are reactionary and unsympathetic to Quebec's colonial challenges.

Reaction in Brooke's presentation of romantic sensibility clarifies her juncture of culture and gender. Rivers exemplifies reactionary impulses in his supposedly progressive attitudes. The "tender tear" he drops at Carisbrook Castle in memory of the "unfortunate Charles the First" and his lament for General Wolfe, the "amiable hero" who "expir'd in the arms of victory," show Stuart nostalgia joining the pathos of military heroism. Histrionic and backward-looking, he renders his pretensions to gentility dubious. He wishes to be "lord of a principality" in Canada to "put our large-acred men in England out of countenance." His aim to be the "best *gentleman* farmer in the province" and desire for "dominion" evidence fantasies about property and power remote from Indigenous people. He values hierarchy that protects his estate in England and freedom to search Quebec with a "valet de chambre" for developable land. The foreign cultures he encounters confirm his nationalism and aggrandize his sensibility. He praises Indians' hardy lifestyle to denigrate "effeminate Europeans." He celebrates "the Huron government" to attack Europe's denial to women of "the common rights of citizenship." If he says women may disobey laws not made by them, his feminism is not radical. He wishes English women to have the franchise so that canvassing for a parliamentary seat will be more enjoyable for men like himself who believe that women's real power is sexual since they will not be a "rebel to their empire." His limited radicalism is clear when he opines that Europe has as much right as the American colonies to complain about political disadvantage: in the context of Brooke's scorn for those colonies, Rivers' comparison is gratuitous. His partial sensibility is highlighted by his claim that Indian women will be civilised only if they are feminised and by his avowal, after decrying French manners, that Emily embodies "the smiling graces of France" and "all the blushing delicacy and native softness of England." Like Arabella who sees the promenade at Quebec as a "little Mall," he imposes English cultural signs on Canada. When he talks of driving out "*en caleche* to our Canadian Hyde Park," he relies on French technology and modes. As with Arabella, cultural volatility testifies to his vitality but reveals, too, contradictions arising from complacency. His indifference to Canadian politics is, like Arabella's, a mask for power. Despite decrying England's parliamentary system, he exploits it when asking friends at Westminster to secure Mme Des Roches' land grant. His romanticism is very limited. On offering Emily his Acadians as "new subjects" and painting her in Edenic terms as the "mother of mankind," patriarchalism, absolutism, and pseudo-worship reveal him to be whimsically regressive.[319]

William Fermor describes Quebec erratically. He accepts Quebec institutions but wants them renewed by the English constitution. Defending the Proclamation by insisting Anglican bishops supervise Catholic rites, he decries it by spurning the assimilation of habitants by an influx of "dissolute" and "idle" Britons. Fear of depopulation at home weighs on him more than laws for Quebec: troubled by "the false and cruel policy" of enclosures in England's Agrarian Revolution, he blames economic and aristocratic power for displacing rural workers and lowering the birth-rate. Despite granting the superiority of French agriculture and the labour required by "the culture of vines," and despite criticizing Britain's taxation of the American colonies and their "mistaken people," he idealises church–state relations in England, asserting the "Supreme Being" blesses its constitution above others. Contradictions between satire and idealisation of England—the clash between his ideas that Quebec's population is a great asset to England and that it must be defined by English political values—show Fermor remote from the accommodating spirit of Murray and Carleton. His eulogy of Carleton's urbane character is unintentionally ironic since he misapprehends the complexities Carleton ably managed: in condescension to Quebec, Fermor stresses the Conquest and the colony's need for British institutions with a dogmatism unlike Carleton's flexibility. His application of gender terms to England manifests an easy sensibility and political rigidity. His view of the "mother country" as the centre of trade and colonists as bees returning to enrich the "paternal hive" conflates gender images in the name of nationalism. His claim that Quebec leaders, by adopting English honours, will spur habitants to commercial efforts for England is utopian. His view that the habitants will not gain from a "change of masters" until reformed by Anglican priests and his rejection of Rousseau's primitivism are rigid. By claiming Indians are virtuous when calling for English priests, Fermor avoids Carleton's pluralism and equates civilisation with the established church.[320]

Yet Brooke exposes patriarchy's contradictions, critically empowering female sensibility. Her heroes even criticise themselves according to their understanding of feminism. Rivers, Fitzgerald, and Temple seem to begin to understand the social construction of gender: romance leads them to try to reform social and sexual convention. But, if Brooke seems to offer radical insights into society's constraints on women, ultimately her book reinforces what it criticises.[321] Emily's emotional refinement displaces courtly politics: "tenderness" outweighs being "empress of the world." Likewise, Arabella scorns male acquisitiveness and naval imperialism: she derides the "lord high admiral of the British fleet." Accepting female criticism of political and military aims, male characters, certainly Rivers, imply that relations between women and men must change, as must institutions governing their relations. Since he is comfortable in a "feminized little circle," he claims a womanly sensibility that affects radical change. Seeing himself as a rural gentleman and, therefore, a "best citizen" and loyal defender of church and state, he urges that the Anglican liturgy be revised by removing "OBEY" from the bride's response in the marriage service and faults government for establishing "domestic tyranny" in its matrimonial act. He speaks on behalf of women since he is one of the "few of [his] sex" to possess the "lively sensibility" of a woman. His androgyny is confirmed by Lucy and Arabella who see "an almost feminine sensibility" in his masculine "firmness of mind and spirit." If, however, Rivers and friends have the capacity to be "melted" to "the softness of a woman" by mothers, sisters, and wives, their feminism is condescending. Far from endorsing a distinctive political outlook, it heightens sexual difference. Rivers' view that "Indian ladies ... do not excel in female softness" matches his instruction to his sister to cultivate "feminine softness and delicate sensibility." If allowing "a little pride in love" to women while holding that man's role is "to submit on these occasions," he differentiates the sexes by telling Lucy that "your sex" must "avoid all affectation of knowledge." His linking of companionate marriage to civic obedience shows that Brooke's males do not take female concerns seriously. Despite feminist pretensions, her heroes are no more averse than society to imposing restrictive roles on women.[322]

Brooke's feminism is unsteady since her women subordinate matriarchy to conventions of rank and nationalism while encouraging reliance on men. Calling Lucy "an exquisite politician" for keeping Temple at home to renew his domestic pleasures, Arabella insists that a woman always finds male more pleasing than female friends. When Emily says she gains a "new existence" from Rivers' "tenderness," she subsumes female claims of romantic transcendence to truisms about sexual difference and marital roles: the women embody an ideology that makes them secondary to men. If she associates England with Rivers' mother on insisting he return to where he was formed, Emily hails England as the "dear land of arts and arms," thereby defending imperialism. Her solidarity with Rivers is shown by sharing his judgment of Clayton.[323]

The limits of Brooke's feminism are exposed when she associates England with women's free choice of marriage partners. Arabella's observation of foreign marital modes is superficial: having praised Aboriginal matriarchy, she spurns it on learning that Indian mothers exercise a "foolish tyranny" in arranging daughters' marriages. Emily and Arabella defend their right to free choice in marriage partners by adopting romantic slogans, not so much inventing definitions of transcendent love as adopting rules voiced by Rivers. If they feminise married love by pretending it transcends money and social circumstance, he introduces slogans such as "souls in unison," "harmony of mind," and "delirium of the soul." His transcendence holds that Emily and he "were formed for each other" and were friends in "some pre-existent state." Inducing the "spirit of romance" in Emily, Rivers offsets the way it makes her unpredictable. The interpolated story of Sophia as "romantic to excess" confirms that Brooke believes women are vulnerable in their "romantic generosity." The illusions of romance weaken women's intelligence. In likening the Church of England to "an elegant well-dressed woman of quality," and claiming that women, unlike men, cannot be infidels, given their natural softness, Arabella unthinkingly links feminist romance to an institution whose theology opposes her feminism. Her application of "petticoat politics" to a "code of laws for the government of husbands" and her tenet that England alone is enlightened about marriage show that Brooke's feminism is not radical but patriotic.[324]

While Brooke articulates the language of romance to denote the transcendent feelings of ideal couples and to validate male subordination to the female, such is not the case. Romantic vocabulary does not exclusively apply to companionate marriage: it also elevates the male over the female as well as honouring the extended family and the gentry as a class. The androgyny assigned to Rivers, on behalf of gender innovation, makes the latter ultimately superfluous. While he spurns the liturgical vow of female "subjection," making equality the basis of marriage, Emily gives her "whole soul" to him. To her, Rivers is "a god" and the "most angelic of mankind." His tenderness bars all others from her soul. She not only finds his "mental beauty ... the express image of the Deity" but effaces herself before him, letting her "every emotion" be ruled by him. If she transforms his benevolence by claiming their souls conform, her romantic self-assertion does not displace theological ideas of self-effacement. Her idolisation of Rivers is not unique: his mother loves him "to idolatry," proving romantic words affect familial authority, as when Emily wishes to secure the permission of Mrs Rivers and her father before she marries.[325]

No private code between heroine and hero, the language of romance tightens society's patriarchalism. If Rivers idolises his sister as well as Emily, Emily idolises Mme Des Roches as well as Rivers. If Rivers' eyes see "nothing lovely but Emily," the only object in his "universe," so "the whole creation" contains no other woman for Temple than Lucy. Perhaps the clearest illustration of conservative romantic codes is Arabella's pride in rebelling against patriarchal authority even as her father, unknown to her, controls her marital choice. Insubstantial romantic action is evident in the predictable ways in which Brooke solves conflicts by contingency. Emily's jealousy of Mme Des Roches and her dispute with Rivers about delaying their wedding seem only to train characters to offset languid moments by posturing with romance as distinct from developing radical visions. If, on leaving Canada, Arabella mocks that "terrestrial paradise" and "divine country," thereby debasing romantic idealism, her deliberate is indistinguishable from accidental irony. When Emily recalls her unwillingness to perform a "romantic parade of fidelity" to Sir George, she so parades for Rivers. The closing masquerade shows that the self-objectification by which Emily honours Rivers relies more on social convention than romantic transcendence.[326]

Illusions of free romanticism reinforce patriarchy in *The History of Emily Montague*. If Rivers creates private domestic spaces for Emily, he is bent on engrossing and absorbing "every faculty" of her mind. He succeeds; she agrees to have "no will" but his, submitting to him as "arbiter" of her fate. The lovers' romantic gestures do not reduce their desire to be recognised by their class. Their pleasure in the "little circle" and "little empire" of rural retreat is ironic: boasted indifference to the "parade of life" heightens their making their estate a political centre. The story of Miss Williams and the orphan lets them parade their benevolence, contempt for aristocrats, and influence in the "great world." Tensions in their romantic self-containment and political program for marriage are not upheld by narrative dialectic, as attested by the arbitrarily complete closure. When Emily wins her father's permission to wed Rivers, the threat of forced marriage dissolves, as in Arabella's case. It is not enough for Brooke to reveal Willmott to be Emily's long-lost father; she arranges that the patriarch independently chooses the same husband for his daughter as she chooses for herself. Coincidences that resolve plot conflicts demonstrate that romantic resistance to patriarchy is a charade. By having the lovers blessed providentially with wealth, Brooke reveals her dependence on formulaic sentimental plays such as Steele's *The Conscious Lovers*. Besides remotivating money in ways the story resists, the closure elides married love, imperial wealth, and patriarchal authority. That the ending rewards rural gentry with financial wealth and social prestige ultimately devalues romance.[327]

With romance championing rural gentry and Anglicanism, the closure devalues narrative and political processes. Its excessive symmetry does not reflect the author's discontent with politics in Quebec and England. Reducing merchants and aristocrats to marital villains and idealising the gentry as true citizens defies belief, the ending asserts Francophobia and Augustan nostalgia: the genteel are socially exclusive patriots, their style of romance cultivating like-mindedness that is dismissive of cultural diversity. In seeming to reconcile ideological conflicts, the closure aggravates them: if matriarchy is admired, patriarchy is reinforced; if the liturgy is attacked, the church is defended; if marriage is an agent of reform, it signals exclusive contentment. Brooke infects politics with romance. Her story does contain progressive ideas, as in the motif of androgyny. But conformity seizes innovation: old ideas govern new. Romance is static, not dialectical: that it offsets marriage's languid moments gives way to a complacency summed in Rivers' phrases of "peaceable possession" and "voluptuous tranquillity." Hardly resolving ideological conflict, the closure raises unanswered problems. If wealth and power are decried throughout but appropriated to the ending and if prudence, maligned in the duration, finally outweighs transcendence, this universalising of themes devalues their mediation.[328]

Brooke predicts little about Canada's future. Her characters, far from closing the gap between political theory and fact, widen that schism: adamant about the Conquest, they would confirm France's defeat by cultivating French sensibility. But, by insisting that that sensibility is best realised by refined English people, they define patriotism in French terms. Their assumption that England can and must assimilate Quebec not only fails to foresee the day when French will replace English law but also blinds them to the political action implied by their romantic illusions. *The History of Emily Montague* says less about Canada than about an empire and the strains of a mother country that afflict Anglican rural gentry who refine its social hierarchy through romantic propaganda, which is their sole means of compensating for political marginalisation.

The Experiments of Pierre Carlet de Chamblain Marivaux

British authors cited the French romancier Marivaux with respect as well as hauteur, with admiration as well as pique. One wonders why he figured so much in eighteenth-century literary history given the ambivalence towards him expressed by Fielding, Richardson, and Fanny Burney (1752-1840). They uncover the nationalism of British fiction because, more than they say, they were affected by Marivaux's experiments in *Le Paysan Parvenu* (1735) and *La Vie de Marianne* (1731–1745), experiments evidenced by translations of those novels: Marivaux's texts were naturalised in ways that exposed the polarities in British fiction when viewed as an institution. Its polar aspects are further clarified by comparing Sterne and Defoe

to Marivaux: systemic relations between him and the British writers test truisms that find Sterne atypical and Defoe marginal.[329]

Assuming literary mirrors cultural history, British writers saw Marivaux as a cultural index. In 1763, Adam Smith (1723–1790) thought France's monarchy had reached "its greatest pitch of glory," like Rome in "the reign of Trajan." In a state's flourishing times, its citizens, continues Smith, turn from "the hurry of life" to "the motions of the human mind." He links Marivaux's genius to Tacitus, the historian who, rather than record events, stressed narrative psychology. If their writing is "of so contrary a nature," Smith says, they are "at great pains to account for every event by the temper and internal disposition of the several actors, in disquisitions that approach near to metaphysical ones." This inward turn of writing, its charting of mental territories, is a corollary of imperial power, national harmony, and domestic comfort.[330] Hugh Blair (1718–1800) lauds the *romancier* likewise: the "works of Marivaux, especially his Marianne, discover great refinement of thought, great penetration into human nature, and paint, with a delicate pencil, some of the nicest shades and features in the distinction of characters." He claims this in 1783 when praising French authors for reforming the "spirit of Novel Writing": they make social and psychological detail the major concern of fiction. French novels are "full of good sense, and instructive knowledge of the world." British authors are "inferior"; they neither "relate so agreeably, nor draw characters with so much delicacy." If Defoe, Richardson, and Fielding write well, Blair reads Marivaux as signifying France's cultural superiority.[331]

A sign of French superiority that afforded Smith and Blair a critical stance on domestic literature, Marivaux was not found exceptional by all commentators. Warburton, anticipating Smith and Blair in appreciating psychological refinement in romance, allows patriotism to modify his connection of fictional reform to cultural supremacy. Like them, he eulogises the French, "this great People (to whom, it must be owned, every Branch of Science has been infinitely indebted)," since, by imitating "real Life and Manners," their fiction amused refined minds and promoted refinement. Yet French culture does not lead him to find Marivaux incomparable: he says Fielding is foremost with Marivaux and that their superior "*Comic art*" equally perfected romance; French superiority involves equivalent praise of Britain and Fielding. Warburton conveys Britain's growing eminence and finds British and French culture comparable.[332]

Resistance to France and romance lies behind the view of James Beattie (1735–1803). Treating romance as a "dangerous recreation," he regards the French writer unenthusiastically: romances "corrupt the heart, and stimulate the passions," breed "a dislike of history" and "substantial" ideas, and fill "the mind with extravagant thoughts" and "criminal propensities." Marivaux is humorous and witty, and his style is simple, natural, and agreeable, but pedagogy and interest in cognition stops Beattie from seeing him as a cultural icon. If romances neither appeal to mature minds nor refine ideas, Marivaux's works, if they possess "a moral tendency," may be read "without danger." But, ignoring claims he charts the mental world, thus not fitting the romancier into Britain's literary history, Beattie makes rational morality devalue French culture.[333]

If Gray and Walpole view their favourite as an emblem of superior culture, this culture is past, not actual: their praise of Marivaux, in disparaging British literature, detracts, too, from French rational optimism. Writing to Richard West (1716–1742) about *Joseph Andrews*, Gray subordinates the British to the French author. His interest in fictional affect remote from Beattie's distrust, Gray aims at fairness. If some of Fielding's incidents are "ill laid and without invention," his humorous depiction of nature and people is laudatory: his "light things" are as "weighty" and "useful" as "grave discourses" about the passions and mind. While Beattie thinks fiction subverts philosophy, Gray celebrates Fielding for his emotional, anti-rational, and non-schematic appeal. For Gray, the greatest "paradisiacal pleasure" is the prospect of reading "eternal new romances of Marivaux and Crebillon." His sense that Marivaux, better than Fielding, achieves paradoxical literary effects matches the sentiments of Mary Collyer (c. 1716–1762) in the preface to her translation of *La Vie de Marianne* (1743). For her, "the love of pleasure is the most natural and easy inlet to young minds," while "grave and serious discourses may sometimes fail of the intended effect."[334] While Gray and Collyer say that bathos may prove elevating, their celebration of Marivaux holds that he achieved the highest sensibility and that to belittle him in the name of systematic reason is culturally regressive.

Walpole, writing to Gray on 19 November 1765, shows that, if Marivaux emblematised French culture, his image was mediated by changing views about intellectual progress in France. Criticising the French for lacking delicacy and gaiety, Walpole objects to philosophes whom he finds superficial, fanatical, dull, and overbearing. Signs of cultural decline are that Claude Prosper Jolyot de Crébillon (1707–1777) is not in fashion and that Marivaux is now a "proverb": the newly coined "*marivauder*" and "*marivaudage*" are synonyms for "being prolix and tiresome." This anti-French view, coming no more than three years after Smith celebrated Marivaux, shows that reactions to him reflect ideologies: such contrariness says as much about the British literary system as about French culture. Walpole's lament for Marivaux implies he does not think highly of British culture, if also that he regards it less unfavourably than that of Enlightenment France.[335]

Rival British views of Marivaux may be summed up by comparing how Clara Reeve (1729–1807) and Chesterfield treat him. She finds the Frenchman's works "of capital merit"; they are "pictures of real life and manners," their sentiments and language "highly polished." But, in praising *La Vie de Marianne* for its realism and refinement, she faults *Le Paysan Parvenu*: this work is "somewhat exceptionable"; its "French morality is not suitable to an old English palate." The books operate distinct moral systems: one is natural, the other too French. But did Marivaux apply one morality in *La Vie de Marianne* and one in *Le Paysan Parvenu* that is neither pure nor traditional? If Reeve's views are not held by Chesterfield, he is ambivalent on other grounds. Affecting Enlightenment positivism, he limits praise by deriding the Frenchman's over-refinement. In one letter, he declares Marivaux "a beaucoup étudié et connoit bien le coeur, peut-être même un peu trop." In another, he mocks his ideas of the heart by saying he "refines so much upon its *plis* and *replis*, and describes them so affectedly, that he often is unintelligible to his readers, and sometimes so I dare say to himself?" If Reeve's patriotism explains her dislike of French rationalism and ambivalence about Marivaux, Chesterfield's urbanity treats the romancier condescendingly and embodies that modish French aloofness that Walpole decried.[336]

The contrariness with which British authors praised Marivaux implies that literary history evolves for political and cultural reasons that are at odds with one another. Divergent views about the romancier also suggest that literary history does not, as an institution, uphold geographical and historical categories: it consists of political and cultural ideologies that strive to appear as systems in their own right, claiming to avoid inevitable arbitrariness. That literary history is a system containing rival systems that require dialectical outlooks may be confirmed by examining the two most extended essays on Marivaux.[337] The first is a two-part article in *The Gentleman's Magazine* of 1749 that compares the French author to Richardson; the second is Murphy's preface to *The Works of Henry Fielding*, published in 1762, comparing him to Fielding. These essays, since opinion was so divided about the merits of the British authors, offer insights into the function of literary history. Placing Marivaux below Richardson and Fielding on opposing literary but similar cultural grounds, they indicate that, far from analysing writers neutrally, literary history strategically compares them, systemically transposing cultural ideology into moral language.

The Gentleman's Magazine claims that *Le Paysan Parvenu* and *La Vie de Marianne*, being "paintings after life," returned French romance to "nature." Anticipating Reeve's admiration of Marivaux's verisimilitude, the anonymous writer does not, however, think the two works morally distinct. Further, while Chesterfield accuses Marivaux of excessive psychologising, this writer charges Marivaux with not detailing "private and domestic" life. For *The Gentleman's Magazine*'s writer, the difference between representing phenomena and mental ideas is an issue. Unlike Smith who appreciates the inward turn of Marivaux's narratives and Chesterfield who thinks the romancier's psychology dissolves phenomenal clarity, this writer claims that Marivaux refuses to exhibit the "particulars which constitute a virtuous life," offering no "representation of the minutiae of *Virtue*" to match Richardson in *Clarissa*. Initially lauding Marivaux's realism, this writer ends up dispraising it. While his criticism is based on generic terms, underlying his formal criteria are national and religious values. If *La Vie de Marianne* is a "kind of chronicle, in which some memorable adventures are well described," *Clarissa* is "an history, where the events of her life follow each other in an uninterrupted succession." This critic's arbitrary generic terms are less categorical than he pretends, for when, after commending Marivaux's realisation of nature, he says that Richardson "paints nature, and nature alone." Setting aside his failure to see *Clarissa*'s editorial reconstruction, this critic's view that French romances never mention God gets at the root of his preference for Clarissa's perpetual confession of religious duty. His remarks about narrative viewpoint also testify to religious prejudice: Marivaux's perspective is less plausible than Richardson's since French romances are improbably retrospective; they "suppose the history to be written after the series of events is closed by the catastrophe." Granting the improbability of epistolary form which assumes characters share an "uncommon taste" for "immediately committing" everything to paper, he still claims writing-to-the-moment is more credible. His contrariness is transparent when he praises Richardson's religious effects in *Clarissa*: he says the novel delineates "the duties peculiar to every hour of a life of perfect virtue" and that the heroine is in the "same station of life" as the reader, so the "unshaken constancy" of her reflections is "within the reach of every capacity." But how could it be that Clarissa is a perfect human and a model easily imitated by readers?[338]

Murphy, like the previous critic, voices systematic views only to expose their ideological prejudices. Like Warburton, he grants Fielding will be respected by posterity as the "illustrious rival" of Marivaux, that "excellent genius." Astutely, he sees Marivaux as a satirist who targets dissimulation, cunning, and arrogance and who reveals "the false pretences of assumed characters" and "subtleties of hypocrisy and exterior religion" to uphold "the delicacies of real honour, and the sentiments of true virtue." But his generosity falters; he echoes Chesterfield rather than anticipates Smith. Praising Marivaux for not being content to "copy" appearances and for tracing the "internal movements" of passions with penetration, Murphy alleges that he too much makes narrative an exploratory process: he is "over-solicitous" and "over-curious." The "traces" he depicts "grow minute and almost imperceptible": touched and retouched, they grow delicate and lose their outline. Murphy prefers the logic on which Fielding bases his "comic fable" to the commitment to "the finer features of the mind" which Marivaux makes in his "*fictitious biography*." His bold plots and efficient characterisation make Fielding superior to Marivaux who labours his "air of originality" too proudly. The latter uncovers "nicer and more subtle workings of the mind" and heart, but Fielding more strongly rouses readers' curiosity.[339]

The opposing ways in which *The Gentleman's Magazine* and Murphy's preface base authorial preference show nationalism inducing them to fault Marivaux's narrative experiments. If, then, he was one focus of British literary history, the contradictory ways he was honoured and dispraised expose tensions within the conscious and unconscious ideology of that history. How Fielding and Burney invoke Marivaux, without admitting indebtedness, further exposes that history, proving that authors were trapped by ideological tensions.

In citing the French writer, Fielding appreciates Marivaux's rhetorical engagement of readers. Yet Fielding's vague allusions conceal a range of motifs drawn from his predecessor and imply a patriotic bias. He cites the romancier in *Joseph Andrews* when he marks his own writing off from romance and chronicle. Without admitting that Marivaux holds to a similar demarcation, Fielding declares that biography is a model for his comic novel since he prizes typical more than documentary truth.[340] That "*Le Paisan Parvenu*" and the "history of Marianne" inspire him to induce readers to "contemplate their deformity," thereby reducing "public shame" by "private mortification," he assigns humanistic rhetoric to the Frenchman without conceding that the latter's experiments with fictional biography challenge humanism. Nor does he admit that Marivaux's ironic modes complicate the reading process deliberately.

He similarly celebrates Marivaux in *Tom Jones* for embodying the comic energy that draws readers to fault themselves and to forgive neighbours. However, by thinking Marivaux a humanist who simply opposes moral self-deception, he is not forthright, given the paradox that he would humble readers by entering the literary canon alongside Marivaux, Shakespeare, and others. The self-assertion afforded by this allusion to Marivaux is strategically cunning. If he does not openly treat the French author as one who figures prominently in cultural debates, his argument that Marivaux simply endorses Christian ethics values nationalistic pride more highly than systemic awareness.[341]

Burney so inconsistently cites Marivaux that one doubts her dependency. In the preface to *Evelina* (1778), she names him, with Johnson, Fielding, Richardson, Smollett, and Rousseau, as one who saved the novel from contempt. But her view is unsteady: her novel's flaws induce her to don the mantle of anonymity while denouncing the luxurious imagination of romances as though speaking univocally. She is, of course, voicing truisms. Her insistence that originality is paramount to fiction is weak when she says one may read her book without moral danger since characters are based on life, not art. Her insistence is curious given her displacement of Marivaux: repeating the list of writers whose authority she admits but whose influence she would minimise, she omits his name. Timid and aggressive tones heighten the omission, making her imitation of *La Vie de Marianne* revealing as to his powerful, if unspecified, influence.[342]

Burney's displacement of Marivaux heightens her experiments with narrative mediation. *Evelina* dramatises forms of writing, creating tensions, in the mode of Marivaux, between conduct-book didacticism and the relativizing processes of autobiography.[343] The anxiety assigned to Evelina reflects Burney's sense of the absorbing complexity of the writing process. If, from the start, Evelina is an accurate social commentator whose naivete does not clash with innate percipience, she still discovers herself by transcribing ideas and feelings. Initially sure that writing is just a form of speaking, she learns that script is reflexive and that shaping ideas in a journal is problematic; "melancholy phantasms" harm self-expression. At times, she is unable to "journalise" since moods prevent her shaping thought; at others, expression is blocked by simultaneous ideas. Since experience and writing are both susceptible to emotional and mental disturbance, Evelina realises her pen may reveal things preferably kept hidden: she sees that correspondence entails a more intimate revelation than is comfortable. Forced by her journal to admit her snobbery and social awkwardness, she learns that writing forms, as well as assumes, identity and that, far from conveying meaning transparently, it requires interpretation. The letter apparently from Lord Orville, actually from Sir Clement Willoughby, confirms these points. Yet, anxieties about script lead Evelina to metonymic ideas that help her understand the personal value of mediation. To her guardian, Mr Villars, she becomes a "book" that needs a reading separate from her letters. To her lover, Orville, she is a text, too: she learns about herself by reading in his face how he reads her person. The metonymic route by which she reaches a sense of selfhood and narrative dialectic ends when she admits that Orville's declaration of love is engraved on her heart but is unscriptable.

Converting a naive letter writer into one whose identity depends on textual mediation, Burney explores the contraries of fictional autobiography like Marivaux.[344]

Fielding's plots are not simply transparent as Murphy says; like Burney, he promotes the psychology of writing and reading. His fluctuations of narrative and identity suggest he is closer to the experimental French author than his conventional, humanist invocation of Marivaux suggests. His voice is not steadily third person: he often uses first-person pronouns and frequently switches between singular and plural forms, this variability complicating individual and representative tones. Addressing readers, he is amusingly problematic: in *Tom Jones*, if he is one moment angry at "reptiles of critics," at the next, his reader is "my good reptile" and "friend." Anticipating Sterne, he stipulates readers' roles in *Tom Jones*, classifying them as young, curious, worthy, or judicious. He dramatises point of view by adopting plural registers. "Founder of a new Province of Writing," given his experienced jurisprudence, he justifies withholding narrative fact by speaking as a cautious empiricist. Among his voices are those of monarch, pedant, preacher, and clown: such stances heighten our sense of mediation. His self-consciousness about authorial digression, rhetorical amplification, and plural viewpoints shows that Murphy is dull to how his author invents rules for affective purposes. By destabilising narrative style, Fielding approaches the ironic mode of Marivaux as much as Aristotelean concepts of plot.[345]

Allusions to Marivaux by Burney and Fielding, being defensive as well as programmatic, evasive as well as creative, confirm that authors uphold and are implicated in the literary system. They champion the French author with ideological uncertainty about his experiments: his exploratory and subversive mediation they subordinate to traditional morality. Ambiguity about French culture inhibits the sense of indebtedness: admiring him, they ridicule those who imitate French manners, linking them to insensibility.[346] If single-minded about France, Richardson exposes contradictions in the literary system. Often compared with Marivaux, he never mentions him. His hostility to France appears in a prefatory letter to *Pamela* opposing its "native Simplicity" to "Strokes of Oratory" that "*frenchify* our *English* Solidity into Froth and Whip-syllabub."[347] Lovelace resides a "good while" at Versailles where he picks up the court's corrupt manners so that his native land becomes a "plaguy island."[348] As a moralist, Richardson cannot mention France positively. The transcendence he gives his heroines enables him to displace its culture. Since Pamela transforms society by converting her master and Clarissa plans her death so that she speaks from beyond the grave with the utmost spiritual force, Richardson commits himself to religious transcendence that is also political. By having the pious Pamela inspire congregations, since raised by God to be "useful in [her] Generation," and ensuring the "divine" Clarissa merits "beatification," he gives them an absolute spirituality and transcendence that is patriotic. Still, his typology in spiritual autobiography is balanced by an involvement of mediation and selfhood recalling Marivaux: offsetting his propaganda on behalf of British perfectibility is a wish to explore narrative that reveals he did not ignore the French author.[349]

His epistolary experiments defy views that the genres adopted by Marivaux and himself are distinct. Richardson problematizes epistolarity. Pamela's and Clarissa's letters are not simple correspondence and autobiography. Unsure of reaching others, his heroines internalise rules of writing: far from dashing letters off, they transcribe them; copies aid identity. Postscripts, subscripts, and re-startings in medias res confirm that, in extending and suspending epistolary rules, their writing is prescriptive and descriptive. If letters effect consolation and self-discovery, they also endanger Pamela and Clarissa. Alert to the polarities of mediation, Richardson makes his heroines' letters signify vulnerability as well as moral reform. Making them confront the materiality of writing, he obliges them to see that the pen must oppose social prejudice strategically in order to defend religious truth: letters must be written and dispatched surreptitiously because they are subject to forgery and theft; they are metonyms of their writers. Hiding letters on the person or in the landscape yields intuitions: Richardson stresses writerly mediation the more he can celebrate his heroines' integrity and spiritual virtues.

While Richardson's style of self-presentation derives partly from Marivaux, his mediation is problematic. His dramatisation of writing transforms letters into journal entries with extended autobiographical reference that counters writing-to-the-moment. His heroines, when writing of themselves, objectify those selves. Like Jacob and Marianne, they describe how they appear as if standing outside themselves.[350] Pamela stresses her confused, guilty look when interrupted at her writing desk by Mr B, describing how her heart throbs through her handkerchief when creeping shamefaced to him. Another such discrepancy arises when she tells how she looked to Mr B when he spied her, through the keyhole of the locked door, lying unconscious. The attack on Richardson's prurience in Fielding's *Shamela* (1741), if unjust, indicates that his heroines are narrators who generate sympathy for themselves by objectifying former vulnerabilities.[351] While Marivaux's autobiographical disjunctions are ironically comic, Richardson's are literal: the former uses them for reflexive ends; the latter's concern for sympathy hinders recursive mediation.

If his objectification of heroines enacts an indebtedness to Marivaux's autobiographical mediation, Richardson's willingness to use it without irony conveys a contradictory, rather than contrary, sense of mediation. His intrusions as compiler and editor manifest an inconsistent mediation: though he wants letters to stand in metonymically for his heroines, he undermines this symbolic mediation by intruding between characters and readers, distracting us with finer literary awareness. That he overdetermines as well as undermines mediation exacerbates his contradictoriness. With seeming unselfconsciousness, he makes his heroines address the medium of manuscript while ignoring that of print. When Pamela, hardly able to hold a pen, describes her "crooked and trembling" lines and Clarissa remarks "how some of the letters stagger more than others," they make stylography personal in a medium seen by readers as print, not script.[352] Similarly, when Pamela, bent on moving readers, refers to her "blotted" and tear-stained paper, she diverts notice from pathos to the intervening printing process that effaces the stains' textuality. This attempt to make writerly mediation a simple, sentimental sign shows that Richardson works less hard than Marivaux to create dialectical tension between different images of mediation. If Pamela's letters prove she cannot be alone without a pen in hand and marriage to Mr B makes writing redundant, Richardson values writing contradictorily: it is essential to identity but is transcended by marriage.[353] Insisting on the absolute closure that Clarissa's letters give her life, he uses Belford's voice to mediate the posthumous reception of her letters. Richardson wants to make Clarissa's letters appear spiritually transcendent, yet, as he realises, their spiritual force derives necessarily from textual mediation.

Since Richardson's novels embody the idea that writing is essential to identity, spiritual growth, and social reform, and since he relies, more than he admits, on devices that Marivaux experimented with in fictional autobiography, we may detect systemic strains in the institution of eighteenth-century British literature. By analysing Marivaux's devices, available to us through the translated texts, we may better define Richardson's contrariness: his dependence on the French writer reveals an outlook that exploits mediation without accepting its systemic constraints. To Richardson, text is open process and closed product; it is instrumental to selfhood, yet ultimately, that identity transcends text; it is reconstituted by editors yet naturally possesses a reforming integrity. Far from pretending, like Richardson, that mediation can be treated single-mindedly, Marivaux knows it involves competing systems: self-reference is psychologically complex and comic; the objectification of self in life and writing is inevitable; self-presentation is strategic and illusory, its indeterminacy making moral and spiritual claims amusingly problematic.[354]

Marivaux's unconcern for fictional closure matches his interest in the paradoxes of autobiography that are expressed by widening narrative gaps. The social eminence enjoyed by Jacob and Marianne neither makes their writing redundant nor guarantees them control of their texts: circumstance does not govern their role as narrators, nor does writerly flexibility inscribe their identities unambiguously. When tempted to view writing as a transcription of life and as a confirmation of identity, they are obliged by the autobiographical process to realise that writing is always a hazardous rhetorical strategy. Written discourse shows them that, if instrumental to identity, writing also unravels selfhood: the necessary subjectivity of writerly mediation disturbs unitary concepts of self. With a comically ironic vision that prefigures Sterne, Marivaux enjoys making his narrators' incomplete sense of the plurality of selfhood heighten the paradoxes of literary form and accentuate the contrariness of literary systems.[355]

Recording the past to justify and celebrate themselves, Jacob and Marianne discover that writing renders identity elusive: narrative is more complex than anticipated. Affecting a frankness beyond artifice, they see, though not so clearly as the reader, that observations and generalisations give way to the relativizing conventions of writerly mediation. To a degree, they are forced to learn that recovery of their selves involves being exclusively secret: the paradox that revelation of self requires withholding of self is borne in on them. For Marivaux, the continuity of narrated and narrating self may not be assumed: recovery of the former self entails a re-creative identification that obliges the autobiographer to move beyond fixed narrative perspectives.[356] That the self is neither transcendent nor reflexively transparent prompted him to experiment with the impact on writing of tensions between conduct and transcription.

Jacob's life story starts with unchallengeable authority, yet within a few pages, he is ensnared in ironies. Asserting he has "never dissembled" the "Truth" of his birth, witness his title, he claims Heaven has rewarded his "Sincerity." Forgetting that his title is generic and anonymous, not unique and transparent, he demeans those who "screen themselves" by "mean Dissimulation" against low origins. He denounces such "Artifice," sure it recoils on those who use it. Assuming the reader is on his side, he admits that he diverts criticism by declaring his humble birth strategically. Far from absolutely sincere, he embodies a complacency which, through dramatic irony, establishes the terms of judgment applicable to him. That his inconsistent retrospection sharpens the reader's narrative memories is keener for Marivaux's pluralising of writerly motives and forms of self-presentation. At one moment, Jacob says he writes to inform readers and to amuse himself. At the next, he declares his book is a "History" not "forg'd for Diversion." Then he withholds his name; to give it would "lay a Restraint" on his "Narrations." Transparency is undermined by generic indeterminacy: varying tone saps control of the narrative future. Discounting his nephews for making him digress, he changes stance in mid-sentence:

> so much the better; for it's proper I should accustom my Readers betimes
> to my Digressions; I am not very positive whether I shall be guilty of many,
> perhaps I may, and perhaps I may not; I can answer for neither; only this I
> am resolv'd, not to confine myself: I am to give you a relation of my Life,
> and if I intermix any thing else, it shall be nothing but what presents itself
> without my seeking.[357]

Volatile digressions make planned spontaneity dubious. Strategic self-representation recoils on his claims to uphold a single, natural narrative. As narrator, he describes his facial features without drawing on other observers. Recalling thoughts and feelings, he pretends that his face made his mind transparent: without justification, he reads his facial image as an unmediated text. Narrative stance perpetuates rather than questions the way, as character, he delighted to view himself in an apparently impartial, third-person mode. When he reports that, being "beau'd out, troth! Jacob made a very promising Figure" or that he was pleased to see "Jacob metamorphos'd into a Gentleman," narrative distance forms a rhetorical self-love, an image of uncritical partiality for self or amour-propre, a sign that Jacob naively writes as if recovery of self can be total. His habitual viewing of self from the outside while detailing thoughts, as if writing makes inner conform with outer life, is the target of irony in Marivaux's narrative dialectic.[358]

The pluralism of Jacob's writing, its subversion of narrative models, is confirmed by his stance on language. He often addresses the reader by stressing narration's verbal aspects:

his names for things and ideas, he claims, respect linguistic convention and the speech community. But his diction can be circular, arbitrary, and self-defeating.[359] About his mistress's unthinking "Libertinism," he insists he has given it "its proper Title" since he names it so. Sometimes merely assertive, at others, he is urbanely sententious. In saying his "Rusticity was void of Dissimulation, and was only the greatest Flatterer by its not knowing how to flatter at all," his equivocation is nicely paradoxical. Variable naming of feelings for Genevieve widens the inevitable gap between mental and bodily life, between writing and speaking. He enters a linguistic "Labyrinth" when trying to match his psychological state to social facts. He experiences a disjunction between consciousness and story that confuses his sense of narrative convention: arrogance about names leads him to admit the instantaneous plurality of mental ideas and to disregard the boundaries between monologue and dialogue, between direct and reported speech, thus rendering his words opaque. If problematic verbal and narrative signs force on him self-conscious deliberation, they oppose him with psychological and phenomenal contraries. When Genevieve says the money given her by their master is a gauge of her fidelity, she tells him, he says, nothing new. Yet, he is "thunder-struck as by a sudden Surprize." Despite professed emotional indifference, he condescends to her and is sexually jealous. His shock at discovering "sparks of the old Fire still alive" is not displaced by his report that it soon extinguishes itself, for Marivaux shows that things and identity are less stable than Jacob supposes, enjoining readers to delight in a narrator who acts and writes so well that he blinds himself to his best conceptions.[360]

Marivaux absorbs readers in mediation when Marianne experiences contrary ideas of fiction and identity. From the start, her narrative recoils on her. She condemns women who sympathised with her when she was first orphaned. To her, as narrator, their sympathy is romantic sensationalism: they gratify themselves by claiming to be "eyewitnesses of everything they were pleased to imagine." Collyer accentuates Marivaux's attack on such literary prejudice by having the women find the orphan's sensational life "written in legible characters" on her body. Yet, if Marianne assails this false story-telling, she must heed it: besides inventing her origin, she must read her own body as yielding narrative meaning. Marivaux further draws attention to narrative mediation by contrary aspects of her self-consciousness. If, at one moment, she prides herself on the congruence of ideas and percepts, at the next, she suffers the disjuncture of mind and reality, experiencing uncertain awareness. Writing her life reflects self-contradiction: when, on arriving in Paris, she finds the "new world" there "not altogether unknown" to her, she learns that perceptions may be contrary. Marivaux pushes this narrative irony far. If, as a character, Marianne omnisciently controls, from time to time, the multiple roles she performs, she cannot, as narrator, always reconcile fallibility and intuition: about her "serious, silent intercourse" with Valville, she cannot say exactly "what [her] eyes said to him." The coexistence of certainty and confusion in her outlook reveals Marivaux's wish to make her mental flexibility stir readers to reflect on mediation. Far from making empirical and innate ideas exclusive, he adopts an inclusive stance towards Marianne's variable agency and flexible awareness that implicitly values mediation itself. Strong evidence for this is

Marianne's account of her reaction to Climal when this would-be lover comes upon her and the obviously favoured Valville. The account of her attempt to follow Climal's lead elicits the contrariness of her conduct and identity:

> I both did too much and too little: in one half of my behaviour, I seemed to know him; in the other, to be entirely ignorant of him. It was a perfect contradiction to itself, and seemed to say yes and no, and yet not perfectly either.[361]

Her contrariness affords Marivaux narrative energy. As his characterisation resists systematic philosophy, so his exploration of multiple relations between narrated and narrating selves defies unitary ideas of identity. His playful experimentation with fictional autobiography proves narrative to be a medium that, in its anti-doctrinaire plurality, is instrumental to humanity.[362]

If this brief exposition of Marivaux's novels in translation shows that his experiments with mediation were available to Richardson, to be more precise about his influence, one must probe the fidelity with which the translations convey those experiments. This requires testing their systemic features. The basic issue is how much the translators alter Marivaux's concerns with mediation. As will become clear, they limit and extend such concerns. Yet, before such concerns may be assessed, one must grant that the translations employ distinct methods: they represent competing modes in the British literary system. Since one prizes picaresque satire and the other moral romance, since one values Marivaux in a manner recalling Defoe and the other in the style of Richardson, we see that he was appropriated by rival ideologies as he was translated. Turning to the translations' features, we note that the title-pages emphasise systemic distinctions. The anonymous translator of *Le Paysan parvenu* keeps the French title primary, while Collyer suppresses it, inventing one that suits her sentimentalism. While the anonymous translator mentions Marivaux's name, Collyer omits it, taking an epigraph from Thomson's *The Seasons* (1726–1744) that emphasises the pleasures of moral education.[363]

Le Paysan Parvenu: Or, The Fortunate Peasant (1739) finds colloquial idioms that capture the cheeky, manipulative tone of Marivaux's Jacob. His fondness for "les choux de mon village" becomes desire for "honest brown Bread in the Country"; "chat en poche" is rendered "Pig in a Poke"; and when he may be "niché entre quatre murailles," Jacob is threatened with having a "Stone Doublet" clapped on him. Yet, the translator misses some idioms. For example, "du pain à discrétion" becomes, with literal awkwardness, "excellent rolls at discretion" rather than *bread ad lib*. So, too, when Jacob congratulates himself on deciding to stay in Paris, the translator reads "le marché" as "la marche," mistakenly saying he took the step of staying. Word-for-word focus leads the translator to flatten the variable tones: s/he introduces inapt colloquialisms: "adresse" becomes "wheedle"; "de mon sentiment" is "jump so"; "sans se soucier" is to "hanker so little after"; "maltraité" turns to "black and blue"; and "est-ce que tu ne m'entends pas?" becomes "wits gone a Wool-gathering." Concern for idioms distracts the translator from psychological subtlety: verbal inventiveness impedes his facility with reflexive meaning, as typified by the clumsy instance when "Ma situation m'attendrit sur moi-même" becomes "The Circumstances I was in made me so compassionate of my self."[364] Marivaux's insinuating, flexible syntax is replaced by a stiffness that recalls Defoe's narrative style but omits his irony. Still, Defoe is the model for the translator's diction and tags. Phrases such as "a mean Dissimulation," "little concurring Accidents," "things of course," and "nothing but Grimace" recall the admonitory reflections of *Moll Flanders* (1722) and *Roxana* (1724) rather than Marivaux's text.[365] The same is true of the following tags: "to speak Truth," "one of those errant Brutes, or Valets, call them which you please," "may perhaps be of Service to my Readers," and "I omit the Pursuit of these melancholy Particulars, an account of them would be too tedious." These stress mediation by addressing the reader but de-emphasise Marivaux's psychological and narrative contraries.[366]

Collyer de-emphasises Marianne's earthy wit, making her demure in the Richardsonian mode. Eschewing brevity, she lengthens sentences; fond of impersonal constructions, she lessens the force of verbs by extending nominal phrases and using an elevated tone. Typically, the single word "visage" grows into "the superior attractions of beauty," and "le jeu d'une physionomie friponne qui les accompagnait" becomes "the external charms of blooming beauty, and the pleasing air that accompanied them," "roguish face" being unduly generalised. Collyer's emotionalism is monotonous: whereas Marianne is "baignée de son sang" (the murdered woman's) in the carriage, Collyer adds that it is "as if she had been taking a last embrace and was loath to bid me an eternal adieu." Amplification prizes expatiation more than irony and fluency more than playful viewpoint. Sentimentality leads Collyer to reduce autobiographical detail: "je me mis à sangloter de toute ma force" becomes "I could make no other reply but sighs and tears, the natural rhetoric of an oppressed and afflicted heart." While Marivaux epitomises Marianne's sexual self-preservation in "un vrai instinct de femme," Collyer refers to the "common effect of inexperience." Likewise, "cet homme-là m'aimât comme un amant aime une maîtresse" becomes a "man not altogether so disinterested as I thought him." By smothering sexual motifs, she reduces Marivaux's concern with fractured awareness and identity. His "l'anéantissement" is merely "melancholy." Sentimentality leads her to objectify selfhood with pictorial imagery: Marianne may be "presque en pleurant de sensibilité," but Collyer has her say "while my eyes could scarce return the tears of sensibility that almost overflowed their banks."[367]

When Collyer translates colloquially, she heightens idioms in Marivaux's text that expose national prejudice. Recalling Richardson and foretelling Burney, she applies idioms to women, such as Mme Dutour, whose grossness she stresses to dignify Marianne's purity. Where Mme Dutour is sexually implicit in saying, "Mais je vois bien ce que c'est," Collyer has her say "I find the old saint has got a colt's tooth in his head." Marivaux calls her sexual compromises "laches maximes," but Collyer insists "they must be shocking to every mind that has the least sense of honor, the least remains of virtue established in the heart." In moral essays that prescribe a sexual code, Collyer views Marivaux's text from Richardson's perspective. So, while Marivaux touches on Marianne's sexual vulnerability in the phrase "en pareil cas," Collyer expands it into "a girl in my circumstances, sure of preserving that inestimable jewel, her chastity." Just prior, Marianne is "resolutely resolved to lose [her] life rather than [her] virtue."[368]

That Collyer translates Marivaux in terms of Richardson's contempt for French mores is clear because, like the British writer, she handles reflexive transparency in over-determined and single-minded ways. To Marivaux's statement that the women who observe the young orphan imagine they see "dans mes traits quelque chose qui sentait mon aventure," Collyer adds that they saw her adventures "written in legible characters." She makes Marianne's body mediate her soul more unambiguously than Marivaux. Thus, she takes "inward satisfaction in the vivacity of [her] countenance" and is sure humility is "visible in [her] behaviour." This view of Marianne's moral radiance lessens Marivaux's concern with fluctuating psychology. Hence, the shallow way Collyer's Marianne lets writing mediate sexual identity. Her Marianne says the coquette "knows how to be many women in one and, by turns, assumes each perfection, suits herself to the inconstancy of her admirers, by presenting them every day a new mistress." This simplifies Marivaux's Marianne. She is personal and direct: "Je fixais l'homme le plus volage; je dupais son inconstance, parce que tous les jours je lui renouvelais sa maîtresse, et c'était comme s'il en avait changé." While Collyer's Marianne accommodates herself to her own plurality, Marivaux's accommodates her plurality to men's fantasies about plurality. Reducing the reflexive processes of self attained by Marivaux, Collyer is impeded by the religious and aesthetic ideology of Britain, evident in her account of the de Rosands, Marianne's guardians. Her account of their garden and aesthetic sense of landscape champions Shaftesbury and Addison. She naturalises Marivaux's text in her attribution of genteel, but heroic, deism to M de Rosand. He dies, not by falling from a horse as in Marivaux, but by fellow Catholic priests denying him liberty of conscience.[369]

Collyer's subversion of French culture by embedding British aesthetic and religious values into Marivaux's novel exemplifies translation's systemic appropriation. That marks of her version differ from those of the translation of *Le Paysan Parvenu* exposes tensions within the host or *target* literary system.[370] The rival styles of translation impose Britishness on Marivaux by privileging the modes of Richardson or Defoe. Marivaux's experimental and dialectical narrative styles are simplified by rivalry in the British literary system between sentimental and picaresque modes. Yet, if competing styles minimise Marivaux's exploration of narrative mediation, they illustrate the interpenetration of mode and ideology. Whereas Marivaux's experiments show that concepts neither motivate nor transcend narrative, the translators, by imposing systematic ideas on his fiction, succeed in illustrating how fiction resists transparency and heightening fiction's reflexive and systemic involvement of form and content.

Sterne's admission that Marivaux was a major influence on him is significant.[371] He translated Marivaux's experiments into British narrative, proving himself keen on the operation of literary systems. The truism that he is atypical and eccentric is belied by his responsiveness to Marivaux. Sterne studied keenly the romancier's explorations of fictional autobiography. The problematisation of literary rules, the reflexive relation of the theory and practice of writing, and the need to make texts resist transparent meaning are issues he will have detected in Marivaux. *Tristram Shandy* and *A Sentimental Journey* show that, like the Frenchman, Sterne did not preoccupy himself with closure or moral codes but preferred mediation as a subject in its own right. Like Marivaux, who was intrigued by the recursiveness of autobiography, Sterne entangled narrators in selfhood to elicit how contrary fictional illusions serve the identity of writers and readers.

Marivaux's influence manifests itself in the volatility of Tristram and Yorick: both express contrary views of readers, writing, and identity. About the gradual familiarity between reader and writer, Tristram says the reader and he are "perfect strangers," then, at the next instant, he calls the reader "my dear friend and companion." Categorical claims recoil on narrators: they are victims of authorship and meta-literary statements. When Tristram says that the more he writes, the more he has to write, and that "this self-same life of mine" will be "the death of me," he realises that writing, far from transcribing experience, has its own life. Seeking to capture his life, he is thrown back on the instrumentality of language, getting ensnared in narrative processes. His wish to be a unique writer, unconfined by "any man's rules that ever lived," is undone by the plural ways in which he classifies his authority. When he calls his book "this dramatic work," "this rhapsodical work," "this cyclopaedia of arts and sciences," and a work of "strict morality and close reasoning," the plurality of his text and the limitations of his literary classifications invite readers to sense the necessary conflict between respect for and rejection of narrative rules.[372]

Marivaux's psychological contraries shape Sterne's dialectical sense of autobiography. Neither Tristram nor Yorick write the story of self straightforwardly: both would figure as heroes, but attempts to triumph are self-defeating. Such recoils are not simply ironic since telling against the self is necessary to life-writing. Sterne's autobiographical dialectic is reinforced by polarities and irreverence to epistemology. The "machinery" of Tristram's life has "two contrary motions"; it is "digressive" and "progressive." While Tristram and Yorick discuss writerly contrariness, they do not steadily understand it since Sterne transgresses boundaries between narrative principle and narrative rationalisation: his narrators are often merely mouthpieces for contraries in the mode of Marivaux. While Tristram attacks the principle of closure with knowing irony on declaring his book is "more perfect and complete by wanting [a] chapter," his claim that writing is "but a different name for conversation" is sapped by constant emphasis on typography and graphic aspects of print. Sterne's challenge to philosophical stances on narrative is clear in his response to how Marivaux deals with mediating the self. Admitting "our minds shine not through the body," Tristram claims that, dipping his pen in ink, he notices "what a cautious air of sad composure and solemnity there appear'd in [his] manner of doing it." Denying transparent meaning to body one moment, he asserts it the next. By presenting opposing concepts of self-presentation like Marivaux, Sterne parodies the Richardsonian style of writing-to-the-moment, converting it into a device that invites the reader to experience the opacity of mediation.[373]

Sterne's contrary narrative moves "backwards and forwards" to "keep all tight together in the reader's fancy." Concern for readers' response means he must satirise Lockean concepts; those cannot be allowed to distract readers from the opacity of mediation. Locke's distinctions between sensation and reflection and between wit and judgment, when voiced by the narrators, cause them problems for the benefit of readers. Far from being comfortably effective in self-representation, those distinctions recoil on narrators, obliging them to see that writing is as likely to open as to close gaps between perceptual and mental awareness. So, Yorick confuses the rules of direct and reported speech, of speech and writing, and of narration and printing, as in his comically self-defeating address to Englishmen in his preface. Like Jacob and Marianne, Tristram and Yorick fuse speech and writing though they know conventions governing speech and writing are distinct. Like Marivaux's narrators too, Tristram and Yorick are variously active and passive before facts of their lives, variously schematic and whimsical about narrative order. The French and British authors give integrity to fiction by making it encompass a range of contrary ideas without relying on conceptual or systematic stances. For Sterne, as for Marivaux, narrative is provocative, absorbing, and fully itself when it defies truisms about the singular self, the equation of sensibility and moral conduct, and writing as transcription of facts and speech.[374]

Insights from Marivaux and Sterne into translation theory and the institution of literature are relevant to Defoe. From these viewpoints, Defoe is not a marginal author. His experiments with mediation anticipate Marivaux and Sterne, creating fictional procedures that were adopted and rejected by Marivaux's translators. In Defoe's fictional autobiographies, conventions of self-representation heighten readers' attention: his narrators are contradictory so that readers may appreciate mediation employing psychological and expressive contraries.[375]

Defoe prizes autobiography for ironic tensions. In *Moll Flanders*, he insists "no Body can write their own Life to the full End of it, unless they can write it after they are dead." Richardson seeks in *Clarissa* to overcome this rule, but Defoe, like Marivaux, embraces it. He prefigures Marivaux, too, in suggesting that the outset of autobiographies must be as indeterminate as their conclusion: Moll has heard the beginning of her life "related so many Ways" she cannot be "certain which is the right Account." Creating tensions between what the stories she has heard "all agree in" and what she cannot give the "least Account" of, Defoe implies that life-writing entails ignorance and knowledge as necessary polarities. The life Moll leads with her Bath lover is a "happy but unhappy Condition," and marriage to the banker sees her both "Merry" and full of "self-reproaches," the wedding making her "entirely easie" and "afraid and uneasy." The reporting of action may be as polar: Moll calls one jaunt "a Robbery and no Robbery." Writerly and experiential polarities make her see that identity is contrary. Newgate compels her to admit that "I was no more the same thing that I had been, than if I had never been otherwise than what I was now." Recovery from penal degeneracy confirms that personal continuity is relative, not absolute: "I was perfectly chang'd, and become another Body." Contraries of identity invite readers to heed narrative mediation more than characterisation. As Moll says: "I leave the Reader to improve these Thoughts, as no doubt they will see Cause, and I go on to the Fact."[376]

Evidence that Defoe did not regard autobiographical form as a transparent medium abounds in *Roxana*. The irony in this first-person novel reveals a narrative intelligence closer to Marivaux than Richardson. With a presumption like Pamela's, Roxana pretends that writing her life lets her stand outside herself and be objective about her conduct. As narrator, she claims the right to "give [her] own Character" impartially as if "speaking of another-body." This claim is soon undercut: after saying she will give "as impartial an Account of [her] Husband" as of herself, she calls him a "weak, empty-headed, untaught Creature." This criticism renders her pretended objectivity ironically reflexive. Like Marivaux's narrators, Roxana's self-objectification is always questionable. While saying of the scene in which she sits among rags in extreme poverty that the "Thing spoke itself," she elaborates how she struck sympathetic visitors: since they did not voice their feelings, she not only verbalises what she claims does not need to be described but invents how others pictured her. Thus, the relation of character and narrator in autobiography is reciprocal. This is reiterated when she describes her brother-in-law's generosity to her children: former pleasure is re-lived in the "relating it again." By making her grant both the irrecoverability of her former self and the reciprocity of character and narrator, Defoe subtly directs the reader's attention to mediation. When she describes her excruciating talk with the captain's wife, each moment of which she expected to be exposed, Roxana concedes that she cannot picture what she looked like: certain that her face betrayed her, she does not present it as such "because I cou'd not see myself." This awareness contrasts with her habit of pretending, like Marianne and Pamela, to recall what her face looked like. For example, when terrified of drowning and unable to see herself reflected in the eyes of a companion, she still pictures her face.[377]

Defoe's exploitation of unstable viewpoints in fictional autobiography links him to Marivaux and Sterne: all three hold that narrative reliability cannot be absolute, that first-person writing necessarily mixes deceit with accuracy, that withholding of self is part of self-disclosure, and that mediation yields a concept of identity that is not unitary and transcendental but plural and contrary. The several cultural and political attitudes to Marivaux voiced by British commentators provide a context for assessing how the affinities of Defoe and Sterne to the French romancier illuminate literary history. That Marivaux's narrative experiments were anticipated by Defoe and upheld by Sterne clarifies systemic contraries in the British literary institution. If some appreciated Marivaux's experiments, all commentators saw them in terms of religious and national values. If some critics praised the Frenchman's literary success, they also reduced him to a device for dignifying their culture; while others, eager to identify with Enlightenment France or to spurn it, condescended to or dismissed him in the extreme. Then again, novelists either appropriated his reputation or techniques, without candidly disclosing that they both relied on and resisted his experiments. In sum, reactions to Marivaux reveal much about polarities in the British literary system and partly explain how prejudices affected native writers committed to innovation. Since

Fielding, Burney, and Richardson naturalised Marivaux's fiction, exploiting its psychological and reflexive traits as they disowned them, inconsistency to the foreign exposes literary history's ideological stance on non-conforming domestic writers.

Defoe, Marivaux, and Sterne share an interest in narrative mediation. This interest, in disrespecting political and religious orthodoxy, explains why they receive equivocal recognition from literary history. Their experimental, playful, and subversive narrative practices render them suspect, leading to the view that Defoe is marginal and Sterne eccentric. The connections binding the three together, because they clarify systemic conflicts within literary history, help revise what that history is, how it has worked, and how it might be renewed. That, besides being read by Marivaux, Defoe set narrative standards by and against which the French author was translated offers a new context for understanding the significance of Sterne's admiration for Marivaux. Their affinities to Marivaux show how Defoe and Sterne fit into the literary history which belittled them: Defoe was as much an experimenter as Marivaux and Sterne, while Sterne's reactions to Marivaux prove the British author was more responsive to modern literature than he is said to have been. In general terms, relating what the three authors have in common to the ideological contradictions of literary history reveals how it comprises rival systems of thought to which theoretical comparisons are essential. What, at first, seems contradictory about the response of eighteenth-century writers to Marivaux can, at a second glance, be seen as contrary: literary history is not one system but a set of competing systems, the polar tensions between which are dynamic. The appropriation and rejection of Marivaux's texts in Britain together with the complicated ways in which they were informed by and influenced British texts show that geographical and temporal boundaries demarcating a given literary period may not be taken for granted. The perspectives from which Marivaux is seen here, namely, polysystem and translation theory, suggest that literary history covers territories that are still undiscovered and operates with boundaries that are not yet fully discerned. The complicated and involved naturalisation of Marivaux's texts demonstrates that narrative contraries in the British eighteenth-century literary system validate comparatists' concepts and methods concerning the revision of the theory of that literary history and improving its practice.

CHAPTER SIX
Civility and Gentility in Nineteenth-Century Novels

By 1800, the novel had advanced its identity well enough to be able to integrate Christian and secular ethics, relate natural and social history, promote civil and aesthetic sensibility, and derive comic and satirical themes from fashion, consumerism, property, and aspirations in church and army. In this context, Jane Austen self-effacingly created moving commentaries that bind personal decorum to civic responsibility and ill manners to immorality.[378] Her appreciation of rural society shaped her depiction of the inner life of worthy characters while detailing abusive attitudes to rank and class in those ruled by selfishness and false intimacy. While concern for the humane education of women affected her, the agrarian revolution encouraged her to devise a code that valued familial and community structures which Mr Knightley upholds from the start. A steward of his estate, not a mere landowner, he is a fully participating member of society. Humble and far from didactic, he keeps his critical sense of observation largely to himself, sure that events will bear him out. Most importantly, he protects and cares for women—both rich and poor, young and old—amending their foibles by example, not precept. In her feminist novel, Charlotte Brontë celebrates the inner life of a downtrodden young woman to show that female suffering may tame male brutality and reform intellectual callousness. In pained emotionality, Jane Eyre resists prejudices by turning liturgical and biblical allusions into self-dramatizing courage. Rochester, her would-be seducer and no civil landowner, is a hedonist like his namesake, the seventeenth-century poet and courtier.[379] Yet, in testing dissenting and romantic codes, Brontë risks depending on explicitly teacherly lessons. In his comic, yet melancholic fiction, Anthony Trollope tackles problems facing institutional religion by developing an aesthetics of wine, its ownership, and its consumption. Yet somewhat troubled by modish consumerism and the rise of temperance societies, he voices a dialectic that is temperate and affecting because informed by conservative and progressive stances. A chronicler opposed to popular journalism, he satirises ecclesiastical professionals but defends clerical gentility, aware that wine rituals should uphold their humanism.

George Knightley as Cultural Ideal in *Emma* (1816)

In *Observations In Husbandry* (1713), Edward Lisle (c. 1666–1722), a clerical landowner, defined a gentleman-farmer: a manager of rural affairs with "unaffected beauty and grace," he administers justice equitably, joining utility to aesthetics: he "sows wisdom and goodness" to bring forth "increase" in the folk.[380] When his son, Thomas, published this work in 1756, the agrarian revolution had passed its acme.[381] A generation later, Arthur Young (1741–1820) thought Lisle "one of the most peculiar writers" to "have appeared in the walk of literature" but found him "undoubtedly valuable": without demagoguery, he wrote "nothing but the plainest narratives."[382]

Lisle's prescriptions suit Austen's ideas of refined masculinity; George Knightley, her gentleman-farmer in *Emma*, is a chivalrous patriot who unites change to continuity, accepts new economic forces, and guides his community by opposing rigid views of hierarchy when Emma and he dispute Robert Martin's qualifications as Harriet Smith's husband.[383] He thinks his tenant a gentleman, but Emma does not. Opposing her views of rank and masculinity, Knightley sees eligibility in his tenant: he never hears "better sense from any one than Robert Martin"; he "speaks to the purpose" and is "open, straight forward, and very well judging." Upset at Emma's "infatuation" with Harriet, Knightley thinks Martin her superior "in sense as in situation," Emma denying that a farmer, even with "sense" and "merit," could be a "good match" for her "intimate friend" and evading Knightley's claim that "to be married to a respectable, intelligent gentleman-farmer" is no "degradation" of Harriet's "illegitimacy and ignorance." While he lauds Martin's "real feeling" and lack of "conceit," Emma asserts that only "a gentleman in education and manner" will satisfy Harriet. Scorning this "errant nonsense," Knightley asserts that Martin's "manners have sense, sincerity, and good-humour to recommend them; and his mind has more true gentility than Harriet Smith could understand."[384]

Grasping controversies about gentleman-farmers, Austen understood the sentimental and revolutionary ideas by which men hoped to renew patriarchy.[385] Thus, she drew on standards of masculine gentility predating the French Revolution, as allusions in *Emma* reveal. George Crabbe (1754–1832), a favoured poet, presents the controversies in "The Gentleman-Farmer." Published four years before *Emma*, the poem exposes the modish radicalism behind agricultural improvement.[386] Its protagonist, Gwyn, buys a property that he plants "far around," letting out "portions of superfluous ground / To farmers near him."[387] He despises this "dull plodding tribe" (l. 3) who tread as "their dull fathers trod" (6), their ways unchanged since before "Corn [was] sown by drill, or thresh'd by a machine"

(9–10). He copies "improvers" who claim "To fill the land with fatness" (13–14) but are social climbers who live "in large mansions ... like petty kings," treat "farms but as amusing things" (15–16), and fraternise "with lords about a breed of sheep" (17–18). His mansion is a "seat," its stately furnishings symbolic of progress (64). A demagogue, he belittles those "shackled" by custom in "mind, body, and estate" (86). He subjects medicine, law, and the church to "rules" of "reason" and "feelings" (165), abstractions allowing him "Forms to despise, professions to distrust; / Creeds to reject, pretensions to deride" (179–80). He worships Edward Gibbon (1737-1794), David Hume (1711-1776), St. John Bolingbroke (1678-1751), Lord Chesterfield, and Tom Paine (1737-1809), free-thinkers who inspired the French Revolution. Gwyn is undone since his ideas grow "As mustard quickens on a bed of dung" (215) and his mistress, opposing his "absolute command" (250), hates "free conjectures" (272). In marriage, she subjugates him to a quack doctor and a Baptist priest.[388]

By contrast, Crabbe's eulogy of Charles Manners (1754-1787), Duke of Rutland, whom he served as chaplain from 1782 to 1787, stresses there is "a taste in morality as there is in the arts." To Crabbe, Manners was a social reformer who resisted fashionable landscape design:

> It was not his delight to form a cascade or adorn a parterre, but rather to pour forth a river and to plant a desert; and a taste congenial with this was displayed in his benevolence. He was not satisfied with the relief he bestowed upon individuals, nor with joy given to a family; but he wanted to invigorate a nation, and make happy a people, and he succeeded....[389]

His ancient family forwarded agrarian and industrial invention.[390] Manners himself renewed aristocratic responsibility in the face of middle-class acquisitiveness.[391] Arguing that, despite private ownership, land remains public space and that aristocrats debase their rank if they do not advance national welfare, Crabbe voices progressive and traditional ideas, matching Austen's belief that the gentry should embody aristocratic ideals and shun fashionable consumerism.[392]

Austen observed other writers on land tenure. Richardson's *The History of Sir Charles Grandison* idealises a landed magnate, its hero a "great planter" on an estate with a radius of five miles. He settles an apothecary to provide health care for tenants. Servants "adore" him with "silent reverence," and worship him by pulling "off their hats to the ground" and bowing "their whole bodies." "Repairs are set about the moment they become necessary. By this means he is not imposed upon by incroaching or craving tenants." His "discernment" is so keen that he issues orders that few "on the spot" could conceive. He manages his Irish and English estates so well that wealth answers "the generous demands of his own heart upon his benevolence." Having studied husbandry and law on his Grand Tour to serve as "his father's steward," he conducts a "personal Survey" of each cottager, inquiring into "his circumstances, number of children, and prospects." Besides forgiving "arrears of rent," he buys back "his own farms" from men with "no prospect of success." Richardson harmonises benevolence and political economy, making Grandison a patriarchal capitalist whose husbandry is communally and nationally progressive.[393]

Austen's Martin cites Goldsmith's *The Vicar of Wakefield* since she will have seen that, in relations between Squire Thornhill, the vicar's landlord, and Burchell, the disguised Sir William Thornhill, Goldsmith probes land tenure.[394] The squire is full of "high life" and "fashionable cant." A careless, libertine huntsman, he seduces tenants' daughters by affecting benevolence while disdaining rural life. When Dr Primrose rents one of his farms, twenty acres with "little enclosures" defined by "elms and hedge rows," things seem idyllic. Local farmers, with "primæval simplicity of manners," till their land, unmarked by urban "superfluity." Yet, affectation harms the Primroses: if, at the prospect of Olivia marrying Farmer Williams, Moses, the elder son, hopes for free access to a "cyder-press and brewing tubs," they suffer "mortification" when unable to arrive at church genteelly, their plough horses unmanageable. Resisting Burchell's humanity, they put themselves in the squire's power. When the vicar cannot pay rent, the steward seizes his cattle. But Burchell helps by working on the farm, helping to save "an after-growth of hay," turning "the swath to the wind." Familiar with ballads, he roves the countryside with toys for children, saves the vicar from debtors' prison, and exposes his nephew, the squire.[395]

The economic dignity of farming is validated by *The Expedition of Humphry Clinker*; Smollett's gentleman-farmer, Matthew Bramble, is a shrewd negotiator about agricultural land. Proudly independent, he superintends his farm with "unspeakable delight" and likes to see tenants thrive. He produces beer from malt of his "own making" and "cyder" from his orchard. His bread comes from his wheat; it is ground in his mill and baked in his ovens. His "five-year old mutton" feeds on the "fragrant herbage of the mountains"; he fattens his "delicious veal"; his poultry is free-range; and rabbits come from his warren. His gardens produce "sallads, roots, and pot-herbs" from a "natural soil, prepared by moderate cultivation." His dairy's "tides of milk and cream" yield "butter, curds, and cheese" which also fatten pigs for ham and bacon. His environs yield game, trout, salmon, and oysters. Farming gives him a "tide of spirits" without "inanition." Charitably, he sells corn at a shilling a bushel "under market price," and forgives tenants who cannot make "regular payments" and poachers who claim nature intends hares for "common use."[396]

However, Bramble blames rural depopulation on "ostentation of wealth" and "affluence without taste or conduct." The "poorest squire" copies the "richest peer" by buying a town house and making "a figure with an extraordinary number of domestics" drawn from farms: "plough-boys, cow-herds, and lower hinds" flock to London and deplete rural labour. To Bramble, "*old English hospitality*" is illusory when Barnard, a college friend, is ruined by the "absurd tyranny" of a luxurious wife who stops him improving his "fortune by management and attention to the exercise of husbandry." In helping him refinance his estate, Bramble denies that a gentleman-farmer need keep horses, hounds, carriages, and servants, rejecting the prejudice that "farming [is] a mystery." Viewed by "fashionable company, as a low fellow, both in breeding and circumstances," Barnard follows "Lyle, Tull, Hart, Duhamel" on farming. He "drained bogs, burned heath, grubbed up furze and fern ... planted copse and willows where nothing else would grow ... gradually inclosed all [his] farms, and made such improvements that [his] estate now yields [him] clear twelve hundred pound a year." To Smollett, agriculture "cannot flourish where the farms are small, the leases short and the husbandman begins upon a rack rent, without a sufficient stock to answer the purposes of improvement."[397]

Agriculture is dignified in *An Inquiry into the Nature and the Causes of the Wealth of Nations* (1776), Smith urging farmers to be political economists since a farmer's revenue comes from labour and stock, and his land is "the instrument which enables him to earn the wages of this labour, and to make the profits of this stock." Taxes, salaries, pensions, and annuities are paid "either immediately or mediately from the wages of labour, the profits of stock, or the rent of land." Yet, gentlemen-farmers do not distinguish income from revenue. He who "farms part of his own estate, after paying the expence of cultivation, should gain both the rent of the landlord and the profit of the farmer." But he likely confuses rent with profit. Hence, if farmers work

> a good deal with their hands, as ploughmen, harrowers, &c. what remains
> of the crop after paying the rent, therefore, should not only replace to them
> their stock employed in cultivation, together with its ordinary profits, but
> pay them the wages which are due to them, both as labourers and overseers.

Smith values farming more than industry. The "art of the farmer," "operations of husbandry," and "many inferior branches of country labour require much more skill and experience than the greater part of mechanick trades." The iron worker handles a fixed material, but he who "ploughs the ground with a team of horses or oxen, works with instruments of which the health, strength, and temper are very different upon different occasions." This variability requires "judgement and discretion." Against such prejudices as Emma's, Smith denies that the "common ploughman" is "the pattern of stupidity and ignorance." Unlike a mechanic, he is unused to "social intercourse." His "voice and language are more uncouth and more difficult to be understood by those who are not used to them." But his understanding is "generally much superior"; "the lower ranks of people in the country are really superior to those of town." Still, tenant farmers must admit the "inferiority" of their "station." Unlike proprietors, they cannot make improvements quickly; a "large share" of their produce goes to rent. They must grant "the yeomanry are regarded as an inferior rank of people" unlike the "better sort of tradesmen and mechanics," let alone "great merchants and master manufacturers." Since "a man of any considerable stock" will not "quit [a] superior in order to place himself in an inferior station," not much "stock is likely to go from any other profession to the improvement of land." Since "great stocks" are not placed in farming by urban capitalists, agrarian advances are firstly made by "small proprietors" and only secondly by "rich and great farmers."[398]

Holding Smith's views on wealth and moral sense, Austen follows him on land tenure. His promotion of small proprietors and tenant farmers was provoked by the false claims of a self-declared improver, Thomas William Coke of Holkham (1754–1842), who represented Norfolk for fifty years in Parliament, his one defeat in 1784 when George III (1738–1820) and William Pitt (1759–1806) were victors.[399] In the year of *Emma*'s publication, Coke in the radical opposition said he had ended the old farming system: his consolidated farms and new husbandry on uncultivated land had boosted employment. The estate he inherited in 1776 had been poor since no manure was used, its sheep were the old Norfolk breed, and it had no cattle. But Young's survey of Norfolk showed that, when improvements did not predate Coke, they were achieved by tenant farmers.[400]

Smith probed farmers' traditional roles and changed debates about their progressive agency with regard to land use, social welfare, and patriotism in the years before and after Austen's birth. Royal patronage was influential too. George III created three experimental farms in Windsor Great Park. Advised by Sir Joseph Banks (1743–1820), he bred sheep from Spain for wool and mutton.[401] He corresponded with Young, editor of the *Annals of Agriculture* (1784–1815), who toured the royal farms. George resembled Burchell: comfortable with farmworkers, he encouraged their children to play cricket and football and to fly kites in the Great Park.[402]

Farming was elevated by Burke, friend to Young and patron of Crabbe. Having inherited an estate in County Cork, he bought Gregories, the former home of Edmund Waller (1606–1687) at Beaconsfield, where he grew clover.[403] An agricultural improver, he wrote to Young in the latter's capacity as secretary to the Board of Agriculture, opposing governmental regulation of day-labourers. Upholding Smith, Burke thought interference in the labour market a Jacobin illusion.[404] *Reflections on the Revolution in France* calls discussion of the "abstract right to food or medicine" pointless; what matters is the "method of procuring and administering them." Burke then lauds "the aid of the farmer and the physician, rather than the professor of metaphysics."[405]

Henry Home, Lord Kames (1696–1782), in *The Gentleman Farmer* (1779), validates farming by political economy and social psychology: agriculture is "the chief of arts" uniting "deep philosophy with useful practice." Gentry will "acquire riches to themselves" and improve Scotland if they aid tenants' agricultural efforts by "kind treatment, by instruction, by example, and by premiums." Annually inviting them to "a hearty meal," landlords would lead them to follow best practices, rewarding the most deserving with "a plough or harrows of the best construction." Like Bramble, Home sees "a throng of work" as "no hardship" to the "active spirit" of a "diligent farmer": he who "conducts his affairs properly may have hours every day, to bestow on reading, on his family, on his friends." Agriculture is "salutary to the mind" since the gentleman-farmer pays "constant attention ... to the soil, to the season, and to different operations." His daily activity and "gathering knowledge" will never "languish" from "low spirits." Farming psychologically balances perception, emotion, and reason:

> The hopes and fears that attend agriculture, keep the mind always awake, and in an enlivening degree of agitation. Hope never approaches certainty so near, as to produce security; nor is fear ever so great, as to create deep anxiety and distress. Hence it is, that a gentleman farmer, tolerably skilful, never tires of his work; but is as keen the last moment as the first.

Since no "occupation rivals agriculture, in connecting private interest with that of the public," each step a farmer takes "for his own good, promotes that of his country!" Like Burke, Home values aesthetics. A gentleman-farmer "disposed to embellish his fields" executes "that pleasing work at the cheapest rate, by employing upon it his farm servants and cattle, every vacant hour." No nabob "impatient for enjoyment," his "refined pleasure of embellishments, arises from a slow progress; which affords leisure to feast the eye upon every new production."[406]

In having Martin read the "Agricultural Reports," Austen shows that Knightley guides his tenant to respect the great agrarian authority. Young, like Austen, explored relations between tradition and progress. One writer whom he found "sensible" was Richard Bradley (1688–1732), professor of botany at Cambridge.[407] To Bradley, a farmer is "a Person whose Business depends more upon the Labour of the Brain, than of the Hands." With keen observation and "right Judgment," farmers gain "good Fortunes" and live "hospitably." Studying "the Nature of every Soil" and learning "to improve one sort by another," a farmer is a "Philosopher."[408] Young disliked Tull for belittling farmworkers: Tull bought his farm "when Plough-Servants first began to exalt their Dominion over their Masters, so that a Gentleman-Farmer was allow'd to make but little Profit of his Arable Lands." The drill he invented to plant crops in rows and maximise seed viability replaced hand sowing. Oxen pulled his seed-drill since servants overfed horses to gall masters.[409] Young judged Tull "the most famous of modern cultivators" who saw "with wonderful quickness the omissions of all preceding writers, and yet split upon one of the rocks he had so much condemned in others ... he composed a folio of reflections, instructions, and opinions which might be just and well founded but carried not with them the proofs of their propriety."[410]

Young's opposition to mechanised farming shows in his view of William Ellis (1700–1758), an equipment distributor, who, like Tull, promoted industrial "Plowing and Sowing." Ellis details "the several Operations of Broad, Bout, Ridge, and Drill-work, by the Two-wheel, One-wheel, Foot, and Three-wheel, and Pulley Drill-ploughs, Horse-breaks, and Sheims, &c.," given his acquisitiveness: "causing Ewes to take Ram at any Time, and lamb twice a year" and producing "the Flesh of suckling Calves ... by several artificial Ways" is easy and profitable. Farmers may learn to produce "dainty Food House-lamb all the Year" in the mode of London. Despite not being widely accepted, Ellis boasts his machines were "serviceable Instruments." In equanimity, Young said Ellis's "husbandry writings" were full of "rubbish" but still contain "more useful common knowledge than half the books of husbandry at present more fashionable."[411]

Another pioneer in agriculture who foretold farming's social worth, Lisle appealed to Young in ways relevant to *Emma*. To Lisle, fashion impeded "honourable conceptions of a country life" that "might engage our gentlemen of the greatest abilities in parts and learning, to live upon and direct the management of their estates." The "yeomanry of England," once "the boast of the nation" and "necessary link in the chain of government, as having an immediate connection with the gentleman on the one side, and the labourer on the other ... have caught the infection" of "mimicking ... their betters." Improving husbandry's image is hard, and it no longer "ranked among the liberal arts" but is seen as the "high road" to ruin. To Lisle, "God is walking" in fields where he visits farmers "with his grace." Since husbandry gives farmers stronger nerves and bones than town-dwellers, Lisle praises rural life in ways Austen follows: townspeople whose commercial interest is widespread have weak ties to neighbours, but the gentleman-farmer "must unavoidably concern himself with the families of the farmers and labourers round about him, and with the tradesmen of the neighbouring towns and villages."[412]

Philip Miller (1691–1771), who translated Duhamel du Monceau's treatise on farming, led Young to study the Frenchman. Du Monceau valued spatial limits: a "refined Husbandry which requires particular care and attention, scrupulously adhered to, may succeed in a small farm, under the eye of an assiduous and intelligent proprietor." Like Burke, he warns there are too many "Theorists who, without having any real knowledge in Husbandry, from their desks pretend to trace systems and lay down rules to Husbandmen, which being merely ideal, too often lead those astray who put any confidence in them." Urging bad customs be "rooted out" by "slow degrees," Du Monceau tells proprietors to improve soil fertility. If not, they remain "simple occupiers" whose "sole view is to make as much as possible of the lands they hold, without regarding how much they impoverish them." Sound landowners increase "their rents" by bringing "works to perfection," but "rich undertakers who engage for rent" harm estates; "mercenary wretches ... spoil the woods, neglect manuring meadows," and ruin "Farmers and poor Cottagers." When the latter cannot pay, "their corn, cattle, and implements of Husbandry, &c. are seized" so that "these undertakers can make a large profit of their leases ... Their obdurate and covetous hearts are utterly insensible to the complaints of the poor wretches they ruin. How different is such a way from that of the good and humane Landlords."[413]

Farming led Young to laud *Essays on Husbandry* (1764) by Walter Harte (1709–1774).[414] Harte scorns "paper-helps about interest, money, bullion"; capitalisation of farmland must be replaced by the provident living of our forbears who preferred "native conveniences of life" to "materials of pride and luxury from abroad." To Harte, rural life demands "full employment for country-labourers." The "breaking up and bringing into culture large portions of ground, formerly waste and neglected" is "an acquisition of value to every state; for such tracts of ground properly managed ... will afford additional employment and subsistence" to many. But custom blocks such reform. Since our parents "neglected to cultivate their lands in person, or establish sufficient laws for the encouragement of husbandry, we, their descendants, adopt the same ideas and conduct without hesitation." The "art" of farming is not "esteemed" since "our parents, not positively, but indirectly, infused in us a distaste for it, and the government has not thought fit … to awaken the husbandman's attention by a proper number of rewards and inducements." Society must realise that "All states owe more to agriculture than any other profession of life."[415] Such sentiments appealed not only to Smollett and Young but to Austen.

Young holds with Burke on agriculture. As he states, "application of theory to matters of government" is "a surprizing imbecility in the human mind," the "science of legislation" and agriculture needing experimentation and induction; "I have been too long a farmer to be governed by any thing but events; I have a constitutional abhorrence of theory, of all trust in abstract reasoning; and consequently a reliance merely on experience, in other words, on events, the only principle worthy of an experimenter."[416] Young calls clover, "one of the grand pillars of British agriculture; insomuch that vast numbers of our husbandmen would be totally unable to pay their rents without the use of it" but it is "utterly unknown by the common farmers in many counties"; "our books of husbandry" praise clover but are "barren enough of real and important trials."[417]

Du Monceau and Burke moved Young to resist "fiery *exclusive* advocates" for new or old husbandry. To Young, Tull was a "prejudiced writer": he thought "the old husbandry totally inadequate to the wants of mankind." But the "spirit of drilling died with Mr. Tull, and was not again put in motion till within a few years." Disputes about "the value of the old and new methods" show Tull's "mode of sowing" not "in common use." His drills do not do what they were meant to perform. Not only are they flimsy, costly, and difficult to procure, but, since seeds must be planted at various depths, no one plough could sow different seeds. Adequate on a few experimental acres, his drill would not last a week on a hard-working farm. To Young, no more than "fifty acres of drilled corn" are found in "the whole island of Great-Britain." Another issue with the new husbandry is the "constant attention" to ploughing, harrowing, and sowing caused by the drill. The old husbandry of broadcasting wheat and water-furrowing let farmers move to other tasks until harvest, but horse-hoeing fills the "water-furrows," so they must be "opened afresh" at great cost. Such husbandry will never enjoy "great progress" given uneven labour demands. Unsuited to wheat, barley, oats, and peas, the drill is fit only for beans and turnips.[418]

In *Annals of Agriculture*, Young, belittling "the old system of restriction, prohibition, and monopoly," promotes "new ideas of reciprocal intercourse and mutual benefit" to "our shallow politicians."[419] This journal presents "An Idea of an Experimental Farm" which, inviting King George to found a farming institute, expounds economic and aesthetic ideas germane to Austen. Young laments that the "happiest of kingdoms" has "millions of acres" of "desarts" since "the mode, conduct, expenses, and profits of cultivating" are unknown, and "questionable points" of "wretched cultivation" in most counties are not "ascertained by experiments." He has in mind country estates given over to "Mr. Brown's winding walks" which pass through acres of "shrubs and velvet lawn" devoid of providing food for "the mind as well as the eye."[420] While Shenstone's ornamental farm, The Leasowes, models utility and beauty, "the present system of decorating ground" lacks "variety of effect."[421] Landscape brings "to the eye a succession of the same images which please this year as they pleased the last, without novelty in the cause, or increase of pleasure in the effect." The "decoration of landskip" shuns social, political, and intellectual sense:

> The beauty of a mere garden-scene is like that of a meer fine face ... It holds little conversation with you; it suggests no new ideas; it furnishes no food to the inquisitive mind ... But when the ornamented walks lead you to something that offers novel information with every season: when you are in the pursuit of unknown facts, to ascertain which, is to promote not your own solitary pleasures and contemplation only, but a science intimately connected with the prosperity of a nation: when every inclosure is pregnant with instruction.... Compared with such an application of a tract of land, what are parks and gardens, shrubberies and decorated grounds, but so many baubles to please children?

In comprehending eighteenth-century views on the improvement of land, Young anticipates how Austen presents the humanistic and cultural values of Knightley's estate.[422]

Austen likely knew Young had been defamed as a farmer who was blind to improvements.[423] In *Review of the Corrected Agricultural Survey of Lincolnshire* (1800), Thomas Stone (d. 1815), bitter about the rejection of his survey, attacked the Board of Agriculture for trusting "the puny efforts of a single individual" and limiting itself to "the feeble and confined endeavours of a private society." Young, says Stone, has an "ill-earned literary reputation." His work for the Board contains "little accurate information" about the "present scarcity and dearth of provisions." Stone hints that Young's editing of "Agricultural Reports" was motivated by fear of stirring farmers to "democratical sedition."[424] Yet, others, who revised the reports, admired Young. Nathaniel Kent (1737–1810) updated the survey for Norfolk, the most agriculturally advanced county. To him, the reports were an ongoing project intended to excite the "intelligent cultivators of the kingdom." He also warned that gentlemen-farmers "neglected the most obvious improvements upon old branches of their estate" and that the "increase of large farms" has a "bad tendency."[425] Austen favoured small, mixed, family farms for the social integrity they gave to rural life.

Since "production of food is the real, serious business of Mr. Knightley's life," he is unique in "the Jane Austen canon."[426] He "epitomizes the virtuous landowner praised by Arthur Young, his spirit of exertion and independence energized under wartime pressure."[427] Saying his name and house "express, without too much subtlety, achievement, age, and of course chivalry," one critic charges Austen with nostalgia, alleging she values the picturesque over the productive and evades issues of landscape aesthetics. She is said to minimise "the perception of difference of rank" in Knightley's relations with Martin and to participate, like Burke, "in the evil she attacks." Another claims she privileges "the pastoral and horticultural over the arable."[428] Such charges are untenable. In giving the "simple story" of his tenant's successful proposal to Harriet, Knightley admits that Martin's "rank in society" is "an evil" he would alter if he could. Nor is Austen single-minded about agriculture; she expects imaginative work from readers in grasping textual implications. *Emma* exercises inferential habits against dogmatic statements about agricultural ideology.[429] As Austen's prayers show, she upheld "a community of believers," her "moral and spiritual terrain" radiating beyond the "elegant houses" of the gentry.[430] Her location of Knightley in the agricultural and political economy sees him engaged and self-effacing, committed to social action and self-correcting.[431] Justice of the peace and parish administrator, he is a keen observer, a strong thinker, an affectionate mentor, and a conscientious agent. If formal and reserved, he is emotional, imaginative, and intuitive.[432] Owning the largest estate in Highbury, he embodies high standards of hospitality and philanthropy in tending the community.[433]

He explains his "modes of agriculture" to Harriet, but we infer his estate management. Steward of Donwell Abbey, he is an older brother whose "local information" must interest John who has spent "the longest part of his life" on the estate; Knightley lives in the imagination of handing it on to John's offspring. Like George III and Burchell, he plays with children: he tosses nieces and nephews "up to the ceiling in a very frightful way," according to Mr Woodhouse. On meeting his lawyer brother, his "communicative" temper comes to the fore. As magistrate, he consults John on points of law or tells administrative anecdotes; as farmer, managing "the home-farm at Donwell," he details his plans, telling "what every field was to bear next year." He engages his brother in the "plan of a drain, the change of a fence, the felling of a tree, and the destination of every acre for wheat, turnips, or spring corn." These details make him a modern farmer who grows arable and fodder crops in rotation.[434] He extends his acreage by draining wet lands; he is prepared to reshape enclosed fields; and he harvests timber tree-by-tree. Producing food for the estate, the immediate community, and distant markets, he is as balanced in farming as in character, as shown by his sheep raising and in which he encourages his tenant. Income from Martin's "large farm" comes from competitively raising sheep. His tenant's "very fine flock" spurs buyers to pay more for his wool than for anybody else's in "the country."[435]

That Knightley is an exemplary sheep farmer is clear from the Gentleman Farmer's *Enquiry* of 1782. Arguing that "inclosing of Commons" ploughs up "sweet Grass" and cuts the production of "fine Wools," it decries "Advocates for inclosing" and "their Opponents" for not informing Parliament about the "Variety" of commons. It complains that, since "Sheep-grazing is the most Gentlemanly Kind of Farming," being more profitable than "other Kinds of Cultivation," wealthy farmers enlarge farms at the expense of small ones who "in general cannot afford to purchase a Flock of Sheep sufficient to pen upon the Land." It recommends that men of "ample Fortune, and public Spirit ... set the Example of allowing ... poor Farmers a Year, or even two Years Rent always in Arrear," so they may lay out money "in keeping a Flock of Sheep"; they would render "a most essential Service to their Country" and "themselves."[436]

Knightley follows Smith. Fully invested in his farm, he extracts no capital from it because he will not display himself fashionably as landlord of Donwell Abbey. With "little spare money," he keeps no carriage horses.[437] He goes on foot or horseback. His healthy living is frugal. His household is small: a house-keeper and a steward. His frugality affords altruism. Besides hiring a carriage to take Miss Bates, Mrs Bates, and Jane to the ball, he sends them apples—"the very finest for baking"—with none of Mr Woodhouse's bad instructions. Supervising his orchard, Knightley sends a sack of "keeping" apples every year.[438] His productivity keeps this orchard as "famous" as in Mrs Bates's "younger days." He sends the ladies extra apples "before they get good for nothing," claiming to have "many more" than he can use and happy that his steward, William Larkins, let him keep "a larger quantity than usual." Larkins, minding his "master's profit," does not fault this liberality since much fruit is marketed. Mrs Hodges, the house-keeper, is not pleased that Larkins carries "the same sort of apples, a bushel at least," to the Bateses. With none "left to bake or boil," she regrets "her master should not be able to have another apple-tart this spring." That he does not jealously guard table supplies and that his retainers serve him faithfully equates household economy to civility. Respect for servants makes it natural that he "would rather be at home, looking over William Larkins's week's account" than looking on at a ball.[439]

No slave to profit, Knightley joins sociability to productivity. His farm is a social vocation. When Mr Woodhouse irritates John, Knightley discusses farm issues to calm his brother: he repeats his "idea of moving the path to Langham, of turning it more to the right that it may not cut through the home meadows" but enlarge his pasture without inconveniencing Highbury. Honouring rights of way and domestic peace, he consults John about the "present line of the path" by turning "to our maps" at the Abbey. He treats the landscape neither arbitrarily nor modishly. When Mrs Elton invites herself to Donwell, he creates a sociable event: his guests eat strawberries that are "ripening fast," his estate "famous for its strawberry-beds." They then take cold meat in the dining-room, Emma reminding herself of Donwell's architecture and landscape. The size and style of the house are "respectable"; it fits the landscape, being "suitable, becoming, [a] characteristic situation, low and sheltered." Its gardens are "ample"; they reach "meadows washed by a stream." There are no improvements; the stream, barely visible from the house, reflects "all the old neglect of prospect." There is "timber in rows and avenues, which neither fashion nor extravagance had rooted up."[440] Unlike Hartfield, the house covers "a good deal of ground"; it is "rambling and irregular, with many comfortable and one or two handsome rooms." To Emma, it is ideal "as the residence of a family of such true gentility, untainted in blood and understanding." She re-discovers Donwell's "pleasure grounds," Knightley not boastfully guiding guests. The grounds offer a "charming walk" in "a broad avenue of limes." Enjoying the scenery, she does not fully grasp its implications. Donwell is close to Abbey-Mill Farm. She had supposed the latter an isolated place to which Harriet would be "banished" by marrying Knightley's tenant. But the Martins' farm is at the "bottom of a wooded bank" with "meadows in front and the river making a close and handsome curve around it." She praises the scene—"the rich pastures, spreading flocks and orchard"—patriotically: "It was a sweet view—sweet to the eye and the mind. English verdure, English culture, English comfort, seen under a sun bright, without being oppressive." Walking to "the old Abbey fish-ponds" and almost "as far as the clover which was to be begun cutting on the morrow," she ignores agricultural signs. Besides being stocked with fish for the house, the ponds irrigate the fields, and the clover to be harvested as a fodder crop produces green manure in rotation and fixes nitrogen in the soil.[441]

Weighty implications arise from Abbey-Mill Farm. The house has "*two* parlours" and a "broad, neat gravel-walk" leading to the front door with "espalier apple-trees" on either side of the walk. A handsome summer-house is "large enough to hold a dozen people."[442] Such features signal that its yeoman family is sociable.[443] The espaliered trees show it horticulturally improves its rented property. Labour-intensive espaliering requires knowledge of shoot and bud formation and of pruning. According to Bradley, "whoever delights in Gardens will not be without espaliers of [apple-trees], as well for the sake of the great quantity of Fruit they will produce, as for the Ornament they afford to a Garden, and the good Shelter they yield to all the under Race of Kitchen-Garden Plants which are encompass'd with them."[444] The Martins' home life is well-rooted; they have had the same "upper maid" for twenty-five years. The food they produce ties them to the community. Mrs Martin sends the "finest goose" from her flock to Mrs Goddard. They have a herd of "eight cows, two of them Alderneys, and one little Welch cow," thus give away or market butter, milk, and cream. Emma sees Harriet will find "security, stability, and improvement" there, being "retired enough for safety, and occupied enough for cheerfulness."[445]

Before she sees his farm, her prejudices about the Martins, the yeomanry, and farming fill the narrative with issues expounded in agricultural texts. Emma knows the Martins live "creditably" as Knightley's tenants but thinks they "must be coarse and unpolished, and very unfit" associates for her *protégée*, who is "almost quite perfect" but for a small lack of knowledge and elegance. Overpraising Harriet, Emma stands off from the Martins as from "another set of beings." She hides her snobbish hypostasis of economic status and rank by describing the "yeomanry" as "precisely the order of people" with whom she can have nothing to do and by seeing Martin as economically above her notice as he is socially "below it." Since the Woodhouses have no "landed property," their "fortune" coming "from other sources," such as government bonds, she spurns Martin for not being "beforehand with the world" since he has "his fortune entirely to make." His property, she flippantly claims, must be "all afloat, all employed in his stock, and so forth." Pretending to economic sense, she claims "it is next to impossible that he should have realised any thing yet." But their farm tells us the Martins are astute yeomen. Emma's superiority rests in her belief that they are not conspicuous consumers who can treat Harriet properly. Sorry that Knightley's investment in farming stops him keeping a carriage, she thinks one befits "the owner of Donwell Abbey," such consumerism defining gentility to her.[446]

Emma holds prejudices about the physique and voice of farmers that match Smith's observations. On first seeing Martin, she voices pejorative clichés: an "entire want of gentility" renders him "so very clownish, so totally without air." Added to his "awkward look and abrupt manner," his voice is uncouth, being "wholly unmodulated." She doubts improvement: "He will be a completely gross, vulgar farmer – totally inattentive to appearances, and thinking of nothing but profit and loss." Her incoherence is notable: having told Harriet that he must be poor, not be rich for a long time, and never be genteel, she says he is

> a great deal too full of the market to think of any thing else – which is just as it should be, for a thriving man. What has he to do with books? And I have no doubt that he will thrive and be a very rich man in time – and his being illiterate and coarse need not disturb *us*.

Her sense of style is as dubious. His letter of proposal is "much above her expectation"; it contains "no grammatical errors"; its "composition" is gentlemanly; it is "strong and unaffected," its "sentiments" creditable. It expresses "good sense, warm attachment, liberality, propriety, even delicacy of feeling." Unable to degrade it by saying "one of his sisters must have helped him" because the letter is "too strong and concise" to be a woman's, she grants that Martin is "a sensible man" with a "natural talent" for expression. But, having corrected herself, she presumes to know his "sort of mind"—one in which "thoughts naturally find proper words." In claiming to know vigorous male minds "with sentiments to a certain point, not coarse," she prevaricates garrulously, like tiresome Miss Bates. Her crude verbosity is renewed when she tells Harriet that by living at Abbey-Mill Farm she will confine herself "to the society of the illiterate and vulgar." Despite the Martins are "well meaning, worthy people," she urges "the evils of the connection." Eventually she sees the "folly" of dissuading Harriet from marrying "the unexceptionable young man" who will place her "in the line of life to which she ought to belong."[447]

To satirise Emma, Austen somewhat parallels the Martins and Woodhouses. Both families read the *Elegant Extracts*, anthologies for schoolchildren.[448] Emma is no mature reader; she has not finished a "course of steady reading"; lacking "industry and patience," she will not subject "the fancy to the understanding." A poor mentor, she would improve Harriet's "mind, by a great deal of useful reading and conversation" but never gets beyond "a few first chapters, and the intention of going on to-morrow." Ironically, Emma has affinities with the Martins and Knightley that root her in agricultural society. She belittles Martin's riding in the countryside like Burchell to get Harriet "walnuts," but, in drawing Harriet to Mr Elton's house, she gladly gets "intimately acquainted with all the hedges, gates, pools, and pollards of this part of Highbury." Since the Woodhouses keep "porkers" that let her father boast of "Hartfield pork," she sends the Bateses a "whole hind-quarter," expecting the leg to be salted and the loin "dressed directly." She is truly hospitable; while he imposes on guests his notion that suppers are "unwholesome," she supplies them "in a much more satisfactory style." Knightley views her as a hostess capable of serving Mr Elton "the best of the fish and chicken." She knows what benefits invalids in "arrow-root of a very superior quality." That match-making for Harriet and scandalmongering with Frank Churchill impede her rural sensibility is owing to false models of gentility and masculinity.[449]

At first, she thinks Mr Elton a "pattern" and "model"; his "gentleness" of manners seems to make them superior to those of Knightley and Mr Weston. When Knightley warns of Elton's acquisitiveness, far from examining the latter's effusiveness, she tells herself Knightley does not understand "the influence of a strong passion at war with all interested motives." Her interior discourse is doubly ironic: Elton lacks passion, and Knightley, having studied its powers, knows he "could not reason" with Martin when the latter is "a man in love." Emma's sense of gallantry blinds her to Churchill's "manoeuvring and finessing." Viewing masculinity in terms of a man doing his duty with "vigour and resolution" and accusing Churchill of having "no English delicacy towards the feelings of other people," Knightley uses terms Emma voices but does not observe.[450]

Knightley is humane and genteel. An acute, sensitive, self-correcting interpreter, he sees "symptoms of intelligence" passing between Jane and Churchill which he cannot measure but which, "having once observed," he cannot tell himself are "entirely void of meaning." Free from "Emma's errors of imagination," he admits his suspicions yet is moved to silence by her "confidence" they are groundless. Since they are acute intuitions, this productive farmer is far from engrossed in agricultural and market facts. His "cheerful manner" inspirits Mr Woodhouse and others. He mentors Emma well since he tells her of her "faults." He upholds domesticity, sensing Miss Taylor's "comfortable provision" from being "settled in a home of her own." He is a romantic. Loving "to look at" Emma and sure she is not "personally vain," he believes she would benefit from falling in love and being "in some doubt of a return." He does not see himself as a love object, lacking the vanity of Elton and Churchill who simply assume their sexual appeal.[451]

Emma is less romantic than Knightley; after the *débâcle* with Elton, she claims she cannot "change for the better" and that, were she to marry, she "must expect to repent it." When she plays at being in love with Churchill, she does not see—even with his hints—that his gallantry is a screen. Yet, when Knightley moves to kiss her hand, she regrets that he desists, his gallantry "simple" and "dignified." By then, Isabella has made her admit his attractiveness by fearing he might marry Jane. As former governess and pupil discuss his hiring of the carriage for the Bateses, Emma realises his "humanity" typifies one likely "to do any thing really good-natured, useful, considerate, or benevolent." She admits that "for an act of un-ostentatious kindness, there is nobody whom I fix on more than Mr. Knightley." Yet, perversely resisting Isabella's hint about Jane and Knightley, Emma cannot imagine him marrying; he cannot have "the least idea of it":

> Why should he marry? – He is as happy as possible by himself; with his farm, and his sheep, and his library, and all the parish to manage; and he is extremely fond of his brother's children. He has no occasion to marry, either to fill up his time or his heart.

She thinks him a bachelor farmer until the ball where his physique strikes her: "His tall, firm, upright figure," she admits, "must draw every body's eyes." His "gentlemanlike" and "natural grace" is manifest when he dances. That he leaves his home because of her father's fear of housebreakers shows him self-effacing and unbound by gender. Believing "A man would always wish to give a woman a better home than the one he takes her from," he goes back on this truism, as Emma concedes when feeling that "in quitting Donwell, he must be sacrificing a great deal of independence of hours and habits."[452] It is an amusing preparation for the denouement that she hides her excitement on discovering that Knightley is not in love with Harriet by pretending to doubt his certainty about Martin's successful proposal. Evasively, yet playfully, she suggests that Knightley will have mistaken what Martin said since they must have been "talking of other things; of business, shows of cattle, or new drills … the dimensions of some famous ox." As the wife of a humane gentleman-farmer, such agricultural topics will fill her married life.[453]

Spiritualised Drama in *Jane Eyre* (1847)

Charlotte Brontë gives her heroine in *Jane Eyre* natural gentility and vague spirituality such that Barbara Hardy finds character and conduct radically incongruous.[454] Hardy thinks Brontë misunderstands spiritual autobiography and, in unfolding Jane's psychological and social awareness, simply assumes a growing religious sense in that awareness. Seeing no relation between young Jane's religious views and the narrator's spiritual condition, Hardy calls Jane's personal and spiritual progress uncertain.[455] Questions stem from this criticism: does Jane's religiosity derive less from dramatized conscience than from unrealised assumptions; does Brontë ignore Jane's spiritual development except in crises that rely on divine law; does Jane claim grace without examining herself so that Brontë fails to treat faith as a human problem?[456]

An answer to the first must grant that Brontë details Jane's education through allusions she either articulates or contemplates. As character and narrator, Jane voices more biblical and liturgical than secular texts. An answer to the second must admit that Brontë insists on Jane's orthodox training and sensibility by emphasising her religious knowledge. Her allusions convey dramatic ironies that heighten her awareness of biblical values. Brontë creates thematic implications from tensions in religious sense that Jane's allusions embody. An answer to the third is unsure. If Brontë's authorial responsibility is greater than Hardy estimates, her theology is dubious. Paradoxically, her book's flaws are attributable to her wish to establish dialectic in Jane's character more than to any specific fictional necessity.[457] Her efforts to derive themes from allusions suggest that Brontë struggles with the nature of faith.

Still, she details the religious forms to which Jane is exposed. First presented as seeking to escape oppression and injustice by cultivating fancy and viewing the world in literary and pictorial terms, Jane has to confront religious ideas that inform the rest of her life.[458]

Preached at by the Reeds' servants, she must face original sin and "corruption." Thus, she confesses to being "a defective being, with many faults and few redeeming points." Tested at Gateshead by Mr Brocklehurst, her "ready and orthodox" replies follow the catechism. Her reaction to his tenet of converting an evil heart is shrewdly critical of complacency. Since childhood is founded on the Bible and Book of Common Prayer at Lowood, her religious ideas are reinforced. Meals, preceded by a "long grace" and hymn, are followed by thanksgiving and another hymn; Sunday evenings are given to learning the catechism and the Sermon on the Mount. Resisting lengthy religious forms and irritated by Brocklehurst's facile ideas about grace and primitive Christianity, she looks at herself and the world through her religious training. When she reacts against the "Babel clamour" of classmates and compares the pasteboard stuck on Helen to a "phylactery," she employs biblical acuity. That she is at ease with how training has informed her habits is clear on her arrival at Thornfield: hoping to find a "safe haven," she offers up "thanks where thanks were due" and implores aid on her "further path."[459]

Self-mortification confirms her religiosity; she depreciates her appearance by calling it "Quaker-like." At Thornfield, she dresses in "Quaker trim." She values asceticism when refusing Mr Rochester's jewellery and insists on remaining his "plain, Quakerish governess." Quaker references do not signal dissent from Christian traditions; they reflect self-respect rather than unorthodox spirituality. Jane does not embody Quakerism. Hence, with unjustifiable indignation, she sees Grace Poole as a fiendish hypocrite with "the demureness of a Quakeress." Dislike of Grace leads her to call Mrs Poole a Quaker when the latter describes providence acting through second causes—a view against Quaker belief. Jane overlooks this, concerned with seeing Quaker demureness as a type of hypocrisy which casts doubt on the times she refers to herself as a Quaker. Despite this irony, Jane's Quaker references uphold her religious training. When she disapproves of Eliza Reed's view that the rubric is the most valuable part of the Book of Common Prayer, Jane is an orthodox Anglican who trusts to the spirit in the letter of church law.[460]

Her orthodoxy is roused by setting. The symbolism of her environs implies the influence of church architecture. Lowood offers a "churchlike aspect," its garden being "convent-like." When excluded from the party at Thornfield, she finds the schoolroom a "sanctum," and, citing Psalm 46, she intensifies the architectural reference by describing it as "a very pleasant refuge in time of trouble." The spiritual reflexivity of her reactions to setting is questionable, however. At issue is not formal education or biblical knowledge but the function of analogies and the degree to which the church shapes imagination. Back at Thornfield after Mrs Reed's death, Jane is moved to view the western sky "as if there was a fire lit, an altar burning behind its screen of marbled vapour." Returning to Rochester leads her to superimpose the image of a sanctuary on the sunset that associates him with natural and ritual splendour. But she stops herself symbolising the house as home. There is little tension between symbolic enthusiasm and restraint, nor are there narrative implications about the "golden redness" of the sunset and the fire that destroys Thornfield. Problematically, Jane seems creative in her application of symbolism, responsible in restraining it, and intuitive by its occurrence, although there is no autobiographical structure for dealing with the abrupt change in character from the narrative stance. Still, Brontë presents, as a characteristic feature, Jane's impulse to associate emotional needs with religious imagery when the latter is subject to irony. Another example occurs just before Jane provokes Rochester to confess his passion and describes the garden at Thornfield as "Eden-like" and the floral scents as the "sacrifice of incense." Despite irony in the name "Thornfield" and her later awareness that the house could only have been "a temporary heaven," no comment addresses the effort to endow the house and grounds with Edenic, ritual associations. If the lightning strike on the horse-chestnut providentially signals Rochester's appropriation of divine sanction, it does not unsettle Jane's symbolising. That she sometimes heightens experience through ecclesiastical symbols is evident when she compares the stillness of Ferndean to "a church on a week-day." Since she habitually relates emotional needs to the church, how does Brontë incorporate, in the autobiographical form, commentary on the value of religious symbols?[461]

One answer may lie in biblical typology; Jane has such a sense, yet it is inconsistent. Studying old-fashioned furniture on Thornfield's third storey, she is alert to emblems; she regards the discarded pieces as "effigies" and "relics." They render the third storey a "shrine of memory." The ancient chests are "types of the Hebrew ark." But emblems do not prevent her from fearing the third storey. That Bertha Mason, with her unholy past, lives there displaces notions of divine covenant arising from the emblem of the ark, Brontë's gothic sense clashing with Jane's symbols. Another example of her emblems being undone by Gothicism occurs when, after Jane declares she would give her life to save Rochester, he asks her to tend the injured Mason. Locked into one of the "mystic cells" on the third storey and fearing for her safety in a way that ironically qualifies her declaration about Rochester, she cares for Mason in a manner that seemingly re-enacts the Crucifixion. She dips her hand "again and again in the basin of blood and water," wiping away the "trickling gore." Doing so, she dwells on the great cabinet, the panels of which figure the carved heads of the twelve apostles with an "ebon crucifix and a dying Christ" above. But her figural sense is muddled: her frightened awareness of Judas as Satan's agent, while appropriate to the horror, displaces Christ's sacrifice for mankind and stops her examining her spiritual state.[462]

Her figural sense is laudable compared to Grace Ingram's; the latter has suffered "martyrdom" at the hands of governesses and thanks God to have done with them. Grace's false piety and social pride make Jane's refusal to suffer the "martyrdom" of a loveless marriage to St John Rivers praiseworthy. Still, there is no clear relation between Jane's sensibility and application of emblems. Neither as character nor narrator is she led to meditation or fortified against superstition by them. When she sees nothing symbolic about the rending of the veil in her dream and is too easily soothed by Rochester's prevaricating explanation, we might ask why she did not recall the Temple at Jerusalem and challenge Rochester's explanation. Again, it is surprising that, when she saves him from fire in his bed by baptising him with water and calling on "God's aid" and when he gives her "anathemas," calling her "witch" and "sorceress" and summoning the "elves in Christendom" to enlighten him, she does not heed their spiritual differences. Her emblematic sense does not prompt her to judge him as she should. Instead, as exemplified when she views Adèle as an "emblem" of her past and Rochester as the "type" of her future, her typology is vague and self-dramatising, preventing a spiritual outlook.[463]

Since typology does not structure Jane's autobiography, what it says about her sensibility is moot. No doubt, Brontë wished typology to reflect well on her heroine. Thus, Jane soon recognises the charade which Grace and Rochester perform, her sense of the history of Israel tracing it to the story of Eliezer and Rebecca. Typology restrains her fantasies of Rochester. When she tries to reach "the hills of Beulah," judgment stops her personalising the emblem: delirium alone would equate the promised land with marriage. Typology also rouses narrative wit. Recalling that pupils at Lowood fell asleep during boring sermons, she notes this re-enacted "the part of Eutychus": the girls fell not from the third loft but from the fourth form; as Paul raised Eutychus from the dead, so they were picked up half-dead from exhaustion. But typology often occasions irony. Recounting her battle with Mrs Reed, Jane cites the twofold "emblem" of the "lighted" and "black and blasted" heath to depict the fierceness of revenge and the wretchedness of remorse. This non-biblical emblem relates to dramatic forestall. When, loving her doll, she dotes on "a faded graven image," the allusion says little about her in the face of propaganda about the inherently sound instincts of children and casualness about her idolatry of Rochester. Her unsteady emblematic sense matches attitudes to people. She reacts to Helen Burns, Rochester, and Rivers with a weak religious sensibility. Given her knowledge of the catechism and the Sermon on the Mount, Jane is oddly surprised by what she calls Helen's "doctrine of endurance." To return good for evil and to love one's enemies are less Helen's doctrines than tenets of Christ's Sermon. Jane resists these tenets by attending more to Helen's person than to the superior light in which Helen regards doctrinal matters. Later, warning Rochester that he attends too much to people and too little to divine truth, she seems not to internalise this warning made to her by Helen. Given how much original sin and damnation have been preached to her, she does not question Helen's unorthodox view that God permits no soul to be damned.[464]

While she finds Helen exemplary, this hardly affects her. When Jane stands on the "pedestal of infamy" before Brocklehurst, Helen tacitly urges her to endure the humiliation. But the "extraordinary sensation" and "new feeling" that Helen's smile encourages does not stay with Jane: she likens the smile to "a reflection from the aspect of an angel" but gives into despair when Helen leaves the schoolroom. In later scenes, she is alert to Helen's spiritual intensity, but alertness does not renew her own spirituality. She may apply Solomon's proverb that love with poverty is better than hatred with riches to her admiration for Helen and Miss Temple, but she does not model herself on it. When Miss Temple leaves Lowood, Jane's restlessness conveys insensibility. That fifteen years after Helen's death she places a stone with "Resurgam" on the grave implies love for Helen and trust in resurrection. But the narrative detaches love for Helen from faith; the personal and doctrinal are unreconciled.[465]

In relating to Rochester, Jane is inconsistently orthodox. He routinely applies religious terms to himself, but she does not upbraid him, being as guilty. She fails to fault him when he arrogantly feigns superiority to convention by drawing a parallel between himself and the faithful centurion, who knew Christ's power to perform miracles was greater than his authority. Failure to criticise this reduction of parabolic truth is unsurprising: when she cites the same parable to describe the servitude imposed on her by Rivers, she also ignores its spiritual import. Although she tells Rochester that repentance cures remorse, that aggressive pretensions to religious inspiration are usually self-deceiving, and that the "human and fallible should not arrogate a power with which the divine and perfect alone can be safely entrusted," her tenets do not shield her from rationalisation but expose her to the irony that she has faults she warns Rochester against. His testimony that Jane trusts her "inward treasure" and obeys "that still small voice which interprets the dictates of conscience" is unreliable not only because he aims to persuade her to accept that the repentant man can ignore social convention but because it also overestimates her spiritual capacity. She resists his flattery by declaring that "a wanderer's repose or a sinner's reformation should never depend on a fellow creature" and by urging that he look for help from "higher than his equals," but her authority to instruct him is questionable. By her admission, she is "a wanderer on the face of the earth." This admission reflects alienation; it appropriates biblical terms for emotional, not spiritual, concerns. She is similarly responsible when she likens herself to a bird that wishes "to taste but of the crumbs" which Rochester scatters and views him as the "master" whose "feast" conveys happiness and whose words are "balm." She alludes to the Eucharist not from sacramental respect but from a wish to dramatise her emotional dependence. When she claims Thornfield has given her "communion" with everything "bright and energetic and high," that she reverences Rochester's mind, and that leaving him is like confronting death, she voices sacramental words for sentimental reasons. Comparing her inability to love him with having her "morsel of bread snatched" from her lips and her "drop of living water dashed" from her cup further reduces sacramental to romantic terms. Her claim to be speaking, not in conventional language but spiritually, as if before God's throne cannot hide false inspiration. This false transcendence spiritually devalues death and the Eucharist. Her claim is histrionic since it establishes a false dichotomy between secular and religious ideas. Soon after this claim, Jane states she is better than Rochester, but her pretension is hollow: she accuses him of temporising since he is as good as married to Grace and rejects being called a bird endearingly. Her charge against his temporising, true in dramatic irony, does not prove her superiority, and her initial image of herself as a bird lowers her to Rochester's level.[466]

Her reaction to his secret marriage proves her sensibility precarious. Her only recourse being to call on God, she despairs. Her mind is "rayless"; she cannot pray. The Psalms vocalise her despair but do not lead to meditation. That she cites them, despite having told Brocklehurst she never read them, implies she has studied them, although textual evidence for this is lacking. That her conscience speaks via the Sermon on the Mount when it reminds her to "pluck out [her] own right eye" and to "cut off [her] own right hand" suggests the lasting effect of her education, but allusiveness does not aid the relation between conscience and despair. It is hard to see why she grows fearless from "inward power" and a "sense of influence" when almost succumbing twice to Rochester's offering himself as the shepherd intent on caring for a lost lamb. Fearlessness comes, not from criticising his appropriation of a pastoral role or from containing despair but from grace. Surprisingly then, she offers herself to Rochester as a model of trust in God and the self, the relation of spiritual power and self-reliance seeming remote. She does not resolve to leave him. She wards off the temptation to stay through "preconceived opinions" and "foregone determinations," this sense an easy acceptance that her emotional disturbance inhibits spiritual deliberation. Her claim that she can strive and endure and that she accepts the law of God as sanctioned by man is unimpressive, her sense more dissociated than she claims.[467]

Jane's reactions to Rivers render her sensibility questionable. Hostile to his doctrines, she finds the man and priest inconsistent. She condemns his bitter sermons; they lack "consolatory gentleness." She faults his "insatiate yearnings" and "disquieting aspirations" in a tone denying her similar enthusiasms, even as she admits they are both unable to possess the peace that passes understanding. Her readiness to condemn him overrules concern about her own religious state. That she laments her "broken idol and lost elysium" while trusting to Rochester's salvation is also incoherent. That she venerates Rivers' principles while measuring the gap between his corruption and Christianity reveals her unsteady perspective on him. When, finally, she treats Rivers as an apostle of primitive intensity, Brontë's heroine reconciles "human tears" with "divine joy," yet she does not balance criticism and praise self-consciously.[468]

Jane Eyre simply assumes Jane's religious sensibility: Brontë does not concentrate on her spirituality. Her account of Jane's religious feelings is confused. Jane lacks a steady perspective on past emotions and thoughts. One moment, she says of her half-comprehended childish notions that they were "strangely impressive" and "profoundly interesting"; the next, she indignantly rejects "solemn doctrines about the angelic nature of children": she emphasises the imaginative sensitivity of her former self from a doctrinaire romantic view about children yet condemns the "dense ignorance" and "morbid suffering" of her childhood. The aggressive tone Jane adopts towards her young self clashes with allusive implications about religious education. When she insists that fear made her a "miserable little poltroon," that her "trifling taste" rendered her unfit to comprehend serious things, and that her juvenile mind was stored with the "rubbish" of folk literature, severe comments expose pretended spiritual growth; such harshness shows that, as narrator, Jane has no balanced perspective on how she developed.[469]

The motif of time illustrates *Jane Eyre*'s inadequacy as spiritual autobiography. While Brontë employs considerable dramatic irony about time, neither as character nor as narrator does Jane organise temporality. As she grows, Jane looks ahead to the future since she wishes to escape the past, yet Brontë makes that past inescapable. Anticipating Lowood, she hopes to enter "a new life." But the future is robbed of newness when Mrs Reed confides in Brocklehurst. Another occasion when Jane cannot shut out the past occurs when she visits

Mrs Reed, despite having vowed she never would. When about to set out for Thornfield and a desired new phase of life, Bessie arrives at Lowood to tell Jane about the Reeds: this irony probes how Jane connects past, present, and future. Before the abortive wedding, she has a "hypochondriac foreboding" that makes her wish the present will never end. If dramatically appropriate, this wish exposes her continual desire to escape time. Following Rochester's disclosure of Bertha, Jane loses all sense of her past life and future prospects. This loss recalls her vague idea of the present when first apprehending death. On both occasions, the present is shapeless. On leaving Rochester, Jane thinks of the past as heavenly and the future as life after the flood, but this emblematic distinction is not realised in how she regards the present. Not having won a religious sense of time, the distinction represents an emotive attempt to deal with frustration. That she is not educated by time's ironies appears in her ineffectuality as narrator: she is coy and reticent in her stance towards temporality if, on occasion, she speaks of the "quiet medium" of time as a source of moral awareness. But this diversity is not harmonised by religious sensibility.[470]

Jane's poor sense of time affects her Bible reading. Her allusions imply she sees herself in terms of Christian history, but her uses of typology are problematic. She can be self-consciously critical when she admits her avoidance of Helen's ideas, saying she did "not ponder the matter deeply" but "like Felix, put it off to a more convenient time." Acts 24:25 suggests she is a type of Felix, the spiritual coward who temporised rather than judged Paul; it implies the narrator has a firm Christian perspective on her earlier self. But other allusions suggest the narrator selfishly distorts typology and ignores the ironic impact that allusions have on one another. When describing her decision not to admit she has heard Rochester's invocation of her, Jane says that she "kept these things" and "pondered them in her heart." But Luke 2:19 is problematic, for Mary's meditation over the shepherds' report of the angelic visitation is an ineffable experience in no way like Jane's wariness about Rochester and belief that hearing him was merely a supernatural coincidence. In seeming to discount Rochester's "mute devotion," she likens herself to the Virgin Mary to prove her spiritual superiority to him. Another ironic allusion occurs after his disclosure of Bertha when Jane says that all her hopes were killed and "struck with a subtle doom, such as, in one night, fell on all the first born in the land of Egypt." Exodus 12:29 illustrates divine punishment, but Jane does not see that it identifies her as an enemy of the children of Israel destroyed by God in the Passover. The allusion is ironic because the deaths of hope and Egyptians are not equivalent and because it clashes with Jane's claim that providence led her from captivity at Thornfield. Allusions, too freely adapted, do not form emblematic patterns. Take the following references to Paul. While breaking away from Rivers, Jane prays to understand the voice which, in calling to her, lets her seem "to penetrate very near a Mighty Spirit." Recalling the ineffable strangeness of the inner sensation, she compares it to the earthquake which set Paul and Silas free from prison. An emblem of grace, the allusion is ineffectual for Jane applies Acts 16:25–26 to vagueness about the separation of soul and body. Whereas the gracious miracle stresses the equivalence of physical and spiritual freedom, her application is one of selfish intent. That Paul is not a type for her is made plain when, recalling Rivers' proposal, she likens his suit to the appeal of the man of Macedonia to Paul. That, being no apostle, she rejects Rivers shows why allusions form no pattern to test religious identity.[471]

Sometimes, her allusiveness implies extreme spiritual faults. In recounting Rochester's relationship with Grace, Jane says that Grace "scorned to touch me with the hem of her robes as she passed." In alluding to Matthew 9:20 and 14:36, Jane parallels herself to those who, desiring to be healed, faithfully approached Christ even as she makes Grace an unwilling saviour. Thus, she aims at giving biblical sanction to her self-pity and contempt for Grace. As narrator, she is more occupied with private myth than typology. This is so of her reaction to Mrs Reed. As character, she freely forgives Mrs Reed on the latter's death-bed, but as narrator, she cannot forget Mrs Reed's cruelty even as she reminds herself that she ought to forgive her "for [she] knew not what [she] did." The discrepancy between the reported action and the narrative stance prompts us to wonder whether Jane forgives Mrs Reed, yet the technical problem means less than the misused allusion; not only does Jane appropriate Luke 24:34 where Christ asks the Father to forgive His crucifiers, but the logic of the appropriation leads us to see that Jane affects the divine response: God alone can respond to the Son's prayer and pronounce forgiveness. When Jane chattily reminds herself to forgive Mrs Reed, whom she has supposedly already forgiven, vanity and pride govern her abuse of the ultimate divine sanction. While through biblical and liturgical allusions she depicts Jane's orthodox education and religious sensibility, Brontë does not use them carefully to confirm Jane's spiritual development. Brontë seems neither to respect traditional emblems nor to realise their structural value in autobiography. Uncontrolled ironies and unsteady narrative stances indicate that she did not treat faith as a human problem. Her religious allusions hint at spiritual themes, generating aesthetic problems rather than lucid autobiographical structures.[472] Allusive ironies in her text seem accidental and impressionistic when compared with Pope's humanistic, yet sustained, criticism of Eloisa.

Oenological Ambivalence in the
Barsetshire Novels (1855–1867)

In his final year, Anthony Trollope put down "24 dozen" bottles each of the 1874 Château Léoville and Château Beycheville.[473] Pride in his cellar led him to install "iron bins" in "fine order."[474] To his grand-daughter, he was a "good judge of wine, especially of claret."[475] In his *Autobiography*, he says, "if a cup of wine has been a joy" to him, it has brought him no "sorrow," his taste of no concern to readers.[476] This disclaimer says much about his literary attitudes. Wine was a topic of debate for Victorians given the rise of temperance societies and the wish of William Ewart Gladstone (1809–1898) to boost Britain by increasing free trade with France and lowering excise on its wines.[477] Favoured by policy and thought healthier than other alcohols, French wines lost status: arguments for claret as a beverage discarded its early symbolism.[478] It had for long been associated with "Toryism," aristocracy and Jacobitism, port standing for the "solid virtues of merchant, squire and the professions" and for Whig constitutionalism.[479] This distinct symbolism is manifest in the names William Younger and A.D. Francis give the Victorian period: to Younger, it is the Age of Claret; to Francis, the Age of Vintage Port.[480] Thus, Trollope used wine to discriminate characters' allegiances.[481] Since politics sapped and fortified wine-drinking traditions as he authored the Barsetshire series, he voiced systematic yet non-dogmatic codes, focussing on histories of claret after the embargoes of the 1670s and of port following the Methuen Treaty of 1703. Christopher Herbert thinks comic sense made Trollope "more impervious" than other Victorians to evangelism. Viewing pleasure in "salvational terms," he scorned "dissolute pleasure-seekers," being "at heart" a "severe Victorian moralist." This "self-contradiction," rooted in the "paradoxes of culture," gives him a "moral amplitude." Wine allusions show that he relied on comic ambivalence, this sense deliberately humane.[482]

Trollope's imagery is not extensive: to one critic, it "never extends ... to explain anything further than itself." Still, wine allusions are an exception: they signal a humanist dialectic. He associated wine with social solidarity and, since it was scarce and taken by the upper classes, with prestige and wealth; he valued tensions between its domestic and political meanings to express an ambivalent mentality. Trollope was no more single-minded about reform than about virtuous collective behaviour; he equally mocked institutional progress and corruption. Holding reform and comedy to be essential, he did not feel their opposing demands could be reconciled by fiction. His need to endorse tradition and to reform contemporary society informs his wine allusions.[483] Their subtlety may be judged by how other nineteenth-century authors treat wine. His balanced attention to its pleasurable and painful effects, to its carefree joys and philosophical problems, may be weighed in the tendencies of fellow writers to be either more doctrinaire or less dialectical.[484] Far from holding the ritualistic and ideological aspects of wine in equipoise, they weight one more than the other: Charles Dickens (1812–1870) and William Makepeace Thackeray (1811–1863) heighten the ideology of wine to depreciate its rituals, while Lord Byron (1788–1824) and Thomas Love Peacock (1785–1866) set its rituals over its ideology.

According to Trollope, his mother "raved" about Byron, happy about his "popularity" and tearful for his "persecution." In *Domestic Manners of the Americans* (1832), Frances Trollope (1779–1863) called Byron a "mighty master" who was admired by true lovers of poetry. But Trollope did not share his mother's enthusiasm, if he appreciated her sociability. His *Autobiography* records that his mother "could dance with other people's legs, eat and drink with other people's palates, be proud with the lustre of other people's finery ... but of all people I have known she was the most joyous or, at any rate, the most capable of joy." Her criticism of liquor consumption in *Domestic Manners* conveys a joy which her son cultivated in life and literature, a kind which perhaps should have given her second thoughts about the cult of Byron. Reporting that hard drinking prevails in America, she complains that liquor is not consumed at "jovial dinners but in solitary dram-drinking"; she is distressed that wine is hardly ever served at dinner and that, when it is, ladies "rarely exceed one glass." American conventions are troubling: mixed dinner parties are rare and, when they take place, ladies and gentlemen eat and converse separately in the same dining-room. Since gender equality and inclusiveness are important to social drinking, she is no happier that married women are excluded from balls and evening parties.[485]

Byron scorned the ethos Frances Trollope sought in wine. Stanza LXXVI of canto XIII of *Don Juan* (1819–1824) mockingly consoles England for its lack of vines and vineyards. Its weather is bleak, but it can purchase choicest claret and Madeira, the "very best of vineyards" being "the cellar." Byron's irony is droll: his verses undo the equation of cellars and vineyards which they seemingly affirm. Far from promoting sociability and ritual pleasure, he retaliates against his native land. Wine allusions in *Don Juan* confirm his struggles with emotional wounds and social stigma. In the libertine mode of Restoration comedy, he likens a married woman's seduction to a "pipe of claret" being "prick'd." Steeped in Elizabethan and Jacobean drama, Trollope does not let wine allusions defend such clichés.[486] But misogyny sees Byron delighting in stale analogies about adulterated women and wine, as when he says they differ from themselves "as wine differs from its label, / When once decanted." If Restoration playwrights likened the opening of bottles to sexual intercourse, they usually undermined libertine analogies with irony.[487] Unlike Trollope, Byron shuns apologies for wine in the tradition of dramaturgical irony. Trollope opposed salacious dramatic wit and recognised that the best playwrights deflate misogyny with ironic wine allusions. If he saw Byron as a good poet, Trollope thought him "wholly powerless on vice." This criticism may be due to the fact that Byron mocked the "bleakness" of his native land since no "Purchased choice of choicest wines" could guarantee social solidarity.[488]

An admirer of Byron, Isaac Disraeli (1766–1848) upheld a subtler wine ideology. In 1822, he told Thomas Moore (1779–1852) that he preferred French wine to port, leading Moore, who had just returned from the Continent, to agree that the "transition is too sudden from the wines of France to the port of Dover." Disraeli enjoyed this blend of geographical and cultural humour. Sympathetic to exiled Stuarts in France, he valued the claret code of Jacobites in Britain. After James II's flight, they drank to him by passing glasses over bowls of water, pledging themselves, with wordless disloyalty, to the *king over the water*. Disraeli knew that, since the 1703 Methuen Treaty favoured port in preferential excise taxes, the resistance to claret had intensified for non-jurors; he traced it to seventeenth-century habits. In "Drinking-Customs in England," printed in his *Curiosities of Literature* (1791), he recalls royalist ritual: the "cavaliers during Cromwell's usurpation usually put a crumb of bread into their glass, and before they drank it off, with cautious ambiguity exclaimed, 'God send this *crum well* down!'"[489]

Peacock also relished wine culture. In "Gastronomy and Civilization," he sees wine as a "symbol of enduring, festive being."[490] Opposing dogma, oenological rituals verify allusive options available to contemporaries. Since "incorruptible republicans" would do well to moisten "their throats with Madeira," he thinks a "jorum of claret" the way to unite politicians.[491] In *Crotchet Castle* (1831) and *Gryll Grange* (1860–1861), wine complements Christianity. In the former, Dr Folliott calls a cellar with a "thousand dozen of old wine" a "beautiful spectacle" and "model of arrangement," deeming it a "talismanic antidote." At dinner, he accepts all wines in a suite of ordered cellarage: Madeira first, followed by hock, champagne, Graves, Sauternes, and Hermitage, leaving claret of the great 1815 vintage to the end.[492] Savouring it, Folliott improves on St. Paul in 1 Corinthians 13:12, confirming Peacock's sacramental paganism: holding his glass to the light, Folliott sees "both darkly and brightly." Dr Opimian, the oenophile in *Gryll Grange*, has a cellar "well stocked" with "best vintages," its order proving his faith that wine gives meaning to daily life. To avoid excess he cultivates a taste for all wines; together they are a "panacea" for worldly care and naive faith in science. A classicist whose "copious libations of claret" propitiate his genius, he reveres the Greeks for mixing salt water and turpentine in wine, and he celebrates marriage as a joyful occasion presided over by "Bacchic ordnance."[493]

Trollope shared Peacock's scientific scepticism and knowledge of pagan wine but rarely makes wine erode Christian ethics with classical sacraments. While he voices Peacock's dim view of progress, he is comparable to Dickens. Like Trollope, Dickens spent much on wine. Indeed, he bought costlier wines than Trollope: in 1850, he paid £35 for a dozen of 1834 port and kept his cellars stocked with first growths of Bordeaux and Burgundy, such as Brâne-Mouton (now Mouton-Rothschild), Chambertin, Clos de Vougeot, and Volnay. What Dickens and Trollope had in common is that, despite their connoisseurship, their wine allusions grow remote from their early convivial fiction and convey declining enjoyment.[494] Still, Trollope's sense of political and cultural tradition stops him from connecting wine to evil like Dickens.[495] Institutional reform governs the latter's allusions. When Mr Bumble, the beadle in *Oliver Twist* (1837–1839), courts Mrs Corney, the almshouse manager, with port meant for sick residents, Dickens lambasts the administration of public charity: the wine reaches not the infirmary's patients but the throats of parish officers. Still, he expects readers to heighten their indignation at civic corruption by grasping Bumble's ignorant taste: his claim the port is fresh and genuine and, having just been taken from the cask, contains no sediment ignores that vintage port throws a crust and that bottle-aging is desirable.[496] Wine is also associated with evil in *Barnaby Rudge* (1841): Sir John Chester embodies an aristocratic wine code; for him, wine "brightens the eyes, improves the voice" and enlivens thought and conversation. In the Gordon Riots, his code equates to bigotry. A connoisseur, he is not only genteelly slothful and luxurious but politically dangerous.[497] Motivated by jealousy, he sponsors mob violence and religious intolerance. While his code is presented negatively, Haredale, his enemy, is rescued by a bacchic, "purple-faced" vintner with whom Dickens sympathises. If Dickens presents an unholy alliance between Protestant aristocrats and the mob, Edgar Johnson says the novel overcame his dislike of the mob and that anger with "accursed gentility" and entrenched privilege made him see that rioters might be effective political agents.[498]

If *Martin Chuzzlewit* (1843–1844) sustains the conviviality for which Dickens is renowned—witness the vintage port and fine wines enjoyed by Mr Pecksniff's pupils at the Salisbury Inn—wine exposes Pecksniff's professional hypocrisy: the architect's pupils design wine cellars but are given the sourest currant wines, which he claims are generous.[499] His vinous susceptibility, when Montague's guest at the Dragon, elicits his greed and gullibility. The wish to make wine images heighten topical evil is evident in Dickens's attack on self-help and the self-made man in *Hard Times* (1854). When Mr Bounderby evades Stephen Blackpool's queries about divorce and the need for legal reform, the manufacturer indulges in his lunchtime sherry: fortifying himself, he spurns the poor man whose lot he feigns sharing. His hypocrisy is implicated when Stephen drinks wine to relieve the pain of a crushed, dying body.[500] Such journalistic sensationalism led Trollope to belittle Dickens as Mr Popular Sentiment at the outset of the Barsetshire series.

With Trollope, Benjamin Disraeli (1804–1881) opposed reducing excise on French wine, but, as Robert Blake says, Trollope disliked Disraeli's glorification of nobility as much as Dickens's journalism.[501] Disraeli's separation of symbolic from pleasurable aspects of wine in *Sybil* (1845) is, in its doctrinaire politics, a context for Barsetshire. Sybil and Walter Gerard, its heroes, call water "nature's wine," linking real wine to false aristocracy. Lord Marney, whose title hails from the dissolution of the monasteries, serves no "choice wines" to inferiors: he gives them claret "on the wane" or "pricked" Burgundy. Yet he cannot enjoy his best claret. Debasement of wine obtains, too, in Baptist Hatton, trader in aristocratic pedigrees. The champagne and Château Lafite he takes at the Athenaeum inspire him with sexual and political fantasies of gaining Sybil's inheritance. The siege of Mowbray Castle's cellar is no crime to Disraeli. When rioters gulp the "choicest wines of Christendom"—the Burgundy, Tokay, port, and Madeira—he does not lament; the ruined wine signals mystical conservatism's victory over political evolution. Trollope neither displaces political tradition so naively nor upholds political theory so vaguely.[502]

Thackeray enjoyed wine as the 1841 and 1848 clarets in his cellar at Palace Green attest. He writes of its pleasures in "Memorials of Gourmandizing" and "The Ballad to Bouillabaise." To George Saintsbury, Thackeray created aesthetic terms to induce contemporaries to savour wine, oenological allusions in *Pendennis* (1848–1850) advancing his terminology of connoisseurship.[503] Yet his application of kinds of wine does not match Trollope's differentiated imagery. Thackeray's fiction "never whole-heartedly celebrates good wine," parties in *Vanity Fair* (1847–1848) "marked by a gross failure in ceremony."[504] His wine-drinkers are targets, his allusions to wine serving either to present sensuous experience obliquely or to deflate pretensions to high life and high art.[505] His pleasures matter less to readers than Trollope's since images in *Vanity Fair* are no more ludic than in *Sybil*, but they are always satirical: wine-drinkers meet with irony; wine is an index of immoral consumption not of aesthetic sensibility or social cohesion. In affected ill-health, Jos Sedley downs seas of claret and Madeira that unman him: rather than court Becky Sharp, he becomes a "prostrate Bacchanalian." Luxury makes him scorn his father's cheap wines, pushing the would-be wine merchant to bankruptcy. Fine wine signals materialism, not domestic or social virtue. Cruelty drives Osborne Sr to buy Mr Sedley's fine wines: dying, Osborne is gratified to possess Sedley's Madeira, contemptuous of his bankrupt mentor. Systematically, wine imagery stresses that avid consumption masks itself as social and political pretension. Sir Pitt Crawley serves Miss Crawley, not his customary malmsey and Madeira, but champagne and claret; he thinks thereby to secure her estate. Equating claret with the French Revolution, she is politically and morally arbitrary. She likes watching relatives scrabble for her money, ready to forgive only those who succumb to her hierarchical claret code. She would have forgiven James Crawley had he got drunk on claret and not gin. Thackeray's view of immoral wine-drinking is epitomised by Mr Osborne and son; George, to extract funds from his parent, praises his father's Madeira, while Mr Osborne takes claret by way of telling his son not to marry Amelia Sedley: rival strategies preclude honest communication, wine is ammunition in inevitable warfare. As when Rawdon Crawley drinks the best claret without paying for it and Becky pretends Lord Steyne's expensive white Hermitage is table wine, Thackeray's characters devalue wine ritual, bathos reinforcing his belief that self-interest erodes social and political life.[506]

Like Trollope, George Eliot (1818-1890) alludes to wine distinctly. A writer whom Trollope loved and whose works he found "full of meat," Eliot may not detail wine images, but they are keys to her narrative.[507] Debates about wine and medicine in *Middlemarch* (1871–1872) probe alcoholic complacency to expose why reform fails.[508] While wine motivates her plot, themes of doubtful treatment and negligence link her to Trollope. Lydgate, a reforming doctor, frowns on port: for him, it has no place in curing alcoholism. But he is trapped by convention. A strong constitution, letting him drink wine freely, leads him to scorn those whom it overwhelms. He buys green glasses for hock, going into debt when he marries by purchasing a "stock of wine." He is professionally careless: had he criticised port truly, his instructions for treating Raffles would have been explicit. But the nurse, upholding the curative value of port and brandy, is told by hypocritical, water-drinking Bulstrode to administer a dose of the latter, which proves lethal. Lydgate's ideas are not actualised: he focusses on medical reform but not its agents. A parallel irony is that he views wine as a sign of status but denies it ritual meaning. That Eliot values ritual is evident when she links dislike of Bulstrode's zeal to that of men who, not vain about cellars, are dismayed by guests who hold wine glasses to the light. That Mrs Garth wears oddities in the way "a very fine wine sustains a flavour of skin" signals that, by applying wine to professional rather than cultural issues, Eliot uses dialectical insights like Trollope's.[509]

Wine functions dialectically in Barsetshire, confirming that Trollope is "everywhere a complicator," offering the "pros and cons" of issues. *The Cambridge Companion to Anthony Trollope* extends this insight by saying he was "an artist of the dialectic" who "stages encounters between the polarities of the day" and wins a "synthetic vision that holds opposing terms continuously in frame" so that "what's old looks new, and that what's new remains familiar." His wine allusions reveal a keen eye for social contexts and symbolic codes. He fuses context and symbolism from an almost mischievous sense of what James Kincaid calls his counterplay of "plot and anti-plot, of gain and loss, of irony and comedy."[510] In the Barsetshire series, wine allusions find fault with systematic social reform and polemical satire. Gentle Reverend Septimus Harding, protagonist of *The Warden* (1855), is assailed by Mr Popular Sentiment in "The Almshouse" for benefitting from ecclesiastical charity. His fiction grossly formulaic, Sentiment makes Harding a demon whose evil is symbolised by thirst for "much daily port wine." But benevolent supervision of Hiram's Hospital leads him often to give "a full glass of port" to Bunce, the head bedesman. Trollope forgives Harding's ignorance of economics and legal history, subordinating this cleric's failure to grasp social structure to his port ritual.[511] Harding's civility to Bunce is opposed by other bedesmen's denigration of the warden: blinded by public detraction, they misjudge his fairness. Far from favouring Bunce as alleged, Harding is not exclusively generous. On surrendering his post, he bids farewell by offering port to all: he blesses each as he hands them a glass. They try to enjoy the wine, but, a "sorrowful repentant crew," they drink it joylessly. Shamed by Harding's courtesy, they lament the motives that led them to slander him.[512]

Harding's port entails self-criticism and social commentary. More basic than political ideology, it involves moral practice and authority.[513] Learning he is subject to a public inquiry, he pours a glass from habit but leaves it untouched; he recalls delights he has enjoyed but not earned. Port's longevity rouses him to link pleasure and critical thought, to contemplate self and society with balanced intensity. In London for legal advice, he takes a mutton chop and port at a sombre, old inn with a sense of "melancholy solitude." Alone, he recalls the duty customers once felt about ordering wine for landlords' benefit. Linking pleasure to responsibility is an imperative. Mourning lost ritual, he honours its code when ordering sherry at a London supper-house only to receive a "horrid mixture procured from the neighbouring public-house." Adulterated wine that is not cellared on site impels him to assail modern hospitality and the diverging living standards of the populace and the wealthy. At this point, Trollope reinforces the satire by berating the legal system that is to rule on Harding's case: the Inns of Court enjoy the pagan luxury upheld by Peacock. Their revels imitate the refined Grecian mode in which the "wildest worshipper of Bacchus never forgot the dignity of the god whom he adored." Trollope extends Harding's sensibility to ecclesiastical criticism. When Bishop Grantly wants Harding as his chaplain so as to have someone with whom to share port, Harding keeps his independence by moving into lodgings, selling his furniture, and reserving his "cellaret" and the "slender but still sufficient contents of his wine-cellar." Self-sufficiency and moderate port is a clerical statement. If the Bishop self-indulgently wants someone to uncork his port, Harding enjoys retirement temperately.[514]

Harding joins liberal principles to a conservativism that sets him above ideological hypocrisy, making him a yardstick by which other clergymen are measured. In *Barchester Towers* (1857), clerical propaganda is exposed by wines other than port; they tend to symbolise false doctrine. Grantly, an expert on claret, boasts cellaring fine wine: the *cave* in the vicarage that Arabin is to occupy Grantly finds "perfectly abominable": it "would be murder to put a bottle of wine into it till it has been roofed, walled, and floored." His rules for storing wine constitute high-church propaganda: his wine makes him superior to those who think a "moderate claret-jug" dangerous. When Arabin becomes dean, Grantly toasts him in "bumpers of claret" to celebrate his victory. Low-church clerics equate scorn for wine with reform, but their inconsistency about the one reveals their hypocrisy about the other. Bishop Proudie's wife dominates him in church politics: he is so spiritually timid that he confronts her only when fortified with sherry. Mr Slope, the bishop's assistant, while, like Mrs Proudie, a zealot for egalitarianism, also like her, harbours social ambitions and reveres hierarchy. Planning the supper for the bishop's installation, he gives careful instructions for serving wine: respect for the "usual gradation" from cathedral-close dignitaries to the lesser clergy leads him to reserve fine wine for the former and to give marsala, at twenty shillings a dozen, to the latter. As Mrs Proudie metes out her time to guests according to their rank, so Slope allots the wine. His hypocrisy is clear when he rejects the "very poor Marsala" that the obsequious Quiverful offers in thanks for preferment. Rejecting the wine, he thinks fit for lesser clergy, Slope is undone by indulgence in fine wine. He invokes the "assistance of Bacchus" when pursuing Mrs Bold: he gulps champagne to dissolve misgivings about her antipathy. A libertine, he allows Mr Thorne's wine to induce him to molest her.[515]

Harding's port ritual, an emblem of the middle way and self-awareness vital to satire, exposes extreme clerical ideologies. To a degree, his ritual is ideological; the Barsetshire novels always make wine-drinking a register of social and political values. Trollope's series consistently adds to the definition of port as a code of sensibility and cultural meaning. *Barchester Towers* shows that the code is traditional and patriarchal rather than nostalgic and matriarchal. Although he respects the Thornes of Ullathorne, the house at which Slope molests Mrs Bold, Trollope laughs at their mode of hospitality. Miss Thorne, nostalgic for the Stuarts and the divine right of kings, in her aristocratic scorn for reform bills and corn laws, runs her house with old-fashioned demeanour. When she urges two bumpers of port on Mrs Bold, thinking this amount medicinal for new mothers, Trollope demurs: poor women are good mothers without port. By making Miss Thorne "a living caricature" of her brother's "foibles," he implies the port code draws on a rural gentility unlike hers. The code's patriarchalism, the implication that men realise culture better than women, is clarified by the eponymous hero of *Doctor Thorne* (1858).[516]

Before becoming Mary's guardian, Thorne is a slovenly bachelor with a "few good bottles of wine in his cellar." Building it to create an ethos in which to rear her, he learns to appreciate wine. Louis Scatcherd, offspring of industrialism, drinks Thorne's port like a toper, but Thorne admires it as a "collector loves his best pictures": "He liked to talk about it, and think about it; to praise it, and hear it praised; to look at it turned towards the light, and to count over the years it had lain in his cellar." Valuing its twenty-year cellarage yet lamenting so little remains, his bitter-sweet ambivalence resembles Harding's. Scatcherd cares nothing for port's aging: he would console his host by ordering claret from London. Drinking Thorne's port tastelessly, he blithely assumes claret a substitute for port. His "prime stuff" is bought from "Muzzle & Drug" at the price of "ninety-six shillings" the dozen, but Thorne spurns it: its cost and adulteration make him declare he never takes claret at home, being content with his "old bin" of port.[517] Opposing Scatcherd's addictive drinking, Thorne stores port, upholding ritual and social responsibility: his scrupulous protection of his ward from Scatcherd's courtship arises from a paternal sensibility.

Thorne's wine code is contrasted by Bideawhile, a time-wasting lawyer whose inanities about port stop him helping Frank Gresham. Recalling that Frank's grandfather enjoyed the 1811 vintage, the lawyer admits to still having a couple of bottles yet claims they are undrinkable since port "won't keep beyond a certain time." His folly about the long-keeping vintage is exposed when he laments that Madeira is not available.[518] Ignorant about geography and history, he says the alternative to port is no longer grown in Switzerland, its vineyards now producing pumpkins: viticultural pretensions show that his false professionalism hides deep cultural insensitivity. His failure to integrate time, place, and value heightens Thorne's rural gentility.

Without adopting dogmatic schemes, Trollope defends the ritual of port by associating claret with aristocratic decadence.[519] When Lord de Courcy serves claret to guests, he adds nothing "to the hilarity of the claret-cup": he poses with wine as with life at Courcy Castle. He takes claret "with an air of virtuous resignation," earning prestige without advancing social cohesion: his hospitality modish, not sincere; political, not communal. The Duke of Omnium likewise offers the best champagne and claret to guests but does not socialise with them. Frank Gresham rejects such Whiggish hospitality. While clerical friends greedily swallow the Duke's claret, he cannot enjoy wine in the host's absence; wine is pleasurable as it effects ritual. His family, infected by aristocratic aspirations, drinks claret with a degree of honesty which reveals that Trollope maintains no easy equation between claret and decadence. A habitual post-prandial decanter allows the Greshams to deal with family problems. Though angry with her son, Frank's mother takes her evening glass before her husband probes their son's feelings for Mary. As father and son talk, a decanter of claret turns their estrangement to closeness. At first, they drink "mechanically" but the wine causes the father to realise his son's manliness. Claret, itself, is not always an ideological barrier to ritual; it may consolidate family unity.[520]

Still, he differentiates between the semiotics of pure port, expensive claret, and cheaper wines like Madeira and brandy in the case of another father and son: Roger Scatcherd and Sir Louis, images of the nouveau riche, reveal why claret is ideologically distinct from port. When Louis attempts to win Lady Arabella's support of his suit for Mary, his abuse of wine etiquette, in alienating Frank's mother, exposes his anti-social self-importance. After she spurns his offer of wine, he declares his ownership of Greshamsbury, swallows his wine triumphantly, and refills his glass twice before passing the bottle. He violates etiquette, having no sense of breeding or ritual. Drink kills Scatcherd and his son, the money won by industrial

genius being self-destructively void of culture. Roger's admirers think him capable, under the influence of Dionysus, of prophetic insights into engineering and business, but Trollope scorns "Eleusinian mysteries," applying the contraction "posiums" to Roger's solitary bouts of drunkenness.[521] Far from dignifying the obsessive industrialist with pagan myths, he asserts that Scatcherd's god-given physique makes him stronger than "ordinary votaries of Bacchus," satirising his compulsion for brandy with fierce irony. Unlike Mr Gresham, Scatcherd lacks paternal sense: he knows Louis will drink himself to death but can do nothing to stop it. The Scatcherds' remoteness from Trollope's wine code is epitomised by Dr Thorne's failure to save Louis. His humane effort to wean the alcoholic by limiting him to two glasses a day fails since Louis lacks willpower. Thorne, finding it intolerable to measure out wine, realises that Louis's suicidal indulgence saps communal values. While claret may be consumed ritually, its connections to fashion, political power, and conspicuous consumption make it less significant than port, around which cluster customs and genteel manners that validate rural, organic, and humanistic principles.[522]

As the Barsetshire series unfolds, Trollope differentiates port and claret in an increasingly complex analysis of wine etiquette that involves narrative strategy with politics. In *Framley Parsonage* (1860–1861), an ironically aristocratic stance satirises Mrs Proudie's conversazione. She plans her entertainment to win renown, but she spends as little as possible. To be fashionable yet hinder liberal eating and drinking, she crowds guests, keeps them standing, avariciously handing round "tea and cake." The narrator remarks that, if servants soon refill glasses at aristocratic parties, the greengrocer class lacking servants cannot serve sherry properly. He sneers at Mrs Proudie's modish imitation by recalling a party when he asked a lady with an empty glass to take wine, assuming it necessary for digestion and not waiting on the servants. The lady, shocked by his gesture, looked as if he had asked her to join "a wild Indian war-dance." He laments "the good old days" when "Christian men and women used to drink wine with each other." His shift from ironic impersonation to elegiac reminiscence makes narrative tone stress that, if aristocrats subvert wine ritual, so do lower-class imitators.[523]

Fascinated with the coexistence in Mrs Proudie of affectation and asceticism and hostile to social debasement of ritual forms, Trollope creates a typology of hostesses in *Framley Parsonage* to defend his wine code. When Mrs Proudie hastens the meal before Harold Smith's lecture by denying the bishop his post-prandial claret, she thinks less of society than of evangelical censorship: she disrupts the lecture too. As the bishop well knows, food and wine are tools of his wife's punitive control. By contrast, Lady Lufton is an effective hostess. While misogynistic Mr Crawley denies her request that he recall Robarts to his clerical office, she does not give up: she induces him to take lunch and recommends Madeira rather than sherry. He becomes humble, admits his ignorance of wine, and takes her advice. Her hospitality brings out the best in him. Miss Dunstable disavows Mrs Proudie's modes, implying support for Lady Lufton's style. The former holds fashionable parties featuring dancing, ices, and champagne. But, after one which fails to reconcile the Duke of Omnium and Tom Towers, she sees the folly of trying to reform society by its own modes. Wishing to drink beer in public, she decries the spiritual vanity of high life and the futile role of society hostess from her sense of the need for meaningful ritual.[524]

Trollope also types male guests. In *The Small House at Allington* (1862–1864), how Crosbie and Eames decline and accept wine, further distinguishing port and claret, stresses that etiquette is inseparable from ritual and ideology. Having plighted her troth to Crosbie, Lily Dale takes him to visit Mrs Eames for whom "bare civilities" are "great favours." He would leave when she produces cake and sweet wine, his excuse that he does not take wine at midday. Trollope locates his refusal by saying the "little sacrifices of society are all made by women, as are also the great sacrifices of life." Leaving to Lily and her sister the role of gracious guests, Crosbie scorns daily ritual: his incivility equals marital ineligibility. Not taking the wine prefigures his betrayal of Lily: spurning Mrs Eames's sacrifice hints at his rejection of Lily's larger one. By contrast, Eames's initial refusal of Lord de Guest's invitation to wine respects ritual aspects of rank. Appropriately, de Guest's second invitation is a response to Eames's virility: saving the earl from the bull, he earns the right to enter de Guest's house and enjoy after-dinner port where decanters help him explain his unrequited love. When the earl playfully has him name his love before tasting the port, the ritual helps Eames process his feelings for Lily and antagonism to Crosbie.[525]

The Small House at Allington translates Crosbie's wine conduct into gross domestic and social manners. Wooing Lily after engaging Lady Alexandrina, he alienates himself from society. Visiting his club, he finds it no longer a haven. Infidelity robs him of a ritual place: his sherry there is joyless. Affording only half a pint, he is reminded of his disappointed economic and social prospects and of his faithlessness to Lily. At Courcy Castle, he is but a "tame chattel," the family scorning him by stopping up champagne's "perennial stream." After being beaten by Eames, he dines with Lady Amelia and Gazebee only to be further humiliated: his sister-in-law denies his request for port, ordering less "heating" claret. His manhood slighted and denied as a guest, all he can do is ask defiantly for brandy and water. Domesticity stresses his isolation: after dinner, he takes a glass with his wife and one by himself to sustain the facade of marital harmony. In the "latter ceremony," he stares into the fire, sensing his deceit and coolness of his marriage.[526]

Unlike Crosbie, Eames develops a taste for port that improves his personal and social relations so that he is exposed only to comic ridicule. His choice of wine over the gin and water taken by vulgar lodgers at Burton Crescent hints at his potential. At first, his taste for port is laughable. Meeting de Guest and Colonel Dale at Pawkins's, he lacks taste: he likes the inferior modern port served there, moved by it to retell his love for Lily. The earl's claim that thirty years ago the house served port as good as that in Guestwick's cellars leads to a plot to use Guestwick port to get Squire Dale to influence Lily in Eames's favour. Dale, recognising the 1820 vintage de Guest has tended for thirty years, sees through the plot. Appealing to Dale's connoisseurship, the earl laughs at John's taste. Eames's words for the port, "uncommonly nice," strike de Guest as appropriate to "champagne, or ginger-beer." He jokes that, since Eames has a pickle in his mouth, he cannot judge the port. While Trollope mocks the earl's prejudice for 1820 port by saying the 1860 vintage will strike seniors of the next age as wonderful, he endorses de Guest's wine code for its effect on Eames. The earl is sympathetic to Eames's romantic failure but critical of his sullen mood; to him, a man must drink with enjoyment to serve social cohesion; one who cannot enjoy wine, even in pain, is unmanly. Instead of getting drunk, Eames accepts the need for courage and joins de Guest's "ceremony" with seeming "gastronomic enjoyment."[527]

Trollope's posture with communal rites and mores, along with his integration of pleasure and politics, deeply informs *The Last Chronicle of Barset* (1866–1867). With comic ambivalence, this novel differentiates port and claret while satirising the declining wine code. Ambition for his son to marry an aristocrat leads Archdeacon Grantly to urge Henry, with 1834 port, to imitate his marchioness sister and drop low-born Grace Crawley. That claret-drinking Grantly makes his case by a superior vintage confirms his condescending strategy with port. His son's satisfaction with one glass of 1834 port and refusal of a better vintage provokes Grantly to drink claret and mock temperance. Unmoved by Henry's claim that modern men take wine with food and not after dinner, Grantly would later bribe him with 1820 port. On that occasion, he retorts, upon his father's abuse of ritual, by toasting Grace. The Archdeacon's incivility is also exposed by Harding's refusal to exert pressure on Henry and to lament the end of the 1820 vintage. Harding recalls that the Archdeacon's father ordered two pipes, thinking curates might like the vintage, if prebendaries and rectors would not. When Grantly protests that the wine is too good for bishops unless of the right persuasion, Harding distances himself from the Archdeacon's bias and his own nostalgia. Instead, he celebrates the former bishop's charity: his plan to give the great vintage to curates proves the Archdeacon's father upheld the tenet, "the poorer the guest the better the cheer." Savouring the last of the 1820 vintage, Harding laments the genteel pleasures of former clergymen: port heightens his self-criticism and impels him to praise reforming priests. While Grantly and claret signify partisanship and destructive domestic schemes, Harding's taste for port involves acute historical memories with a civilised imaginativeness about ritual pleasure. While his wine code absorbs Harding in retrospection, it entails sensibility more than conduct, highlighting society's inability to integrate duty and pleasure fully. In *The Last Chronicle of Barset*, since no one grasps the code like Harding, unbalanced reactions to it signal cultural decline. Bishop Proudie, not wishing to prosecute Mr Crawley in the ecclesiastical courts, does so to stop his wife making his "daily modicum of wine" lose its flavour. His indulgence does not validate Crawley's abstinence; pride blinds the curate to his sick wife's need for wine as medicine and leads him, one Christmas when Framley Court sends food and wine, to reject the gift. He takes wine only if forced to. When Dr Tempest insists that he take some, he resigns his benefice with dignity, even admitting the humane and "salutary violence" of Tempest's offering. Still, he never grants the ritual uses of wine so that, while Grantly comes to accept him as an equal, his view that Crawley is unbendingly eccentric is fair.[528]

If dismayed by how Proudie and Crawley sap wine's functions, Trollope heightens his apology by depicting Eames's unfulfilled sensibility. Far from upholding de Guest's code of port, he drinks with growing imprudence: at work he takes sherry against office rules; joining a modish set led by Dobbs Broughton, he lacks discretion. Broughton, a claret drinker, is a corrupt businessman. His office cellaret is stocked with good wine, but his premises adjoin those of a merchant who sells Himalaya wines at twenty-two shillings and sixpence a dozen. These wines signal his gross capitalism: a shady dealer in the money-market whose marriage is a sham, he is an alcoholic killed by drink. When Eames first meets him, Broughton has secured first-growth claret from an exceptional vintage: the 1841 Lafite. He exacts respect from the wine, forcing guests to take its provenance as a personal emblem. He boasts that, having bought ninety dozen bottles for £104 pounds, he could get £120 for them. Conway Dalrymple will not drink that claret, given the terms on which it is offered, but Eames does not scruple. If Broughton's claret conveys Eames's indifference to ritual, it heightens Crosbie's acute reaction to the moneylender. Wanting his bill extended, he faces a drunken, avaricious businessman who offers wine, not help. His rejection of the wine undoes the earlier distinction between Lily's two lovers.[529]

Eames's surrender to fashion and betrayal of port's cultural history heighten narrative dialectic: as the wine code declines, it gains meaning. On one hand, Trollope levels the contrast between Eames and Crosbie; on the other, he creates one between Broughton and Toogood to widen the gap between port and claret. Toogood, the lawyer who defends Crawley, as spokesman for port, is a foil to Broughton. Domestic virtues make him a gracious host, his jocular boasting about his old port voicing true liberality. His taste for wine is one with his distaste for modern modes: with bitter irony he tells Mr Walker that he dares not proffer a glass of wine since fashion dictates that one must wait to be served and drink as if alone. Rejecting this mode, they grasp the decanters at their elbows, defending the taking of wine socially and politically. Drinking in unison, they plan Crawley's defence, and Toogood attacks "the claret-drinking propensities of the age." He decries "Gladstone claret," the wine let into Britain by the 1861 act which abolished excise on French wine in the name of re-establishing Bordeaux as a beverage.[530]

At Toogood's house with Walker, Eames indulges in port but with scant awareness of its meanings. Like most characters in *The Last Chronicle of Barset*, he weakens culture by forgetting political history. Julia de Guest serves him her late brother's "superexcellent port" as consolation for his failure with Lily. Yet the port signals the distance between Eames and Lily, stressing their equally deficient sense of convention. Lily offers John the prospect of Lady Julia's old port to console him while feigning to drink it. Her condescension repels Trollope. Comparing Lily to a simple wine and telling Eames he cannot "learn the flavour of wines by sipping sherry and water," Madalina Desmolines, despite her sexual jealousy, is not far off the mark. Mocking Lily's formulaic praise of Eames's worldly success, Trollope says that "we drink our wines with other men's palates." This comment makes Lily's indifference to wine expose society's disengagement of pleasure and value. Far from exhibiting reciprocal enjoyment and principle, most consumption of wine in the final Barsetshire novel involves self-interest, moral inertia, or pathos. Onesiphorus Dunn, a "good judge of wine" who supervises the bottling of friends' wine, is a faceless parasite. Archdeacon Grantly, giving his son claret and discussing the Plumstead foxes to persuade him to live like a rural gentleman, is less intent on domestic and political value than on being histrionically irate about the decline of country life. Images of Squire Dale dozing over port sent in to his London inn from a public house; of Bishop Proudie, the lonely widower, taking wine to ward off despair; even of Harding drinking his daily glass of port in stoic isolation until the day of his death are bathetic rather than joyous, sombre rather than vital.[531]

Wine imagery in the Barsetshire novels is sustained yet incremental; it is an instrument to explore tensions between pleasure and responsibility, between communal action and political history. Allusions to port and claret are metaphors shaped by opposing contexts. As such, they have strong semiotic functions: they complement polemical and aesthetic aspects of narrative ambivalence. Trollope associates wine not only with comic pleasure and loss of comedy but also with the promotion and degeneration of cultural knowledge. His presentation of drink shows how doctrinaire reform and fashionable convention erode communal values. Despite his love for claret, he dignifies port for reasons that may be summarised after exploring the political basis for differentiating these wines in other Victorian writers.

Port and claret in *Bleak House* (1852–1853) reflect Dickens's topicality rather than a long view of society. Claret-drinkers, Harold Skimpole and Bayham Bagder are absurd. Skimpole, an image of Leigh Hunt (1784–1859), takes claret for reminding him of the sun, his egotism debasing etiquette, while Badger so self-effacingly admires his wife's first husband that Swosser's wine blocks his sense of hospitality. If claret suits unworldly insipidity, port highlights legal corruption; lawyers in "port-wine committee" batten on the Jarndyce and Jarndyce lawsuit, Mr Tulkinghorn, the "butler of the legal cellar," is the chief drinker of port. His "priceless binn" he drinks alone, except, as with Mr Snagsby, when bending others to his will; port testifies to anti-social pleasure and professional evil. Mellow by fifty years, it is a "Radiant nectar" filling his room with a "flavour of southern grapes" amid London dust and legal aridity. When he lies shot to death with an unfinished bottle on his table, port images the recoil of cruel fantasies he cherished.[532]

If George Meredith (1828–1909) raised the "philosophy of the palate to a loftier plane" than Peacock, his differentiation of port is like Dickens's in that it applies to minor characters but does not register the social and political forces in Trollope. Dr Middleton is marginal in *The Egoist* (1879)—a connoisseur cleric in Peacock's line by whom Meredith mocked his father-in-law. Middleton champions "piety and epicurism," sure that he who is not moved to wit by vintages is unfit for this world and the next. His creed stresses port's organic purity; he likens vinification to the cultivation of literary skill, devising a taxonomy matching Burgundy to Pindaric dithyramb and port to Homeric hexameter. His schematic appreciation of hock, Hermitage, and Burgundy and view that port is a cultural legacy closed to most men and all women is paternalistic luxury. His "whimsical, robustious, grandiose-airy" creed is exploded when his daughter thwarts his wish for permanent access to Sir Willougby Patterne's "cool vaulted cellar." Opposing her father's reactionary authority and misogynist defence of aristocratic patronage, Clara represents Meredith's challenge to patriarchy and to the sophistication of wine symbolism.[533]

That Trollope's wine taxonomy was moderate is shown by the attack on port in *A History and Description of Modern Wines* (1851) by Cyrus Redding (1785–1870). Redding damns port since imported pipes contain twenty-four gallons of brandy to eighty-one of wine. Since no "wine is worthy to be drunk in a highly-civilized country which is not made of grapes alone," he demands that England be afforded pure wine. Irate that port was "forced on us by our rulers" and that the monopoly granted the Douro company in 1756 ensured imports would be adulterated, he says that port has further declined recently because of commercial incentives to adulteration. Spurning wine's traditional associations, he makes it symbolise political corruption, angry that taste for it has led to adulteration of claret with brandy and wines from Cahors and Hermitage. Finding port dull, heavy, and alcoholic, he praises claret for being cool, light, and exhilarating. Blaming taste for port on Whig politics, he promotes claret since it is preferred by "refined and wealthier classes."[534]

A connoisseur of Bordeaux wines who despised port's adulteration, Trollope's sensibility and cultivated ambivalence avoided overpraising claret. Port in Barsetshire represents a cultural legacy he wanted to perpetuate. His awareness of the equal, but rival, claims of political progress and traditional customs moved him to set up a counterpoint between port and claret which evidences not only his negative capability and extension of metaphors but his wisdom about how values are destroyed as well as created, and how the consumption of food and drink involves, for better and worse, public policy and social trends.[535] He depicted a political history of wine and invented a dialectic of port and claret in order to renew community.[536] His discriminations of these wines show that, as well as being an intelligent critic of his society's competing ideologies, he is an accomplished practitioner of comedy. By making port and claret into a set of competing social and literary signs, he ably combines humour and pathos, conveys the instability of custom and political programs, and forges a narrative style which, if reliant on traditional patterns, incorporates irresolution and exploits dialectic. As such, Sadleir's metaphor describing Trollope's genius is highly appropriate:

> To him everything is material for observation, nothing for declamation or for vanity. He approves virtue and deprecates vice, but he refuses to become excited either over ugliness or beauty. Like a connoisseur of wine he sips at this vintage and that, selects to his taste and lays a cellar down. We, who inherit it, have but to drink at will, and in the novels that he left behind to savour the essence of life as once it was, as it still is, as in all likelihood it will remain.[537]

CHAPTER SEVEN
E. M. Forster
A Modern Humanist?

The three novels treated (not in order of publication) in this chapter promote concerns with ecology and the industrial-commercial world. Hence, the Wilcoxes of *Howards End* are agents of pollution despite their athletic pretensions; they ignore the mutual natural history of their family house and its wych-elm. However, Leonard Bast, the working man, ruined by their casual indifference, becomes a literary romantic who denies his poor heart health. Educated in classical mythology, Rickie of *The Longest Journey*, indulges in romantic fantasies which destroy him because he can neither resist scepticism nor understand philosophical idealism. His moral superiority to his illegitimate half-brother, Stephen Wonham, a true man of nature, is self-destructive. The Anglo-Indians of *A Passage to India* are so oblivious to that country's geography and ecology that its material realities never offer them steady transcendent symbolism despite their occasional glimpses and hopes. How visionary impulses arise for Adela Quested and Mrs Moore are momentary and disillusioning. Forster's point of view is upheld by a modern theology that would integrate classical and progressive values from a humanist perspective: in this context, friendly humans fail to cross cultural divisions, natural prejudices inhibiting true cosmopolitanism.[538]

In this context, Forster is a contrarian who embodies a romantic sensibility about nature ecology while he eloquently expresses scepticism about civilisation. Metaphysical double-mindedness lets him write as a controversialist. His dialectical expositions are shaped by comedy and satire and by the ethos of Dryden, Austen, and Trollope. Through ironic opinions and self-effacement, he aims not only at urban, suburban, colonial, and imperial mindsets but also at other ideological bases of modernism. His fictions early promise thoughtful advances but counter them finally with scenes of cultural stasis. His dialectic shows that generic boundaries between comedy and tragedy are permeable. Rooted in humanism and biblical knowledge, his narratives oscillate between realism and spiritualism to defy certitudes about sex and gender and to mystify truisms about capitalism and commerce. His rhetoric is often gnomic, aphoristic, and allegorical, addressing serious topics evasively and light-heartedly.[539]

His most powerful imagery derives from a dialectic that traverses boundaries between matter and spirit: physical categories dissolve and spiritual visions rise from within rocks and down from the sky, mysteriously upholding and spurning optimistic sensibility.[540]

Tragic Faith in *A Passage to India* (1924)

> Religion is more than an ethical code with a divine sanction. It is also a means through which man may get in to direct connection with the divine.[541]
>
> My motto is: "Lord, I disbelieve - help thou my unbelief." [542]

Religion and atheism were mutually informing to Forster. While his paradoxical sense of faith and modern trust in comparative religions are well known, they warrant further analysis.[543] Forster speculates about "sacred bewilderment" since he appreciates the fruitful discontent that religion causes.[544] Narratorial discontent in *A Passage to India* clarifies how he links modernism to problems of faith. Nathan A. Scott, the cultural historian, and Paul Ricœur, the philosopher of religion, hold that modern developments in theology and literature are reciprocally enlightening.

To Scott, in exegetical "figuralism" Old Testament events and characters foretell the New Dispensation.[545] It upholds a reality that views worldly events as providential, as in *Absalom and Achitophel*. This premodern equivalence of religion and literature fell with realism's growing autonomy; nineteenth-century historicism saw humans enmeshed in objective circumstance. The metaphysic of fact disjoined material and spiritual reality, ending traditional figuralism. Scott shows how twentieth-century radical theologians refused to lament this sacramentalism, happy to discard classical dualities about the natural and supernatural. They urged that Christian faith requires desacralization of the cosmos, stressing that Christ's dispensation obliges man alone to be responsible for the world. This responsibility constitutes modernism's dilemma: it raises the question of whether the global environment can be rehumanised in genuine reciprocity.[546] Scott argues that theologians and authors have renewed trust in the world via the anthropological concept of "savage thought" in which heterogeneous realities coalesce so that distinctions, such as between the one and the many, have no primal significance. Since, in primitive thinking, nothing is objective and everything may stand in a relation of reciprocity, the contact between nature and man is a sacrament of presence rather than a matter of alienation. Primitive thought prompts the impulse in theology and literature to discover holiness in the banal. To Scott, radical theology, by welcoming urbanism, and modern literature, by embracing collage, reconceive holiness. Seeking the "numinous" in daily reality, theology and literature adopt a sacramentalism that is radically secular and postreligious; neither upholds a sacred world apart from the mundane.

For Scott, modernism displaces supernaturalist postulates of classical theism and recognises that traditional theology promotes no genuinely reciprocal relation between God and man. Modern sacramentalism depends on a paradoxical vision of the commonplace that rests on primitive and postreligious ideas. Scott agrees with Dietrich Bonhoeffer (1906-1945) that the world may be viewed as trustworthy and sacramentally real only if spiritual concerns are explored in a non-religious way and God addressed in secular modes.

Forster's modernism is clarified by Ricœur's addressing God in a non-religious way.[547] His starting point is that atheism, avoiding the taboos imposed by religion, opens the way to faith. He turns to Friedrich Nietzsche (1844-1900) and Sigmund Freud (1856-1939), showing how their analyses of culture and creed, in terms of fear and disguised wishes, inform the philosophy of religion. Ricœur expounds Nietzsche's view that religious ideals are illusions of slavish wills that weakly project themselves into heaven, creating a forbidding god: Nietzsche's nihilism affirms the nothingness in religion's origins. In Ricœur's mind, confronting nothingness begins the return to the real origins of faith. Like Scott, Ricœur upholds primitive and postreligious aspects of renewed faith to elaborate an existential theory of language. Following Martin Heidegger (1889-1976), he holds that, when a person utters a meaningful word, he listens to his own saying in an obedient manner that antedates taboos. That language gives access to non-ethical thought and lets the individual understand that, while his will is autonomous, it can be embraced by being. Ricœur's thesis is that the saying and listening which derive from sincere utterance are related to the source of being: because sincere words are not at our disposal, they mediate a relation to the Word and lead to an existential trust in which the desire to exist fully originates. To Ricœur, this faith, free from divine interference, is a tragic one—like Job's; his faith was tragic since God exposed him to life's dangers to test his human worth. Thus, it is necessary that modern theology and literature reflect the essentially problematic nature of faith.

Forster delves into faith as problem in *Howards End*. Through the Schlegel sisters, he voices discontent with liberal humanism. Margaret's wish to be free from cultural constraints makes her regret the "sin" of missing concerts; she knows culture is infected with weak taboos. Stressful modernity makes her deny the Arnoldian principle of seeing life steadily and whole. Yet, the narrator sees London's urbanism as "religion's opportunity" to re-establish a concept of divinity. Shunning the "decorous religion of theologians," he senses that the modern city needs God to be "a man of our sort." Given ineffectual traditional theology, he would make sense of religious desires: "only in the days of [the] decadence" of the gods does a "strong light" beat "into heaven." Dramatising Helen's reaction against Nietzsche, Forster agrees with her that "the Invisible lodges against the Visible." Like the sisters, he feels obliged by the decline of religion to reconceive holiness. Thus, the sisters realise their love for one another is "rooted in common things" and that their "salvation [is] lying round them." They see the holy in the banal after confronting nihilism. When Margaret insists that "even if there is nothing beyond death we shall differ in our nothingness," she accepts that nihilism helps to define faithful existence. Even lowly Leonard Bast has a tragic faith: he is "blessed" by living his "sense of sinfullness."[548]

The dialectic of modernism and faith in *A Passage to India* stems from Forster asking why the modern world replaces classical theism with a new sacramentalism from his consideration of how to derive faith from existential properties of language and from his thoughts on how to address spiritual issues in non-religious ways. From Ricœur's standpoint, Forster confronts religion with atheism for the sake of faith. After his trial, when Dr Aziz decides to celebrate the Hindu-Moslem "entente" poetically, he does not write the poem since he believes the "song of the future must transcend creed." So, he tells Fielding that he does not want to be a "religious poet." This atheist replies there is "something in religion that may not be true, but has not yet been sung." That religion is not exhausted as a source of literary expression implies Forster's manner of operating in the novel.[549]

Far from dismissing religion, he satirises its displacement by assailing Anglo-Indians for lacking divine concepts. Their religion is vestigial—appropriated by sociability. They cling to a club that protects their exclusive gregariousness. Consoling them in their own image, the club exposes the masquerade of their taboos. After the alleged assault on Adela Quested, Mrs Blakiston moves among the "subdued but elated" women of the club like "a sacred flame," and the men, exempt from sanity, intoxicate themselves with righteousness by revering Ronny Heaslop as a "martyr" bearing "the sahib's cross." But club members lack any sense of the holy spirit or sacrifice; they reduce these ideas to a need for drama. They debase the idea of God not with faith in humanity but with pretensions to superiority. To Mrs Moore, they "like posing as gods." The club happily reveres the Turtons as "little gods." Mr Turton reveals himself "like a god in a shrine."[550] Thus, Forster illustrates the decline of traditional theology and the evasion of atheism. When Heaslop tells his mother that the weather is the "alpha and omega" of India's problems, his biblical allusion, void of apocalyptic meaning, supports glib racism and spiritless banality.[551]

Forster uses religious allusions seriously when he examines theology purposefully. That the sky produces glory and benediction, that Aziz finds it more blessed to receive than to give, and that the missionaries struggle with salvific inclusiveness reflect a wish to probe theology. Not always imitating biblical language ironically, Forster cites it plainly as when he reports Fielding's belief that Heaslop has "heaped coals of fire on his head" and when he wonders whether for Adela "the Word that was with God" is not also God. Whether adapting biblical texts or not, with them, he probes relations between religion and faith and suggests that a faithful sensibility belongs more to those reacting against religion than to those who unthinkingly accept its forms. At the climax of Adela's trial, while initially worrying about spiritual disgrace and clinging to her "suburban Jehovah" in her dependence on taboo, she soon moves past forms. Admitting Aziz's innocence, she is unconscious of all, even of her "Atonement and confession." If, momentarily, she lets herself be examined by life, this temporary trust transcending dogma.[552]

If faith transcends religion, Forster insists upon a necessary tension between them. Thus, Fielding is upset when his wife admires Hinduism without respecting "its forms" because he relies on "the language of theology" to confirm that his marriage is "blessed." Marital faith eludes him since he does not "bother much over belief and disbelief." Seeing himself as "a holy man minus the holiness," he does not think of humanity and holiness dialectically. He faults barrister Hamidullah for not letting faith "rule his heart," but theological inexperience prevents faith from ruling his own heart. Trying to realise the benediction of nightfall as he scans the distant Marabar Hills, he cannot grasp the gracious moment: "He experienced nothing himself; it was as if someone had told him there was such a moment, and he was obliged to believe." His eventual desire to know faith makes his reliance on theology troubled by his wife's unconcern with religious forms. In Fielding's loss of secular confidence and discontents about faith, Forster accents his own ironical perspective on humanism. Yet, he also shows that Fielding's humanism is properly tested by finding the dialectical tension between religion and faith discomfiting.[553]

This tension shows why Forster severs faith from geography. When he insists the Anglo-Indian form of prayer is unknown in England and that Heaslop's religion is "the sterilized public-school brand," he stops seeing faith nationalistically. Satirising English and Anglo-Indian forms of religion, he disowns straightforward political analogies to attend to universal aspects of the problems of faith. He almost equates Aziz's admiration of a mosque with that of an English church, while stressing Aziz's intolerance of alien creeds and twice saying of Aziz's faith that it is as limited as the average Christian's. By scorning the "facile contrast between the spiritual East and the materialistic West," he increases tensions between atheism and faith.[554]

Dialectical concern marks the gap between his characters' social and moral thinking. Most relate customs and established beliefs with difficulty to bases of knowledge and truth. In their dissociated sensibilities, Forster traces illusions and nihilism to disintegrated sacramental views of the world. Apropos is Fielding's sensibility. Surprisingly upholding the tradition that a decline in morals follows loss of faith, this inconsistent humanist is only a little discomforted by his inability to argue for his own and Britain's presence in India. Despite valuing the subversive "interchange" of ideas, he explains himself personally and the British government by precedent. This defensiveness shows that his participation in interchange is limited; he does not connect social and moral ideas. The Indians, however, are no more successful in linking personal feelings and principle. They too easily assume mental conventions are equivalent to spirituality. If they acknowledge this illusion, their recourse is to a bureaucratic social and political coherence which proves that, rather than confronting mental conventions, they avoid renewing them. Conventional in outlook, Aziz's sensibility is dissociated: he views his relation to collective experience naively. That he can "meditate" lying his way to Calcutta exposes the gap between his social and religious thinking. He holds that "the mere existence of unfaithfulness" injures a friend or God, but he cannot conceive of its existence harming society. Aziz typifies Forster's characters in that his religious beliefs are totally separate from his communal responsibility.[555]

The dullness Fielding, Aziz, and the Indians embody in dissociating private and public values is not as thick as that of the Anglo-Indians. The gulf between their personal and social existence is made deeper by pretending no gulf exists. Although they claim to respect communal thinking, their sociability is illusory. After the alleged molestation of Adela, they opt to become a mad "herd." Deciding on "emotion," they discard "the lantern of reason ... putting aside their normal personalities and sinking themselves in their community." In calculated spontaneity and stilted self-surrender, they disjoin individual and collective life. A perverse unreality knits their cohesion, given how much their relation of private and public meaning is self-deceived.[556]

The Anglo-Indians embody illusions at the expense of individualism by degrading the problem of faith: taboos erode their civility. By contrast, Forster insists that civilisation does not reduce Indians' integrity; it does not let them fuse social and moral thinking. He admires the civilisation in the "restfulness" of their ordinary "gestures." Benediction applies to the grace of those gestures: they convey "the Peace that passeth all Understanding."[557] This biblical allusion does not convey a humanistic reduction of religion for, although that grace is "the social equivalent of Yoga" and being earned is unlike religious grace, he compares it to religious grace. Since the civilisation of the gestures is self-contained, untranslatable, and incapable of being understood except on its own terms, it cannot affect the relation of social and moral thinking. Aziz may be made "complete" and "dignified" by civilisation, but he remains "hard," vengeful, and ideological. Forster treats civilisation as ambivalently as religion. It is sporadic and ghostlike; it neither aids communication nor impedes regressive nationalism.[558]

Modernity in *A Passage to India* propels ideas of faith to discontent with civilisation and religion. Avoiding humanist solutions to nihilism, Forster employs concepts of religious failure like those that Scott and Ricœur discuss: he shows that religion represents the ultimate failure to close the schism between social and moral thinking and that failure must occasion a new faith. The failure of civilised people like Adela and Fielding to assess spiritual reality he makes disturbing, but he makes more disturbing the failure of a "well-equipped" religious mind like Mrs Moore's to see holiness in daily life. Her failure is moving since her alienation from God follows a profound attempt to connect religious ideas and faithful experience. While she runs from her failure, Forster scrutinises its inevitability: a vision is expressible only in its own terms, and "mysteries" are as hidden from the "adept" as from the "unbeliever."[559]

Since religion does not mediate faith, he holds that its bases are uncomfortably minimal and that little is achieved in faith. A revelation may be complete, yet its paradoxical effect makes one feel it is still to come. Hope and fulfilment, if exclusive categories of faith, are contraries necessary even "in heaven." Spiritual experience is not comforting, cannot be realised in spatial or temporal terms, and is "apprehended" only when "unattainable." The paradigm informing the narrative is that the distinctness of religion and faith obliges one to treat faith dialectically with religion. With no model of spiritual comprehension available, Forster's fictional goal is to prove that social and moral thinking may be mended only by religion's failure to express faith.[560]

His narrative mode, given its flexibility, is a suitable instrument of modernism's problem with faith: it fluctuates between humour and solemnity, realism and allegory. Calm yet quizzical, experienced but troubled, the mode provides no stable fictional illusion; Forster diversifies his voice with primitive and postreligious tones which evade standard ethics. This confirms his wish to confront a "profound and elemental primitivism," to delimit the "archetypal emptiness" which precedes, and to regard material reality as predating "the logical and ethical distinctions of human speech."[561] To Lionel Trilling, a corollary of Forster's concern with the past is his belief in a present free from eschatological expectations of the future.[562] His primitive and postreligious voices exemplify that to understand the nature of ethics one must first think non-ethically.

The narrative presents characters, at one moment, solemnly and, at the next, jocularly, bathos satirising self-sufficiency and cultural amorality. When Forster says Anglo-Indians "had tried to reproduce their own attitude to life upon the stage, and to dress up as the middle-class English people they actually were," ironical prolixity and understatement emphasise their total unawareness of their banality. This bathetic pointedness is common. When the narrator says, after they stiffly sing the national anthem in the club, that they "poured out, offering one another drinks," the joke consists in the delayed equation of their leaving the club and their being what they consume. A similar joke, tracing descent of firmness into fluidity, occurs when Mrs Turton, after scourging Anglo-Indian males for lacking vindictiveness, subsides "into a lemon squash." The Anglo-Indians' banality appears when their complacent importation of kingship prompts humour: they not only believe in "the divinity that hedges a king" but hold that it "can be transplanted."[563] Remotivating Shakespeare's metaphor exposes their literal-mindedness, cultural insularity, and ignorance about the nature and climate of India. Bathos applies not only to them. After describing, with fluctuating seriousness and ironic fulsomeness, the "streams" of the Nawab Bahadur's well-chosen words, the narrator calls him "this old geyser." Again, after commenting on Aziz's possessive but unorthodox sense of hospitality, the narrator distances us from Aziz by depicting his violent emotionalism: "The black bullets of his eyes filled with soft expressive light." Thus, banality arises from both a feeble sense of identity and weak taboos.[564]

The bathos limiting our identification with characters is matched by setting—assertion and qualification defy assumptions about the natural order. The first chapter offers two views of Chandrapore, and, within each, contraries record material uncertainty. In the first paragraph, the river front has "no bathing steps" yet there is "no river front"; in the second, Chandrapore is "a city of gardens" yet is "no city." Indeterminate points of reference in setting disturb humanity's sense of living in the natural world. When the Nawab Bahadur's car crashes and a spurious unity descends on Adela and Heaslop, this unity is defined by contrasting the transitory gleam of a firefly and enduring night. Yet the narrator decries the absoluteness of the night as "a spurious unity." He treats "the high places of Dravidia" similarly: seemingly a ground for being that is "primal" and "older than all spirit," they are unstable since they alter slowly.[565]

That Forster stresses nihilism and doubts human conformability to matter enhances his modulations of voice. His view that identity is spiritless and that morality disregards creation as supportive of human endeavour explains why he frees his voice from recognisable ethical stances, making it oscillate between primitive and postreligious stances. The narrator describes Indians at the "Bridge Party" by commenting that "the East, abandoning its secular magnificence, was descending into a valley whose farther side no man can see," negative generalisation in tension with personification and metaphor: the voice is cryptic, no verifiable ethical stance connects the generalisations. The comments seem to parody biblical expression yet link a primitive respect for the natural order to postreligious respect for the secular: they free themselves from ethics by disjoining the verbal and the moral. On saying Godbole's spirituality is a matter of "Completeness, not reconstruction," the omniscient voice delimits the experience without morally assessing it. That is to say, the narrative is judgmental without being prescriptive; it expresses a primitive acceptance of spiritual phenomena in postreligious terms. This non-ethical stance recurs when the narrator upholds Fielding in the latter's preference of "truth of mood" to "verbal truth" and condemns Dr Lal for ignobly demolishing Aziz's civil lie.[566]

Equivocating with primitive and postreligious terms, the narrator subverts conventional morality. In sympathy with Hindu worship, he asserts that "All spirit as well as all matter must participate in salvation," thus assailing non-primitive, immaterial notions of holiness. But, when he avers that the sun, "debarred from glory" being a "creature," may not be mythologised as the eternal promise and cannot correspond to the "never-withdrawn suggestion that haunts our consciousness," he speaks from a postreligious stance against the figural imagination. At times, then, the narrator speaks as if he can talk on behalf of the primitive world, as when he claims that the inarticulate and inanimate world is "in tune with the infinite," while, at others, as when he asserts that "no high-sounding words" are appropriate to the "spiritual muddledom" of the "double vision," he expresses a postreligious contempt for the cosmological assumptions of traditional art and morality, this contempt is epitomised in the view that "we can neither act nor refrain from action, we can neither ignore nor respect Infinity." Although equivocation with primitive and postreligious stances leads to nihilism, the hope of a return to the origin of faith is not precluded. In lauding Moslem poetry for its amoral yet civilising role, the narrator rehearses its representativeness: "it voiced our loneliness ... Our isolation, our need for the Friend who never comes yet is not entirely disproved." If this nihilism subverts ethics, it holds primitive logic and postreligious uncertainty in brief equipoise to indicate the tragic nature of faith.[567]

Narrative tensions between primitive and postreligious phrases define Forster's concern with being and speaking. He explores existential aspects of language which carry the conviction that, though minimally present in verbal essence, belief is "endemic" in language.[568] Words have an independent life, and language is not at the disposal of humans. The bazaar youths playing polo on the Madan could not have said they were "training" since "the word had got into the air." The Marabar Caves are beyond human speech: the "word" that they are extraordinary had "taken root in the air, and had been inhaled by mankind." Existential words are poignant. After experiencing the horror of double vision, Mrs Moore loses interest in communication so that her affectionate words to Aziz seem "no longer hers but the air's," and in court, the criticism of Adela's physique is said to fall "from nowhere, from the ceiling perhaps."[569]

Complementing autonomous language is the motif that words are mortal since humans do not endow them with enough being. For Forster, as for Scott and Ricœur, verbal usage indicates more than cultural values; it provides occasions for discovering individual being. When the Anglo-Indian ladies at the Bridge Party speak, they say nothing: "their words seemed to die as soon as uttered." The Nawab Bahadur's superstitious guilt saps his politeness so that his conversation lacks essence: "His words died into Arabic." When Adela, without insight and conviction, would explain to Fielding Mrs Moore's knowledge of Aziz's innocence by the term "telepathy," the "pert, meagre word" falls "to the ground." Although such words exist apart from individuals, they must draw on being if they are to ground responsibility and hope.[570]

Since bringing words into being is difficult, the topic occupies *A Passage to India*. Hence, the Moslems' public attitude to poetry and the primitive quality of their listening. They do not analyse words; they live and breathe them. Obedient listening lets them exist in a fuller than usual way. For moments, they transcend indifferent nature, words their vital element: "they regained their departed greatness by having its departure lamented, they felt young again because reminded that youth must fly." Yet, the being touched on in poetic paradoxes is nostalgic; it is insufficient to preclude "trivialities" and shallow discontents. There is nothing truly holy in their words. A merely conventional acceptance of them "as immortal" permits them to exist in "the indifferent air." Traditional poetry cannot mediate their being. Aziz's poetic sensitivity does not affect his being. He lets himself be "deceived" by Mrs Moore's voice, his concupiscence shattered by her appearance. Sensitivity does not improve his listening nor give purpose to his speaking. He does not present himself to Mrs Moore in the mosque by words. She comes at his "essential life" by seeing through his repetitious, exaggerated, and contradictory speech. Aziz appreciates magic in poetry but countenances it unsteadily in life. At one moment, he hates to hear "the name Moore," yet, at the next, he talks piously about finding her name "very sacred." Words do not bring him integrity or a renewed faith in being. When, feeling the disgrace of his untidy room, he asks his servant Hassan to clear up, Hassan "found it possible not to hear him; heard him and didn't hear, just as Aziz had called and hadn't called." Ambivalence exposes his difficulty in making words draw on being. Without vitality, they do not refresh his faith in living.[571]

Forster's existentialism reaches an acme in the courtroom scene. After criticising institutionalised word magic, he gives Adela an experience that transcends her usual existence and verbal lifelessness. When the "invocation" of Mrs Moore stops proceedings, unknowingly the populace repeats the syllables of her name, making it a talisman. When the magic exhausts itself, the chant stops with ritualistic complacence: it is "as if the prayer had been heard, and the relics exhibited." The chant is merely formulaic. By contrast, having rehearsed syllable by syllable what she is to say, since afraid something she will not detect will form beneath her words, Adela overcomes her fear. Despite her "monotonous tones" and "flat, unattractive voice," she reaches a vision in which she is passive and active. It defies her belief that troubles are diminished if defined, forcing her to discard the romantic tenet that life is perpetually exciting, a tenet usually compelling "her lips to utter enthusiasms." As the vision begins, she stops fearing the "sound of her own voice." Returning to the Marabar Caves, she speaks "across a sort of darkness." Her saying involves an estranging double perspective: she is of and not of the "fatal day" which occurs and which she creates. She so lives her "doubt" that it becomes "solid and attractive," an "indescribable splendour." Although speech is "more difficult than vision," she faithfully confesses in "hard prosaic tones" the effects of her vision. For a while, she exists fully because, paradoxically, her words are not at her disposal, yet she is creative with them. Her gracious experience reaches far beyond traditional theological concepts.[572]

Adela briefly enjoys contact with being since she surrenders her taboos to verbal trust. This faithful being precedes fact and value, displacing her dualistic sense of the world as objective reality and the will as moral repository. Forster presents her fullest being in tension between primitive and postreligious theology; her gracious contact is exhausting, not consoling. After the vision, she feels "emptied" and "valueless"; without virtue, she sees herself as "isolated from the rest of the universe" and is made to confront the notion that existential faith is tragic. Her being is not strong enough to face nihilism with the minimal spiritual truths of existentialism. Refusing to remain subdued by what she best works in, she reverts to "rationalism," tries to interpret her vision which always disappears, and limits her sacrificial humility by making it come from rather than "include her heart." She surrenders her vision, her traditional personality unable to tolerate the tension between primitive and postreligious ideas.[573]

Free from Christian and humanist ideas, Godbole accepts this tension. For him, "nothing can be performed in isolation"; individual suffering, if real, is not ultimately significant, and good and evil are prior to thought. His depreciation of personality frees him from concern with ideas when celebrating divine love. He cares not whether Mrs Moore is a "trick of his memory or a telepathic appeal." His desire is to imitate God loving Mrs Moore and Mrs Moore invoking God's love. Nor does he mask personal inadequacy with mysticism. His religious performance does not strike him as much, but he trusts it is more than his identity. He exemplifies Mrs Moore's tenet that the "sincere if impotent desire" wins blessing and that, while "everyone fails … there are so many kinds of failure." His failure to make religion match belief is weak, given his unawareness of tragic faith, but it is also strong because his vision approaches an existential paradigm.[574]

Mrs Moore's failure to renew faith in a desire to be arises from a nihilism that shows how dependent she becomes on intellectual reconciliation of classical theology and humanism. When her vision reveals that "Everything exists" but "nothing has value," she is so disgusted that the universe offers no repose to her soul that she rejects theism and human relations. Thwarted desire for divine protection makes her spurn humanist trust in the holiness of relationships. She tries so hard to convince others that personal relations are not progressive that her conviction takes the form of "a person" offering her "a relationship." Here, Forster ironically suggests there is a being beyond personhood and that Mrs Moore's discontent with theology and humanism is not fruitful because its recoil produces an image of what she would destroy. Her dogmatism aside, Mrs Moore retains the potential for being. On leaving India, she glimpses the possibility of reacting to things in themselves rather than "in terms of her own troubles." Yet she fails to see that a relation to the world defined by theology can be positively challenged by atheism.[575]

His passions stop Aziz from developing a tragic sense of faith. Blood controls his opinions; his mind changes itself and is not moved by reason. Emotional complacency distances him from being. Mourning his wife sincerely, because seldom, he deceives himself that she can live in his mind. He does not realise that to love the dead "increases their unreality" and that "the more passionately we invoke them the further they recede." His passions spring from an uncritical desire to hear his religion praised. This soothes "the surface of his mind," letting "beautiful images" form under it. In his complacency, he does not treat criticism of religion as a way of exploring creation's trustworthiness. But he has the potential to confront being. When he argues for the place of sensibility in advancing India, he says so without aesthetic decadence yet in a voice that mediates his being. This voice, seeming "to arise from a dream," he can alter even as he speaks from below "his normal surface." His voice signals a capacity to exist more deeply. Yet passions prevent him from sustaining his examination of being. That he lacks the right footwear for India shows that he is not enough immersed in the world. He does not scrutinise material and immaterial relations. About Aziz's abortive bicycle ride, Forster meditates that "the cyclist's only hope is to coast from face to face, and just before he collides with each it vanishes." Thus, primitive trust in the otherness of material reality makes it lose its threatening objectivity. The ambivalence of "face," its reference to human distinctness as well as to planes of material reality, conveys the existential belief that a trust in being informs mankind and the creation. But Aziz's outlook lacks primitive trust in the world and postreligious feeling for what binds humans. Provocatively, the atheist Fielding, not Aziz, learns that relationships are not self-contained since there has to be "a link outside each participant that is necessary to every relationship."[576]

Forster explores this *link* between modernism and faith. Obliging atheist Fielding to explain the "link" to himself in the "language of theology" and criticising Adela's failure to see that "the Word that [is] with god" is also God, he tests the view that the divine is essential to human existence and is mediated by language. His narrative ambivalence holds that faith in being, which exists beyond individual apprehension, stems from primitive thinking that opposes humanist progress and postreligious reaction that denies classical theism. Sustaining a dialectic between religion and faith, understanding that religious ideas need not be spiritually evasive and countenancing a religious view of the frailty of humanism, Forster confronts unorthodox means of trusting being and the world. Narrative ambivalence, which depends on the paradox that language is beyond human disposal yet is the origin of spiritual being, shows that he valued spiritual problems and tragic faith. *A Passage to India* presents religion, atheism, and humanism from unorthodox perspectives, which have their parallels in radical theology.

His essay, "What I Believe," applies the motif of tragic faith to humanism. Admitting an aversion to creed, he acknowledges an obligation to make a creed of his unbelief. Trusting in the "indwelling spirit" of kind, creative humanists, he restates this trust in postreligious terms. Alert to declining liberal humanism, he points to the solipsism which results from this decline, insisting that the fragmentary world is an opportunity for renewing sacramental reality. He embraces the paradox that man's separation from his fellows in a faithless world is the very condition which makes him capable of intercourse with them. To reinforce the fruitfulness of essential loneliness, he quotes Job's words: "Naked I came into the world, naked I shall go out of it."[577] Citing the prophet of tragic faith, he defines a promise of spiritual renewal: the absolute loneliness of mortality is a human condition that motivates love and creativity. By exploring the inadequacies of religion and humanism in *A Passage to India*, he invites readers to see that recognising the tragic nature of faith may renew our trust in the modern world.

Spiritual Ecology in *The Longest Journey* (1907) and *Howards End* (1910)

Places have a genius, though the less we talk about it the better.[578]
She recaptured the sense of space, which is the basis of all earthly beauty, and, starting from Howards End, she attempted to realize England. She failed—visions do not come when we try, though they may come through trying. But an unexpected love of the island awoke in her, connecting on this side with the joys of the flesh, on that with the inconceivable.[579]

In these epigraphs, Forster suggests a dialectical renewal of body and spirit, nature and imagination, locale and infinity. After visiting Greece in 1903, he wrote "The Road from Colonus" (1904). In this *fantasy*, the Hellenism of which obliquely parallels Sophocles's tragedy of Oedipus, he stresses a banality that crushes an old man's inspirations, experienced in a shrine to "the Virgin, inheritor of the Naiads' and Dryads' joint abode."[580] The novels discussed here extend this humanist dialectic of classicism and Christianity: *Genius loci* is real but ineffable; aesthetic affection for place leads doubtfully to bodily and spiritual pleasure. Thus, Forster's philosophy is misnamed "liberal humanism"; the label ignores his "anti-antimodernist circumvention"; modernism's limits do not define his authorship. Satirising public-school ideals, urbanism, and commerce, he tests middle-class life by "a practical alternative to spiritualism" that opposes tradition to modernism.[581] He subordinates capitalism to geography, sites symbolically mediating human relations. To an extent, his sense of identity is empirical. Yet, like Sterne, he mocks Locke's sense of selfhood and enduring ideas, mental associations resisting chronology and putting idealism and materialism at odds. His secular theology leads his homoerotic characters to holy places; his criticism of cosmopolitanism validates topographical and sexual unorthodoxy.

Taking an analogy for marriage from Percy Bysshe Shelley (1792–1822)—"the dreariest and longest journey"—in the second edition of *Epipsychidion* (1839), Forster makes Rickie Elliot, the focal character of *The Longest Journey*, weak yet admirable. Offspring of a loveless marriage and dull to sterile gender conventions, Rickie is dislocated. The obtuse plot and motif of sudden death mock immortality, and the three-part story, "Cambridge," "Sawston," and "Wiltshire," offer deep implications about spatial imagination. Forster begins humorously with how Rickie sees the world. The adverb *there* is repeated as his Cambridge friends debate reality after Berkeley: how do being and perceiving relate; do objects exist only when perceived? Metaphysical talk passes Rickie by. He cannot grasp his friend Ansell's belief that some things exist objectively while others are given reality by "diseased imagination." To Ansell, perception may be both lazy and over-determined. Since Rickie forgets the arrival of Herbert and Agnes Pembroke, Ansell denies them reality, given their conventionality. Herbert depresses people with his "clerical cut." Forster saps the Pembrokes' sense of place; the picture of a city with waterways in Rickie's room that Agnes thinks is Venice despite not having been there, while visitors "who had been to Stockholm knew [it] to be Stockholm" proves the point. That city and Rickie's mother are juxtaposed: "looking rather sweet," she is "standing on the mantelpiece." That Rickie's mother conceived Stephen Wonham, his half-brother, in Stockholm comes later. Forster's irony is keener for second-time readers who, thus, read place imaginatively.[582]

Rickie's sense of place trivialises myth; he will not let place's subversive potential inform his imagination. Elms in the college quadrangle are dryads—lady trees who "had for generations fooled the college statutes" by living with students. Sexualising the scene, he extends neither image nor subversion, his impressions facile. The dell he visits in the "season of its romance" seems as big as Switzerland or Norway.[583] It is also a church that transfigures his actions. "Like the ancient Greeks," he laughs at "his holy place" yet leaves it "no less holy." Aspiring to its spirit, he feels "extremely tiny and extremely important." To friends, his sublimity is mere posture—a preciosity he ultimately disowns. Joining Agnes in the dell, he recalls wishing to touch nature like the Greeks and to realise England's beauty by imagining trees and fields are "alive." But he accepts her denial of myth. The self-abasement he nurses with his deformed leg and the belief he will never achieve the passion of Agnes and Gerald yields to her. Her need for a love object ignores his earlier consolation of her grief. When Gerald and Agnes kiss, Rickie is displaced: now he looks "down coloured valleys," now "at pinnacles of virgin snow." A "riot of images" takes him to the "springs of creation" and "primeval monotony." Such disorder he cannot shape. When Gerald dies, Rickie turns Agnes into an exotic image, despite Ansell's scorning such puerility. To Ansell, she is "not there," but Rickie insists that, if not born in Greece, she is an intelligent princess from "overseas" with "more reality than any other woman in the world." Losing touch with the world, he commits "an unpardonable sin." His mythologising ignores the locality of images. His topography is undercut by imperial and sexual idolatry. Patriotic in imagination, he is sure the English have "been nearly as great as the Greeks" and that "England is immense. English literature certainly." He thinks the English superior since the Greeks "lacked spiritual insight, and had a low conception of woman." Forster exposes this complacency, denying that literature and humanism endorse nationalism. Similarly, *Howards End* mocks "the native imagination" for failing to vivify "one fraction of a summer field, or [to] give names to half a dozen stars." It takes in only witches and fairies. The Pembrokes' sense of Rickie's writing dulls his imagination. Agnes is scornful: "He muddles all day with poetry and old dead people, and then tries to bring it into life. It's too funny for words." They treat literature with typical British materialism.[584]

Rickie's idolatry and patriotism are globally pretentious. To Ansell, there is "no great world at all, only a little earth, for ever isolated from the rest of the little solar system." Love keeps Rickie from meeting Agnes at the Cambridge Union since it keeps "Cambridge in its proper place" and makes him "a citizen of the great world." His pretence is undone by a dream, proving he loves his college rooms more than her; they are the only place he calls his own. His focus on inner space means he fears "the splendours and horrors of the world" and avoids the "genius of the place." While Rickie invests Agnes with sibylline mystery, place matters little to her. After Gerald's death, she gets used to "any place." If less appealing than Rickie's fear, her indifference exposes his preciosity. By denying Agnes and Herbert voices and giving their suburban house articulation, Forster rejects Rickie's aestheticism: criticism of Agnes and him links gender and place. Sexual identity becomes a theme since, despite their caring too much and too little for place, they conventionally gender nature as female. His effort to create place is bathetic. Returning to Cambridge, he enjoys views from the train; the trip is "his pilgrimage towards the abode of peace," but the city greets him with "open drains." Unable to block Rickie's liking for landscape, Agnes recoils from it. Returning to Sawston via "the Virgilian counties," she hates him looking from the train window and seeing nature as "some dangerous woman." Conflicted stances to place expose their unacknowledged sexual sublimation.[585]

Despising Mrs Failing, his father's sister, Rickie accepts her denial of locality. Dreaming of Arcady, she deplores Wiltshire, her aesthetics "sterile." When fatally wounded on the railway, Rickie grants her denial, despite having tried to resist her sterility. Stephen's vulgarity and "empirical freedom" terrify Rickie, making him want to sink into the earth rather than admit male sexuality. Before learning his mother is also Stephen's, he will not be guided by Stephen in the country. After a solitary walk to Cadbury Rings, Mrs Failing slyly discloses his half-brother. This shocks his new sense that views the country as a system spread before him: Wiltshire is the "heart of our island" and "our national shrine." Impressed by England's size, he cannot picture a larger. His recall of the Cambridge dell reveals the ironic mix of system and impression in his sense of place and disclaimer of imperialism. His reading of Shelley in the Rings ignores the overlay of British, Roman, Saxon, and Danish history in Wiltshire. He is as blind to the pagan burial mound in the Rings as to brotherhood with Stephen: the mound is the past he seals like an unhallowed grave when Mrs Failing shocks him. His love for fields ends when he faints among the dead whom he denies. Recovery opens him a little: "The earth he had dreaded lay close to his eyes, and seemed beautiful." But he never owns the generative power of Stephen's father.[586]

Rickie asks Agnes to treat Stephen as a symbol. She spurns his request. To Rickie, Stephen is a symbol offered only once. Agnes is glad Mrs Failing would send Stephen abroad. Far from affecting Agnes, Rickie gives in to her and becomes "a sexual snob," ignoring Stephen when he calls to say farewell. Agreeing with Agnes that Stephen lacks "full human rights," Rickie betrays his symbolic creed. Marriage further betrays his ideals; he prays for deliverance "from the shadow of unreality that had begun to darken the world." Agnes and Herbert master him by preaching a Great Britain isolated from Europe in the name of world rule; imperialism subdues their intellect and quells any "uneasy memory of spiritual deserts, spiritual streams." When she would send Stephen off, Mrs Failing thinks "with satisfaction of our distant colonies." To the vicar, leaving England is not going abroad; the colonies are simply "Greater Britain."[587]

Stephen loathes geopolitical and sexual truisms. The colonial view of North America as a "boundless continent" is to him senseless. Too "near to the things he loved to seem poetical," he will not be a remittance man, preferring a classical quest at home. In a drunken "symbolic act," he strips, crosses the mill-pond, dresses anew, and sets off cross country. He refuses to mythologise place or love Wiltshire "more than the whole world." While Rickie frets over Salisbury's sprawl and proposes that rural life resist the "modern spirit," Stephen is "an animal with just enough soul to contemplate its own bliss." To Ansell, Stephen truly figures in the landscape: he seems Greek and to have come from a distant place about which he never talks and to have been a guest of the gods with whom he has eaten.[588] A bastard of parents whose embrace found "one little interval between the power of the rulers of this world and the power of death," he is hallowed by biblical and classical allusions. Born on the continent, he is the son of a farmer whose talk of Wiltshire soil made it a "living being" and who viewed manure as "a symbol of regeneration and of the birth of life from life." His fertility symbolism grows from facts shared with Mrs Elliot whose belief that "the living world is beautiful beyond the laws of beauty" was stifled by a husband from whom she begged bread but who gave her "not even a stone."[589]

An unlettered humanist, Stephen is a particularist; he holds that one "belongs to the place one sleeps in and to the people one eats with." Walking north from Wiltshire, he wins a spiritual ecology that prefigures *Howards End*. He reaches a river as black and "majestic as a stream in hell." Rising in Wiltshire, it is tainted by Midland modernity. The waters he grew up by and on which he floated ritual boats flowed unspoilt to the English Channel. His sense of Wiltshire as England's watershed divides his antipathy to London from his love of the rural: Londoners are "on the road to sterility," this disgust figured as a river never reaching the sea. His dislocation is more creative than Rickie's when the latter stops his brother killing himself at Sawston. Rickie saves the drunkard to resurrect their mother: his deed means that "she whom he had loved had risen from the dead and might rise again." His Christology is undone by admiration for Stephen as one "who probably owned the world." Confused theology and easy secularism aside, Rickie's outlook is harmful: he makes Stephen a figure of lost maternal love since he will not let symbols grow from immediate love. To free himself from kinship and gender rules, Stephen yearns to be treated as a man, not a brother, and to rescue Rickie from Agnes and Herbert. Rickie responds by trusting Stephen's voice only in so far as it has overleaped the grave. Rickie accepts that sex is subject to generational change, but his need to find his mother in his brother impels him to think about voice as close to "racial essence" and divinity. No wonder he succumbs to Agnes's denial of Stephen. She denies him human rights since his voice recalls Gerald and turns her to him as to her first lover. Self-disgust leads her to call him "illicit" and "abnormal." If Stephen's voice recalls his mother to Rickie and Gerald to Agnes, it defies kinship. After confronting Mrs Failing, Rickie hopes for spiritual love; he would sacrifice conventions for love of Stephen. But final discovery of his drunken brother shows otherwise. He prays for a brother, not a man, and for himself, having taken people as "real." In religious despair, he is sure Stephen will defile his mother by dying debauched. He saves Stephen a second time with dutiful weariness but without self-love. Adopting Mrs Failing's nihilism, he will not face death: he is taken not by accident or spiritual sloth but by sexual, domestic, and imperialist conventions.[590]

Sudden death is a motif in *Howards End*, pointing readers beyond nihilism: "People have their own deaths as well as their own lives, and even if there is nothing beyond death we shall differ in our nothingness." Dying suddenly, Ruth Wilcox is a spirit. Aristocratic in temperament, she worshipped the past in "ancestors." Like Stephen, she exists as "a voice." Her trust in heritage surpasses kinship, as her idea of "property" shows. Ownership of Howards End, her birthplace, roots her. Sick of urbanity—equated to the automobile and industrial revolution—she tells Margaret Schlegel, her spiritual heir, to enjoy being "a girl." Ruth shuns progress; caring nothing for the franchise, she is no activist. She values inner growth. She tolerates her husband's scorn of the Continent, accepting that her family's Anglicanism has dimmed her Quaker upbringing since she wants Howards End transfigured into "the Holy of Holies." She bequeaths the house to Margaret as "a spirit," the plot validating her desire and thwarting the Wilcoxes' unbelief.[591]

Denying Margaret's request to stay at Howards End with Helen, Mr Wilcox evades Ruth's will, hiding illicit conduct in abstract talk about "the rights of property itself." His sense of entitlement is patriarchal. Margaret delights in Howards End and its wych-elm—to her "a comrade"—since both resist patriarchy: "House and tree transcended any simile of sex." Tree and house are like neither man nor woman. Far from glimpsing "truer relationships" beyond the grave, she sees them arising from "within limits of the human." After Mrs Avery unpacks the Schlegels' furniture, Margaret feels Howards End's vitality, sure houses are "alive." To Mr Wilcox, residents' associations make houses "sacred," but Margaret explores their spiritual ethos. To her, men spoil houses by making them "nice for women": patriarchy ruins interior design. She shares Mrs Avery's view that the Wilcoxes cannot make Howards End live since the "house lies too much on the land." To Margaret, the house and site kill what is dreadful and enliven what is beautiful. A very English farm, it makes Margaret see life steadily and whole. Envisioning "its transitoriness and eternal youth," she connects all humanity through its Englishness.[592]

The sisters end up at Howards End, enjoying the reciprocity of being and place, but the rootless Wilcoxes travel from self-imposed duty. When Paul flees, he enters "exile in Nigeria" for family business, his sense of place remote from personality. The Wilcoxes have no love for wherever they go; detachment renders their unity illusory. They cannot live near one another, a fact they hide behind propaganda that sends them to "where the white man might carry his burden unobserved." Visiting Oniton, Margaret learns the "Wilcoxes have no part in the place, nor in any place": this country house does not tie them to the parish or local myth. Henry is only at home in Simpson's, the restaurant on the Strand, which feeds "guests for imperial purposes" and hails "the solidity of the past." His London is commercial. He serves as "a reassuring name on company prospectuses," capitalism letting him feel he owns the world. He stands by the Thames, proud of his shares in the lock at Teddington, with the river only flowing "inland from the sea." Henry's reversal of tidal ebb and flow is exposed by ignorance of the insurance industry, while Leonard Bast, its victim, is praised for testing culture by walking out into the countryside.[593]

Henry, an imperialist with a dysfunctional family, harms people because, while he scorns the Schlegels' cosmopolitanism, he advances it by fulfilling ambitions at the cost of turning the earth "gray." To his clan, England is capitalised "Suburbia," imaged in the Hilton railway station, while Margaret pictures London stations through the landscapes of their termini. Since the Schlegels' aunt, Mrs Munt, denies the sisters' German origin and would stop them investing in "Foreign Things," her Englishness is ridiculed. She is blind to the "six Danish tumuli" outside Hilton, her nationalism no answer to Wilcoxian imperialism. Geographical and sexual imagination fail as much from insularity as from imperialism. Mocking English cynicism about romance, Forster describes "Chelsea Embankment" where Henry and Margaret walk as an "open space" based on German design: Henry is dull to its continental urbanity even as he stifles his prejudices against Germany, when citing British and German commercial rivalry in West Africa, to chat up Margaret. The family ignores

Ruth's will by calling Margaret the worst kind of "cosmopolitan." Prejudice makes them agents of cosmopolitanism, but the Schlegel sisters abandon urbanity as they adopt Ruth's appreciation of Howards End. They value temperance, tolerance, and sexual equality more than "the whole British Empire." Daughters of an intellectual whose imperialism was "of the air," they disown propaganda for Pan-Germanism and British Imperialism.[594]

With a strong spatial imagination, Margaret denies the "orderly sequence ... fabricated by historians," life having "signposts that lead nowhere." Her sense of space also forms itself against theology: the successful life involves a "waste of strength that might have removed mountains"; the least successful is "not that of the man who is taken unprepared, but of him who has prepared and is never taken." She displaces the mustard seed of Matthew 17:20 with effort before crushing circumstance. Both sisters want to be tested by the outer world. If Helen is soon disillusioned by Paul's panic, Margaret slowly sees the family's failings; temperance lets her share life with Helen at Howards End. Margaret tolerates Henry's vacuity yet abandons the middle way to become an activist: her feminism stems from spatial and sexual imagination. Early on, the Schlegel sisters describe domestic space through gender. In their father's time, their house in Wickham Place was "irrevocably feminine." They must save it from effeminacy, the Wilcoxes theirs from brutality. The sisters hold that gender is inscribed in domestic space. The dining-room at Duce Street smacks of loot; capitalism masks itself in the "ancient guest-hall" where lord sat among thanes. The Wilcoxes' home images warriors, their gender differentiation prehistoric. To Margaret, Henry "camps" in Duce Street, and his lunch sandwich represents a "prehistoric craving." His heroic code holds that "Man is for war, woman for the recreation of the warrior"; his gender divide is "the imperishable plinth of things." As promoter of urban growth, Henry advances a harmful "nomadic" civilisation by severing personal ties from nature. Margaret probes his temporal and architectural inconsistencies. To offset his obtuseness, she tries to accept his gender divide. But her failure to have him save the Basts shows that "the methods of the harem" must give way to human rights. The more she would balance idealism and reality, the more she is chastened by place. Oniton's faults behind its visual appeal confront her with "an overpowering shame" and Henry's fallibility. With "mask" off, London is "a caricature of infinity" which confirms that domestic space and picturesque beauty waste as much as inspire love.[595]

Given this ambivalence, can place address human rights and sexual identity? The sisters view the Purbeck Hills as a site for imagination that "becomes geographic and encircles England." Before marriage, Margaret will not choose between imperialists and those who see Britain as whole yet add nothing to her power; she admits no schism between doing and seeing. Surveying the land—"England was alive, throbbing through all her estuaries"—she would connect external and internal places. When first at Howards End, she regains the sense of space lost in the drive from London and mentally joins the empires of England and Germany. The house's heartbeat caused by Mrs Avery does not vanquish Margaret's insight. Displaced by Oniton, she would regain her sense of space by imagining England from Howards End. Her vision fails but confirms her love for the land, the joys of the body, and the ineffable. These rewards of spatial imagination make her spurn active, unthinking men. Before learning of Henry's infidelity, the drive to Oniton leads her to resist the "concourse of males": "their whole journey from London had been unreal. They had no part with the earth and its emotions. They were dust, and a stink, and cosmopolitan chatter, and the girl whose cat had been killed had lived more deeply than they."[596]

Margaret's spatial imagination spurns patriarchy, imperialism, and cosmopolitanism, Forster's comedy of gender roles justifying her activism. His characters call one another men or boys and women or girls, tying gender construction to place. Infatuated with the Wilcoxes' scorn for her, Helen does not treat Paul as a person. This boy plays "no part" in her romance: she sees "one kind of man" as distinct from "another sort." Despite her code of personal relations, she is so abstract that she does not divide "young men whom one takes an interest in from young men whom one knows." Margaret hardly does better with Leonard; his diffidence renders him a "fool of a young man." The sisters doubt Tibby's identity. Their house "a regular hen-coup," Helen thinks him no "real boy"; he does not care for men. If the right sort visits, they get "the wrong side of him." Margaret will not have Tibby scolded but goads him to virility. Work, she urges, was bred into men "in the last century": empire is boring but not "the heroism that builds it up."[597]

Forster's gender views can be severer than when mocking Helen and Margaret. If Leonard is a young man, Helen thinks him an "ill-fed boy." Forster calls him "boy" given his spitefulness to his betters and his democratic slogan that "All men are equal." To Leonard, the sisters are not ladies since they joke about "stealing an umbrella." He calls them girls in retaliation against their Arnoldian culture despite his effort to fulfil the spiritual prose of John Ruskin (1819–1900), itself an escape from Jacky, his common-law spouse. A revivalist awaiting conversion, he is punished for sexual pretensions. None of "your weak knock-kneed chaps," he claims to be virile but has a heart condition. Jacky cannot cure his sexual passivity. Margaret's attempt is as fruitless: moved by his country walk, she thinks him a "naive and sweet-tempered boy," but when she presents him to Henry and Evie Wilcox as a real man, they smirk.[598]

The Wilcoxes suffer gender delusions. Jealousy turns Henry brutish: Margaret's defence of Leonard makes him fight like a "farmyard" cock. She is too polite to say his virility stems from "the magic triangle of sex," but he exposes himself by seeing the Schlegel sisters as "girls" and hens. Since Evie will not see them as girls, her gender views are flabby. Marriage to Margaret quells Henry's jealousy, letting him assume her fidelity. He tolerates her, "one of his holiest beliefs" being that "women may say anything." Hypostasising "the female mind" as incapable of economic thought, the Wilcoxes spurn modern ideas of gender. Charles Wilcox believes in "temptresses"; they complement the strong man he affects. His father is ambivalent: he sees Charles "as little boy and strong man in one." Margaret observes that their ilk has not found "the life of the body."[599] The more they think gender fixed, the more a comic transfer exposes them. Evie, the athletic woman who daunts Margaret by staring at nothing and entering marriage blithely, scowls "like an angry boy." Aware of Henry's blindness to illimitable views,

Margaret would enlarge "the space" of his strength. Tolerating his masterly resistance, she is masterly in her own way: "If he was a fortress she was a mountain peak, whom all might tread, but whom the snows made nightly virginal." She is tempted to lapse from comradeship and give Henry "the kind of wife" he wants. She plays the girl "until he could rebuild his fortress and hide his soul from the world" on admitting his infidelity to Ruth and believing Margaret not womanly enough. His sexual contempt for the sisters is ungrounded, since the love that Helen and Margaret find "in common things" proves "the inner life" pays and vivifies the world. When Margaret drives "her fingers through the grass" at Howards End, the hill moves. Her speech defying Henry to "use repentance as a blind" does not harm her. She follows Christ in not judging Helen: "Christ was evasive when they questioned Him. It is those that cannot connect who hasten to cast the first stone." The "peace of the present which passes understanding" falls on Margaret since the countryside inspires her to adapt the gospels and since she fights for women against men. Opposed to commercialism's "inner darkness," she resists ideological sterility: proportion is to be reached only by "continuous excursions" into "reality and the absolute." She realises the "barrier of sex," if falling, is high and hazardous for women, and she defies the gender divide that is reified by public-school virility in the Bible's claim that "Male and female created he them." Stirred by Henry's infidelity to think the sexes may be "races" with distinct moralities and love a "device of Nature's to keep things going," she decides sexual impulses are less mysterious than sexual tenderness, the gap between farmyard and humans being wider than "Science" can measure and "Theology" ponder. When she excuses Henry to Helen, Margaret calls for "charity in sexual matters": so little is known about them that society's verdict is "futile." She roots this code at Howards End, finding in a shared love of place with Helen a power less to do with sexual difference than with gender indeterminacy.[600]

The claim that the Schlegel sisters turn Howards End into a "sterile quarantine" and that Margaret is too wedded to the melioristic notion of a third sex is moot since it reads Forster as more abstract than he was: the sisters' residence at Howards End results from a feminist critique of society and an earthy commitment to reproduction. The contention that *The Longest Journey* emphasises masculinity, given Forster's vague apocalypticism, similarly ignores his creation of fruitful tensions between familial values and powerful contingencies arising from geographical setting.[601] Nearer the mark is the proposal that, if Rickie, Stephen, and Ansell set humanity over against nature's redundancies, they draw masculinity "somehow" from the soil. This "somehow" indicates how Forster's treatment of setting is unique.[602] If sympathetic to his romantic wish to base human continuity on ties to nature, critics discount his spiritual sense of place by judging Margaret's transfiguration into Mrs Wilcox as poor characterisation.[603] Forster's dissociation of heterosexuality from identity suggests why he might not have seen reproduction as either a natural bond or a guarantee of vital tradition. Thus, he questioned imperialism's certainties about heterosexuality.[604] Still, his narratives operate on a broader base. If we see that he used Christian humanism to express dissatisfaction with liberalism and orthodox religion and if we grant that he exploited the existential properties of language and voice to realise disembodied values, we begin to appreciate that figural ideas of place and gender were for him sacramental.[605]

CHAPTER EIGHT
The Book Trade

One aspect of literary history complementing the explications in the previous chapters involves what book production tells about the cultural values of writing and reading. Economic and political facts about the book trade broaden literary contexts, reminding us that authors, far from isolated creators, are obliged to conform to business practices that do not always serve them. Even acclaimed authors like Austen experienced the whims of publishers and prejudices of reviewers. At the end of the eighteenth century, female authors still confronted gender discrimination; ideological systems in the trade also unsettled male writers. Scholars often aim to recover the work of supposedly minor authors in the belief that the literary canon was too exclusive: historians of the trade rightly question the power of institutional publishing cartels. One powerful institution—the *Dictionary of National Biography*—first appeared between 1885 and 1900. This work, listing seven hundred authors, called Alexander Bicknell, the subject of this chapter, "an industrious littérateur of the last quarter of the eighteenth century, whose writings received their due meed of ridicule or faint praise in the *Monthly Review*, and are now forgotten." But from what we may deduce, he was a university-educated, humble member of the established church who struggled long and hard for authorial identity and public recognition. He had moments of success with popular and educational topics. Despite winning patrons and subscribers, success was short-lived. His final essays show that, in his own mind, his reputation as a hack was irredeemable. His troubled career gives rise to issues related to the cultural history of reading and to constrictive marketing practices since he often celebrates and imitates major writers of the turn of the eighteenth century discussed earlier in this book. While this chapter draws his biography from his bibliography, in detailing the range of his generic efforts, it shows that he tried to uphold humanistic education by meeting the philosophical challenges it faced at the end of his life. Together with his promotion of linguistic and historical pedagogy, his interest in medieval romance, tragic women, and pictorial narrative illustrates the ongoing influence of the Renaissance.

A Literary Journeyman:
Alexander Bicknell (d. 1796)

The original *Dictionary of National Biography* assigns Bicknell thirteen "books and pamphlets" along with eight publication dates. One title-page says he edited *Travels through the Interior Parts of North America* (1778) by Jonathan Carver (1710–1780), the Massachusetts writer, and *Apology for Her Life* (1785) by George Anne Bellamy (1727–1788), the Irish actress. Revising the entry for the *New Oxford Dictionary of National Biography* raised questions about why the initial entry implied that his titles were noticed in the *Monthly Review* alone. There were many more reviews and newly discovered title-pages that increase our understanding of his literary aspirations: periodicals in the 1780s and 1790s expand his bibliography. If newly discovered essays confirm his failure to win renown, they are resources for what may be deduced from prefaces, dedications, and other para-literary forms about his outlook on authorship, patronage, and the book trade.[606] Tracking him in periodicals illustrates how he dealt with the contempt of literati and aspired to a place in the literary canon.[607]

His first publications were anonymous but soon manifested professional intent when title-pages linked works. When his name appeared on title-pages, he had ghost-written books that were later cited on title-pages. As his career advanced, he wrote under his full name, placing select prior works on title-pages. Early periodical essays bore his full name, but later ones were identified only by his initials "A.B."[608] That these letters matched generic initials of boxes in coffee-houses shows he was not averse to hiding himself in declining circumstances.[609] His final books, published under his name, did not list earlier ones. The ground on which he built an identity and finally produced books and essays that were unconcerned in promoting his name is evident in the fact that, while he sustained relations with publishers, the titles of which he was most proud were self-published. This career pattern appears in novelistic, historical, theological, and periodical texts. In magazines, he tested ideas for books and promoted published ones. The original *DNB* underreported his output, limiting his range of genres while over-relying on the *Monthly Review*.[610]

His first title, *The Benevolent Man*, is an anonymous novel published in 1775 by J. Lewis at his circulating library in Charles Street, Westminster.[611] Dedicated to William Legge (1731–1801), second Earl of Dartmouth and secretary of state for the American Department, this two-volume work seeks his lordship's protection, "this trifling Essay" a "Vehicle" for "Admonition." It balances moral reform and social activism with political deference, as topical allusions and rhetorical appeals witness. It lauds Lady Mary Wortley Montagu (1689–1762), Baron Thomas Dimsdale (1712–1800), and Robert Sutton (1708–1788) as inoculators who saved "the fairest part of the creation from the ravages of a dreadful disorder"; it celebrates Jonas Hanway (1712–1786), the philanthropist, for creating workhouses, and it begs Lord North (1732–1792), the prime minister, to spur legislation to advance such benevolence; it heralds John Howard (1726–1790), the prison reformer, and Charles Whitworth

(1752–1825), the distinguished politician and diplomat, for freeing thousands from debtors' prisons to "liberty and society"; and it praises Garrick, the Barrys, and the "lovely Baddeley," the stage being an important cultural institution.[612] Bicknell calls the British throne a model of "connubial happiness" while chiding city husbands for resorting to prostitutes. Defending class hierarchy, he calls for a "proper distinction" between schools for daughters of the great and of "tradesmen and mechanics." The former need "genteel accomplishments," the latter "domestic and useful" skills. A patriot, he laments educating girls in France where they are turned "against the customs and religion of their native country."[613]

His second title, also anonymous, is *The History of Lady Anne Neville, Sister to the Great Earl of Warwick*, its two volumes printed for T. Cadell in 1776.[614] The *Monthly Review* damned its mixture of fancy and fact but judged it harmless since "written in too vicious a style to survive its first winter."[615] Since Lady Anne (c. 1414–1480), a distinguished book collector and confidante of Margaret of Anjou (1430–1482), had a refined soul like the Duchess of Kingston, Bicknell dedicates his "trifling" composition to the latter. Lauding Elizabeth Chudleigh (1720–1788) in the dedication of 13 October 1775 and seeking her protection to save his book from oblivion, he admits he cannot boast of "former Labours, or an established reputation" but voices sympathy for abused and notorious women.[616] Chudleigh was under proceedings for bigamy: mistress to Evelyn Pierrepont (1711–1773), Duke of Kingston, she wed him in 1769 while married to Augustus Hervey (1724–1779), later Earl of Bristol. Once found guilty, she lived in Calais on a legacy from the duke.[617] Bicknell's openness to French writers appears in his prefatory admission of indebtedness to Abbé François Prévôst (1697–1763). Not intent on accuracy about the Wars of the Roses, he promotes humanity by distinguishing between error and vice in a woman whose arranged marriage led to wretchedness, early widowhood, and court intrigue. Erotically heightening Anne's life, he likely thought popular history might defend Chudleigh.

Isabella: or The Rewards of Good-Nature, A Sentimental Novel, a third anonymous title, was published by J. Bell in London and C. Etherington in York in 1776.[618] The title-page of its two volumes identifies the writer as author of *The Benevolent Man* and *The History of Lady Anne Neville*, saying the novel is intended "chiefly to convey united amusement and instruction to the fair-sex." If Bicknell gains identity through continuity of titles, his concern for female readers and feminine topics accepts patriarchalism in the literary establishment. The *Monthly Review* faults his equation of social and literary aims, damning the novel's sensational formulae; its language is "diffuse and ill modulated." While endorsing its concern for female education, the reviewer claims the novel's sole merit is that its heroine is "a very amiable picture of conjugal tenderness and prudence," turning social prescription into literary insult.[619]

Bicknell popularised medieval times in his next anonymous title: *The History of Edward Prince of Wales, commonly termed the Black Prince*.[620] It was printed for J. Bew in 1776.[621] The *Monthly Review* names him in its table of contents but not in the review, which says the book lacks "industrious researches"; its generalisations command no respect: he simply popularises a royalist guidebook. The dedication to the Prince of Wales, George Augustus Frederick (1762–1830), calls him true descendant of Edward Woodstock, the Black Prince (1330–1376).[622] In loyalty, he offers a model to a prince who will match his ancestor's fame. To be more readable than Arthur Collins (c. 1682–1760), he omits source references: simplifying historiography and drawing on Jean Froissart (1337–1405), he asks readers to grant him authenticity.[623]

He popularised history again in *The Life of Alfred the Great, King of the Anglo-Saxons*, with mounting confidence since, published in 1777 by Bew, publisher of the former title, it named "A. Bicknell" for the first time on a title-page. It was listed as a new publication by the *Gentleman's Magazine* of December 1777; the *Monthly Review* delayed its contempt:

> A subject that might have claimed the pen of a Robertson or a Hume,
> a subject truly great, and, in every respect, adapted to the times, is here
> occupied by a writer who is not even an Oldmixon, or a Guthrie.[624]

Undiscouraged, Bicknell was tenacious: the *Life* formed the basis of a play he penned at this time and a chapter in a commentary on providence which he produced in the following decade.

In 1777, he undertook controversy when Bew brought out *Philosophical Disquisitions on the Christian Religion, Addressed to Soame Jenyns, Esq. and W. Kenrick, L.L.D.* In this work, he anonymously tried to reconcile Jenyns (1704–1787), whose *A View of the Internal Evidence of the Christian Religion* had five editions in 1776, and William Kenrick (1725–1779), whose *Observations on Soame Jenyns's View of the Internal Evidence of the Christian Religion: Addressed to its Almost-Christian Author* also came out in 1776. The *Monthly Review*, blind to the author, derided the claim that Jenyns and Kenrick would have better defended Christianity had they realised that the soul's pre-existence clarifies the mysteries of nature and religion.[625] The review damns *Essay on Regimen* (1740) by George Cheyne (1673–1743), denying the world is full of spirits and attacking citations of Plato, Shakespeare, Milton, and Pope; poetic licence cannot confirm faith. The reviewer's dissenting materialism spurns Jenyns as an incontrovertible defender of Christianity.[626]

Bicknell's service to literary tradition was again clear in 1779 when his anonymous two-volumes-in-one paraphrase of Edmund Spenser's *Faerie Queene*, *Prince Arthur: An Allegorical Romance* was published by G. Riley and sold by F. Newbery in London.[627] With another title-page, it appeared that year in Cambridge.[628] Dedicated to Viscountess Charlotte Howe (1703–1782), it exploits the revived taste for romance to guide young readers.[629] Bicknell seeks to reveal the beauties of Spenser under the allegory and to inculcate the love of glory in all classes.

Pedagogy aided Bicknell in defending class hierarchy, the ecclesiastical establishment, and literary tradition in his next work. In 1780, he again took up controversy with his eighth title, *The Putrid Soul. A Poetical Epistle to Joseph Priestley. LL.D. F.R.S. on His Disquisitions Relating to Matter and Spirit*. Published by J. Bowen in the Strand, its title-page named "A.

Bicknell" author of *The Life of King Alfred* and compiler of Carver's *Travels*. These titles resist the *Monthly Review*; they claim commercial success and oppose orthodoxy to the honoured radical materialist. Bicknell presents himself as "an unlearn'd Muse," citing his *Philosophical Disquisitions* along with *Treatise on a Pre-existent State* (1762) by the Reverend Capel Berrow (1715–1782) and Cheyne's *Essay* to defy Priestley's "degrading tenets" and to locate his poem in a canon. Hostile to Priestley throughout his career, Bicknell likely thought he could gain renown by defaming the materialist.

Priestley (1733–1804), a Calvinist by upbringing, embraced unorthodoxy at the Daventry Academy; training for the Presbyterian ministry, he followed David Hartley (1705–1757) in denying religious ideas of identity, free will, and the distinction between soul and body. Despite his Unitarianism, Priestly became a tutor at the Dissenting Academy of Warrington where he taught oratory, criticism, grammar, history, and law. *The Rudiments of English Grammar* appeared in 1761, having nine editions in his lifetime. Less popular than *A Short Introduction to English Grammar* (1762) by Robert Lowth (1710–1787), it told grammarians that Latin was no model for English syntax. Elected to the Royal Society in 1766 for historiography, Priestley thought education should further administration and commerce but not ecclesiasticism. Faced by discrimination, he sided with John Wilkes (1725–1797). Refuting doctrines of atonement in *The Scripture Doctrine of Remission* (1761), he argued in *Disquisitions Relating to Matter and Spirit* (1777) that objections to materialism are false: matter is not passive, impenetrable, solid, or unable to initiate action; objects are centres of force, their solidity best viewed as a power of repulsion. Since they interact, mind and body are forms of the same substance. According to the title-page of *Disquisitions*, Priestley opposed the "*Doctrine of the Pre-existence of Christ*."[630]

Baffled by Priestley's fame, Bicknell aimed to rival his educational theory; however, the *Monthly Review* disabused him in its vehement review of *The Putrid Soul*: the author is "so completely deficient" as "poet, philosophe, and theologist" that we cannot "determine in which character he disgraces himself most"; his system is a compound of crude, heterogeneous principles drawn from "the dregs of Platonism" and "last runnings of modern mysticism" and placed in "a cracked poetical phial" as an antidote to "Dr. Priestley's highly rectified spirit of matter." The reviewer derides the "long-forgotten hypothesis of the lapse of human souls in a pre-existent state" and "flight of impure spirits, after their departure from this world, to some of the remoter planets, where they will undergo a degree of punishment, proportioned to the guilt they have contracted, till by progressive steps ... they recover their original purity." Mocking "the resolution of souls into their first principle," the reviewer charges Bicknell with "gross and profane raillery" beyond the "wildest visionaries of the Christian church." Thus, the *Monthly Review* scorns the religious sublime of Thomson, Young, Collins, and Christopher Smart (1722–1771), echoed by Cowper, Blake, William Wordsworth (1770–1850), and Samuel Taylor Coleridge (1772–1834).[631]

Bicknell was active as ghost-writer and magazine contributor in the eight years before his name reappeared on a title-page, namely *The Patriot King; or, Alfred and Elvida*. This self-published tragedy, printed for "Alexr. Bicknell," went on sale at his house, No. 26, Red Lion Street, near Red Lion Square, in 1788.[632] Available at bookshops, it was slighted in the *Monthly Review* which says theatre managers of 1778 refused the play, the nation defended against invasion from France and Spain "by other means." The plot depicts Alfred's resistance to King Haldane's invasion and the warring lust of the Danish monarchs. To the reviewer, Alfred's character lacks the sublime sentiments of Thomson's, sinking rather to "Mr. John Home's Alfred."[633] As for Bicknell's spiritualism, the reviewer scorns the invisible spirits taken from Thomson and the transfer of setting to Norway where, in imitation of Shakespeare, preternatural beings and magicians appear. In defeating Haldane and saving Queen Elvida from the jealous Gunhilda, Alfred redeems his country and his love. Ignoring Bicknell's patriotic focus on marital fidelity, the review ends anticlimactically: "The diction is not so quaint as in some late productions, but it does not any where rise to that dignified simplicity which tragedy requires."[634] The *Gentleman's Magazine* differs. It details the title-page which records Bicknell's authorship of *The Life of King Alfred* and *The History of Edward the Black Prince* and his editorship of Carver's *Travels* and *An Apology for the Life of George Anne Bellamy*. It reprints the play's preface, endorses the list of subscribers, and charges theatre-managers with caprice. The play is his "first effort of genius" since his other works are "mere compilations," the last named doing him "least credit." It finds the subscribers "respectable," and, since the list contains the name of Sir Barnard Turner who died in 1778, it finds the play's publication long intended. It notes Bicknell wrote prologue and epilogue and that the latter is dated 1779. With fewer bibliographical details, the review in the *General Magazine and Impartial Review* finds the subscribers "very respectable" and focuses on style: there is "something to blame, and much to commend" in the tragedy; it contains

> much good writing, and will not prove an unacceptable present for the closet. They who are fond of the tales of other times, will read it with pleasure, and will probably have little fault to find, unless they censure the author's numerous imitations of Shakespeare: but is not some degree of praise due to him who has taste and talents sufficient to imitate that great master at all?

In dismissing the reprinted play, the *Monthly Review* is malign: *Alfred, an Historical Tragedy. To which is added, A Collection of Miscellaneous Poems. By the same Author* is cited as an octavo volume published by Robinsons in 1789 at four shillings, the author's name withheld. The notice is harsh: "The writer of *a tragedy* should be *a poet*. Whether the author of *Alfred* comes under that description, the reader may judge for himself from the following specimen. We have not selected the most exceptionable lines in the performance. The *fable* is wholly unworthy of notice." To accent dispraise, it lauds the poems: "The 'Miscellaneous Poems' are so much superior to the tragedy in point of harmony (although the thoughts contained in them are trite and common), that we can scarcely believe them to be the productions of one and the same pen." By damning his consistency, the *Monthly Review* attacks his identity. Its refusal to recall its first review and to evaluate the reprinting shows it assuming an unassailable institutional power to prevent Bicknell from being viewed as an independent voice with an identifiable corpus.[635]

The prologue and epilogue of *The Patriot King* match concerns throughout his writing life. The former is royalist and patriotic in making Alfred's story an occasion to renew loyalty to George III, and the latter, spoken by Melpomene, praises Garrick for turning the tragedies of Shakespeare and Otway into ennobling national agents, unlike frivolous comedies based on foreign works. Bicknell's nationalism is reflected in the pride with which he drew up, in March 1788, a list of works to be advertised in the first edition, the list naming: *The Life of King Alfred, The History of Edward the Black Prince, The History of Lady Anne Neville, Isabella, The Benevolent Man, Prince Arthur, Philosophical Disquisitions, and The Putrid Soul*. The list includes two untraced poetical volumes: *A Monody (After the Manner of Milton's Lycidas) on the Death of Mr. Linley, Junior* and *More Odes upon Odes; or, A Peep at Peter Pindar; or, Falsehood Detected; or, What You Will*. The 162 subscribers warrant pride; the thirteen fellows of the Royal Society, Banks included, must have been encouraging (given Bicknell's dislike of Priestley who is not on the list, although Priestley's friend, Richard Price, is). Five MPs, five MDs, eleven reverends, and nine knights or higher titles are there. Eminences include Robert Adam, architect (1728–1792); Burney, music historian; William Chambers, architect (1723–1796); John Jebb, medical doctor and reformer (1737–1786); John Coakley Lettsom, philanthropist and benefactor to Carver's London widow (1744–1815); and Thomas Warton (1728–1790), Poet Laureate.[636]

Since his poetical volumes are not extant, probably appearing anonymously, one turns to *Doncaster Races* as his next work.[637] The title-page of this two-volume "tale of truth," subtitled *The History of Miss Maitland*, claims Bicknell edited original materials. Published in London by C. Stalker, this epistolary work lacks a date on the imprint, the British Library Catalogue proposing 1790, perhaps since it was reviewed that year by the *Monthly Review*. But the *General Magazine and Impartial Review* noticed it in 1789.[638] The title-page names Bicknell as the author of *History of Lady Anne Neville, Isabella*, and *The Patriot King* and editor of Bellamy's *Apology* and Carver's *Travels*. Bicknell's wish to be known as compiler shows in the advertisement where he calls himself improver of the letters. He edited them because of their amiable heroine and the "instructive extraneous matter" he could intersperse. He trusts the tale will, like his other works, receive "universal approbation" given his pen's "embellishing additions." The *Monthly Review* had none of this, treating it as "a mere novel" and ignoring the extraneous material. Its scorn images excessive "manufacture"; the "usual œconomy of the inundations that still continues [sic] to pour on us" leads to novels so similar that "comparative merit" is indefinable, this "species of composition" being "worn-out." The review is disgusted with Bicknell and novelistic conventions: a gentleman, renouncing a prior engagement, marries a stranger whom he meets at Doncaster Races. His abandoned betrothed watches over him with passionate concern which only novelists could invent. Disguised as a man, she schemes, by means of a West Indian fortune left by an uncle who dies for this purpose, to save her beloved from the ruin into which his immoral wife leads him. Human feelings revolt at this, more so when the profligate wife dies from consumption, so the infatuated woman may step into the place for which she was first intended and which she has dearly purchased. The *General Magazine and Impartial Review*, not degrading the genre, thinks differently; the novel is "not without its merit." If unoriginal, the characters are not "servile copies." Bicknell finishes the characters "in the style of a master of no mean abilities." Beyond this painterly praise, the review admires the history of Egypt in one character's letters, reprinting nineteen entertainingly instructive paragraphs. Bicknell should be imitated "for the service of the ladies"; his enrichment of their fancy by "useful intelligence and instruction" is exemplary. This review admires the travelogues and concern for female readers; the *Monthly Review* is hostile to the *General Magazine and Impartial Review*.

As populariser of domestic education, Bicknell was subject to periodical rivalry evident from a title he did publish in 1790. *Painting Personified*, a two-volume exposition of works by leading artists, came out in London from R. Baldwin. The *Monthly Review* used the occasion to abuse such surveys. The reviewer cites Shaftesbury: he who reads many works is not well-read; he is exposed more to bad than good models, his head filled with "bombast, ill fancy, and wry thought." Wondering whether the volumes have a subject, the reviewer expects them to turn him into a blockhead. Mocking the fictional biography in popular prints, he reduces Bicknell's "poetical rhapsodies" to verbiage. Earlier, the *General Magazine and Impartial Review* says the work affords "great entertainment": the commentaries on pictures display taste and judgment, Bicknell enhancing them with analyses for which the artists should be grateful; the pathos assigned to serious works will improve the rising generation, and the humour read into comic paintings amuses too. The review reprints Bicknell's essay on the "Loss of the Halswell" (1786), a painting of the sensational shipwreck of the East Indiaman by Robert Smirke (1752–1845).[639]

This praise is unsurprising; a year earlier, the *General Magazine and Impartial Review* printed Bicknell's "Caricatures Explained," an essay on *Family Piece* (1781) by Henry William Bunbury (1750–1811) that begins with lines from Pope's "Eloisa to Abelard," which also serve as the epigraph to *Painting Personified*.[640] Bicknell presents himself as reading pictorial rhetoric for the public good "through the medium of your excellent and widely-circulated Magazine." If his essay pleases, he will produce a series on Thomas Rowlandson (1756–1827) and Bunbury. It seems from the later publication and review that his first effort did please readers. The *Monthly Review* is further questionable because his essay displays, in its satire of the Griskin Family sitting for a group portrait, the vulgarisation of art by *cits* and support for aesthetic idealism.

Curiously, the *Monthly Review* was positive about his final three titles. In 1790, he self-published *The Grammatical Wreath; or, A Complete System of English Grammar* which was entered at Stationer's Hall and sold by R. Baldwin of Paternoster Row and J. Debrett of Piccadilly, the former having published *Painting Personified*. The *Grammatical Wreath* digests English grammars for youth, native speakers, and foreigners, so says its title-page that has epigraphs from Virgil and Lowth.[641] Sneering at Priestley's *Rudiments* for stressing grammatical problems, the preface defends Bicknell's synthesis, stressing grammarians' erratic terminology. The advertisement at the volume's end differs from that in *The Patriot King*: it reports that *The Life of King Alfred* was dedicated with permission to William Murray (1705–1793), the powerful jurist and first Earl of Mansfield, omits *Philosophical Disquisitions*, and includes *The Patriot King*. Since he modifies his bibliography, it is odd that the advertisement mentions neither *Doncaster Races* nor *Painting Personified*, the latter published early that year.[642] Oddly, too, he does not cite edited works he had included on title-pages and in captions of periodical essays. Reshaping his bibliography in the advertisement, he does not identify himself by former works on the title-page of *The Grammatical Wreath*.

If he was thereby attempting to preclude criticism, the *Monthly Review* appreciates his aim to build a copious system of English grammar from the best parts of existing grammars, accepting his claim to have added original elucidations. It finds his rules concerning prepositions and accentuation long and perplexing and thinks the book will be used by masters more than pupils. Again, the review in the *General Magazine and Impartial Review* came out earlier and was more positive: the work embodies "much reading and labour." With its "peculiar discernment and accuracy in thought and expression," it brings order out of confusion; it records the substance of all former writers, manifesting genius, taste, and judgment. It usefully simplifies several branches of learning, abridging the philological system so that it will be a valuable acquisition to "every publick seminary of learning and every student of the English idiom." The review dislikes the puffery on the title-page but endorses Bicknell's self-estimation.[643]

His thirteenth extant title, *A History of England and the British Empire Designed for the Instruction of Youth; to which is Prefixed an Essay on the English Constitution*, also curtails self-promotion. It was published by W. Lowndes in London in 1791 and reissued in 1794. Aiming at youth, Bicknell perhaps thought it pointless to identify his works on the title-page. The *Monthly Review* judged it comparatively. Wondering why compendia of English history flood the market, the reviewer ranks Bicknell's among the best for being well executed. Yet he doubts their value; intelligible to the knowledgeable, they are above students. The maps and table of European Sovereigns contemporary with English kings render Bicknell's volume unique however.[644]

The reluctance to use para-literary forms for self-advertisement continues in his final book, *Instances of the Mutability of Fortune, Selected from Ancient and Modern History, and Arranged according to Their Chronological Order*, published by J.S. Jordan of London in 1791 and reissued in 1792, that year noticed by the *Monthly Review*. Bicknell does not identify himself on the title-page by former works. This is remarkable since he had worked on this text as early as 1783 when the first *Instances* appeared in the *European Magazine*.[645] He is likely the maker of verse mottoes on the title-page and at the head of each *Instance*, but no source is given for them. The book has no preface. Its introduction is long by two paragraphs. Footnotes cite historians whose work he digested (i.e., Josephus, Plutarch, Procopius,

Marmontel, Prideaux, and Guthrie); his *Life of Alfred* is the basis for the instance of Alfred.[646] He probably promoted the book, yet his strategy for defending his career was becoming more indirect by appealing to readers of magazines.

After he started writing for the *Town and Country Magazine* in January 1791, a review of *Instances* appeared there in April 1792. It is neutral except for a tag saying the author might have provided more examples. Bicknell may have written this review since the magazine printed a second review, including the preface and excerpts, in October 1793.[647] Repeating the first review's claim that the *Instances* fulfils authorial intent, the second calls Bicknell's method that of "the divine and the moralist." This may signify his reconciliation to writing from his ecclesiastical training. The *Monthly Review* is, as usual, condescending but not dismissive: such collections are easy to make but are acceptable if executed with judgment and spirit. The biblical stories from Adam to Nebuchadnezzar may gain attention in their new dress. The *Instances* from Croesus to Massaniello, not unpleasantly narrated, will be "convenient and grateful to many." Singling out Cromwell whose abilities and faults heighten the tyrannical grandeur of his royal antagonist, the review endorses Bicknell's emphasis on piety and virtue, concluding that the *Instances* will prove entertaining and instructive.

The reviews in the *General Magazine and Impartial Review* and the *Monthly Review* were hard won. Almost undone by ghost-writing, Bicknell turned increasingly to magazines. Under his full name, he published a poem, "Vauxhall," in the *General Magazine and Impartial Review* in 1787: the Garden of Eden has moved to London's pleasure gardens where cheerful harmony dispels the solemn silence of the time of Adam and Eve, and where, given the "choicest viands" and "richest wines," Hygeia, Momus, and Bacchus should preside.[648] For the next issue, he wrote a letter on a topic in *The Benevolent Man*, continuing his role as protector of women. An illiterate declaration of love from an Irish fortune-hunter to the daughter of a London tradesman, the letter warns maidens and widows whose fortunes are "prey to need and dissipation." The victim is a "gay city damsel" educated at a genteel boarding school where she acquired a taste for a noble style of living to which birth does not entitle her. Bicknell warns young women not to correspond with suitors without the approval of parents, clandestine matches bringing disgrace to families. The next month, "A. Bicknell" derides aristocratic fashion yet upholds hierarchy in "Observations on the Mottos Annexed to the Arms of the Nobility." Coaches emblazoned with heraldic arms deserve satire: were the mottoes inside coaches, peers would not degenerate from ancestors. The essay, unlike earlier dedications to nobles, caustically surveys the mottoes.[649]

Work for the *General Magazine and Impartial Review* likely aimed to repair the ill-fame of his commercially successful titles. Carver's *Travels through the Interior Parts of North-America, in the Years 1766, 1767, and 1768* appeared in 1778, sold by J. Walter of Charing Cross and S. Crowder of Paternoster Row. Turning Carver's journals into *Travels*, Bicknell stressed the North West Passage more than the fur trade and told of Indians who had been civilized by Europeans. He heightened Carver's agency, added passages translated from Belgian and French travellers, missionaries, and historians: Antoine Louis Hennepin (1626–1704);

Louis Armand, Baron de Lahontan (1666–1716); and Pierre François Xavier de Charlevoix (1682–1761), his writing "ornate, involved, and often flowery."[650] Improver of the explorer's text, Bicknell called himself compiler of *Travels* on the title-page of *The Putrid Soul*, following Carver's death in 1780, and editor on the title-pages of *The Patriot King* (1788) and *Doncaster Races* (1790).[651] A correspondent to the *Gentleman's Magazine* in August 1780 wanted "to know more of Mr. Bicknell, who calls himself editor of the former edition" of *Travels*. Still relatively unknown, Bicknell shrewdly linked himself for a decade to Carver's book.[652] His spiritualism was upheld by Carver, as "Anecdote of the late Captain Carver" by "A.B." in the *European Magazine* of November 1783 shows: Carver had a dream before leaving America in 1769. Predicting independence for the colonies, it upholds spiritual foresight: an arm, descending from a cloud, holds England's royal standard which the winds shred.[653] Carver told this dream in 1778 to Bicknell when he was working on Carver's book and rejecting Priestley's materialism. Bicknell was no doubt moved by a fellow struggling author: Carver, having gained permission from the Board of Trade to publish his papers, incurred losses when having to buy them back from the publisher. Bicknell was then writing *The Patriot King* and securing subscribers: *Travels* is revealingly dedicated to Banks, one of Bicknell's subscribers. In helping Carver, Bicknell enhanced his literary identity in his own eyes.

But accounts of actresses he was rumoured to have composed harmed him. *An Apology for the Life of George Ann Bellamy, late of Covent Garden Theatre. Written by Herself* sprang from the Literary Society in 1785.[654] Being "dedicated fulsomely" to the Prince of Wales and George Brudenell, Duke of Montagu (1712–1790), it was reviewed and excerpted positively in the *European Magazine*.[655] But a review with excerpts in the *Gentleman's Magazine* was hostile, claiming *apologia*, used by defenders of primitive Christianity, had been perverted to uphold stage and stews: to defend Bellamy's immorality is egregious, her life was one continued course of vice, folly, and extravagance. The sole benefit of the book might be to warn young women about treading "the slippery boards of a theatre."[656] In 1787, attitudes to Bicknell hardened when *The Memoirs of Mrs Sophia Baddeley, late of Drury Lane Theatre* appeared. The name of Mrs Elizabeth Steele, a friend of Baddeley's, is on the title-page. Yet it was mistakenly supposed to be written by him.[657] Explanations are easy to find: known to be sympathetic to unfortunate and romantic women, Bicknell was keen on the theatre as *The Patriot King* shows; when he praised Baddeley in *The Benevolent Man*, she was past her acting prime and known as a courtesan, and there are stylistic parallels between the biographies of Bellamy and Baddeley.[658] The *European Magazine* seized on one: it pointed out that the epigraph from *The Rape of the Lock* about forgiveness of Belinda on the title-page of Baddeley's biography had been applied to Bellamy, the "fair but unfortunate daughter of pleasure." Recognising professional help and supposing a continuity of ghost-writing, the magazine is sure the *Apology* is a pretext for "the mass of abominable trash before us": the former's success explains the latter's publication. Yet, Bellamy was a saint compared to Baddeley whose memoirs, clothed in "elegant language," lack decorum, consistency, and truth, Steele and coadjutor stabbing "the bosom of domestic happiness." The review namelessly sneers at Bicknell: while Steele provided the book's matter,

> be it known (and too well, indeed, is it known already) that for putting those materials together, she was indebted to the *disinterested* aid of one of the most *industrious* and *universal* book-makers in England, but who, *mirabile dictu*! has already been discarded by his fair employer, and exposed by her in the public prints for his *inability* or *misconduct* in the task of correcting and arranging the disgraceful materials necessary to compose the wretched history of an unhappy Courtesan.[659]

Blaming by ironical praise, idealising domestic life, and upholding a double standard of sexual morality, the review bears the institutional weight of a system that aimed to crush Bicknell. A month before, the *General Magazine and Impartial Review* attacked Baddeley's *Memoirs*; the pious, sentimental labour of Bellamy and her amanuensis is the model for Baddeley's autobiography. Mindful of her beauty and stage skills, the review wishes her vices had remained in the grave. From "pecuniary gratification," the book harms the living and dead by detailing infidelities: it creates domestic strife by informing wives of what were best unknown. A "mere journal, never elegant, and not always grammatical," this book, neither entertaining nor instructive, tells how a beautiful actress plunges into dissipation and prostitution and how men by casual affairs expose themselves to the vitiated tastes of those who "relish the worst of all *literary carrion*." The reviewer trusts that Steele and "her *goose-quill* friend" will exhaust readers rather than cause the harm better authors might have occasioned.[660]

Bicknell's supposed second memoir of an actress is a turning point in his literary identity: he listed his editorship of Bellamy's autobiography on the title-pages of *The Patriot King* and *Doncaster Races* but never advertised collaborating with Steele. He was likely galled by the notoriety his name attracted from association with Baddeley in magazines that once promoted his works and whose good opinion he needed to regain. The notoriety arising from his book on Bellamy and the one on Baddeley may explain the delayed publication of *The Patriot King*. His identity was certainly harmed by patriarchal attitudes to the theatre and sex which the *European Magazine* and *General Magazine and Impartial Review* shared with the *Monthly Review* and which were turned upon him by these formerly accommodating periodicals. Yet his resilience is attested by the reviews which his books later earned in magazines that had formerly castigated him. His final effort to win laurels involved fourteen articles in the *Town and Country Magazine* between 1791 and 1795, the year before he died.[661] The effort was muted; he signed them only with his initials. But he exploited essayistic self-reflexivity in ways that shed light on his sense of himself and the economic and social forces governing the book trade.

Since the *Town and Country Magazine* addressed contributors on its editorial page, the notes addressing Bicknell help assess his reputation. In January 1791, the editor notes that, despite arriving late, "Hampstead Generosity" appears "to afford Encouragement to a new and valuable Correspondent." In April 1792, the editor acknowledges poems from A.B., but in July, he advises that an acrostic and an "Epistle to Dr. Priestley from A.B., on his political and religious principles" will not appear since it is "not adapted to the Plan and Complexion of our Miscellany." In October 1792 and September 1793, he complies with A.B.'s wishes, but in March 1795, he tells A.B. that "A Collection of Good Things" will not be published. These notes show that Bicknell lacked a steady sense of the magazine's aims, partly because he remained too bent on retaliating against Priestley. Still, the editor generally treats him with courtesy and professional respect.

Of his contributions to the magazine, the first is a satire, and later ones are autobiographical pieces on authorship; the essays as a whole combine social issues with thwarted literary identity. "Hampstead Generosity; or the Preservation of a Human Life a Breach of the Sabbath" holds that local by-laws punish the working poor unfairly but ignore the patrician class that buys their services. It tells of a coach-driver who drowns on the village's western edge: after the coach overturns, no bystanders help since it is the Sabbath. Bicknell ironically stresses that the villagers' hydrophobia does not preclude strong liquors. A resident of Pond Street in Hampstead who collects stories from spectators, Bicknell decries false Christianity and calls for genuine religion.[662]

His second article, "Difference Between Genuine and Adulterated Pride," is a moral essay. His third, "Observations on the Different Modes of Salutations," views poverty in the light of gaps between polite epistolary formulae and threats. Based on French journalism, this essay cites a landlord who threatens to despoil a tenant but who closes his letter as a most obedient servant. Bicknell's next is fifteen "Queries," verbal puzzles (for example, "1. Why is a bad woman like a good epigram?" and "5. Why is an unpopular minister like a propped house?"). A fifth piece, "Enough Is Sufficient," explains how he accepted the loss of a small estate by writing retirement poetry, only to realise contentment depends less on comparing oneself to the unfortunate than cultivating pursuits: to have no external goals is to fall into spleen. His sixth, "Medical Application of Money," follows Rabelais by showing how money opens up people; that is, lawyers will speak for hours at the prospect of a fat fee. A laxative, money opens prisons, the House of Lords, and the Church of England and effects litigation, fraud, injustice, oppression, and bribery. Lacking cash to grease the editor's palm, A.B. does not expect to see his piece published! After this whimsical, yet bitter, exposé of preferment and patronage, his seventh article treats literature: "Observations on Modern Literature." In this article, he states that current publications are unoriginal: "Our present *labourers at the quill*" avoid the temple of fame, choosing to amble in the paths of mediocrity and to visit the vaults of Dullness. Allusions to Pope support the claim that literary genius is sterile whereas science is prolifically creative. On the one hand, luxury and sloth cause genius to decline; on the other, penury is its enemy: the former enfeebles, the latter cramps it. Bicknell focusses on poverty: it chains the man of genius; wants prevent him from study;

and claims on his purse interrupt his meditations. When landlord, milkwoman, and tailor come collecting, they drag him from the muses. Pindar and Cicero could not have withstood the "severe tax of *present payment*." Needy authors deliver but half-formed embryos. Dryden, Steele, Addison, and Pope remain models given patronage in their days: genius must recall the Augustan Age.[663] Bicknell here places disparaging terms applied by reviewers to him in context: essayistic self-consciousness deflects literary clichés from himself and critiques the economic priorities of the publishing industry.[664]

His next piece, "The National Advantages of a Good Appetite," uses Guthrie's stories about Handel's huge appetite to boast a larger one: London eateries pay A.B. to stay away since he eats ten times what he pays for. A gluttonous friend to fishmongers, butchers, and poulterers, he keeps the price of food high, enabling farmers to pay the land tax![665] His ninth, "On the Misapplication of the Term Christian," attacks the abuse of the idiomatic phrase "like a Christian" when it is applied to pets; Christians should not equate humans and animals. "The Autumn. Written in November 1792" calls harvest-time and the seasonal cycle divine favours. He contrasts the natural and human worlds: children of nobles do not perpetuate parental virtues as acorns do oaks. Yet climate makes good vines yield bad grapes. Melancholic and self-sympathetic, he recalls his best days were clouded, but he laid up provisions from education and experience. At life's end, he hopes to have been useful. His eleventh piece, "A Letter from a Young Gentleman in the Neighbourhood of London, to His Sister in the Country," is formulaic in content and tone. He mentions an only sister, Nancy, who lives near Salisbury, but little is deducible about his life in London.[666]

His twelfth piece, "On the Effect of the Atmosphere on the Health," cites Milton's view that weather affects creativity and Johnson's inconsistency on the topic in *The Rambler* and *The Life of Milton*. To Bicknell, since weather helps and harms superior authors, inferior ones who write for a living are more vulnerable. They have to calculate the effects of wind, atmosphere, and site; an automaton in Kensington sunshine may shine east of Temple-Bar, the gloom of Bolt-Court perhaps condensing ideas and the north wind rousing rich images![667] Landlords and laundresses infesting the retreats of genius would be gentler and creditors less fierce were the effects better known; attorneys would stay home rather than harass penniless authors; and landladies would study the barometer before demanding rent. Since MPs are exempt from certain taxes, why may not writers who work for the nation receive similar benefits? Were the editor so to assist impecunious authors, he would be immortalised. Behind this mock-heroic hyperbole lies bitterness about the material conditions of literary journeymen.

His thirteenth piece, "The Progress of an Author," treats this theme autobiographically. On burning ninety-seven pamphlets, he narrates his life. Born to the disease of writing like Pope and early becoming a scribbler, he turned professional writer despite being ill-trained. While *The Rambler* says a writer should first read, his reading left no firm impression; his sole resources were "the third volume of *Tristram Shandy*, a *Bath Guide*, and a tract of *Swedenborg's*." Narrow circumstances made study fruitless. Living amid noisy families and hounded by washerwomen, tailors, and pastry cooks, he exploited imagination when information failed in imitation of indigent geniuses like Apollo, Pliny, Hooker, Shakespeare, and Dryden. He copied Shakespeare, turned theological controversialist, wrote sonnets and madrigals, and defended the constitution. Admitting commercial failure, he is consoled that he did not seek fame, a portrait by Sir Thomas Lawrence (1769–1830), a tomb in Westminster Abbey, a variorum edition of his works, or a costly quarto of his literary remains. Yet he expects renown since his pen remained independent, evident in the condemnation meted out equally by the "*Monthly* and *Critical* Reviewers."[668] The children of his great-great-grandchildren will taste his pen's fruits when the fever of party cools. His final days will appease his stationer and printer because he accepted a curacy worth £30 per annum.

His final piece for the *Town and Country Magazine*, "Advocate for Poor Clergymen, to the Editor, July 26," explores curacies. While clergymen's widows are funded, the inferior clergy are not. Curates afflicted by ill health are unfortunate; they have no option but to die in workhouses. Those too sick to preach cannot feed themselves by teaching. The remedy is to have beneficed clergy and wealthy laity create a fund that will give supplementary income of £20 or £30 to poor curates. Bicknell hopes readers will promote his plan and save the church from contempt.[669]

Besides their commitment to writing, which lasted until near life's end, what do Bicknell's articles for the *Town and Country Magazine* add to his identity and humanism? They confirm his knowledge of French and Latin and the likelihood that he was university educated. Their literary and clerical themes reinforce his long-held spiritualism. They show he imitated Steele and Addison and was conversant with the branches of rhetoric, including pulpit oratory. His citations of Johnson, Milton, and Pope respect Augustan humanism and remind us that his interest in literary history is reflected in imitations of Spenser, Shakespeare, and Thomson. His essays reveal his belief in a literary canon based on patronage rather than on the economics of the book trade. He grasped the self-consciousness of the periodical essay, exploiting confessional and defensive tones. Agonisingly familiar with the critical terms used against hacks and his own books, he appropriated them wittily and seriously. Presenting himself as victim of circumstance, he created a voice expressing economic deprivation and literary aspiration, social conservatism, and otherworldliness. Both defender and victim of hierarchy, he analysed the forces that oppressed him. He may once have seen writing as an alternative to preferment in the church, but it served neither ambition nor basic needs, and, if he did turn to a curacy, that did not help, for he died a year after his last essay in St. Thomas' Hospital—an institution for the indigent.[670] His last months will have been rendered distressing by poverty, illness, loneliness, and literary oblivion. One wonders if discomfort was alleviated by fantasies of success or made more acute by awareness of the artificialities of literary identity? Since he suffered the rigidity of literary reviewers as they, unlike Johnson, sought to widen the gap between celebrated authors and hack writers, one is moved to speculate about how much more painful his discomfort might have been had he foreseen that the *Monthly Review*'s scorn would be institutionalised in the *DNB*?

In sum, Bicknell saw himself as one who often addressed young readers. He was drawn to sympathise with women who were rendered notorious by patriarchal sexual attitudes which, in a limited way, he qualified as he represented. An opportunist who conformed to publishing trends, he resisted these trends to the extent he would not demean women. Unable to make a living with his pen, he wrote for magazines without compensation in order to justify his life. Few publishers he worked for were insignificant; some operated in powerful cartels. In expanding his bibliography and deducing patterns of writerly behaviour, this chapter seeks to make up for the dearth of public records about Bicknell and to show that his career yields evidence of the challenges faced by one literary journeyman whose seeming anonymity likely stands for the common lot of would-be professional authors in the last quarter of the eighteenth century.

Endnotes

1. For the whole text, see Swift 1963, 399–418.
2. Baugh and Cable 2002, 258–63 and 267–69. Johnson faulted Swift's *Proposal for Correcting, Improving, and Ascertaining the English Tongue* (1711) in an academy but was positive about Swift's style: "His sentences are never too much dilated or contracted; and it will not be easy to find any embarrassment in the complications of his clauses, and inconsequence in his connections, or abruptness in his transitions ... His style was well suited to his thoughts, which are never subtilised by nice disquisitions, decorated by sparkling conceits, elevated by ambitious sentences, or variegated by far-sought learning" (1952, II: 192 and 211).
3. Swift 1963, 404.
4. Swift 1963, 417. On Swift as a humanist, see Fussell 1969, 11. Whereas Johnson approved of corporal punishment for beating language into pupils, Swift opposed it (Damrosch 2019, 14).
5. Swift 1963, 413–14. On Swift's contrary senses of mystery and reason, see Williams 1958, 31–38.
6. Cohen 1977, 75
7. Hale 1994, 194–97. The following paragraphs draw on Burke's *Reflections* (1968, 94, 175, 187, 181–82, 194–95, and 278) since there is no greater upholder of Swift's humanism.
8. Nussbaum 2010, 2, 18, 23, 29, and 53.
9. Postman 1999, 32, 35, 36, 48, 51, 53, 74, and 79. For recent technical criticism of the Internet, see Keen 2007 and Carr 2010.
10. Manguel 1998, 39.
11. Iser 2011. "The Reading Process: A Phenomenological Approach." In Towheed et al 2011, 80–81.
12. Harpham 2002, 2, 5, and 12–13.
13. Darnton 2011. "First Steps Towards A History of Reading." In Towheed et al 2011, 23–35.
14. Perkins 1992, 177–78.
15. Grant 1969, 113–33.
16. Frye 1982, 139–55.
17. Roper 1965, 13–14 and 187. Biblical sources of Dryden's narrative include 2 Samuel 14–18 (for Absalom's rebellion against David); Luke 15:11–32 (The Parable of the Prodigal Son and David's initially mild treatment of Absalom); Genesis 25–27 (for the birth of Esau and Jacob, and the stealing of the former's birthright by the latter).
18. Zwicker 1972, 16–23, 88, and 99.
19. Atkins 1980, 40 and 57.
20. McFadden 1978, 250.
21. Hamilton 1967, 5 and 15.
22. Line numbers in *Absalom and Achitophel* refer to vol. 1, pp. 215-43 of Dryden 1958.
23. St. Stephen (c. a.d. 5–c. a.d. 34), the first Christian martyr and a deacon in the early church at Jerusalem, denounced the authorities who accused him of blasphemy and had him stoned to death. See the Acts of the Apostles, chapter VI.
24. Zwicker 1972, 39.
25. See, for example, Lord 1972, 188–90.
26. For the negative view, see Lord 1972, 188.
27. The first view is voiced by Meyers 1973, 93.
28. Genesis 25: 24–34 and 27: 18–24.
29. Sir William Jones (1631–1682), the Attorney-General who prosecuted the Popish Plot.

30. Garrison 1975, 242.
31. Zwicker 1984, 93 and 100.
32. King 1969, 81–82, and 68.
33. To West, Dryden voices "a rhetoric of moderation that stakes a claim to a more reasoned consideration of political information than that achieved by the Multitude"; the poet's rhetoric "retains an enthusiastic register, not only in its presentation of loyalty to the Stuart cause but also by testing out how far enthusiasm's range might be able to reach under duress." Dryden's enthusiasm is strongest when oscillating between "modes of loyalty and extravagant daring," between "preserving the royalist cause" and revelling in the "ironic instability of loyal steadfastness" (2018, 66 and 72).
34. Krieger values the collapse of the polarity of religion and love more than the apparent religious resolution. However, he proposes the poem's ideological inconsistencies are beyond Pope's control (1969, 3 and 28–47).
35. Johnson declares that Pope's poem celebrates the religious consolation and pious retirement of Eloisa and Abelard (1952, II: 236–37).
36. Trowbridge avers that, while Pope removes the "theological argument" of his sources, Eloisa is never deceived about her equally strong religious and sexual desires (1973, 11–34). Seeing no tension between religion and passion, Kalmey attributes it to the "enduring Christian context" in the medieval letters, the translations, and Pope's poem (1980, 247–65). Pettit (1968, 320–32) and O'Hehir (1968, 333–49) question the struggle between grace and nature as an explanation of the poem. For Pettit, Eloisa is "essentially erotic" yet emotionally able to transcend eroticism. For O'Hehir, there is a fundamental Christian irony in the poem, which requires Eloisa to see that nature and grace are not opposites in Christ. While refusing to identify Pope with Eloisa, O'Hehir proposes that Eloisa recognises that she must lose her life to gain it. Keener regards Eloisa's inability to distinguish between religious and erotic feeling as grounds for satire in the poem. But his view that Pope is comfortable with her attack upon orthodoxy seems questionable (1974, 49–58). Hagstrum maintains that, in *Eloisa to Abelard,* Pope "celebrates not the triumph of divine grace or of theological dialectic but the glorious persistence of passion" (1980, 132). Hagstrum refuses to countenance the struggle between grace and nature: intent on Pope's manifestation of personal romance, he claims the poet reduced the mystical rapture of the sources to heighten eroticism. To Hagstrum, Eloisa's libertinism is a dignified reaction against institutional repression. Opposing Johnson, Hagstrum contends that religion is unattainable for Eloisa (1980, 121–30).
37. Line references to Pope's poems are to the one-volume edition of the Twickenham text of *The Poems of Alexander Pope,* edited by John Butt (London: Methuen, 1968), unless otherwise stated. To Hagstrum, Eloisa's "vision of her own future is not bliss in the beyond with a redeemed Abelard but a 'kind' (343), shared, and quiet grave" (1980, 129).
38. Peter Abelard (1079-1142) was a philosopher and theologian recognised for solving the problem of universals and for original use of dialectics. He was also a poet and musician. Héloïse d'Argenteuil (1101-1164) was a French nun, writer, scholar, and abbess.
39. O'Hehir makes the point that holy knees are more adamantine than the rocks (1968, 342).
40. Mack comments on the poem's "immersion in Catholic feeling" and its allusions to the "various structures of devotional meditation" (1985, 326).
41. Frank 1966, 9 and 11. Nicolson and Rousseau argue that more attention should be paid to the effect that Pope's considerable medical history had on his poetry (1968, 7–82). Nichol points out that Pope had ill-health in common with Queen Anne (2021, 178).
42. For the text of the essays, see Ault and Cowler (1936, I: 134–40). They are numbers 132 and 169 of *The Guardian.* For a bibliographical analysis, see Stephens 1982, 719–20 and 744–45.
43. Pope, however, does not ultimately expect to persuade Miss Blount with "Good Humour"; he means it to be less persuasive than his offer of friendship. Nor in *The Rape of the Lock,* when Clarissa advises Belinda to exemplify "good Humour," is this term meant to be as convincing as

Clarissa's emphasis on mortality (V, l. 30). However, Dixon claims that good humour is persuasive since it is "a gentle and appealing version of Stoic equanimity" (1968, 166).

44. Winn discusses Pope's reliance on Voiture's amatory rhetoric to suggest involvement with the Blounts enabled him to alter epistolary rhetoric (1979, 89–118). Objecting to moral love poetry, Trickett faults *Epistle to Miss Blount* for didactic heaviness. But her preference for poetic "responsiveness to the world of appearance" belies Pope's sensibility (1967, 166 and 169–71).

45. Other poems evidence Pope's mature views. In *An Essay on Man*, death is "the great teacher" (I, l.92); it is "the lurking principle" which "Grows with [man's] growth and strengthens with his strength" (II, ll. 134–36). Death must be welcomed (II, ll. 259–60) since it is inextricably connected to hope (III, ll. 71–78).

46. For Campbell's and Hazlitt's views, see Hunt 1968, 88–91. Brower warns that, while Pope's serious concerns in *The Rape of the Lock* have been overstressed, they should not be disregarded (1959, 146) and Cunningham regards the poem as "a trap for those who label it or who treat it consistently seriously or with consistent levity" (1961, 13).

47. Price describes Pope's underworld as "an erotic nightmare of exploding libidinous drives" (1964, 153).

48. On the presence in the "satiric catalogue" of "scenic effects of contemporary opera and pantomime," see Tillotson 1940, 183 and the note to line 43 ff.

49. Ludovico Ariosto (1474–1533) wrote *Orlando Furioso* between 1516 and 1532. A playful but pessimistic episode to which Pope refers is Astolfo's voyage to the moon to recapture Orlando's lost wits. The episode is self-affirming and self-deconstructing, according to Carthy (2009, 104: 71–72), and its satire of the Renaissance court and human hopes and desires as well as the ambivalent treatment of patronage and court poets serve Pope's purposes well.

50. See Brooks 1968, 135–53; Budick 1974, 144ff.

51. In *Vanity Fair*, when Lord Steyne bows over Rebecca Crawley citing "the hackneyed and beautiful lines, from the *Rape of the Lock*, about Belinda's diamonds 'which Jews might kiss and infidels adore,'" Rebecca replies: "But I hope your lordship is orthodox" (Thackeray 1963, 463).

52. For the view that Pope's mythical perspective stems from "an innocence older than Christianity," see Grove 1979, 85–87.

53. Delany proposes that, since he upheld aristocratic and sexist values, Pope satirised only the upper-middle classes. But her social limitation of satire is unduly restrictive (1975, 46–61).

54. To Rabb, seemingly trivial consumer "toys" have cognitive significance; they offer temporary gratification and distract shoppers from moral symbols and ecological signs (2019, 109–12).

55. Rogers gives several reasons why Pope moved the "rape" of Belinda to Hampton Court from her home in London (2021, 21–40). One was the work of Antonio Verrio (1636–1707), who enhanced the palace's grandeur; another was Queen Anne's early success effecting political equilibrium there. For more on Verrio, see chapter three.

56. Since "Clarissa's speech cheapens Sarpedon's rhetoric," Cunningham claims that it presents a "realistic and enlightened" morality (1966, 13–14). Ehrenpreis denies that Clarissa is a figure of moral enlightenment (1974, 14).

57. Fussell argues that the wisdom Pope offers to Belinda is secular. He regards Clarissa's speech as a moral elegy unrelated to Christianity (1969, 283–86). This claim is questionable because Pope does not expect wisdom to withstand mutability.

58. Walls holds rightly that passions overcome all characters, their strong physical expressions being unconstrained (2021, 138–39).

59. Wahl, "The Fear of Death" in Feifel 1965, 18–25. See Kübler-Ross's account of the harm that repression of ideas of death causes (1970, 11–15) and her *Death: The Final Stage of Growth* (1975).

60. *Tom Jones* is "a variable text. It isn't conducted on a single plane, in one genre, but rather organized by the intersection of conflicting codes of value and contrasting kinds of representation" (Black 2019, 85).

61. Fielding 1961, 116. Tinkler describes the influence of Renaissance history-writing on the eighteenth-century novel, tracing its letter collections and dialogue forms back to Petrarch and Erasmus (1988, 511–12). Black emphasises "the continuity of romance as a literary phenomenon interesting in its own right" (2019, 5). See also Black, "Henry Fielding and the Progress of Romance," in Downie 2016, 237-63.

62. Black 2019, 83.

63. The major study of Fielding's legal ideas states he was no reformer since conservative views induced in him an almost slavish respect for the harsh criminal laws of the time (Zirker 1966, 132–40). Claiming he manipulated plots of novels to evade social problems, Zirker rejects the celebration of Fielding as humanitarian reformer in Jones who asserts that "Fielding's views on punishment and his emphasis of the value of prevention were far in advance of the ideas and practice of the eighteenth century" (1933, 226). Zirker rejects this view (1966, 37–42). But his dismissal of Fielding as reformer ignores his integrated legal, political, social, and religious ideas. Conceding that Fielding came late and reluctantly to the legal profession, Rogers insists that the author of *Amelia* made this novel reflect the "reforming zeal" of his social pamphlets (1979, 193). However, Rawson in the introduction to *A Journey from This World to the Next* says that Fielding's "morality transcends his own explicitly formulated socio-legal principles in contexts where the full human situation invited a deeper and larger view" (1973a, xxii).

64. On Fielding's concern for reform in society as an organic whole, see Sherburn 1959, 251–53.

65. Fielding 1961, 42. For the good Samaritan, see St Luke 10:33–36.

66. Fielding 1961, 244 and 242–43. For Fielding's attitudes to the professions, see Hatfield 1968, 127–51: "high esteem" made him "painfully conscious" of threats to corrupt them. His scorn for Lawyer Scout is matched by satire of the "vile Petty-fogger" in *Tom Jones* (Fielding 1973b, 328).

67. Fielding 1961, 18–19, 57, 142, and 102.

68. Fielding 1961, 17, 33, and 126.

69. Fielding 1961, 233 and 236.

70. Fielding 1973b, 724 and 505.

71. Fielding 1973b, 421, 272, and 495–96.

72. Fielding 1973b, 464, 167, 269, 159, and 432. See 2 Corinthians 3:6. Allworthy is "a very competent Judge in most Kinds of Literature" and an excellent justice of the peace (Fielding 1973b, 46).

73. Fielding 1973b, 97, 99, 103, 262, 519, 523, 558, 674, and 703.

74. Fielding 1973b, 45, 77, 237, 682, and 750–51.

75. To Miller, Fielding "conveys an attitude towards his materials by assuming the jargon-voice of a particular profession" (1970, 278). In *Joseph Andrews*, when the robber escapes from Mr Towwouse's house and the constable is said to be an accessory, Fielding impersonates a stupid magistrate with a literal-minded sense of evidence (Fielding 1961, 59). By this impersonation, Fielding implies that personal history, character, beliefs, motives, and circumstances should be considered as legal evidence. In *Tom Jones*, various legal stances matter since Fielding makes his characters' rhetoric indicate their moral attitudes. Mrs Wilkins is one whose legalistic sense of justice is transparent in her insensitive and ineffective speech while Fielding himself appreciates the "perfect Oratory" of the ancients and celebrates William Pitt as "a Rival in Eloquence to *Greece* and *Rome*" since sound rhetoric is essential to justice and public morality (Fielding 1973b, 31, 37, 428, and 566). On Fielding's rhetoric, see Miller 1966 and Perl 1981.

76. Fielding 1973b, 299, 397, 68, 108, 129, and 132.

77. Fielding 1903, XIII: 9 and 17.

78. Fielding 1903, XIII: 65 and 126.

79. Fielding 1962, 5–7. Battestin says *Amelia* contains Fielding's "maturest thinking about human nature and about the grounds of order in society"; it ends in a "comic apocalypse" affirming that "fiction is the mirror of a higher reality than life's tragic muddle" (1974, 613–14).

80. Fielding 1962, I: 14–15 and 47; II: 61.

81. Fielding 1962, II: 248 and 253–55.

82. Fielding 1962, I: 149 and 154; II: 106–07, 121, and 131–32.

83. Fielding 1962, II: 149, 157, and 159.

84. Fielding 1962, II: 229 and 296.

85. Fielding 1962, II: 134, 214, 304; I: 125 and 10. This motif governs the early chapters of *A Journey from This World to the Next*. When he describes the spirits of the dead meeting with the spirits about to enter life and presents Minos judging the candidates for Elysium, Fielding emphasises the interchangeability of social ranks and the relative advantages and disadvantages of all stations because of his spiritual values.

86. Fielding 1907, 16–17, 29–30, 74, 76–78, and 105. Rawson notes an "intensified see-sawing between apparently contradictory elements" in Fielding's later social outlook, citing particularly his faith in benevolence and sense of natural depravity (1972, 96). Such oscillations do not seem to become more intense or to reflect a loss of ideals, as Rawson claims.

87. "Most of Fielding's pronouncements [on the law] relate to topical circumstances, such as an apparent wave of violent robberies, a riot in the streets, or a controversial *missing persons* case. However, the cast of mind underlying the writing of these works is philosophical as well as pragmatic. While Fielding was a practical reformer and active participant in day-to-day controversial discourse, he was also a deeply reflective man, with a fuller knowledge of humane learning—history, literature ancient and modern, and political theory—than almost all of his colleagues on the bench" (Rogers 2007, 138).

88. Preston 1970, 114 and 117.

89. Battestin (1959) gives a fine account of Fielding's latitudinarianism; Swann explains Fielding's indebtedness to Shaftesbury yet suggests that, in as much as he differs from that philosopher, he is close to Hume's empiricism (1929, 46–64). While this suggestion is not detailed, Harrison (1975), especially in chapters five and six, charts a moral dialectic in Fielding that places him beyond the influence of Shaftesbury and the Latitudinarians.

90. MacLean details Fielding's admiration of Locke, showing the novelist reacting to his epistemology (1936, 16, 35, and 55); Hatfield (1968) describes Fielding's reaction to Locke's theory of language; Miller contends that, while opposing Locke's nominalism, Fielding employed the philosopher's vocabulary of mental events (1976, 65); Kropf describes Fielding's exploration of ideas about mental growth and his variable relation to Lockean assumptions (1974, 113–20); to Kramnick, empiricism's simple representational ideas do not fit the syntax of cognition which more resembles script than pictures; complicated ideas not coming from the association of simple ideas, they cannot form "a sentence of a mental language" (2018, 105–06).

91. Locke 1887, 30, 60–1, and 64.

92. Fielding 1973b, 99, 107, 39, and 89.

93. Locke 1887, 38.

94. Fielding 1974, 171, note 1.

95. Locke 1887, 40.

96. Fielding 1973b, 129 and 81.

97. Locke 1887, 41–42.

98. Fielding 1973b, 174.

99. Locke 1887, 71, 166–67, 116, and 196.

100. On this point, see Battestin 1968, 188–217.

101. Fielding 1973b, 106, 185, and 743.

102. Locke 1966, 32, 35, 65, 73, and 87.

103. Fielding 1973b, 439 and 424.

104. Fielding 1973b, 66 and 616.

105. See Alter's account of the inferences required of readers (1968, 43ff.).

106. Fielding 1973b, 641, 88–89, 114, 305, and 35–36.
107. Fielding 1973b, 298 and 296.
108. Fielding 1973b, 173 and 126.
109. Fielding 1973b, 86 and 47; Locke 1966, 38–39.
110. Fielding 1973b, 475, 49, 109, 223, 252, 94, 564, 163, 373, and 456.
111. Like Fielding, Locke links quick-sightedness into evil with unawareness of fallibility (1965, II: xxxiii and 335). Sophia is unique; aware of her fallibility, she perceives other minds accurately.
112. Fielding 1973b, 115, 207, 67, and 471.
113. Fielding 1973b, 117 and 534.
114. Fielding 1973b, 512 and 545. For his definition of simple modes, see Locke 1965, II: xiii, 133.
115. Fielding 1973b, 63.
116. Fielding 1973b, 127, 156, 73, 178, and 261.
117. Fielding 1973b, 427–28, 287, and 119.
118. Fielding 1973b, 499–500.
119. Rousseau (1982) shows that by 1770 natural histories outnumbered all other science books, their linguistic impact greater than that of natural philosophy: "Science books and their readers in the eighteenth century" in Rivers 1982, 202, 220, and 225.
120. Soupel 1982, 10, 24–25, and 30.
121. McKeon 1987, 68–73 and 19–22.
122. "English provincial realism is not exclusively a discourse of secular empiricism ... realism's concern with the observed world does not mean that it is antagonistic to a theologically inflected world view .... the persistence of natural theology in varied forms into at least the middle of the nineteenth century reflected the twining of piety with the Enlightenment goal of the pursuit of science" (King 2019, 3–4).
123. Mabey discusses White's reliance on Ray and Derham (1986, 11–12). White cites these titles (1949, 51 and 105). Thomas links natural history to aristocratic power (1984, 13, 133, 184, 209, 227, and 283), claiming that biological classification reinforced social hierarchy (1984, 40 and 61).
124. Priestley 1965, 318–19.
125. Brooke 1985, 383.
126. Keith provides a fine analysis of White's literary techniques (1974, 50–57).
127. Maddox says White's focus on upper-class Anglicans was sharpened by opposition to the French Revolution (1986, 45–57). Thomas's claim that White saw the natural world in a "direct, unstylized" way assumes the new science was "totally hostile to symbolic thinking" (1984, 266 and 67). Williams voices the same assumption (1973, 118–19).
128. White 1949, 112, 163, 127, 168–69, 217, 122, 137, 187, 25, and 279.
129. White 1949, 146, 124, 186, 194, 2, 211, 169, 267, 212, 277, and 108. For White's interest in the viewpoint of animals, see Hammond 1949, 377–83. Defoe anticipates White's view of country houses (1974, I: 167–68).
130. White 1949, 72. White's stance is analysed by Trowbridge 1979, 79–109 and Curtis 1979, 137–41.
131. White 1949, 200, 141, 205, 19, 227, and 229. White's words for the "father of the flock" resemble Lovelace's (Richardson 1985, 449).
132. Mathurin Jacques Brisson, the French naturalist, lived from 1723 to 1806. White 1949, 141, 3, 75, 162, 19, 31, 244, 87, 47, 89, 35, 34, 49, 101, 109, 73, 36–37, 145, and 47 (second time).
133. White 1949, 35, 52, 156, and 220. To the King, he who makes "two blades of grass" grow "where only one grew before" deserves "better of mankind ... than the whole race of politicians put together" (Swift 1960, 109).
134. Turner 1985, 164, 173, and 6. Joseph Pitton de Tournefort (1656-1708) journeyed through Spain, Portugal, and the Levant, collecting plant species.

135. Turner 1985, 204, 183, 54, 66, and 110. Thomas Pelham-Holles, first Duke of Newcastle (1693–1768) had a country house at Halland in the parish of East Hoathly where Turner was Overseer of the Poor as well as a shopkeeper.
136. Woodforde 1978, 230, 261, and 50.
137. Woodforde 1978, 53, 99, 402, 566, 219, 396, 299, 332, 310, and 132.
138. See White 1949, 39, 42, 151, 189, 192, 219, 249, and 262 for his knowledge of travelogues. Cf. Maddox 1986, 47.
139. Defoe anticipates White in criticising Pliny, valuing "physick" gardens and exotic plants and seeing wildlife as a capital return and source of rare gifts (1974, I: 248; I: 47; I: 79 and II: 269).
140. Defoe 1974, I: 72; I: 210; I: 127; I: 56; I, 98 and I: 100. To White, at Tunbridge wheat-ears "appear at the tables of all the gentry that entertain with any degree of elegance" (1949, 161).
141. Defoe 1974, II: 168 and II: 293.
142. Pliny the Elder, Gaius Plinius Secundus (a.d. 23/24–79), was a naturalist, natural philosopher, and naval and army commander in the early Roman empire. He was a friend to Vespasian, Titus Flavius Vespasianus (a.d. 9–79), the emperor who ruled from a.d. 69 to 79.
143. Fielding 1907, 9, 105, 102, 116, and 71. Hays says Pliny created an "anthropology of the absurd" (1972, 28).
144. Wendt 1965, 23, 41, 46, 105, and 62. On White's view of Johnson, see Mabey 1986, 153.
145. Smollett 1981, 17, 30, 2, 118, and 160. Smollett lists fish and fruit for sale at Boulogne and Nice to imply France's superior plenitude (1981, 23 and 153).
146. Defoe 1969, 85, 86, 91, 107, 129, and 102.
147. Defoe 1969, 92,107, 113, 112, 86, and 102. Anticipating White's anthropocentric analogies, Defoe shows his narrative hand when, in *A Tour*, he says that cartographers ignorant about northern Scotland "fill it up with hills and mountains, as they do the inner parts of Africa, with lyons and elephants, for want of knowing what else to place there" (1974, II: 410).
148. Defoe 1969, 89 and 82.
149. Fielding 1961, 255, 26, 116, 201, and 233.
150. Fielding 1973b, 120, 263, 368, 649, 67, 477, and 130. Fielding, citing Philip Miller's *The Gardener's Dictionary* (1731), says natural classification must employ experience (1973b, 373).
151. Aesop (c. B.C. 620–560) was a legendary Greek storyteller whose oral tales describe cunning animals and stupid humans.
152. Richardson 1971, 43, 81, 121, 155, 137, 148, 77, 78, 162, 370, 100, 151, 113, 118, 303, and 211. When Pamela refers to Mrs Jewkes' "huge Paw," she is recalling the Book of Samuel (1971, 121). See Numbers 11:5 for the reference to onions and garlic.
153. Richardson 1985, 164, 327, 352, 437, 1349, 1306, 892, and 1121. Phyllirea, an ornamental evergreen from the Mediterranean, was imported into England in the seventeenth century.
154. Richardson 1985, 66, 283, 77, 119, 557, 449, 480, 1221, 559, 917, and 659.
155. Richardson 1985, 647, 165, 473, 492, 439, 541, 891, and 1126. For Nathan's parable of the rich man, the poor man, and the latter's single lamb that goads King David to admit his sexual hypocrisy regarding Uriah and Bathsheba, see 2 Samuel 12:1-7.
156. Johnson 1976, 43, 45, 49, 53, and 70.
157. See Kuhn 1970, 26–27, 67, 38, and 81.
158. Smollett 1967, 94, 392, 66, 150, 152–53, 252, 260, 369, and 385.
159. Goldsmith 1982, 55, 88, and 92
160. On worship of trees, see Thomas 1984, 212–23.
161. Kuhn 1970, 139, 194, 88, and 227
162. Kuhn 1970, 232–33, 237, 278, 252, 277, 275, 251, and 304.
163. Edgeworth 1980, 14 and 17.
164. Austen 1966, 173, 110, 87, 119, 223, 421, 197, 133, and 86.

165. For related attitudes to natural history in White and Austen, see King's Chapter 1. "Reverent Natural History, the Sketch, and the Novel: Modes of English Realism" in White, Mitford, and Austen" (2019, 47–88).
166. Addison, Swift, and Pope insisted that music debased words, and musical theoreticians, John Brown (1715-1766) and Daniel Webb (1718/19–1798), resisted the idea that music expresses emotions (Winn 1981, 199–202). Scorn for opera and libretto-writing came from notions that musical destroys poetical harmony (Meyers 1956, 17–30). Despite a general contempt for opera, Handel's were much celebrated (Schmidgall 1977, 31–35). On the power of Handel to command the rapt attention of audiences, see Brewer 1997, 403–06. Gibbons recounts the Masonic appeal of Handel's *Orlando* (1733) when opera's audience appeal seems to have been in decline (2010, 65–82). Handel's aesthetic refinement is clear from his "very substantial picture collection, of oils and engravings"; it "seems likely that connoisseurship of the visual arts was the principal hobby of his later years" (Burrows 2015, 442). Pope's eulogy is found in Book IV, line 64 of *The Dunciad*.
167. Tillotson et al 1969, 880 and 923.
168. Handel struggled to maintain relations with the Court in Hannover when he moved to England and later with the divided courts of George I and son. Struggles led him to befriend aristocrats who did not live at courts so that he might concentrate on his musical creativity and on friendship with such as Georg Philipp Telemann (1681-1787).
169. Fielding 1974, I: 169.
170. Fielding 1962, I: 200 and II: 174.
171. Richardson 1972, I: 106, 108, and 239.
172. Stanhope 1929, 97.
173. Richardson 1972, IV: 374 and VI: 88. Note Grandison's transposition of Dryden's lines which substitutes "good" for "brave" (IV: 345) in honour of Harriet Byron. See also II: 239 for Grandison's preference of Handel to Scarlatti and admiration of *Alexander's Feast* (1736).
174. Defoe 1968, 316ff.
175. Boswell reports that Johnson wrote the preface to Burney's work (1953, 1345).
176. Boswell 1961, 131–32.
177. Deutsch 1955, 139–43.
178. Deutsch 1955, 158–60.
179. *Musica mundana* is the cosmic idea of the well-tuned creation and *musica humana* the moral power of music to arouse and control emotions and spirit. To Wendorf, Dryden's "A Song for St. Cecilia's Day, 1687" is the best example of poetry harmonising these ideas (1981, 136–44).
180. Deutsch 1955, 306.
181. Deutsch 1955, 206.
182. Dryden 1958, II: 239.
183. Deutsch 1955, 340.
184. Wendorf 1981, 135–38.
185. Deutsch 1955, 533.
186. Deutsch 1955, 614.
187. Deutsch 1955, 476.
188. Laurence Whyte, "On Mr. Handel's Performance of his *Oratorio*, call'd the *Messiah*" (Deutsch 1955, 547).
189. Deutsch 1955, 608–09.
190. Deutsch 1955, 820.
191. Deutsch 1955, 822–23.
192. Langhorne 1797, 34–38.
193. On the commemoration concerts held to fund the Society of Decayed Musicians, see Brewer 1997, 402–06. The second concert featuring opera selections was held in the Pantheon.
194. *The London Magazine* 1784, 497.

195. Meyers 1956, 15.

196. Cowper 1967, 233, ll. 633–37; Cowper 1969, I: 352; Meyers 1946, 219.

197. On Seward's view of genius which saw her championing humble poets and deriding clever satirists like Cowper, see Brewer 1997, 580–81; Seward 1974, III: 5–14; Pope 1968, 770 (*The Dunciad* Bk. IV, ll. 65–68).

198. Reynolds 1975, 78–79.

199. On "dialectical contraries," see Thorslev 1989, 103–12. The early pages of Thorslev (1984) describe eighteenth-century dialectic. Blake's maxim appears in Plate 3 of *The Marriage of Heaven and Hell*, titled "Attraction and Repulsion, Reason and Energy, Love and Hate, are necessary to Human existence" (Blake 1966, 149).

200. Dryden 1962, I: 69–70 and II: 59.

201. Defoe 1976, 139. On the relations between philosophical dialectic and narrative procedures, see Merrett 1989, 171–85.

202. Crane 1952, 380; Hipple 1957, 136.

203. Lipking 1970, 166–67.

204. Holtz 1970, 21–38.

205. To Hagstrum, this period heightened acuity in the visual arts. Not before "did writers to the same extent see and understand paintings, possess such considerable collections of prints and engravings, and read so widely in the criticism and theory of the graphic arts. And in no previous period ... could a poet assume a knowledge of great painting and statuary in the audience he was addressing" (1958, 130); to Lipking, we "see according to conventions" and "our minds paint pictures ... in conformity with the pictures they already know" (Wendorf 1983, 10).

206. Steiner 1988, 23. To Mitchell, the "space-time problem" is never resolved: it involves "a dialectical struggle in which the opposed terms take on different ideological roles and relationships at different moments in history" (1986, 98).

207. See Mitchell 1986, 43–44.

208. For social and political tensions in the Augustan theory of art, see Barrell 1986, 1–68.

209. For the involvement of pictorial and political signs, see Bermingham (1986). She pays considerable attention to contradictions within paintings and social ideology.

210. Defoe 1974, I: 167–68, 177–78, and 183.

211. Defoe 1974, I: 196. In praising the workmanship and antiquarian value of the Earl of Twedal's family pieces, Defoe singles out one modelled on a portrait of Charles I formerly hung at Whitehall (1974, II: 297).

212. Verrio was rewarded highly by Charles II and James II. Catholic and pro-French, he refused to serve William and was persuaded to complete the decoration of the staircase at Hampton Court only with great difficulty (Gaunt 1980, 140).

213. Defoe 1974, II: 368, 424; I: 304–05.

214. Defoe 1974, I: 194; II: 297 and 106.

215. Defoe 1852, 191–92, 202, and 198.

216. Defoe 1974, I: 177–78.

217. Richardson 1972a, 107, 139, 23, 40–41, 63, and 45. Richardson's analogy between portraiture and narrative upholds the portraitist's "double–and sometimes contradictory–obligations" (Wendorf 1983, 108). Wendorf further explores Richardson's double agency as visual and verbal portraitist (1990, 135–50). By contrast, Lipking calls Richardson an uncomplicated thinker in the line of Locke (1970, 109–26).

218. Richardson 1972b, 12, 17, 25, 20, 36, and 39. Synaesthesia is crucial to the sister arts because images involve "multisensory apprehension and interpretation" (Mitchell 1986, 14ff.).

219. Richardson 1972b, 44, 221, 55, 47, 66, 191, and 204.

220. Richardson 1971, 22, 183, 174, 200, and 39.

221. Richardson 1971, 57 and 96–97. Steiner applies chronological and narrative order to medieval religious paintings (1988, 14–42).
222. Addison and Steele 1964, IV: 250–52. *The Spectator* no. 555 appeared on Saturday, 6 December 1712.
223. Addison and Steele 1964, II: 170–72. *The Spectator* no. 226 appeared on Monday, 11 November 1711.
224. Cooper 1964, I: 96 and 135.
225. Addison and Steele 1964, I: 259–61. *The Spectator* no. 83 appeared on Tuesday, 5 June 1711.
226. Wendt 1965, 257. For Johnson's anti-heroic, domestic stance, see Folkenflik 1984, 65–118.
227. Gray 1912, 258, 252, and 89.
228. Stanhope 1929, 124, 227, 232, and 167.
229. Shenstone 1802, 38. Shenstone's scorn for art theory partly derives from his admiration for the "moral Hogarth" (1939, 290, 293, and 403).
230. Shenstone 1939, 388 and 391. Alcock's portrait is the frontispiece of this edition. On portrait typology, see Stewart 1974, 3–43, and Wendorf, "Iconic Pictures: Van Dyck and Stuart Portraiture" (1990, 65–107).
231. Shenstone 1939, 249.
232. In "The Visual Arts," Shepherd provides an excellent account of relations between the sister arts and Richardson's narrative styles (2017, 195–204).
233. Richardson 1985, 509 and 1515. For the reliance of portraiture on "encoded" gestures and poses recommended by etiquette books, see Bermingham 1986, 20–28.
234. Battestin 1983, 8.
235. For his portraits, see the frontispiece of Smollett 1988 and Plate 1 of Giddings 1967.
236. Holtz 1970, 37. A reproduction of Sterne's portrait appears in *The Tate Gallery* 1987, 237.
237. On the contrary allusiveness of Hogarth and Reynolds, see Pevsner 1964, 53 and 68. On Reynolds's self-portrait, see Leonard 1969, 74. Lady Cathcart's portrait is found in *The Tate Gallery* 1987, 222.
238. For an analysis of Hogarth's self-portrait, see Wendorf 1990, 183–85. A fine reproduction is found in Einberg and Egerton 1988, 111. Paulson describes Hogarth's attitude to portraiture (1974, 185–201 and 344–51).
239. Paulson 1974, 213–15 and 275.
240. Highmore's series is reproduced in *The Tate Gallery* 1987, 156–59. See also Einberg and Egerton 1988, 50–59.
241. Richardson 1971, 21, 16, 10, 144, 58, 107, and 148. To Farr, Mrs Jewkes's facial and bodily ugliness is a device promoting heterosexual unions. Her disability stands in "metonymically for the unrestrained impulses of libertinism that must be curbed and channeled into virtuous sentiment" (2019, 72–74).
242. Richardson 1971, 262 and 385. For a full account of how Richardson separates his visual thinking from Pamela's, see Brown 1993: 129–51.
243. Kramnick's explication of the dialectical relations of intention and action clarifies Lovelace's philosophical but manipulative worldliness (2010, 211–15).
244. Richardson 1985, 399, 492, and 555. Oliver illustrates Richardson's symbolic discourse encoded in dress and costume when she analyses the painting by Francis Hayman (1708-1776) of the abduction scene in *Clarissa* (2008, 114-15).
245. Richardson 1985, 485, 333, 1338, 208, 1306, 1415–16, and 1357.
246. Richardson 1985, 1351, 1361, and 1387–88.
247. Fielding 1973b, 160 and 567–68.
248. Fielding 1967, 41 and 61–62.
249. Fielding 1973b, 51, 62, 104, and 214.
250. Fielding 1907, 30.

251. Fielding 1967, 17 and 182; Fielding 1973b, 387.

252. Fielding 1967, 234 and 152.

253. Fielding 1973b, 116–17, 48–50, and 256.

254. Fielding 1973b, 195, 622, 553, 589, and 754.

255. Smollett 1981, 46, 229, 231, 272, 277, 271, 256, 272, 278, and 257.

256. Smollett was art and cultural critic for the *Critical Review*, which he edited between 1756 and 1763. Familiar with English engravers and artists, he studied the Flemish school of art. More to the point, he understood the "drift" of the art market away from aristocratic patronage to "a buying public," auction houses, "gallery exhibitions, reviews by professional critics, reproductions of famous works sold by subscription, and the artist as celebrity" (Gibson 2007, 11–17).

257. Smollett 1983, 227–28, 332, 334–36, and 772. See also Smollett 1983, 787–88n.2.

258. To Farr, *The Expedition of Humphry Clinker* is "an ideal literary text for a critical disability-medical reading"; it depicts "the disabling effects of chronic disease alongside a wide range of medical interventions." Like Richardson, Smollett links illness and disability to courtship irregularity before ending with "bodily wellness and matrimonial harmony" (2019, 103–05).

259. Smollett 1967, 177, 107, 340–41, and 184.

260. Sterne 1983, 143–45, 176, 222–23, 252, 436, and 126. Recently, Lipski has suggested that Sterne exploited Hogarth's aesthetic discrimination between straight and waving lines in order to shape readers' senses of direct and oblique narrative mediations (2020, 61–72).

261. Sterne 1984, 85, 5–6, 17–18, 71, and 73.

262. Sterne 1984, 146, 164, 180, and 175.

263. MacKenzie 1967, 85; Goldsmith 1966, IV: 79.

264. Austen 1980, 217–20. Duckworth notes that Elizabeth's discovery of Darcy's portrait leads to "the most radical change" in her "perspective" (1971, 122–23).

265. On Raphael's reputation in England, see Hagstrum 1958, 162–66.

266. See Jauss 1974, 11–41 and Weimann 1974, 43–61. On pedagogy, see Graff 1987 and 1992.

267. Goberman's recording came out from Everest (3127/2) in 1962. For Gay's allusions to popular songs and Italian opera, see Bronson 1966, 298–327 and Kurtz 1975, 52–55. For a recent explication of Gay's skilful treatment of the text's interactions with the ballad opera's sixty-nine popular tunes, see Atkins 2006, 25–26.

268. On the affective aspect of popular culture and pedagogy, see Grossberg 1986, 177–200.

269. Kuhn 1970, 79 and 110.

270. Hirsch 1967, 6–10.

271. While his view that eighteenth-century prisons bred crime applies to Gay's satire, Foucault's historical sense ignores the mixed plurality of cultural phenomena (Merquior 1985, 101–07).

272. Recent studies promoting critical pluralism and the difference between literary and critical texts include Fromm 1991 and Hirsch 1991.

273. Gay 1969, xii–xxix.

274. For Gay's collaboration with Handel, see Irving 1940, 283–85.

275. On the new historicism, see Buchbinder 1991, 98–119 and Veeser 1989, ix–xvi.

276. On criticism of pantomime, see Pope 1940, 183–84.

277. Loftis 1963, 63–93 and Doody 1985, 30–56 and 119–58.

278. Bender 1987, 87–103.

279. On Gay's sets of ambivalence, see Donaldson 1975, 65–80.

280. On the performance history of heroic tragedy, see Arthur H. Scouten and Robert D. Hume, "'Restoration Comedy' and its Audiences, 1660-1776" in Hume 1983, 46–81.

281. Bender uses Bakhtin's term positively (1987, 87).

282. For the impact of reformers on dramatic decline, see Brown 1981, 145–84.

283. Gay 1969, 6 and 63. On speech-act theory and performative meaning, see Austin 1965 and Pratt 1977.

284. Gay 1969, 55, 67, 44–45, and 15.
285. Gay 1969, 6, 23, 7–8, and 9–10.
286. Gay 1969, 16, 9, 63, 15, 28, 31, and 80.
287. Gay 1969, 38 and 34–35. Fowler (1981) explains the objective aspects of discourse and semiotics.
288. Brecht refers to "the Coronation" to link Macheath's reprieve to the monarchy. While Gay satirises social networks, Brecht attacks institutions such as the crown, the church, and the middle class from a specifically economic viewpoint (Wright 1989, 28–30).
289. For a full and complex account of radical conservatism, see Clark 1985 and 1986.
290. Empson 1966, 182. He points out that Gay's women make "betrayal itself a lascivious act" and confuse love with death (1966, 182–83).
291. Gay 1969, 11, 26, 21, 10, 26, 52–53, and 68.
292. Gay 1969, 35, 41, 44, and 41.
293. Spacks 1965, 129.
294. Irving 1940, 32, 151, 186–87, 209–13, and 289.
295. See LaGrandeur 1991, 69–79.
296. On proliferating London and provincial theatres, on architectural changes accommodating larger audiences, on new staging devices, and on evasion of the restrictive Licensing Act of 1737 by producing Restoration plays, see Dickson, 2018, "An introduction to 18th-century British theatre." In *British Library Discovering Literature. On-line.*
297. Feminist scholars clarify interactions between narrative and dramatic modes. Anderson (2009) says the artificiality of staged action lets novelists create a revealing dialectic between disclosure and disguise. Marsden (2006) presents the popularity of suffering women on the stage for the benefit of female spectators and in opposition to moral objections to displays of female sexuality. Against the idea of declining dramatic mediation, Marsden (2019) holds that the common heightening of audiences' emotional response in the latter half of the century aimed to elevate the moral status of the theatre.
298. On the notion that idealising domestic femininity in literary sentimentalism "embodies long-held cultural mistrust of women," as it serves a "male fantasy" of controlling and relegating them to a perpetually lowered status, see Oliver 2008, 16.
299. Brooke 1985, xliii and 1.
300. Despite Mr Brooke's fruitless association with Quebec merchants, he was paid as their chaplain until his death (McMullen 1983, 79–83).
301. On the Brookes' Anglicanism and "genteel poverty," see Edwards 1981, 171–82.
302. While the novel tries to "deal honestly" with the "Canadian scene," it is "dominated by a bourgeois moral system" valuing "prudence, caution, and respectability" (Pacey 1946–47, 147–50). The novel is "indicative of the tension of the times" (New 1972, 37). Brooke's hostility to aristocrats is clarified by Jarrett (1973) and Cannon (1984); both emphasise the increasing economic and political power of aristocrats.
303. On the Marriage Act, see Marshall 1962, 225–27. Cannon describes the growing intermarriage among aristocrats and the relative marital immobility of the middle class (1984, 74–92). McMullen gives biographical reasons why the Brookes objected to the Marriage Act (1983, 9). Rivers definitively connects the Marriage Bill to the constitution (Brooke 1985, 371).
304. Brooke 1985, 7, 285, 50, and 98. Messenger defends Arabella's "complexity of self-awareness" against Pope's belittling of the character in *The Rape of the Lock*. She assigns an "all-pervasive" irony and keen sense of "irreconcilable contradictions" to Arabella: she is a self-conscious, not frivolous, coquette (1986, 162, 164, 165, and 170). But Brooke was in command neither of her epistolary medium nor of the strategic requirements of narrative dialectic.
305. Brooke 1985, 101, 188, 98, and 281.
306. McNaught 1969, 45.
307. McNaught 1969, 47–48.

308.Morton 1963, 153.

309.Morton 1963, 154; Brooke 1985, 250.

310.Eccles 1972, 223–24.

311.Brooke 1985, 26, 140, 3, 154, and 260; Garon 1976, 260.

312.Brooke 1985, 241, 22, 41, 250, 271, 141, 274, 221, 271–72, 49, 147, and 377.

313.Brooke 1985, 24, 38, 30, 80, 139, 23, 355, 373, 30, 301, 303, 379, and 407.

314.For an economic explanation of the failure of trade to support the characters' optimistic hopes, see Binhammer 2010, 295-319.

315.Brooke 1985, 5, 179, 330, 311, 388, 407, and 348.

316.Brooke 1985, 51–52, 74, 58, 95, 320, 121, 347, 124, 284–85, 404, 116, and 342.

317.Brooke 1985, 266, 264, 297, 381, 311, 154, 341–42, 58, 301, 312, and 323. Macey relates the growth of dowries to the "financial revolution" and the development of the national debt (1983, 89–93). In "Marriage," Cannon details the tightening bonds between class, wealth, and marriage. He shows that, despite talk about companionate love, arranged marriages increased in number and increasingly fortified social hierarchy (1984, 71–92).

318.To Ouellet, economic rivalry between aristocratic and bourgeois values eroded nationalistic concepts. He notes the growing power of aristocrats in government bureaucracy (1980, 53–102). His account explains why Brooke both admires the governors' gentility and rejects their aristocratic sympathy for the displaced seigneurs and noblesse.

319.Brooke 1985, 3, 5, 24, 26, 71, 11, 34–35, 158, 119, 57, 49, 13, 90, 277, and 260.

320.Brooke 1985, 220, 222, 242, 232–33, 241, and 250. By contrast, Marivaux's plays have a "colonial subtext" that defies the hypocrisy of the Christian moral economy in France's Atlantic colonies and probes the evils of slavery in plantation economies (Sanders 2019-20, 271-96).

321.On these issues, see Boone (1987) and Rabine (1985). Boone describes how conceptions of marriage and narrative techniques, whether traditional or progressive, are corollaries, while Rabine, analysing the recoil of radical ideology upon itself in a series of romances, elaborates why progressive concepts in romance tend to be self-defeating.

322.Brooke 1985, 295, 310, 326, 342, 205, 371, 42, 133, 198, 277, 400, 13, 93, 187, and 206.

323.Brooke 1985, 378, 340, and 212.

324.Brooke 1985, 56, 59, 185, 138, 324, 360. 358, 80, 107, and 230–31.

325.Brooke 1985, 205, 189–90, 192, 226, 247, 249, and 254.

326.Brooke 1985, 177, 219, 165, 224, 226, 287, 74, and 320.

327.Brooke 1985, 331–32, 341, and 366.

328.Brooke 1985, 314.

329.Vivien Bosley invited me to speak at the Marivaux Colloquium in 1988, sparking my interest in the French author (Merrett 1989a). Milan Dimić explained systemic concepts of literature to me. Thus, I am indebted to Hawkes (1977), Lambert and van Gorp (1985), and Dimić and Garstin (1988). I employ "systematic" and "systemic" distinctly: the first adjective applies to the construction of a system from the maker's external viewpoint, the second to elements of a single system and the interactions of plural systems viewed structurally, organically, and internally.

330.Smith 1971, 108.

331.Blair 1965, II, 308–09.

332.Warburton 1751, IV, 169.

333.Beattie 1783, 570–73.

334.Gray 1874, 388; Collyer 1965, 4. Collyer's preface says Marivaux's novel "is a production that reflects a glory on the French nation" (1965, 5). Her translation appeared in 1743, Gray's letter to West dating from April 1742. Their remarks about pedagogy and Marivaux as a national, cultural emblem are close in spirit.

335.Walpole 1837, II, 313.

336. Reeve 1785, 129. Chesterfield wrote in December 1750 and April 1751 (Stanhope 1892, I, 384 and 431). He likely met Marivaux thirty years before (Desvignes-Parent 1970, 25 and 32).

337. "The very use of the concept of system implies that we are aware of conflicts and parallelisms between systems and sub-systems" (Lambert and van Gorp 1985, 51).

338. *The Gentleman's Magazine*, vol. 19 (1749), 245–46 and 345–49.

339. Murphy 1762, I, 42–44.

340. For a comparison of Fielding, Richardson, and Marivaux, consider Frederick Green's views: comparing Fielding to Marivaux in order to contrast Richardson and the French author, he suggests that Marivaux is much more subtle than Fielding (Green 1966, 388–89). For Marivaux's experimental humanism, see Coulet and Gilot 1973.

341. Fielding 1962, 158 and 1974, II, 686.

342. Burney 1982, 7–9. Cf. Collyer 1965, xxxviii.

343. On why the "significance of autobiography" should be sought for "beyond truth and falsity," see Gusdorf 1980, 28–48.

344. Burney 1982, 26, 130, 255, 239, 263, 288, and 352.

345. Fielding 1974, 525–27, 77, and 235. On Fielding's variable philosophical stance see Merrett 1980b, 3–21 and chapter two above.

346. If Orville's refinement exemplifies French culture, Lovel the fop represents Burney's sense of corrupt French manners (Burney 1982, 82 and 79). Fielding's doubts about France are clear in the characters of Beau Didapper in *Joseph Andrews* and Lord Fellamar in *Tom Jones*. His doubts were informed by hostility to Jacobitism.

347. Richardson 1971, 7. Pamela recoils from the French dances she learns (Richardson 1971, 77).

348. Richardson 1985, 161, 261, and 785.

349. Richardson 1971, 401, 407, and 1985, 1369–70. Warner's study of *Clarissa* (1979) explores systemic tensions in the text to challenge Richardson's supposed humanist intentions.

350. To Marshall, Marianne is a "victim of her own story" from self-objectification (1988, 54–63).

351. Richardson 1971, 40, 82, and 42. The anonymous author of *Pamela Censured* similarly criticises the novel's prurience (1976, 28, 32, and 44).

352. Richardson 1971, 159–60 and 1985, 368.

353. Richardson 1971, 25 and 1985, 408.

354. Marivaux's delight in literary problems is discussed by Rosbottom in terms of the "literature of compromise" (1974, 36–47).

355. To Greene, paradoxes in Jacob's characterization make him an "open character" (1965, 193).

356. Rosbottom 1974, 220.

357. "Et tant mieux, car il faut qu'on s'accoutume de bonne heure à mes digressions; je ne sais pas pourtant si j'en ferai de fréquentes, peut-être oui, peut-être non; je ne réponds de rien; je ne gênerai point; je conterai toute ma vie, et si j'y mêle autre chose, c'est que cela se présentera, sans que je le cherche" (Marivaux 1981, 41).

358. Anon. 1735, 1–2, 5–6, 13, and 217. The anonymous English translation of *Le Paysan parvenu* listed in the Works Cited is the one cited throughout.

359. Bourgeacq summarises the ironies of Jacob's diction (1975, 217–25).

360. Anon. 1735, 8, 16, 31–32, and 40.

361. "En un mot, j'en fis trop et pas assez. Dans la moitié de mon salut, il semblait que je le connaissais; dans l'autre moitié, je ne le connaissais plus; c'était oui, c'était non et tous les deux manqués" (Marivaux 1978, 108). Note Collyer's reduction of the contraries to a contradiction.

362. Collyer 1965, 10–11, 16, 31, 51–52 and 65. "Marivaux a créé à travers les variations du récit et leurs conséquences, un romanesque nouveau où l'acte de raconter lui-même devient romanesque" (Jugan 1978: 183).

363. The hurried informality of the translated *Le Paysan Parvenu* is reflected in the fact that it neither announces volume numbers on the title-page nor is complete. Collyer's deliberateness is mirrored by such an announcement and by the prolixity of her translation.

364 Pagination for textual parallels: Marivaux 1981, 65, 68, 66, 84, 45, 67, 54 (two examples), 57, 65); the translation of 1735, 36, 39, 37, 59, 11, 39, 22 (two examples), 27, 26, 37.

365. Anon 1735, 1, 2, 15, and 27.

366. Anon 1735, 4, 44, and 46.

367. Pagination for the parallels in this paragraph: Marivaux 1978, 50 (twice), 52, 55, 56, 72, 66, 70; Collyer 1965, 7 (twice), 9, 15, 17, 35, 29, 33.

368. Marivaux 1978, 78, 81(twice); Collyer 1965, 42, 45 (twice), and 43.

369. Marivaux 1978, 53 and 83; Collyer 1965, 10, 16, 33, 47, 12–13, and 18–19

370. Lambert and van Gorp 1985, 44.

371. The writers who most influenced Sterne were Rabelais; Joseph Hall, the Elizabethan satirist; and Marivaux (Collyer 1965, xiv). The relation between Sterne and French sentimentalists is treated by Brissenden 1974, 110 ff.

372. Sterne 1940, 11, 286, 8, 18, 35, 122, and 218.

373. Sterne 1940, 73, 313, 108, 75, and 215. Also compare *Tristram Shandy*: "Writing, when properly managed (as you may be sure I think mine is) is but a different name for conversation" (Sterne 1940: 108) with *La Vie de Marianne*: "je n'ai garde de songer que je vous fais un livre, cela me jetterait dans un travail d'esprit don't je ne sortirais pas; je m'imagine que je vous parle, et tout passe dans la conversation" (Marivaux 1978, 71).

374. Sterne 1940, 462; Sterne 1984, 13.

375. On Defoe's sense of contraries in terms of his verbal habits, see Merrett 1989b, 171–85.

376. Defoe 1981, 5, 8, 120, 184, 187, 254, 279, 281, and 337.

377. Defoe 1964, 6–7, 17, 25, 284, and 127.

378. Wall, describing Fanny's non-acquisitive observation of symbolic features at Sotherton in *Mansfield Park*, illustrates Austen's rhetorical humanism (2014, 177–79). To Black, "Austen's exemplary novels are romances in both theme and form, organised by updated conceptions of chivalry and traditional love stories alike. They may be "experienced as romantic fantasies" and studies of "everyday life." He continues: "Romance is the reminder that we have never been as fully modern as we say, and the remainder of a much longer, wider, and weirder literary history than that told by our familiar stories. Such accounts tend to work between binary poles—epic and novel, myth and history—with romance as the excluded middle .... As a genre defined by its intermediate status as a 'compromise' between epic and novel, romance is an enabling hinge in literary history, an in-between mediating genre" (2019, 5 and 89).

379. John Wilmot (1647–1680), 2nd Earl of Rochester.

380. Lisle 1757, xxi.

381. "As historians push the Industrial Revolution forward to the later eighteenth century, so they pull the agricultural revolution back into the seventeenth-century" (Hill 1969, 150).

382. Young 1770a, ix–x.

383. "Knightley's name is well and intentionally chosen, for not only does he continually bring into the daily life of Highbury the spirit of chivalry ... but more importantly he exemplifies the kind of behaviour Jane Austen considers necessary for the maintenance of a morally founded society" (Duckworth 1971, 156).

384. Austen 1974, 59, 61–63, and 65.

385. To Colley, the calling into question of the ruling élite during the period of the American and French revolutions led to the formation of a new and unitary class that came to dominate land ownership during Austen's lifetime (1992, 152–61).

386. On Austen's respect for Crabbe, see Merrett 1980, 53 and Merrett 2004, 97 and 116–18.

387. Crabbe 1967, 148–61. This reference is to lines 45–47. Subsequent references appear in parentheses.
388. On "energizing possibilities of social bounds and physical boundaries" in "The Gentleman-Farmer" as contexts for *Emma*, see Winborn 2004, 100ff. Since his life is "marked by distraction, by a precarious distension beyond the limits of his home," Gwyn points up Knightley's self-restraint and social commitment.
389. Crabbe 1788, 11–12.
390. When Defoe visited Belvoir Castle in 1726, the family had "risen by just degrees to an immense state both of honour and wealth"; its estates stretched from Lincolnshire into Nottingham and Derbyshire because of "lead mines and coal-pits" (Defoe 1974, II: 91 and 103).
391. Cannadine says "the landed establishment" gained territory, titles, power, and influence until the early 1870s through its exploitation of the industrial and agricultural revolutions (1990, 10–15). On Burke's use of the estate to symbolise the nation, see Duckworth 1971, 45–46.
392. Everett relates landscape design to "changing conceptions of improvement" under "the growing influence of doctrines of political economy, and the replacement of the traditional ethic of benevolence—increasingly regarded as uncertain, intrusive, and unjust—with a greater emphasis on market-influenced social relations" (1994, 7). Pearce (2020) details Austen's neoclassical aesthetic; her moral figuration of things signifies her modern humanism.
393. Evidence of Grandison's estate management is taken from Richardson 1972, Part 3, Volume VII, Letter VIII, 285–89.
394. Friedman in his five-volume edition of Goldsmith says the "great popularity" of *The Vicar* "came after Goldsmith's death in 1774." In the last quarter of the century, "there were at least twenty-three London editions and twenty-one editions in English published elsewhere" (1966, IV: 11).
395. Goldsmith 1982: 70–71, 184, 50, 49, 104, 75–76, 150, and 57. Goldsmith's "The Traveller" and "The Deserted Village" display the incompatibility of farming values, taken as the basis of "national well-being," with commercial progress (Everett 1994: 62).
396. Smollett 1967, 150–51, 255–56, 33, 43, and 53.
397. Smollett 1967, 66, 118, 197, 329, 362–63, 365–66, 369, and 252. Model agricultural pioneers include: Jethro Tull (1674-1741), Walter Harte (1709-1774), and Henri Louis Duhamel du Monceau (1700-1781). Smollett promotes agricultural innovation for Scotland (1967: 281–83).
398. Smith 1776, I: 64, 158, and 478–79.
399. Brooke 1972, 258.
400. Coke innovatively offered twenty-one-year leases and had tenants rotate turnips, barley, grass, and corn after 1815 (Beckett 2006). Despite Duckworth's claim, it is hard to imagine Knightley as "an heir of Coke and Townshend" (1971, 156): he is not vainglorious, and he encourages his tenant farmer in political economy.
401. Brooke 1972, 211 and 304.
402. Hibbert 1998, 197.
403. For Burke, "the spirit of a gentleman, and the spirit of religion," since they inspire "love, veneration, admiration, or attachment," will reform "our institutions" more effectively than the "mechanic philosophy" of the Jacobins (1968, 172–73).
404. Kramnick 1977, 158–59.
405. Burke 1968, 151–52. Although Burke defends France's "men of landed estates" as partners of farmers, he reprehends the "old tenures" and laments, speaking as "not a good, but an old farmer," the incursions of capitalism into French agriculture to defy claims that moneylending, aggravated by confiscated church lands, advances agriculture (1968, 243 and 308).
406. Home 1779, v–xi and xv–xvii.
407. Austen 1974, 29; Young 1770a, xi.
408. Bradley 1726, vii–ix.
409. Tull 1731, xi–xvi.

410. Young 1770a, x.
411. Ellis 1750, iii–vii; Young 1770a, x–xi.
412. Lisle 1757, xi–xx.
413. Du Monceau 1764, ix, xv–xvi.
414. Young 1770a, xvii.
415. Harte 1764, 20 and 11–14.
416. Young 1793, 2–4. *The Example of France a Warning to Britain* contains "a few short essays, inserted originally in the Annals of Agriculture" (Young 1793, 3).
417. Young 1770a, I: Book V, 4–5.
418. Young 1770b, 345, 314–15, 325, 333–34 and 340–42.
419. Young 1785, 18–22. Young edited forty-five volumes of the *Annals of Agriculture* from 1784 to 1815. The Board of Agriculture was created in 1793. Two General Views of each county were published (Overton 1996, 129). These were the Agricultural Reports.
420. Young 1785, 457. When Capability Brown (1716-1783) died, "around four thousand landscape parks" had been created by him and his imitators. A landscape park consisted of open expanses of grass and "irregularly scattered trees," the "open turf" appearing to flow up the walls of the main residence (Williamson 1995, 82 and 77).
421. Shenstone created the Leasowes personally in 1745 as a *ferme ornée* (Williamson 1995, 60).
422. Young 1785, 463–65.
423. Overton 1996, 129.
424. Stone 1800, v–xii and 356–59.
425. Kent 1796, xii; Kent 1775, 10 and 211.
426. Lane 1995, 163.
427. Winborn 2004, 122.
428. Everett 1994, 194–98.
429. To Kramp, Knightley is a trusted civic leader who upholds tradition while sensing that the "post-Revolutionary nation" is ready for "significant social shifts." This Whig view leads Kramp to say the culture of *Emma* is slowly accepting "the collapse of traditional systems of order," such as the aristocracy and archaic modes of masculinity. To say that Knightley adopts "the behavior of the Jacobin farmers" by working the soil vigorously too easily imposes the ideology of the French Revolution on Austen's ideas of the agrarian revolution (2007, 109, 112, and 115).
430. Stovel 1996, 204–05.
431. Butler relates the near silence of Knightley and the total silence of his alter ego, Martin, to substantiality: Martin's solidity comes from a well-defined involvement with the material world; by contrast, the novel's discourse is flimsy. Since action occurs in the inner life, its theme is the scepticism about qualities that make it up—intuition, imagination, original insight (1975, 273).
432. Johnson finds Knightley an impressive figure; he is a model of chivalry who performs male duties in neither an anachronistic nor an overly progressive way. A new type of English male, he "desentamentalizes and deheterosexualizes virtue," making it available to women as well as to men (1995, 191–99).
433. Strangely, Butler finds Knightley's "paternalistic ideas" at odds with his "social instincts" which, she claims, are in "a state of atrophy" (1982, 107).
434. Productivity was improved by "convertible husbandry and the Norfolk four-course rotation." The former ended the distinction between grass and arable land, the latter rotating "around the farm." Convertible husbandry integrated livestock into arable farming. Grain crops alternated with fodder crops to reduce pests and diseases; nitrogen was fixed in the soil by clover and recycled by livestock eating roots and seeds. Weeds were controlled by hoed turnips. Rotation allowed increased yields of grain and "higher stocking densities." Norfolk four-course rotation (wheat, turnips, barley, clover) was not widespread until after 1800 (Overton 1996, 116–19).

435. Austen 1974, 361, 81, 100, 225, 23, and 28. "Martin is one of the new breed of tenant farmers ... While some of the old yeomen farmers had gone under with enclosure, a minority, those most adaptable and intelligent, had prospered, taking advantage of new methods and new markets opened up by better roads" (Lane 1989, 197).

436. *Enquiry* 1782, 21–24.

437. After giving annual figures for keeping horses, Young says: "If horses kept for use alone, and not for shew, have proved thus expensive to me, what must be the expence to those farmers who make their fat sleek teams an object of vanity! It is easier conceived than calculated" ("On the Expences of Keeping Horses" in Young 1785, 132).

438. According to cookbooks, chief dessert apples were Pippins, Rennets, Codlins, and Biffins.

439. Austen 1974, 213, 238–39, and 257.

440. Capability Brown and his imitators planted trees in clumps and curvilinear shapes.

441. Austen 1974, 107, 354–55, 358, 54, and 360–61. Clover is a small, three-leaved herb, eighteen species native to Britain. Sown alone or mixed with rye-grass, it was a staple of green-manuring in crop rotation. Animals ate clover at pasture and dried as winter feed.

442. Austen 1974, 186. Espalier is a shoulder-high lattice-work of stakes on which fruit trees are trained. Trained fruit is accessible, being protected from winds yet open to the sun and air.

443. On Austen's appreciation of the design and sociability of parlours and her wish that readers draw deductions from such material details, see Tristram 1989, 12–16.

444. Bradley 1718, 22. Bradley describes pruning for espaliers as follows: "upon an Espalier well order'd, we ought to see Wood laid in of three Summers, the one with Fruit, others to the knot for Blossoms ... and the third sort new Shoots to follow in their turn ... About Midsummer is the best time to tie the Shoots of that Summer to the espalier, and disburden the Tree ... of its superfluous Shoots" (1718, 24–25).

445. Austen 1974, 28, 27, and 482. Pure-bred Alderneys were imported from the Channel Islands. Their large udders yield lots of rich milk for making excellent butter. Bramble gives an Alderney cow to a widow on his estate since it will provide her with an income (Smollett 1967, 33).

446. Austen 1974, 23, 28–29, 136, 30, and 213.

447. Austen 1974, 32–34, 50–51, 54, 179, and 413.

448. Emma and Mr Woodhouse read the *Elegant Extracts* (Austen 1974, 79 and 81). In his preface, Vicesimus Knox (1752-1821) says he compiled the work to "be used in schools either in recitation, transcription, the exercise of the memory, or in imitation." It contains "models, which are the best means of exciting genius" (1805, viii). His anthology, originally compiled for Tunbridge School, is "adopted to the use of young persons of both sexes" (1808, I).

449. Austen 1974, 37, 69, 35, 83, 172–73, 24–25, 14, and 391.

450. Austen 1974, 34, 67, 146, and 149.

451. Austen 1974, 343, 351, 11, 39, and 41.

452. Austen 1974, 84, 386, 223, 225, 326–28, 428, and 429.

453. Austen 1974, 473.

454. Hardy 1964, 51–70. Keefe is also critical; he calls the novel a "quasi-religious odyssey," its structure reflecting *The Pilgrim's Progress,* but Jane's ultimate triumph is an irreligious emanation of Brontë's fantasy life (1979, 96–129). For the view that the novel's religion is orthodox, see Martin 1966, 81–100. Jay offers a fine account of Brontë's beliefs (1979, 244–60).

455. Brontë's narrative is upheld by Tillotson and Craik. Tillotson asserts that the reader watches a "personality discovering itself not by long introspection but by a habit of keeping pace with her own experience" (1961, 294–95), while Craik, who takes Brontë to be the pioneer of fictional autobiography, insists that neither author nor reader ever disagrees with Jane (1968, 75). Both simplify the dynamics of first-person narration as established by Defoe and Sterne; both overlook the intended and accidental ironies of the double narrative perspective. Linder discards notions of

autobiographical structure in attempting to find narrative integrity; she describes two narrative points of view, claiming they do not come together until the end (1978, 66–67).

456. Critics often describe Brontë as unconcerned with the problem of faith. Moglen says Brontë possessed "a religious aspiration that transcended traditional belief" (1976, 107), and Peters insists that legal language disqualifies the novel as a Christian parable and makes self-judgment, rather than faith, the controlling theme (1973, 147). To Stoneman, "Jane Eyre can be a heroine for the modern world because she does not deny herself in submission to a supernatural cause or a social convention, but only in defence of her self-respect" (2013, 47).

457. The "enduring appeal" of Brontë's novel must "lie in its curious mixture of radical and conservative elements" (Stoneman 2013, 47).

458. To Stoneman, the 'hidden injustice of imperialism ... underpin[s] this novel" (2013, 43)

459. Brontë 1973, 27, 79, 32, 46, 61, 47, 74, and 99.

460. Brontë 1973, 99, 130, 261, 157, and 237.

461. Brontë 1973, 49, 168, 246, 250, 324, 259, and 436.

462. Brontë 1973, 106–07 and 212.

463. Brontë 1973, 179, 410, 286–87, 150, and 289. Calling her a solitary pilgrim, Blom maintains Jane is so "self-involved" that she "sees others only as adjuncts or impediments to her own fulfilment" (1977, 89 and 104). Ironically, Jane's concern with self overrides her spirituality.

464. Brontë 1973, 186, 153, 61, 38, 28, 56, and 59. The story of Eliezer and Rebecca appears in Genesis 24. The oft-repeated phrase "graven image" first appears in Exodus 20:4. Smith provides sources for Beulah (Isaiah 62:4) and Eutychus (Acts 20:9): see Brontë 1973, 471 and 468. Smith notes that Helen shares her creator's faith that no soul will be damned (Brontë 1973, 468).

465. Brontë 1973, 68 and 75.

466. Brontë 1973, 125, 402, 137–39, 203, 221, 230, 247, and 255. See 1 Kings 19:12 for "still, small voice"; Genesis 18:5 and Judges 19:5 for "morsel of bread"; John 4:10 for "living water." The "face of the earth" is an idiom common to the Old Testament. Ross's opposing claim is that Jane's flight from Rochester to the moors teaches her about the human form as distinct from that of animals, insects, and deformed bodies; she learns "the human form is not so commonplace" and that "preserving one's own humanity is a precondition of spiritual enlightenment" (2020, 93).

467. Brontë 1973, 299, 301, 306, and 322.

468. Brontë 1973, 356, 329, 416, and 458.

469. Brontë 1973, 8–9, 109, 31, 50, and 113.

470. Brontë 1973, 25, 37, 90, 282, 298, 80, 325, 15, and 423.

471. Brontë 1973, 56, 453, 298, 364, 425, and 407.

472. Brontë 1973, 187, 242, and 20.

473. Trollope 1983, II: 938; Peppercorn 1982, 343.

474. Trollope 1953, 303; Trollope 1983, II: 877.

475. Terry 1987, 244.

476. Trollope 1953, 314–15.

477. Briggs 1985, 19 and 33–37.

478. Briggs 1985, 26–30.

479. Hewett and Axton 1983, 140.

480. Younger 1966, 418; Francis 1972, 286–314.

481. Harvey 1980, 69.

482. Herbert 1987, 43, 48, 18, and 53. To Goodlad, the "achievement of Trollope's Barsetshire Novels was ... to insist that though England was 'a commercial country' its exceptionality was founded on a nobler conception of sovereign property than that to which 'buying and selling' gives rise" (2015, 72).

483. Gindin: 1971, 5; Sadleir 1961, 154–55 and 164–65; Herbert 1987, 52–53.

484. "Trollope, we contend, is an artist of the dialectic. His writing stages encounters between the polarities of the day. It drives toward a synthetic vision that holds opposing terms continuously in frames, thereby that what's old looks new, and that what's new remains familiar" (Dever and Niles 2011, 2)

485. Trollope 1953, 19 and 21; Frances Trollope 1984, 75 and 256.

486. Byron 1935, 614 and 395. In *The Recruiting Officer* (1706), Worthy keeps "the Maidenhead" of a "fresh Pipe of choice *Barcelona*" for Captain Plume's piercing, implying men may enjoy women violently and like wine (Farquhar 1930, II: 51). To Herbert, Trollope attacked anti-feminism, the tradition of comic drama leading him to explore women's sexual charm (1987, 74–87). For his conforming to and resisting Victorian sexual mores, see apRoberts 1971, 82 and Terry 1977, 71–74. On Trollope's familiarity with historical English drama, see Epperley 1988.

487. Byron 1935, 655. In *Love and a Bottle* (1698), Lovewell says "Our Women are worse than our Wine"; if "Claret" contains little French wine, women are adulterated with the devil. He is countered by Roebuck who holds that women and wine are both necessary; sex makes him "like a Bumper of Claret, smiling and sparkling" (Farquhar 1930, I: 25). To Crompton, Byron's anti-feminism was "a fashionable posture among cynical radicals" in the Regency (1985, 239–41).

488. Herbert 1987, 74–87; Merrett 1988, 180–83; Trollope 1983, 2, 1033 and I, 513; Byron 1935, 614.

489. Ogden 1969, 129; Disraeli 1969, II: 300.

490. Polhemus 1980, 76.

491. Peacock 1967, IX: 397 and 400.

492. Broadbent says the 1815 vintage was small but of the highest quality; it seems to have equalled those of 1798 and 1811 (1980, 35).

493. Peacock 1967, IV: 23; IV: 75; V: 19; V: 377.

494. Hewett and Axton 1983, 140, 146, and 147.

495. For Trollope's relation to contemporary novelists, see apRoberts 1971, 111–12; Gindin 1971, 42 and 53–55; Kincaid 1977, 51–53.

496. Dickens 1966, 218. Bottle-age and the throwing of a crust are essential to vintage port.

497. Dickens 1954, 102 and 243.

498. Johnson 1952, I: 313–16.

499. Dickens 1968, 138 and 147–48.

500. Dickens 1907, 62–65 and 240–43.

501. Briggs 1985, 25; Blake 1967, 217.

502. Disraeli 1926, 149–50, 257–58, and 419. On Disraeli's differences from Peacock and on Trollope's dislike of Disraeli, see Blake 1967, 190–220.

503. Saintsbury 1933, 6ff.

504. Hardy, 1972, 121 and 126.

505. Carey 1977, 86 and 93.

506. Thackeray 1963, 61, 381, 590, 100, 93, 334, 123, 202, 361, and 428. On Thackeray's uses of wine, see Carey 1977, "Food and Drink," 79–102. To Thackeray, port was one of the "admirable institutions" needing to be satirised (1980, 77).

507. Trollope 1983, II: 689 and 627.

508. Harrison 1971, 306–08.

509. Eliot 1956, 68, 513, 489, 255, 384, 520, 91, and 179.

510. apRoberts 1971, 41; Dever and Niles 2011, 2; Kincaid 1977, 28.

511. Harding, "a dutiful pastor" and "the moral centre of the Barsetshire novels," is "not the corrupt caricature of reformist rhetoric," since Trollope's "more subtle message is to concede the legitimacy of moderate reform even while demonstrating that the law, the supposed moral compass of a secular modernity, is inadequate to provide authoritative judgment on questions of rightful

ownership" (Goodlad 2015, 73). Goodlad explains how Trollope looks back to Burke and Walter Scott for his symbolic, gradualist conception of history.

512. Trollope 1980f, 207, 29, 51, 53, 269, and 274–75. Harding "represents a metaphor for Trollope resonant in all his writings" (Terry 1977, 246).

513. Wright says "for political ideology" Trollope "substituted common sense, moderation, the middle course" (1975, 64). Cockshut explains that liberal principles and conservative sensibilities place Trollope beyond political categories (1980, 161–81).

514. Trollope 1980f, 131, 212, 225, 186, 263, 294, and 284. For a revealing case of legal decadence, see McMaster 1986, 53. In nineteen days of feasts for officers of the Old Bailey, one hundred and forty-five dozen bottles of wine were consumed. The feasts were interrupted for pronouncement of death sentences.

515. Trollope 1980a, I: 102; I: 207; I: 31; II: 260; I: 88; I: 91; I: 133; II: 144.

516. Trollope 1980a, I: 230 and 216. For Kincaid, Thorne is a more elemental and radical Harding, who by "refusing to let go of values that are dying ... saves them" (1977, 118).

517. Trollope 1980b, 38 and 451. Compared with the 1874 vintage cases of Château Léoville that cost Trollope seventy-two shillings each (see note 473 above), Scatcherd's "prime stuff" at ninety-two shillings a case ought to be first growth. Yet what "Muzzle & Drug" supplies must be adulterated, Trollope's wine jokes were based on precise details and sly innuendoes.

518. Trollope 1980b, 585. Skilton says that Bideawhile's ignorance of the Port of 1811, "the year of the comet," one of the best vintages ever, makes him out to be an utter fool (Trollope 1980b, 631). See also Broadbent 1980, 368.

519. This association is common in eighteenth-century comedy (Merrett 1988, 179–93).

520. Trollope 1980b, 213, 215, 260, 263, 399, and 401.

521. In his *Autobiography*, Trollope uses the word "symposium" with a full sense of its social meaning (Trollope 1953, 39).

522. Trollope 1980b, 466–67, 124–25, 139, and 488.

523. Trollope 1980c, 202–04.

524. Trollope 1980c, 68, 319, 181, 241, and 359. Robarts is guilty of too keen an attachment to Dean Arabin's claret (1980c, 319).

525. Trollope 1980e, 136–37, 151, 187, 201, 235, and 238. Eames's refusal contrasts with George de Courcy's failure to develop a manly independence, evident in his sponging on his parents and in his taking the "paternal wines" for granted (Trollope 1980e, 174).

526. Trollope 1980e, 270, 443, 367, 383, and 523.

527. Trollope 1980e, 359, 363, 641, and 643. Ginger beer figured in campaigns for sobriety (Harrison 1971, 38 and 300–01). De Guest's put-down of Eames, champagne, and ginger beer signals Trollope's jocular reaction against social reform.

528. Trollope 1980d, 24, 219–20, 108, 90, 195, 671, and 883.

529. Trollope 1980d, 150, 373, 238–39, 250–51, and 442. For the excellence of the vintage and the notoriety 1841 Lafite earned with its inflated prices, see Penning-Rowsell 1985, 454–55.

530. Trollope 1980d, 403, 407, and 410. Gladstone's attempt to make French wine a beverage failed (Harrison 1971, 248–51).

531. Trollope 1980d, 365, 355, 292, 850, 554, 562, 788, 461, 730, and 861.

532. Dickens 1970, 559, 165–66, 4, 12, 286, and 626.

533. Able 1933, 84–85; Meredith 1968, 239–40.

534. Redding 1851, 239, 348, 237, and 246.

535. To Small, Trollope's strong reality effects are "at odds with the dominant traditions of English realism." His "hypothetical non-alliance with his own readers makes plain the degree to which Trollope's attraction to characters who go against self-interest had its roots in Tory anti-authoritarianism, at least as much as in its liberalism.... [He] creates an imagined reader who errs

on the side of a too ready and presumptive sympathy ... [and] tends to oppose himself to, rather than align himself with, the reader" (2012, 400 and 412–13).

536. Faith 1988, 74.

537. Sadleir 1961, 372–73. For White's effect on Trollope's novels, see King 2019, 229-44.

538. On Forster's admiration of Austen, see *The New Republic*, 30 January 1924. Calling Austen Forster's "favourite author," Stevenson sees *A Passage to India* "aligned with modernism's new awareness of epistemological complexities" (2007, 210 and 216). On economic bases of Forster's comic similarities to Austen, see Dorsey 1990, 54-59. To Frank, Forster develops Trollope's experimental stance on testaments and legitimacy in *Howards End* (2004, 311-30).

539. Contextualizing "Howards End," Bradshaw finds Forster's liberal values frail (2007, 171).

540. On Forster's humanism, see Sarker 2007, 3: 1038–40. To Sultzbach, landscape and non-human life counter Forster's humanism: "to be human is only realized by confronting what it means to be a creature in a larger environmental habitat that informs so-called essential human features." In *A Passage to India*, nature trumps imperialism's humanist hypocrisies (2016, 62 and 25).

541. Forster, "Notes on the English Character" (1996, 9).

542. Forster, "What I Believe," in the opening paragraph of *Two Cheers for Democracy* (1938).

543. To Trilling, Forster has a "tenderness for religion because it expresses, though it does not solve, the human mystery" (1943, 19–20). Weber shows that *A Passage to India* employs Christian terminology (1971, 98–110). Crews suggests Forster has a "theological preoccupation without a theology to satisfy it" (1962, 14). Martin (1974) sees Forster as an agnostic because of liberal humanism. Proponents of Forster's modernism, Bradbury says *A Passage to India* "contains one of the most powerful evocations of modern nullity" (1973, 95) and Thomson calls it an original response to the "psychological demands of the twentieth century" (1967, 28).

544. Parry 1979, 129–41.

545. Scott (1971), "The Decline of the Figural Imagination" and "The Sacramental Vision." Scott also links modernism to the problem of faith: *The Broken Center: Studies in the Theological Horizon of Modern Literature* (New Haven: Yale University Press, 1966) and *Negative Capability: Studies in the New Literature and the Religious Situation* (New Haven: Yale University Press, 1969).

546. To Sultzbach, Forster's pastoralism "attempts to highlight the limitations of the humanist ideal and the improbability of environmental harmony in a modern age." She notes "the posthuman potential" of *A Passage to India* "where the nonhuman is the primary 'other'" (2016, 26 and 62).

547. For Ricœur, see "Religion, Atheism, and Faith" in MacIntyre and Ricœur 1969, 59–98.

548. Forster 1973, 147, 158, 107, 136, 235, 296, 311, and 315.

549. Forster 1978, 257 and 265. To Childs, "with regard to religion, humour always plays a large part in the novel .... In some ways it appears that existence is comically meaningless, and that God's absent presence renders all religion absurd" (2007, 192).

550. Forster 1978, 173, 176, 43, 23, and 154. Comically, Forster describes the religious conduct of so-called Christians in terms of their imitation of religions native to the Indian continent.

551. Forster 1978, 43. Cf. Revelations 1:8.

552. Forster 1978, 3, 134, 32, 181, 233, 207, and 219. Cf. Proverbs 25:22; Romans 12:20; and John 1:1.

553. Forster 1978, 310, 102, 112, 164, and 181. Colmer agrees that, in his creation of Fielding, Forster treats humanism ironically, further claiming that Forster does not justify faith in the "humanistic endeavour" (1967, 14 and 13).

554. Forster 1978, 21, 245, 13, 49, and 295, and "Notes on the English Character" (1996, 9–10).

555. Forster 1978, 56, 103–08, and 94.

556. Forster 1978, 156.

557. Philippians 4:7.

558. Forster 1978, 239. Adela strives "in vain against the echoing walls" of the civil Indian ladies, and Aziz, after enjoying the fellowship of polo-playing, is soon overcome by the "poison" of nationality (Forster 1978, 37 and 51–52).

559. Forster 1978, 252, 128, and 278.

560. Forster 1978, 294 and 304.

561. These phrases come respectively from Wilde 1964, 135; Stone 1966, 335; Levine 1971, 178.

562. Trilling 1943, 22

563. *Hamlet* Act IV, Scene 5.

564. Forster 1978, 34, 21, 206, 23, 85, and 134.

565. Forster 1978, 2, 80, and 116.

566. Forster 1978, 33, 277, 65, and 52.

567. Forster 1978, 270, 106, 105, 198, and 97.

568. On this concept, see Ong, "Voice as Summons for Belief" in Abrams 1958, 80–105.

569. Forster 1978, 51, 117, 141, and 208.

570. Forster 1978, 34, 80, and 251.

571. Forster 1978, 10, 96, 15, 292, 310, and 92.

572. Forster 1978, 215, 202–03, 125, 216–17, and 219.

573. Forster 1978, 220, 227, 229, and 233.

574. Forster 1978, 168, 281, and 45.

575. Forster 1978, 140, 127, and 199.

576. Forster 1978, 49–50, 96, 108, 11, and 300.

577. Forster 1972, 73. See Job 1:21.

578. Forster 1960, 63.

579. Forster 1973, 202.

580. Forster 1947, 97.

581. May 1997, 10.

582. Forster 1960, 22, 15, and 13.

583. To Stevenson, Forster "developed a late version of the Romantic vision which initially resisted pressures of modernity and industrialisation" in order to emphasise the "inner qualities of spirit, imagination, or intuition and their affirmative responses with an unsullied, non-urban world ... yet such affirmations invariably contain notes of uncertainty and precariousness" (2007, 211).

584. Forster 1960, 8, 23–24, 77, 45, 53–54, 51, and 55. For the reference to *Howards End*, see Forster 1973, 264.

585. Forster 1960, 68, 71, 63–64, 38, 60, and 179.

586. Forster 1960, 108, 281, 118, 132, 103, and 137.

587. Forster 1960, 142, 145, 156, 210, and 244.

588. "Stephen Wonham often seems a spirit of the true English countryside. But he is also a socialist activist" (Finch 2012, 244)

589. Forster 1960, 218, 242, 219, 267, 269, 215, 217, 242, 232, and 235. Cf. Matthew 7: 9.

590. Forster 1960, 217, 245–46, 250–51, 255, 257, 259, 277–78, and 280.

591. Forster 1973, 311, 19, 69–70, 74–75, 88, 83, and 96.

592. Forster 1973, 323, 203, 292, 151, 303, 295, 270, 297, and 266.

593. Forster 1973, 22–23, 201, 246, 149–50, and 128–29.

594. Forster 1973, 320, 13, 9, 6, 11–12, 22–23, 126, 128, 99, 156, and 25–27.

595. Forster 1973, 104, 41, 160, 258, 256, 258, 227–28, and 277.

596. Forster 1973, 165, 172, 198, 222, 210, and 212.

597. Forster 1973, 23, 29, 33, 40, 108, and 110.

598. Forster 1973, 42–43, 52, 46–47, 51, 118, and 144.

599. Forster 1973, 145, 152, 125, 214, 322, and 216.

600. Forster 1973, 95, 184, 179, 226, 243, 296, 331, 305, 309, 312, 287, 329, 192, 63, 208, 237–38, and 255. Biblical allusions in this paragraph are to John 8:7; Philippians 4:7; and Genesis 1:27.

601. Stone 1966, 265, 257, and 214.

602. Crews 1962, 62.

603. Wilde 1964, 44 and 118.

604. Martin 1997, 256 and 263.

605. Merrett 1984, 74 and 77. Bradshaw holds that Forster's liberal values, far from sturdy, are frail. It is worth considering his suggestion that the Schlegels in their blindness and bigotry have a kinship with the Wilcoxes (2007, 171 and 157).

606. To Collins, patronage ended in the eighteenth century. Yet, dedications invited patronage until the 1730s, earlier authors receiving small fees for them, the fees rising since a "rate of exchange" was set for "prefatory laudations." This system of payment supposedly collapsed in the reign of George II. By 1780, dedications were "merely a graceful and expected introduction to a work" (1927, 181 and 183). That this system was displaced because it demeaned authorship is challenged by Griffin (1996, 1–12 and 13–44). In "The persistence of patronage" (1996, 246–85), he shows why the modified system lasted through the century. Griffin supports historians, such as Cannon (1984) and Clark (1985), who spurn Whig notions of progress. Brewer details issues about the rise of professional authors, the difficulty of distinguishing between professional and hack writers, and strained relations between authors and booksellers (1997, 141–66).

607. Donoghue sees the reviewing system as an institution upheld by the *Monthly Review* and the *Critical Review* (1996, 34–55). Despite opposing ideologies, these magazines were preoccupied with regulating reading standards, disparaging romance and novel forms, and promoting theoretical disjunctions between critics, authors, and readers.

608. Bicknell will have known his initials were the signature of literary journeymen, as Charles Surface indicates in Sheridan's *The School for Scandal*, V, iii: "Aye, aye, Stanley or Premium, 'tis the same thing, as you say; for I suppose he goes by half a hundred names, besides A.B. at the coffee-house" (Lindsay 1995, 480).

609. Coffee-houses gathered news from contributors who put messages in elaborately carved boxes (Ellis 1956, 171 and 224). There were many ties between the book trade and coffee-houses (Johns 1998, 111–13).

610. Ralph Griffiths (c. 1720–1803) founded the *Monthly Review* in May 1749. He was sole manager and editor until his death. Its prestige saw it lasting another forty-one years. Griffiths employed expert reviewers like Owen Ruffhead (1723–1769), Burney, Murphy, and John Hawkesworth (c. 1715–1773) rather than hacks. Reviewers worked in isolation to guarantee impartiality. The *Monthly Review* was hostile to church and state in its commitment to dissent unlike its rival, the *Critical Review* (1756–1817), which, until the French Revolution, operated under Tory and ecclesiastical patronage and after which it embraced extreme reforms (Sullivan 1983, 231–34; Roper 1978, 20–22 and 174–78). Smollett was the latter's editor from 1756–1763.

611. Its full title is *The Benevolent Man; or, the History of Mr. Belville: in which is introduced, the Remarkable Adventures of Captain Maclean, the Hermit*. Addressing female concerns and written for a circulating library, it addresses male citizens and politicians too, confirming Brewer's view that circulating libraries catered more to male than female readers and that, despite the propaganda of literary reviews, fiction did not cater solely to women readers (1997, 179–83).

612. Spranger Barry (1719–1777), the Irish actor, took for his second wife Mrs Dancer (1734–1801), the actress. Sophia Baddeley (née Snow, 1745–1786), an actress, singer, and courtesan, eloped at age eighteen with the actor Robert Baddeley (1732–1794).

613. Bicknell 1775, I: 35–36, 194–95, 239–40, 200–01, 100, 105, and II: 112–13.

614. Thomas Cadell (1742–1802), a leading London publisher, operated a sophisticated wholesale and agency network. He left trade with a large fortune, having published the work of major authors, such as Smith, Gibbon, and Hume (Raven 1992, 47–50).

615. *Monthly Review* (1776) vol. 55: 66.

616. Bicknell 1776, vi.

617. Rizzo 1994, 67–71.

618. John Bell (1745–1831) traded in the Strand where he displayed "commercial flair" and profited from innovations in library series and newspapers (Raven 1992, 50). He produced the works of Shakespeare (9 vols., 1773–74), *Bell's British Theatre* (21 vols., 1776–80), and *The Poets of Great Britain* (109 vols., 1776–82). The latter met with hostility from more established London publishers: Bell was denied credit, help with distribution, shelf-space in bookshops, and advertising in newspapers (Bonnell 1989, 63).

619. *Monthly Review* (1776) vol. 55: 157.

620. Its full title is *The History of Edward Prince of Wales, Commonly Termed The Black Prince, Eldest Son of King Edward the Third, with a Short View of the Reigns of Edward I, Edward II, and Edward III. And a Summary Account of the Institution of the Order of the Garter.*

621. John Bew traded at No. 28, Paternoster Row, London's publishing centre, from 1774 until 1795 when he died. He specialised in tracts and periodicals but also retailed prints. His business exploited the growing "middle-income market" (Raven 1992, 48).

622. *Monthly Review* (1777) vol. 57: 81. The dedication is dated 13 August 1776, a day after the prince celebrated a birthday at Windsor Castle.

623. Arthur Collins (1696–1760) published *The Life and Glorious Actions of Edward Prince of Wales* in 1740. An antiquarian and historian of the peerage who suffered economic hardship, he found it difficult to secure patronage (Nichols 1967, 89–93).

624. *Gentleman's Magazine* (1777) vol. 47: 602; *Monthly Review* (1778) vol. 58: 402. The reviewer's hostility to William Guthrie (1708–1770) may be due to the latter's having served Smollett as assistant editor on the *Critical Review*. Guthrie received patronage from Robert Walpole (1676–1745) and the coalition succeeding him (Griffin 1996, 52 and 57). Boswell's praise of Guthrie exemplifies the arbitrariness of distinctions between literary and hack writers (Griffin 1996, 68). Griffin shows that major authors at the end of the century received patronage of one sort or another and that many regarded themselves at one time or another as hacks. Bicknell was indebted to Guthrie's histories of the crown and the peerage.

625. *Monthly Review* (1777) vol. 57: 331. The *DNB* recognises Bicknell as author of *Philosophical Disquisitions* but the *ESTC* does not. It has been attributed to the Reverend Samuel Badcock (1747–1788), whom Kenrick had tried to involve on his side of the debate (Rompkey 1984, 59).

626. Bicknell likely sided with Jenyns for ideological as well as theological reasons. A landlord and placeman, Jenyns was a conservative Whig who opposed John Wilkes. He was a member of the Board of Trade before which Carver solicited patronage for his journals. As compiler and editor of Carver's book in 1777 and 1778, Bicknell would have wanted to ingratiate himself with Jenyns.

627. Francis and John Newbery specialised in children's titles. They produced 47 between 1751 and 1760, 111 between 1761 and 1770, and 218 between 1791 and 1800 (Raven 1992, 40).

628. Its title was *Una and Arthur* (Hamilton *et al* [1990, 400]).

629. "Of some 250 verifiable imitations and adaptations (not including works only influenced by, or alluding to, or echoing Spenser), at least 50" are from 1746 to 1758 (Hamilton *et al* [1990: 396]).

630. Passmore 1965, 10; Schofield 1997, 99 and 205; Passmore 1965, 24.

631. *Monthly Review* (1780) vol. 63: 467–68.

632. Red Lion Street and Red Lion Square were probably named after the Red Lyon Inn, a hostelry in Holborn opened in 1611. In describing the first free-standing London theatre built in the garden of the Red Lion by John Brayne in 1567, Park Honan reports that, according to PRO KB27/1229 m.30, it was a "'Messuage or farme house called and knowen by the Sygne of the Redd Lyon'" (1999, 101). Hanway, the philanthropist praised by Bicknell in *The Benevolent Man*, lived in Red Lion Square where he died in 1786. Bicknell's allusions to Milton in the *Town and Country Magazine* are poignant since after the Restoration the poet lived in a humble dwelling in Red

Lion Fields. The square, developed by Nicholas Barbon in 1684, was reputedly the burial place of the regicides. In his *Tour*, Defoe noted the "prodigious pile" of buildings in the district, many of them underway in the mid-1720s (1974, I: 328). It formed a "nest of alleys" in the reigns of the first two Georges and gained a reputation for immorality. Nor was it safe for pedestrians. Red Lion Street was known for dealers in plaster casts (Thornbury and Walford n.d., IV: 545–50).

633. In 1740, Thomson and David Mallett (1705-1765), under royal patronage, wrote *Alfred*, a masque performed in the gardens of the Prince of Wales's house, evading the prohibitions of the Licensing Act (Collins 1927, 158–59). Thomas Arne (1710–1788) wrote the music, later turning it into an oratorio in 1745 and then an opera in 1753. It is best known for its finale: "Rule, Britannia!"

634. *Monthly Review* (1788) vol. 78: 522–23.

635. *Gentleman's Magazine* (1788) vol. 58, Pt. 1: 427; *General Magazine and Impartial Review* (May 1788): 256; *Monthly Review* (1789) vol. 81: 179. The Robinsons were leading publishers: George Robinson I (1737–1801) traded in Paternoster Row from 1764, with George II, John, and James from 1785, and with George II and James from 1794–1801 (Raven 1992, 48). That major publishers reprinted Bicknell's self-published work suggests it met with favour and commercial success. The reprinted version of the play had not been registered by the *ESTC* at the original time of researching this piece.

636. Given the hostility of the *Monthly Review* to Bicknell, it is interesting that Burney, one of its reviewers, should have subscribed to his play. See note 610 above.

637. *General Magazine and Impartial Review* (June 1787, 22) presents *More Odes upon Odes* (published by Lowndes in quarto at two shillings and sixpence) as anonymous. It says the poet's effort to imitate Peter Pindar, while accusing him of "false tales" and "bad taste," recoils on him.

638. *Monthly Review* (1790) vol. 2. n.s.: 463; *General Magazine and Impartial Review* (May 1789): 214–18. This latter magazine flourished for six years from July 1787, offering many original articles when reprinting and piracy were staples of magazine editing. Its reviews were exclusive; Thomas Bellamy, the editor, prided himself on their prompt appearance. The reviews had a rare "air of generous and unpretentious appraisal," perhaps due to Bellamy's and his readers' lack of literary sophistication (Sullivan 1983, 131–32). Raven names Charles Stalker with Bew, Hookham, and Cooke as prolific publishers who marketed good-breeding to the middle classes (1992, 151). *Doncaster Races*, in attacking gambling and promoting wifely fidelity, typifies the moral sense consumed by middle-class readers (Raven 1992, 190–92).

639. *Monthly Review* (1791) vol. 4, n.s.: 109; *General Magazine and Impartial Review* (March 1790): 117–20. NB. The correct spelling is "Halsewell."

640. *General Magazine and Impartial Review* (February 1789): 53–61. Bicknell identifies himself at the head of the essay as "author of The Patriot King, etc., etc."

641. The dedication records his address as still in Red Lion Street.

642. Since the review of *The Grammatical Wreath* appeared a month before that of *Painting Personified*, this might explain the non-appearance of the latter in the self-advertisement. This assumes the *General Magazine and Impartial Review* mirrored publication dates accurately.

643. *Monthly Review* (1791) vol. 5, n.s.: 100; *General Magazine and Impartial Review* (February 1790): 67.

644. *Monthly Review* (1791) vol. 5, n.s.: 100. Bicknell may have had Priestley's *A Chart of Biography* (1764) in mind when working on the apparatus of this work.

645. *Monthly Review* (1792) vol. 9, n.s.: 116; *European Magazine* (November 1783) vol. 4: 328–30; (December 1783) vol. 4: 417–21; and (February 1784) vol. 5: 105–09. The *European Review* spanned forty-five years from 1782 to 1826. Devised by a group calling itself "the Philological Society of London," it had James Perry as its first editor. He established its format in the first two volumes, joining the features of a magazine and a review. In the early years, the magazine often dealt with social and court life. Each issue also featured engravings (Sullivan 1983, 106–11).

646. Bicknell 1791, 242.

647. *Town and Country Magazine* (1792): 173 and (1793): 463–66.

648. *General Magazine and Impartial Review* (July 1787): 105–06. Since Bellamy, proprietor and editor of this magazine, "never hired professionals or paid for contributions" (Sullivan 1983, 132), Bicknell could not have had a mercenary motive in writing for it.

649. *General Magazine and Impartial Review* (August 1787): 145–47; (September 1787): 180–84.

650. Parker 1976, 31.

651. The status of his ghost-writing will have been clear to Bicknell; the advertisements placed in his self-published works, *The Patriot King* and *The Grammatical Wreath,* mention none of his three texts. It is difficult to explain why he identified himself through these works on title-pages but not in the advertisements.

652. *Gentleman's Magazine* (August 1780) vol. 50: 374. Carver's *Travels* appeared in the fall of 1778, ten years after he wrote his journals. Bicknell's name does not, according to Parker (1976), appear in this or the second edition which came out in 1779; no substantial changes having been made. The correspondent to the *Gentleman's Magazine* likely saw Bicknell's claim to be compiler (not editor) of Carver's book on the title-page of *The Putrid Soul.* The popularity of Carver's book is indicated by a Dublin piracy of 1779, but a counter-indication is that sheets from the 1779 London edition were reissued in November 1780 in London.

653. *European Magazine* (November 1783) vol. 4: 346–47. Bicknell's biblical digests that came out in *Instances* also appeared in the *European Magazine* at this time.

654. The popularity of this 'autobiography' is attested by its fourth London edition in 1786. It was published in five and six volumes by J. Bell, the London publisher of Bicknell's *Isabella.*

655. Melville 1900, 243; *European Magazine* (February 1785), 97–100; (March 1785), 180–82; (April 1785), 251–53; (June 1785), 427–28. Before Bicknell advertised this in *The Patriot King* and *Doncaster Races,* it was known that he was the author: the *DNB*'s entry on Bellamy says he arranged and transcribed it, while Melville says that he wrote and arranged it (1900, 243). To the reviewer, "these extracts will serve to justify the opinion we have given of this volume. Mr Bell should recollect, that the best wine, if drawn too near the lees, will become foul" (1785, 428).

656. *Gentleman's Magazine* (March 1785) vol. 55: 204–07 and (April 1785) vol. 55: 294–98. The reference comes from page 205 of the first number.

657. The *DNB* entry on Baddeley reports that Mrs Steele was "her companion, and claims to have been her friend ... but the discredit of the publication has been assigned to Alexander Bicknell." According to a letter written in 1802 by Stephen Sayre, Baddeley's lover, Steele's assistant on the project was William Jackson, Elizabeth Chudleigh's secretary during her trial for bigamy. He helped government ministers blacken the character of opposition politicians, such as Charles Fox (Rizzo 1994, 363–64). Sophia Snow Baddeley and Elizabeth Hughes Steele were whore and madam, business partners, and lovers. Baddeley was a star actress between 1764 and 1771 and London's most desired courtesan from 1769 to 1773 (Rizzo 1994, 199).

658. Bicknell 1775: I, 201.

659. *European Magazine* (July 1787), 41. Here, this magazine shares the insulting tones of the *Monthly Review* which had disparaged Defoe as "a book-maker" (1776) vol. 55: 157.

660. *General Magazine and Impartial Review* (June 1787), 20.

661. Archibald Hamilton was owner and editor of the *Town and Country Magazine,* which he founded in 1769. The magazine, producing as many as 20,000 copies in the 1780s, declined in the 1790s, ceasing publication in 1795. Since Hamilton had co-founded with Smollett the *Critical Review* and long served that review as chief editor, upholding its Tory ideology, it is unsurprising that he appreciated Bicknell's political and social outlook.

662. *Town and Country Magazine* (January 1791), 20–21.

663. Bicknell's regret for the passing of patronage may show that he was out of step with the book trade. To Collins, by 1760, there was little point to such arguments as Bicknell makes: authors

could do well without patronage, so thought the patrician class for whom writers became increasingly marginal. Collins grants patronage revived somewhat in the early reign of George III under royal influence; for example, Guthrie extorted the renewal of his pension from Prime Minister John Stuart, 3rd Earl of Bute (1713-1792) in 1762. Whereas Johnson, Smollett, and Goldsmith saw themselves rising from the ranks of the hack, Collins insists that booksellers did not aggravate the misery of hacks since it did not pay them to do so: publishers such as Cadell, Robinson, and Newbery (with whom Bicknell dealt) were known to treat authors generously. Still, Collins admits that writers' prospects were difficult unless they had independent means, powerful patrons, or a "fair social standing." The latter was crucial in setting the price of copyright (Collins 1927, 191, 200, 24, 33, 41–47, 28, and 30). In the life of poet William Collins in *The Lives of the Poets*, Johnson says the power of booksellers drove poor men to write fluently and badly. Bicknell follows Johnson rather than see that the number of patrons was declining and that political and cultural motives for patronage were weakening. His writing for magazines seems not to have led him to recognise the growth of middle-class readership. One concludes that efforts to forge a literary identity did not win him financial independence, sustaining patrons, or cultural influence. Griffin's criticism of Collins's inconsistencies and view that the patronage system did not decline adds to the seriousness with which Bicknell's complaints should be treated (1996, 253–54).

664. The dates of the six essays from the *Town and Country Magazine* discussed in this paragraph are: (April 1791), 175; (September 1791), 401–02; (August 1792), 375; (December 1792), 569–70; (February 1793), 66; and (March 1783), 109–10.

665. On Handel's love of gourmet food and appetite for wine which may have contributed to his blindness, see Van Til 2007, 45 and Blakeman 2009, 20–21.

666. The dates of the four essays from the *Town and Country Magazine* discussed in this paragraph are: (March 1793), 113–14; (April 1793), 155–57; (October 1793), 459–60 [note the publication lag of almost a year]; (June 1794), 241–42.

667. The reference to Bolt Court may be a retort to Johnson; it was well known that he lived in Bolt Court, Fleet Street, where he died on 13 December 1784.

668. Bicknell refers to Lawrence, the portrait painter and president of the Royal Academy. The *Critical Review* (vol. 68 [July 1789], 75) and the *English Review* (vol. 15 [June 1790], 465) found the plot of *Doncaster Races* absurd and appalling (Raven 1992, 72).

669. The dates of the final three essays from The *Town and Country Magazine* discussed in previous paragraphs are: (March 1795), 81–82; (August 1795), 284–85 [but dated Richmond, April 10: note shorter publication lag]; and (August 1795), 299.

670. "St. Thomas's, in Southwark, founded as an almonry in 1213, had been rebuilt as a hospital, by public subscription, between 1701 and 1706" (Rudé 1971, 84). Bicknell would have suffered humiliation there since hospitals were "charitable and 'reforming' institutions in which the poor were constantly reminded of their lowly station in life and their obligations to God and to their social betters" (Rudé 1971, 84–85). Yet when he was resident, cleanliness and ventilation had improved, and the death-rate had fallen to one-in-fifteen (George 1966, 62). Defoe describes the hospital's foundation and its relation to Guy's Hospital in the *Tour* (1974), I: 369–70.

Bibliographical Note

Essays in this book first appeared in France, Germany, Holland, the United States, and Canada. Each has been re-contextualised with up-to-date scholarship, re-written, abbreviated, and cross-referenced, with titles changed and printing errors corrected. Note formats and Works Cited are unified. Chapters briefly introduce critical engagement with humanism and the liberal arts. Birth and death dates of authors (when known) are given at their first appearance, as are publication dates. Original titles were: "Diction and Verbal Sequence in Dryden's *Absalom and Achitophel*: The Rhetorical Confirmation of Religious Typology," *Etudes Anglaises* 45, 2 (1992): 129–42; "Irony and Theology in *Eloisa to Abelard*," *Wascana Review* 18, 1 (1983): 40–51; "Death and Religion in *The Rape of the Lock*," *Death and Dying*. Ed. Evelyn J. Hinz (Winnipeg: Mosaic, 1982), 29–39; "The Principles of Fielding's Legal Satire and Social Reform," *Dalhousie Review* 62, 2 (1982): 238–53; "Empiricism and Judgment in Fielding's *Tom Jones*," *Ariel* 11, 3 (1980): 3–21; "Natural History and the Eighteenth-Century English Novel," *Eighteenth-Century Studies* 25, 2 (1991-92): 145–70; "England's Orpheus: Praise of Handel in Eighteenth-Century Poetry," *Mosaic* 20, 2 (1987): 97–110; "Pictorialism in Eighteenth-Century Fiction: Visual Thinking and Narrative Diversity." *Time, Literature and the Arts in Honor of Samuel L. Macey*. Ed. Thomas R. Cleary (Victoria: University of Victoria, 1994), 157–91; "*The Beggar's Opera* and Literary Historiography: Critical Pluralism as Strategy for Teaching a Canonical Text." *Bridging the Gap: Literary Theory in the Classroom*. Ed. J. M.Q. Davies (W. Cornwall, Connecticut: Locust Hill, 1994), 181–201; "Les Formes Théâtrales Anglaises, 1660-1780," *L'Aube de la Modernité*. Ed. P.-E. Knabe, R. Mortier, and F. Moureau. Vol 16 of *A Comparative History of Literatures in European Languages* (Amsterdam and Philadelphia: John Benjamins, 2002), 205–224; "The Politics of Romance in *The History of Emily Montague*," *Canadian Literature*, 133 (1992): 92–108; "Marivaux Translated and Naturalized: Systemic Contraries in Eighteenth-Century British Fiction," *Canadian Review of Comparative Literature*, 17, 3–4 (1990): 227–54; "The Gentleman-Farmer in *Emma*: Agrarian Writing and Jane Austen's Cultural Idealism," *University of Toronto Quarterly*, 77, 2 (2008): 711–37; "The Conduct of Spiritual Autobiography in *Jane Eyre*," *Renascence* 37, 1 (1984): 2–15; "Port and Claret: The Politics of Wine in Trollope's Barsetshire Novels," *Mosaic*, 24, 3–4 (1991): 107–25; "E.M. Forster's Modernism: Tragic Faith in *A Passage to India*," *Mosaic* 17, 3 (1984): 71–86; "Spiritual Places in *The Longest Journey* and *Howards End*: E.M. Forster's Gendered Criticism of Imperialism and Cosmopolitanism," *Proceedings of the 7th International Literature of Region and Nation Conference*. Ed. Susanne Hagemann (Frankfurt: Peter Lang, 2000), 255–68; "Problems of Self-Identity for the Literary Journeyman: The Case of Alexander Bicknell (d. 1796)," *English Studies in Canada* 28, 1 (2002): 31–63.

Works Cited

Able, Augustus Henry. 1933. *George Meredith and Thomas Love Peacock: A Study in Literary Influence*. Philadelphia: Folcroft.

Abrams, M.H. (ed.). 1958. *Literature and Belief*. New York: Columbia University Press.

Addison, Joseph and Richard Steele. 1964. *The Spectator*. Ed. C. Gregory Smith. 4 vols. London: Dent.

Alter, Robert. 1968. *Fielding and the Nature of the Novel*. Cambridge, MA: Harvard University Press.

Anderson, Emily Hodgson. 2009. *Eighteenth-Century Authorship and the Play of Fiction: Novels and the Theatre, Haywood to Austen*. New York: Routledge

Anon. 1735. *Le Paysan Parvenu: Or, The Fortunate Peasant*. London: John Brindley.

Anon. 1976. *Pamela Censured (1741)*. Ed. Charles Batten. Los Angeles: Clark Memorial Library.

apRoberts, Ruth. 1971. *The Moral Trollope*. Athens, OH: Ohio University Press.

Atkins, G. Douglas. 1980. *The Faith of John Dryden: Change and Continuity*. Lexington, KY: The University Press of Kentucky.

Atkins, Madeline Smith. 2006. *The Beggar's 'Children': How John Gay Changed the Course of England's Musical Theatre*. Newcastle-upon-Tyne: Cambridge Scholars Publishing.

Ault, Norman and Rosemary Cowler (eds.). 1936. *The Prose Works of Alexander Pope*. 2 vols. Oxford: Blackwell.

Austen, Jane. 1966. *Mansfield Park*. Ed. Tony Tanner. Harmondsworth: Penguin.

Austen, Jane. 1974. *Emma*. Vol. 4 of *The Novels of Jane Austen*. Ed. R.W. Chapman. 5 vols. 3rd ed. The Oxford Illustrated Jane Austen. London: Oxford University Press.

Austen, Jane. 1980. *Pride and Prejudice*. Ed. James Kinsley and Frank W. Bradbrook. Oxford: Oxford University Press.

Austin, J. L. 1965. *How to Do Things with Words*. Ed. J.O. Urmson. New York: Oxford University Press.

Backscheider, Paula (ed.). 1979. *Probability, Time, and Space in Eighteenth-Century Literature*. New York: AMS Press.

Badir, Magdy Gabriel and Vivien Bosley (eds.) 1989. *Le Triomphe de Marivaux*. Edmonton: Department of Romance Languages, University of Alberta.

Bareham, Tony (ed.). 1980. *Anthony Trollope*. London: Vision Press.

Barrell, John. 1986. *The Political Theory of Painting from Reynolds to Hazlitt: 'The Body of the Public.'* New Haven: Yale University Press.

Battestin, Martin C. 1959. *The Moral Basis of Fielding's Art: A Study of Joseph Andrews.* Middletown, CT: Wesleyan University Press.

Battestin, Martin C. 1968. "Fielding's Definition of Wisdom: Some Functions of Ambiguity and Emblem in *Tom Jones*." *ELH* 35: 188–217.

Battestin, Martin C. 1974. "The Problem of *Amelia*: Hume. Barrow, and the Conversion of Captain Booth." *ELH* 41: 613–48

Battestin, Martin C. 1983. "Pictures of Fielding." *Eighteenth-Century Studies* 17: 1–13.

Baugh, Albert C. and Thomas Cable. 2002. *A History of the English Language*. 5th ed. Upper Saddle River, NJ: Pearson Education.

Beattie, James. 1783. *Dissertations Moral and Critical*. London: W. Strahan.

Beckett, J.V. 2006. "Coke, Thomas William, First Earl of Leicester of Holkham (1754–1842)." *Oxford Dictionary of National Biography*. Ed. H.G. Matthew and Brian Harrison. Oxford: Oxford University Press. Online edition. Ed. Lawrence Goldman. http://www.oxforddnb.com/view/article/5831 (Accessed June 26, 2007).

Bender, John. 1987. *Imagining the Penitentiary: Fiction and the Architecture of Mind in Eighteenth-Century England*. Chicago: University of Chicago Press.

Bermingham, Ann. 1986. *Landscape and Ideology: The English Rustic Tradition, 1740–1860*. Berkeley: University of California Press.

Bevis, Richard W. 1980. *The Laughing Tradition: Stage Comedy in Garrick's Day*. Athens, GA: University of Georgia Press.

Bevis, Richard W. 1988. *English Drama: Restoration and Eighteenth Century, 1660–1789*. London: Longman.

[Bicknell, Alexander]. 1775. *The Benevolent Man*. 2 vols. Westminster: J. Lewis.

[Bicknell, Alexander]. 1776. *The History of Lady Anne Neville, Sister to the Great Earl of Warwick*. 2 vols. London: T. Cadell.

Bicknell, Alexander. 1780. *The Putrid Soul. A Poetical Epistle to Joseph Priestley. LL.D. F.R.S. on his Disquisitions relating to Matter and Spirit*. London: J. Bowen.

Bicknell, Alexander. 1791. *Instances of the Mutability of Fortune, Selected from Ancient and Modern History, and Arranged According to Their Chronological Order*. London: J.S. Jordan.

Binhammer, Katherine. 2010. "The Failure of Trade's Empire in The History of Emily Montague." *Eighteenth-Century Fiction* 23 (2): 295–319.

Black, Scott. 2016. "Henry Fielding and the Progress of Romance." In Downie 2016, 237–63.

Black, Scott. 2019. *Without the Novel: Romance and the History of Prose Fiction*. Charlottesville, VA: University of Virginia Press.

Blair, Hugh. 1965. *Lectures on Rhetoric and Belles Lettres*. Ed. Harold F. Harding. 2 vols. Carbondale: Southern Illinois University Press.

Blake, Robert. 1967. *Disraeli*. London: Methuen.

Blake, William. 1966. *Complete Writings with Variant Readings*. Ed. Geoffrey Keynes. London: Oxford University Press.

Blakeman, Edward. 2009. *The Faber Pocket Guide to Handel*. London: Allen & Unwin

Blom, Margaret Howard. 1977. *Charlotte Brontë*. Boston: Twayne.

Bonnell, Thomas F. 1989. "Bookselling and Canon-Making: The Trade Rivalry over the English Poets, 1776–1783," *Studies in Eighteenth-Century Culture* 19: 53–70.

Boone, Joseph Allen. 1987. *Tradition Counter Tradition: Love and the Form of Fiction*. Chicago: University of Chicago Press.

Boswell, James. 1953. *Boswell's Life of Johnson*. Ed. R.W. Chapman. London: Oxford University Press.

Boswell, James. 1961. *Journal of a Tour of the Hebrides with Samule Johnson LL.D. 1773*. Eds. Frederick A. Pottle and Charles H. Bennett. New York: McGraw Hill.

Bourgeacq, Jacques. 1975. *Art et Technique de Marivaux dans "Le Paysan Parvenu": Etude de Style*. Monte Carlo: Editions Regain.

Bourke, Richard. 2015. *Empire & Revolution: The Political Life of Edmund Burke*. Princeton: Princeton University Press.

Brack, O.M. (ed). 2007. *Tobias Smollett, Scotland's First Novelist*. Newark: University of Delaware Press.

Bradbury, Malcolm. 1973. *Possibilities: Essays on the State of the Novel*. London: Oxford University Press.

Bradley, Richard. 1718. *New Improvements of Planting and Gardening, Both Philosophical and Practical*. London: W. Mears.

Bradley, Richard. 1726. *The Country Gentleman and Farmer's Monthly Director*. London: James Woodman and David Lyon.

Bradshaw, David (ed.). 2007. *The Cambridge Companion to E.M. Forster*. Cambridge: Cambridge University Press.

Bradshaw, David. 2007. "*Howards End*." In Bradshaw 2007: 151–72.

Brewer, John. 1997. *The Pleasures of the Imagination: English Culture in the Eighteenth Century*. New York: Farrar Strauss Giroux.

Briggs, Asa. 1985. *Wine for Sale: Victoria Wine and the Liquor Trade 1860-1984*. Chicago: University of Chicago Press.

Brissenden, R.F. 1974. *Virtue in Distress: Studies in the Novel of Sentiment from Richardson to Sade*. London: Macmillan.

Broadbent, Michael. 1980. *The Great Vintage Wine Book*. New York: Knopf.

Bronson, Bertrand H. 1966. "*The Beggar's Opera*." In Loftis 1966: 298–327.

Brontë, Charlotte. 1973. *Jane Eyre*. Ed. Margaret Smith. London: Oxford University Press.

Brooke, Frances. 1985. *The History of Emily Montague*. Ed. Mary Jane Edwards. Ottawa: Carleton University Press.

Brooke, John. 1972. *King George III*. New York: McGraw-Hill.

Brooks, Cleanth. 1968. "The Case of Miss Arabella Fermor." In Hunt 1968: 135–53.

Brower, Reuben A. 1959. *Alexander Pope: The Poetry of Allusion*. Oxford: Oxford University Press.

Brown, John Russell and Bernard Harris (eds.). 1965. *Restoration Theatre*. London: Edward Arnold.

Brown, Laura. 1981. *English Dramatic Form, 1660–1760: An Essay in Generic History*. New Haven: Yale University Press.

Brown, Murray L. 1993. "Learning to Read Richardson: 'Pamela,' 'Speaking Pictures,' and the Visual Hermeneutic." *Studies in the Novel* 25 (2): 129–51.

Buchbinder, David. 1991. *Contemporary Literary Theory and the Reading of Poetry*. South Melbourne: Macmillan.

Budick, Sanford. 1974. *Poetry of Civilization*. New Haven and London: Yale University Press.

Burke, Edmund. 1968. *Reflections on the Revolution in France*. Ed. Conor Cruise O'Brien. Harmondsworth: Penguin.

Burney, Charles. 1964. *An Account of the Musical Performances in Westminster*. Amsterdam: Frits A.M. Knuf.

Burney, Fanny. 1982. *Evelina*. Ed. Edward A. Bloom. Oxford: Oxford University Press.

Burns, Edward. 1987. *Restoration Comedy: Crises of Desire and Identity*. Basingstoke: Macmillan.

Burrows, Donald. [2012] 2015. *Handel*. 2nd. ed. New York: Oxford University Press, Oxford Scholarship Online.

Butler, Marilyn. 1975. *Jane Austen and the War of Ideas*. Oxford: Clarendon.

Butler, Marilyn. 1982. *Romantics, Rebels and Reactionaries: English Literature and Its Background 1760–1830*. New York: Oxford University Press.

Butt, John (ed.). 1968. *The Poems of Alexander Pope*. The one-volume version of the eleven-volume Twickenham Edition. London: Methuen.

Byron, Lord. 1935. *Don Juan and Other Satirical Poems*. Ed. Louis I. Bredvold. New York: Odyssey.

Cannadine, David. 1990. *The Decline and Fall of the British Aristocracy*. New Haven: Yale University Press.

Cannon, John. 1984. *Aristocratic Century: The Peerage of Eighteenth-Century England*. Cambridge: Cambridge University Press.

Carey, John. 1977. *Thackeray: Prodigal Genius*. London: Faber.

Carr, Nicholas. 2010. *The Shallows: What the Internet Is Doing to Our Brains*. New York: W.W. Norton.

Carthy, Ita Mac. 2009. "Ariosto the Lunar Traveller." *The Modern Language Review* 104 (1): 71–82.

Chambers, Douglas. 1996. *The Reinvention of the World: English Writing 1650–1750*. London: Arnold.

Childs, Peter. 2007. "*A Passage to India*." In Bradshaw 2007: 188–208.

Clark, J. C. D. 1985. *English Society 1688-1832*. Cambridge: Cambridge University Press.

Clark, J.C.D. 1986. *Revolution and Rebellion: State and Society in England in the Seventeenth and Eighteenth Centuries*. Cambridge: Cambridge University Press.

Clifford, James. (ed.). 1959. *Eighteenth-Century English Literature: Modern Essays in Criticism*. New York: Oxford University Press.

Cockshut, A. O. J. 1980. "Trollope's Liberalism." In Bareham 1980: 161–81.

Cohen, Murray. 1977. *Sensible Words: Linguistic Practice in England 1540-1785*. Baltimore: The Johns Hopkins University Press.

Cohen, Ralph (ed.). 1974. *New Directions in Literary History*. London: Routledge & Kegan Paul.

Colley, Linda. 1992. *Britons: Forging the Nation 1707-1837*. London: Pimlico.

Collins, A. S. 1927. *Authorship in the Days of Johnson*. London: Robert Holden.

Collyer, Mary Mitchell. 1965. *The Virtuous Orphan: Or, the Life of Marianne Countess of ******. Ed. William Harlin McBurney and Michel Francis Shugrue. Carbondale: Southern Illinois University Press.

Colmer, John. 1967. *E.M. Forster: "A Passage to India."* London: Edward Arnold.

Cooper, Anthony Ashley, Earl of Shaftesbury. 1964. *Characteristics of Men, Manners, Opinions, Times*. Ed. John M. Robertson. 2 vols in 1. Indianapolis: Bobbs-Merrill.

Coulet, Henri et Michel Gilot. 1973. *Marivaux: un humanisme experimental*. Paris: Librairie Larousse.

Cousins, A.D. and Daniel Derrin (eds.). 2021. *Alexander Pope in the Reign of Queen Anne: Reconsiderations of His Early Career*. New York: Routledge.

Cowper, William. 1967. *Cowper: Poetical Works*. Ed. H.S. Milford. London: Oxford University Press.

Cowper, William. 1969. *Correspondence*. Ed. Thomas Wright. 4 vols. London: Haskell House.

Crabbe, George. 1788. *A Discourse Read in the Chapel at Belvoir Castle after the Funeral of His Grace the Duke of Rutland*. London: J. Dodsley.

Crabbe, George. 1967. *Tales, 1812, and Other Selected Poems*. Ed. Howard Mills. Cambridge: Cambridge University Press.

Craik, W.A. 1968. *The Brontë Novels*. London: Methuen.

Crane, R.S. (ed.). 1952. *Critics and Criticism*. Chicago: University of Chicago Press.

Crews, Frederick C. 1962. *E.M. Forster: The Perils of Humanism*. Princeton: Princeton University Press.

Crompton, Louis. 1985. *Byron and Greek Love: Homophobia in 19th-Century England*. Berkeley: University of California Press.

Curran, Louise. 2016. *Samuel Richardson and the Art of Letter-Writing*. Cambridge: Cambridge University Press.

Curtis, S.E.G. 1979. "A Comparison Between Gilbert White's *Selbourne* and William Bartram's *Travels*." In *Actes du VIIe congrès de Littérature Comparée*. Ed. Milan Dimić and Juan Ferrate. Stuttgart: Erich Bieber: 137–41.

Cunningham, J.S. 1961. *Pope: The Rape of the Lock*. London: Arnold.

Cunningham, J.S. (ed.) 1966. *The Rape of the Lock*. London: Oxford University Press.

Damrosch, Leo. 2019. *The Club: Johnson, Boswell, and the Friends Who Shaped an Age*. New Haven: Yale University Press.

Darnton, Robert. 2011. "First Steps Towards a History of Reading." In Towheed et al 2011, 23–35.

Das, G. K. and John Beer (eds.). 1979. *E.M. Forster: A Human Exploration*. London: Macmillan.

Defoe, Daniel. 1852. *Religious Courtship: Being Historical Discourses on the Necessity of Marrying Religious Husbands and Wives Only*. Halifax: Milner and Sowerby.

Defoe, Daniel. 1964. *Roxana*. Ed. Jane Jack. London: Oxford University Press.

Defoe, Daniel. 1968. *Augusta Triumphans*. In *Selected Poetry and Prose of Daniel Defoe*. Ed. Michael F. Shugue. New York: Rinehart: 309–19.

Defoe, Daniel. 1969. *Captain Singleton*. Ed. Shiv. K. Kumar. London: Oxford University Press.

Defoe, Daniel. 1974. *A Tour through the Whole Island of Great Britain*. Ed. G.D.H. Cole and D.C. Browning. 2 vols in 1. London: Dent.

Defoe, Daniel. 1976. *Robinson Crusoe*. Ed. J. Donald Crowley. London: Oxford University Press.

Defoe, Daniel. 1981. *Moll Flanders*. Ed. G.A. Starr. Oxford: Oxford University Press.

Delany, Sheila. 1975. "Sex and Politics in Pope's *Rape of the Lock*." *English Studies in Canada* I: 46–61.

Desvignes-Parent, Lucette. 1970. *Marivaux et L'Angleterre*. Paris: Librarie Klincksiek.

Deutsch, Otto Erich. 1955. *Handel: A Documentary Biography*. London: A. & C. Black.

Dever, Carolyn and Lisa Niles (eds.). 2011. *The Cambridge Companion to Anthony Trollope*. Cambridge: Cambridge University Press; Cambridge Collections Online.

Dickens, Charles. 1907. *Hard Times*. Ed. G.K. Chesterton. London: Dent.

Dickens, Charles. 1954. *Barnaby Rudge*. Ed. Kathleen Tillotson. London: Oxford University Press.

Dickens, Charles. 1966. *Oliver Twist*. Ed. Peter Fairclough. Harmondsworth: Penguin.

Dickens, Charles. 1968. *Martin Chuzzlewit*. Ed. P.N. Furbank. Harmondsworth: Penguin.

Dickens, Charles. 1970. *Bleak House*. Ed. Alberta J. Guerard. New York: Holt.

Dickson, Andrew. 2018. "An Introduction to 18th-Century British Theatre." In *British Library Discovering Literature* (2018). On-line: https://www.bl.uk/discovering-literature.

Dimić, Milan V. and Marguerite K. Garstin. 1988. *The Polysystem Theory: A Brief Introduction, with Bibliography*. Edmonton: The Research Institute for Comparative Literature.

Disraeli, Benjamin. 1926. *Sybil*. Ed. Walter Sichel. London: Oxford University Press.

Disraeli, Isaac. 1969. *Curiosities of Literature*. Ed. Benjamin Disraeli. 2 vols. New York: George Olms Verlag Hidesheim.

Dixon, Peter. 1968. *The World of Pope's Satires*. London: Methuen.

Donaldson, Ian. 1975. "'A Double Capacity': *The Beggar's Opera*." In Noble 1975: 65–80.

Donoghue, Frank. 1966. *The Fame Machine: Book Reviewing and Eighteenth-Century Literary Careers*. Stanford: Stanford University Press.

Doody, Margaret Anne. 1985. *The Augustan Muse: Augustan Poetry Reconsidered*. Cambridge: Cambridge University Press.

Dorsey, Shelley. 1990. "Austen, Forster, and Economics." *Persuasions* 12: 54–59.

Downie, Alan (ed.). 2016. *The Oxford Handbook of the Eighteenth-Century Novel*. Oxford: Oxford University Press.

Dryden, John. 1958. *The Poems of John Dryden*. Ed. James Kinsley. 4 vols. Oxford: Clarendon.

Dryden, John. 1962. *Of Dramatic Poesy and Other Critical Essays*. Ed. George Watson. 2 vols. London: Dent.

Duckworth, Alistair M. 1971. *The Improvement of the Estate: A Study of Jane Austen's Novels*. Baltimore: Johns Hopkins University Press.

du Monceau, Henri Louis Duhamel. 1764. *The Elements of Agriculture*. Trans. Philip Miller. 2 vols. London: P. Vaillant *et al*.

Eccles, W.J. 1972. *France in America*. Vancouver: Fitzhenry and Whiteside.

Edgeworth, Maria. 1980. *Castle Rackrent*. Ed. George Watson. Oxford: Oxford University Press.

Edwards, Mary Jane. 1981. "Frances Brooke's *The History of Emily Montague*: A Biographical Context." *English Studies in Canada* 7: 171–82.

Ehrenpreis, Irvin. 1974. *Literary Meaning and Augustan Values*. Charlottesville: University of Virginia Press.

Einberg, Elizabeth and Judy Egerton (eds.). 1988. *The Age of Hogarth: British Painters Born 1675-1709*. London: Tate Gallery.

Eliot, George. 1956. *Middlemarch*. Ed. Gordon S. Haight. Boston: Houghton.

Ellis, Aytoun. 1956. *The Penny Universities: A History of the Coffee-Houses*. London: Secker and Warburg.

Ellis, William. 1750. *The Modern Husbandman, Complete in Eight Volumes*. London: D. Browne *et al*.

Empson, William. 1966. *Some Versions of Pastoral*. Harmondsworth: Penguin.

The English Short Title Catalogue 1473–1800. CD-ROM 1998. Ed. The British Library Board. [*ESTC*]

Epperley, Elizabeth R. 1988. *Anthony Trollope's Notes on the Old Drama*. No 42. ELS Monograph Series. Victoria: University of Victoria.

Erskine-Hill, Howard and Anne Smith (eds.). 1979. *The Art of Alexander Pope*. London: Vision Books.

Everett, Nigel. 1994. *The Tory View of Landscape*. The Paul Mellon Centre for Studies in British Art. New Haven: Yale University Press.

Faith, Nicholas. 1988. *The Story of Champagne*. London: Hamilton.

Farquhar, George. 1930. *The Complete Works of George Farquhar*. Ed. C. Stonehill. 2 vols. London: Nonesuch.

Farr, Jason S. 2019. *Novel Bodies: Disability and Sexuality in Eighteenth-Century British Literature*. Lewisburg, PA: Bucknell University Press.

Feifel, Hermann (ed.). 1965. *The Meaning of Death*. New York: McGraw-Hill.

Fielding, Henry. 1903. *The Complete Works of Henry Fielding*. Ed. William Ernest Henley. 16 vols. London: William Heinemann.

Fielding, Henry. 1907. *The Journal of a Voyage to Lisbon*. Ed. Austin Dobson. London: Oxford University Press.

Fielding, Henry. 1961. *Joseph Andrews and Shamela*. Ed. Martin C. Battestin. Boston: Houghton Mifflin.

Fielding, Henry. 1962. *Amelia*. Ed. George Saintsbury. Introduction by A.R. Humphreys. 2 vols. London: Dent.

Fielding, Henry. 1967. *Joseph Andrews*. Ed. Martin C. Battestin. *The Wesleyan Edition of the Works Of Henry Fielding*. Oxford: Clarendon Press.

Fielding, Henry. 1973a. *A Journey from This World to the Next*. Ed. Claude Rawson. London: J.M. Dent.

Fielding, Henry. 1973b. *Tom Jones*. Ed. Sheridan Baker. New York: Norton.

Fielding, Henry. 1974. *The History of Tom Jones A Foundling*. Eds. Fredson Bowers and Martin C. Battestin. *The Wesleyan Edition of The Works Of Henry Fielding*. London: Clarendon.

Finch, Jason. 2012. "E.M. Forster and English Place: A Literary Topography." *Neophilologische Mitteilungen* 113 (2): 241–45.

Folkenflik, Robert. 1984. "Samuel Johnson and Art." *Samuel Johnson: Pictures and Words*. Los Angeles: William Andrews Clark Memorial Library. 65–118.

Forster, E.M. 1924. "Jane, How Shall We Ever Recollect?" *The New Republic*, 30 January.

Forster, E.M. 1947. *Collected Short Stories*. Harmondsworth: Penguin Books.

Forster, E.M. 1960. *The Longest Journey*. Harmondsworth: Penguin Books.

Forster, E.M. 1972. *Two Cheers for Democracy*. Ed. Oliver Stallybrass. London: Edward Arnold.

Forster, E.M. 1973. *Howards End*. Ed. Oliver Stallybrass. London: Edward Arnold.

Forster, E.M. 1978. *A Passage to India*. Ed. Oliver Stallybrass. London: Edward Arnold.

Forster, E.M. 1996. *Abinger Harvest* and *England's Pleasant Land*. Ed. Elizabeth Heine. London: Andre Deutsch.

Fowler, Roger. 1981. *Literature as Social Discourse: The Practice of Linguistic Criticism*. Bloomington: Indiana University Press.

Francis, A.D. 1972. *The Wine Trade*. London: Black.

Frank, Catharine. 2004. "Fictions of Justice: Testamentary Intention and the (Il)legitimate Heir in Trollope's *Ralph the Heir* and Forster's *Howards End*." *English Literature in Transition, 1880–1920* 47 (3): 311–30.

Frank, Catharine O. 2016. *Law, Literature, and the Transmission of Culture in England, 1837–1923*. London: Routledge.

Frank, Erich. 1966. *Philosophical Understanding and Religious Truth*. New York: Oxford University Press.

Fromm, Harold. 1991. *Academic Capitalism & Literary Value*. Athens, GA: University of Georgia Press.

Frye, Northrop. 1982. *Divisions on a Ground: Essays on Canadian Culture*. Ed. James Polk. Toronto: Anions.

Fussell, Paul. 1969. *The Rhetorical World of Augustan Humanism*. London: Oxford University Press.

Gallant, Christine (ed.). 1989. *Coleridge's Theory of Imagination Today*. New York: AMS.

Garon, André. 1976. "La Britannisation, (1763–1791)." In Hamelin 1976: 249–82.

Garrison, James D. 1975. *Dryden and the Tradition of Panegyric*. Berkeley: University of California Press.

Gatrell, Vic. 2006. *City of Laughter: Sex and Satire in Eighteenth-Century London*. New York: Walker.

Gaunt, William. 1980. *Court Painting in England from Tudor to Victorian Times*. London: Constable.

Gavin, Michael. 2015. *The Invention of English Criticism 1650–1760*. Cambridge: Cambridge University Press.

Gay, John. 1969. *The Beggar's Opera*. Ed. Edgar V. Roberts. Lincoln: University of Nebraska Press.

[A Gentleman Farmer]. 1782. *An Enquiry into the Nature of English Wools, and the Variations of Breed in Sheep*. London: T. Evans.

George, M. Dorothy. 1966. *London Life in the Eighteenth Century*. Harmondsworth: Peregrine.

Gibbons, William. 2010. "Divining Zoroastro: Masonic Elements in Handel's *Orlando*." *Eighteenth-Century Life* 34 (2): 65–82.

Gibson, William. 2007. *Art and Money in the Writings of Tobias Smollett*. New York: Associated University Presses.

Gibson, William. 2007. *Art and Money in the Writings of Tobias Smollett*. Lewisburg: Bucknell University Press.

Giddings, Robert. 1967. *The Tradition of Smollett*. London: Methuen.

Gindin, James. 1971. *Harvest of a Quiet Eye: The Novel of Compassion*. Bloomington: Indiana University Press.

Goldsmith, Oliver. 1966. *Collected Works of Oliver Goldsmith*. Ed. Arthur Friedman. 5 vols. Oxford: Clarendon.

Goldsmith, Oliver. 1982. *The Vicar of Wakefield*. Ed. Stephen Coote. Harmondsworth: Penguin.

Goodlad, Lauren M.E. 2015. *The Victorian Geopolitical Aesthetic, Realism, Sovereignty, and Transnational Experience*. Oxford: Oxford University Press.

Graff, Gerald. 1987. *Professing Literature: An Institutional History*. Chicago: University of Chicago Press.

Graff, Gerald. 1992. *Beyond the Culture Wars: How Teaching the Conflicts Can Revitalize American Education*. New York: Norton.

Grant, George. 1969. *Technology and Empire: Reflections on North America*. Toronto: Anions.

Gray, Thomas. 1874. *Poems and Letters*. London: Chiswick Press.

Gray, Thomas. 1912. *Gray's Poems, Letters, and Essays*. Ed. John Drinkwater. London: Dent.

Green, Frederick C. 1966. *Literary Ideas in 18th Century France and England: A Critical Survey*. New York: Frederick Ungar.

Greene, E. J. H. 1965. *Marivaux*. Toronto: University of Toronto Press.

Griffin, Dustin. 1996. *Literary Patronage in England, 1650–1800*. Cambridge: Cambridge University Press.

Grossberg, Lawrence. 1986. "Teaching the Popular." In Nelson 1986: 177–200.

Grove, Robin. 1979. "Uniting Airy Substance: *The Rape of the Lock* 1712-1736." In Erskine-Hill and Anne Smith 1979: 52–88.

Gusdorf, Georges. 1980. "Conditions and Limits of Autobiography." In Olney 1980: 28–48.

Hagstrum, Jean H. 1958. *The Sister Arts: The Tradition of Literary Pictorialism and English Poetry from Dryden to Gray*. Chicago: University of Chicago Press.

Hagstrum, Jean H. 1980. *Sex and Sensibility: Ideal and Erotic Love from Milton to Mozart*. Chicago: University of Chicago Press.

Hale, John. 1994. *The Civilization of Europe in the Renaissance*. New York: Atheneum.

Hamelin, Jean (ed.). 1976. *Histoire du Québec*. Montreal: France-Amérique.

Hamilton, A.C., Donald Cheney and W.F. Blisset (eds.). 1990. *The Spenser Encyclopedia*. Toronto: University of Toronto Press.

Hamilton, K.G. 1967. *John Dryden and the Poetry of Statement*. Brisbane: University of Queensland Press.

Hammond, Lansing V. 1949. "Gilbert White, Poetizer of the Commonplace." In Hilles 1949: 377–83.

Hardy, Barbara. 1964. *The Appropriate Form: An Essay on the Novel*. London: Athlone Press.

Hardy, Barbara. 1972. *The Exposure of Luxury: Radical Themes in Thackeray*. London: Owen.

Harpham, Geoffrey Galt. 2002. *Language Alone: The Critical Fetish of Modernity*. New York: Routledge.

Harrison, Bernard. 1975. *Henry Fielding's Tom Jones: The Novelist as Moral Philosopher*. London: Chatto and Windus.

Harrison, Brian. 1971. *Drink and the Victorians: The Temperance Question in England 1815-1872*. London: Faber.

Harte, Walter. 1764. *Essays on Husbandry*. Bath: W. Frederick.

Harvey, Geoffrey. 1980. *The Art of Anthony Trollope*. London: Weidenfeld and Nicolson.

Hatfield, Glen W. 1968. *Henry Fielding and the Language of Irony*. Chicago: University of Chicago Press.

Hawkes, Terence. 1977. *Structuralism and Semiotics*. Berkeley: University of California Press.

Hays, H. R. 1972. *Birds, Beasts, and Men: A Humanist History of Zoology*. Baltimore: Penguin.

Herbert, Christopher. 1987. *Trollope and Comic Pleasure*. Chicago: University of Chicago Press.

Hermans, Theo (ed.). 1985. *The Manipulation of Literature: Essays on Translated Literature*. London: Croom Helm.

Hewett, Edward and W.F. Axton. 1983. *Convivial Dickens: The Drinks of Dickens and His Times*. Athens, OH: Ohio University Press.

Hibbert, Christopher. 1998. *George III: A Personal History*. London: Viking.

Hill, Christopher. 1969. *Reformation to Industrial Revolution: 1530–1780*. Vol. 2 of *The Pelican Economic History of Britain*. Harmondsworth: Penguin.

Hilles, Frederick W (ed). 1949. *The Age of Johnson*. New Haven: Yale University Press.

Hipple, Walter John. 1957. *The Beautiful, the Sublime, and the Picturesque in Eighteenth-Century British Aesthetic Theory*. Carbondale: Southern Illinois University Press.

Hirsch, David H. 1991. *The Deconstruction of Literature: Criticism after Auschwitz*. Hanover, NH: Brown University Press.

Hirsch, E.D. 1967. *Validity in Interpretation*. New Haven: Yale University Press.

Holtz, William V. 1970. *Image and Immortality: A Study of "Tristram Shandy."* Providence, RI: Brown University Press.

Home, Henry, Lord Kames. 1779. *The Gentleman Farmer. Being an Attempt to Improve Agriculture by Subjecting It to the Test of Rational Principles*. 2nd. ed. Edinburgh: John Bell.

Honan, Park. 1999. *Shakespeare: A Life*. Oxford: Oxford University Press.

Hume, Robert D. 1976. *The Development of English Drama in the Late Seventeenth Century*. Oxford: Clarendon Press.

Hume, Robert D. 1983. *The Rakish Stage: Studies in English Drama, 1660–1800*. Carbondale: Southern Illinois University Press.

Hunt, John Dixon (ed.). 1968. *Pope: The Rape of the Lock*. London: Macmillan.

Irving, William Henry. 1940. *John Gay: Favorite of the Wits*. Durham, NC: Duke University Press.

Iser, Wolfgang. 2011. "The Reading Process: A Phenomenological Approach." In Towheed *et al* 2011: 80–81.

Jacob, Margaret C. 2019. *The Secular Enlightenment*. Princeton: Princeton University Press.

Jarrett, Derek. 1973. *The Begetters of Revolution: England's Involvement with France, 1759–1789*. London: Longman.

Jauss, Hans Robert. 1974. "Literary History as a Challenge to Literary Theory." In Cohen 1974: 11– 41

Jay, Elisabeth. 1979. *The Religion of the Heart: Anglican Evangelicalism and the Nineteenth-Century Novel*. Oxford. Clarendon Press.

Johns, Adrian. 1998. *The Nature of the Book: Print and Knowledge in the Making*. Chicago: University of Chicago Press.

Johnson, Claudia L. 1995. *Equivocal Beings: Politics, Gender, and Sentimentality in the 1790s Wollstonecraft, Radcliffe, Burney, Austen*. Chicago: University of Chicago Press.

Johnson, Edgar. 1952. *Charles Dickens: His Tragedy and Triumph*. 2 vols. Boston: Little, Brown.

Johnson, Samuel. 1952. *Lives of the English Poets.* Ed. Arthur Waugh. 2 vols. London: Oxford University Press.

Johnson, Samuel. 1976. *The History of Rasselas, Prince of Abissinia.* Ed. D.J. Enright. Harmondsworth: Penguin.

Jones, B.M. 1933. *Henry Fielding: Novelist and Magistrate.* London: George Allen and Unwin.

Jugan, Annick. 1978. *Les Variations du Récit dans "La Vie de Marianne" de Marivaux.* Paris: Editions Klincksieck.

Kalmey, Robert P. 1980. "Pope's *Eloisa to Abelard* and 'Those Celebrated Letters.'" In Mack and Winn 1980: 247–65.

Keefe, Robert. 1979. *Charlotte Brontë's World of Death.* Austin: University of Texas Press.

Keen, Andrew. 2007. *The Cult of the Amateur: How Today's Internet is Killing Our Culture.* New York: Doubleday.

Keener, Frederick M. 1974. *An Essay on Pope.* New York: Columbia University Press.

Keith, W.J. 1974. *The Rural Tradition: A Study of the Non-Fiction Prose Writers of the English Countryside.* Toronto: University of Toronto Press.

Kenny, Shirley Strum (ed.). 1984. *British Theatre and the Other Arts, 1660–1800.* Washington, DC: Folger Books.

Kent, Nathaniel. 1775. *Hints to Gentlemen of Landed Property.* London: J. Dodsley.

Kent, Nathaniel. 1796. *General View of The Agriculture of the County of Norfolk.* Norwich: Crouse, Stevenson and Matchett, and London: George Nicol.

Kern, Jean B. 1976. *Dramatic Satire in the Age of Walpole 1720–1750.* Ames: Iowa State University Press.

Kincaid, James R. 1971. *Dickens and the Rhetoric of Laughter.* Oxford: Clarendon.

Kincaid, James R. 1977. *The Novels of Anthony Trollope.* Oxford: Clarendon.

King, Amy M. 2019. *The Divine in the Commonplace: Reverent Natural History and the Novel in Britain.* Cambridge: Cambridge University Press.

King, Bruce (ed.). 1969. *Dryden's Mind and Art.* Edinburgh: Oliver and Boyd.

King, Bruce. 1969. "*Absalom and Achitophel*: A Revaluation." In King 1969: 65–83.

Kinne, Willard Austin. 1967. *Revivals and Importations of French Comedies in England 1749–1800.* New York: AMS.

Knox, Vicesimus. 1805. *Elegant Extracts Or, Useful and Entertaining Pieces of Poetry.* London: J. Johnson *et al.*

Knox, Vicesimus. 1808. *Elegant Extracts: Or, Useful and Entertaining Passages in Prose.* 9th ed. London: J. Johnson *et al.*

Kramnick, Isaac. 1977. *The Rage of Edmund Burke: Portrait of an Ambivalent Conservative.* New York: Basic Books.

Kramnick, Jonathan. 2010, *Actions and Objects from Hobbes to Richardson.* Stanford: Stanford University Press.

Kramnick, Jonathan. 2018. *Paper Minds: Literature and the Ecology of Consciousness.* Chicago: University of Chicago Press.

Kramp, Michael. 2007. *Disciplining Love: Austen and the Modern Man*. Columbus: The Ohio State University Press.

Krieger, Murray. 1969. "*Eloisa to Abelard*: 'The Escape from Body or the Embrace of Body'" *Eighteenth-Century Studies* 3: 28–47.

Kropf, C.R. 1974. "Educational Theory and Human Nature in Fielding's Works." *PMLA* 89: 113–20.

Kübler-Ross, Elisabeth. 1970. *On Death and Dying*. New York: Macmillan.

Kübler-Ross, Elisabeth. 1975. *Death: The Final Stage of Growth*. Englewood Cliffs, NJ: Prentice Hall.

Kuhn, Albert J. (ed.). 1970, *Three Sentimental Novels: A Sentimental Journey, The Man of Feeling, The History of Sandford and Merton*. New York: Holt Rinehart.

Kuhn, Thomas. 1970. *The Structure of Scientific Revolutions*. 2nd ed. Chicago: University of Chicago Press,

Kurtz, Eric. 1975. "The Shepherd as Gamester: Musical Mock-Pastoral in *The Beggar's Opera*." In Noble 1975: 52–55.

LaGrandeur, Kevin. 1991. "Aporia and the Emptied Teacher: Deconstruction and the Unraveling of (Con)'Texts.'" *College Literature* 18: 69–79.

Lambert, Jose and Hendrik van Gorp. 1985. "On Describing Translations." In Hermans 1985: 42–53.

Lane, Maggie. 1989. *Jane Austen's England*. London: Robert Hale.

Lane, Maggie. 1995. *Jane Austen and Food*. London: Hambledon Press.

Langhorne, John. 1797. *The Poetical Works*. London: C. Cooke.

Leonard, Jonathan Norton. 1969. *The World of Gainsborough 1727-1788*. Alexandria, VA: Time-Life.

Levine, June Perry. 1971. *Creation and Criticism: "A Passage to India."* Lincoln: University of Nebraska Press.

Linder, Cynthia A. 1978. *Romantic Imagery in the Novels of Charlotte Brontë*. London: Macmillan.

Lindsay, David W. (ed.). 1995. *The Beggar's Opera and other Eighteenth-Century Plays*. London: Dent.

Lipking, Lawrence. 1970. *The Ordering of the Arts in Eighteenth-Century England*. Princeton: Princeton University Press.

Lipking, Lawrence 1983. "Quick Poetic Eyes: Another Look at Literary Pictorialism." In Wendorf 1983: 3–25.

Lipski, Jakub. 2020. *Painting the Novel: Pictorial Discourse in Eighteenth-Century English Fiction*. New York: Routledge.

Lisle, Edward. 1757. *Observations in Husbandry*. 2d ed. 2 vols. London: C. Hitch *et al.*

Locke, John. 1887. *Some Thoughts Concerning Education*. Ed. The Rev. R.H. Quick. London: C.J. Clay for Cambridge University Press.

Locke, John. 1965. *An Essay concerning Human Understanding*. Ed. John W. Yolton. 2 vols. London: J. M. Dent.

Locke, John. 1966. *Of the Conduct of the Understanding*. Ed. Francis W. Garforth. New York: Teachers College Press, Columbia University.

Loftis, John. 1959. *Comedy and Society from Congreve to Fielding*. Stanford: Stanford University Press.

Loftis, John. 1963. *The Politics of Drama in Augustan England*. Oxford: Clarendon.

Loftis, John (ed.). 1966. *Restoration Drama: Modern Essays in Criticism*. New York: Oxford University Press.

Loftis, John. 1973. *The Spanish Plays of Neoclassical England*. New Haven: Yale University Press.

Lord, George deForest. 1972. "*Absalom and Achitophel* and Dryden's Political Cosmos." In Miner 1972: 156–90.

Mabey, Richard. 1986. *Gilbert White: A Biography of the Author of "The Natural History of Selbourne."* London: Century.

Macey, Samuel L. 1983. *Money and the Novel: Mercenary Motivation in Defoe and His Immediate Successors*. Victoria, BC: Sono Nis Press.

MacIntyre, Alasdair and Paul Ricœur. 1969. *The Religious Significance of Atheism*. New York: Columbia University Press.

Mack, Maynard. 1968. *Essential Articles for the Study of Alexander Pope*. Hamden, CT: Archon Books.

Mack, Maynard. 1985. *Alexander Pope: A Life*. New York: W.W. Norton.

Mack, Maynard and James A. Winn (eds.). 1980. *Pope: Recent Essays by Several Hands*. Hamden, CT: Shoe String Press.

MacKenzie, Henry. 1967. *The Man of Feeling*. Ed. Brian Vickers. London: Oxford University Press.

MacLean, Kenneth. 1936. *John Locke and English Literature of the Eighteenth-Century*. New Haven: Yale University Press.

Maddox, Lucy B. 1986. "Gilbert White and the Politics of Natural History." *Eighteenth-Century Life* 10: 45–57.

Magnet, Myron. 1983. *Dickens and the Social Order*. Philadelphia: University of Pennsylvania Press.

Manguel, Alberto. 1998. *A History of Reading*. Toronto: Vintage Canada.

Marivaux, Pierre Carlet de Chamblain. 1978. *La Vie de Marianne*. Ed. Michel Gilot. Paris: Garnier-Flammarion.

Marivaux, Pierre Carlet de Chamblain. 1981. *Le Paysan Parvenu*. Ed. Henri Coulet. Paris: Gallimard.

Markley, Robert. 1988. *Two-Edg'd Weapons: Style and Ideology in the Comedies of Etherege, Wycherley, and Congreve*. Oxford: Clarendon Press.

Marsden, Jean I. 2006. *Fatal Desire: Women, Sexuality and the English Stage, 1660–1720*. Ithaca, NY: Cornell University Press.

Marsden, Jean I. 2019. *Theatres of Feeling: Affect, Performance, and the Eighteenth-Century Stage*. Cambridge: Cambridge University Press.

Marshall, David. 1988. *The Surprising Effects of Sympathy: Marivaux, Diderot, Rousseau, and Mary Shelley*. Chicago: University of Chicago Press.

Marshall, Dorothy. 1962. *Eighteenth Century England*. London: Longmans.

Martin, Richard. 1974. *The Love That Failed: Ideal and Reality in the Writings of E.M. Forster*. The Hague: De Gruyter Mouton.

Martin, Robert Bernard. 1966. *The Accents of Persuasion: Charlotte Brontë's Novels*. New York: Norton.

Martin, Robert K. 1997. "'It Must Have Been the Umbrella': Forster's Queer Begetting." In Martin and Piggford 1997: 255–273.

Martin, Robert K. and George Piggford (eds.). 1997. *Queer Forster*. Chicago: University of Chicago Press.

May, Brian. 1997. *The Modernist as Pragmatist: E.M. Forster and the Fate of Liberalism*. Columbia: University of Missouri Press.

McFadden, George. 1978. *Dryden the Public Writer, 1660–1685*. Princeton: Princeton University Press.

McKeon, Michael. 1987. *The Origins of the English Novel 1600–1740*. Baltimore: Johns Hopkins University Press.

McMaster, Juliet and Bruce Stovel (eds.). 1996. *Jane Austen's Business: Her World and Her Profession*. Houndmills, Basingstoke: Macmillan.

McMaster, R. D. 1986. *Trollope and the Law*. Basingstoke: Macmillan.

McMullen, Lorraine. 1983. *An Odd Attempt in a Woman: The Literary Life of Frances Brooke*. Vancouver: University of British Columbia Press.

McNaught, Kenneth. 1969. *The Pelican History of Canada*. Harmondsworth: Penguin.

Melville, Lewis. 1900. *Stage Favourites of the Eighteenth Century*. London: Hutchinson. "George Anne Bellamy," 243–79.

Meredith, George. 1968. *The Egoist*. Ed. George Woodcock. Harmondsworth: Penguin.

Merquior, J.G. 1985. *Foucault*. London: Collins.

Merrett, Robert James. 1980a. "The Concept of Mind in *Emma*." *English Studies in Canada* 6: 39–55.

Merrett, Robert James. 1980b. "Empiricism and Judgment in Fielding's *Tom Jones*." *Ariel* 11: 3–21.

Merrett, Robert James. 1984. "E.M. Forster's Modernism: Tragic Faith in *A Passage to India*." *Mosaic* 17: 71–86.

Merrett, Robert James. 1988. "Bacchus in Restoration and Eighteenth-Century Comedy: Wine as an Index of Generic Decline." *Man and Nature* 7: 179–93.

Merrett, Robert James. 1989a. "Marivaux and England: Fictional Exchange." In Badir and Bosley 1989: 57–68.

Merrett, Robert James. 1989b. "Narrative Contraries as Signs in Defoe's Fiction." *Eighteenth-Century Fiction* 1: 171–85.

Merrett, Robert James. 2004. *Presenting the Past: Philosophical Irony and the Rhetoric of Double Vision from Bishop Butler to T.S. Eliot*. English Literary Studies. Victoria: University of Victoria.

Messenger, Ann. 1986. *His and Hers: Essays in Restoration and Eighteenth-Century Literature*. Lexington: University of Kentucky Press.

Meyers, Robert Manson. 1946. "Fifty Sermons on Handel's Messiah." *Harvard Theological Review* 39: 217–41.

Meyers, Robert Manson. 1956. *Handel, Dryden, & Milton*. London: Bowes and Bowes.

Miller, H.K., E. Rothstein and G.S. Rousseau (eds.). 1970. *The Augustan Milieu*. Oxford: Clarendon.

Miller, Henry Knight. 1966. "Some Functions of Rhetoric in *Tom Jones*." *PQ* 45: 209–35.

Miller, Henry Knight. 1970. "The Voices of Henry Fielding: Style in *Tom Jones*." In Miller *et al* 1970: 262–88.

Miller, Henry Knight. 1976. *Henry Fielding's Tom Jones and the Romance Tradition*. Victoria: University of Victoria.

Miner, Earl (ed.). 1972. *Writers and their Background: John Dryden*. Athens, OH: Ohio University Press.

Mitchell, W.J.T. 1986. *Iconology: Image, Text, Ideology*. Chicago: University of Chicago Press.

Moglen, Helene. 1976. *Charlotte Brontë: The Self Conceived*. New York: Norton.

Morton, W.L. 1963. *The Kingdom of Canada: A General History from Earliest Times*. Toronto: McClelland and Stewart.

Murphy, Arthur. 1762. *The Works of Henry Fielding*. 4 vols. London: A. Millar.

Myers, William. 1973. *Dryden*. London: Hutchinson University Library.

Nelson, Cary (ed.). 1986. *Theory in the Classroom*. Urbana: University of Illinois Press.

New, William H. 1972. "Frances Brooke's Chequered Gardens." *Canadian Literature* 52: 24–38.

Nichol, Donald W. 2021. "Renewing the Classics in the Age of Queen Anne: The Making of Pope's *Iliad*." In Cousins and Derrin 2021: 175–196.

Nichols, John. 1967. *Literary Anecdotes of the Eighteenth Century*. Ed. Colin Clair. Fontwell, Sussex: Centaur.

Nicholson, Colin. 1996. *Writing & the Rise of Finance: Capital Satires of the Early Eighteenth Century*. Cambridge: Cambridge University Press.

Nicolson, Marjorie and G.S. Rousseau. 1968. *"This Long Disease, My Life": Alexander Pope and the Sciences*. Princeton: Princeton University Press.

Noble, Yvonne (ed.). 1975. *Twentieth Century Interpretations of the Beggar's Opera*. Englewood Cliffs, NJ: Prentice-Hall.

Nussbaum, Martha C. 2010. *Not for Profit: Why Democracy Needs the Humanities*. Princeton: Princeton University Press.

Ogden, James 1969. *Isaac D'Israeli.* Oxford: Clarendon.

O'Hehir, Brendan. 1968. "Virtue and Passion: The Dialectic of *Eloisa to Abelard.*" In Mack 1968: 333–49.

Oliver, Kathleen M. 2008. *Samuel Richardson, Dress and Discourse.* London: Palgrave Macmillan.

Olney, James (ed.). 1980. *Autobiography: Essays Theoretical and Critical.* Princeton: Princeton University Press.

Ong, Walter J. 1958. "Voice as Summons for Belief." In Abrams 1958: 80–105.

Ouellet, Fernand. 1980. *Economic and Social History of Quebec, 1760-1850.* Toronto: Macmillan.

Overton, Mark. 1996. *Agricultural Revolution in England: The Transformation of the Agrarian Economy 1500–1850.* Cambridge: Cambridge University Press.

Pacey, Desmond. 1946–47. "The First Canadian Novel." *Dalhousie Review* 26: 147–150.

Parker, John (ed.). 1976. *The Journals of Jonathan Carver and Related Documents, 1766-1770.* St. Paul: Minnesota Historical Society Press.

Parry, Benita Parry. 1979. "*A Passage to India*: Epitaph or Manifesto?" In Das and Beer 1979, 129–41.

Passmore, John. 1968. *A Hundred Years of Philosophy.* Harmondsworth: Penguin.

Paulson, Ronald. 1974. *Hogarth: His Life, Art, and Times.* Abr. ed. New Haven: Yale University Press.

Peacock, Thomas Love. 1967. *The Works.* Ed. H.F.B. Halliburton and C.E. Jones. 10 vols. New York: AMS.

Pearce, Mary. 2020. "Of Things in Austen: Or, Encounters with Trinkets, Harps, and Sofas." *Persuasions On-Line* 40: 2.

Pearson, Jacqueline. 1988. *The Prostituted Muse: Images of Women & Women Dramatists 1642-1737.* New York: Harvester-Wheatsheaf.

Penning-Rowsell, Edmund. 1985. *The Wines of Bordeaux.* 5th ed. San Francisco: Wine Appreciation Guild.

Peppercorn, David. 1982. *Bordeaux.* London: Faber.

Perkins, David. 1992. *Is Literary History Possible?* Baltimore: The Johns Hopkins University Press.

Perl, Jeffrey M. 1981. "Anagogic Surfaces: How to Read *Joseph Andrews.*" *The Eighteenth Century* 22: 249–70.

Peters, Margot. 1973. *Charlotte Brontë: Style in The Novel.* Madison: University of Wisconsin Press.

Pettit, Henry. 1968. "Pope's *Eloisa to Abelard*: An Interpretation." In Mack 1968: 320–32.

Pevsner, Nikolaus. 1964. *The Englishness of English Art.* Harmondsworth: Penguin.

Polhemus, Robert. 1980. *Comic Faith: The Great Tradition from Austen to Joyce.* Chicago: University of Chicago Press.

Pope, Alexander. 1940. *The Rape of the Lock and Other Poems*. Ed Geoffrey Tillotson. London: Methuen.

Porter, Roy. 2000. *Enlightenment: Britain and the Creation of the Modern World*. London: Penguin.

Postman, Neil. 1999. *Building a Bridge to the 18th Century: How the Past Can Improve Our Future*. New York: Vintage.

Pratt, Mary Louise. 1977. *Toward a Speech Act Theory of Literary Discourse*. Bloomington: Indiana University Press.

Preston, John. 1970. *The Created Self: The Reader's Role in Eighteenth-Century Fiction*. London: Heinemann.

Price, Martin. 1964. *To the Palace of Wisdom*. Carbondale and Edwardsville: Southern Illinois University Press.

Priestley, Joseph. 1965. *Priestley's Writings on Philosophy, Science, and Politics*. Ed. John A. Passmore. New York: Collier.

Rabb, Melina Alliker. 2019. *Miniature and the English Imagination: Literature, Cognition, and Small-Scale Culture, 1650–1765*. Cambridge: Cambridge University Press.

Rabine, Leslie W. 1985. *Reading the Romantic Heroine: Text, History, Ideology*. Ann Arbor: The University of Michigan Press.

Raven, James. 1992. *Judging New Wealth: Popular Publishing and Responses to Commerce in England, 1750–1800*. Oxford: Clarendon.

Rawson, C.J. 1972. *Henry Fielding and The Augustan Ideal Under Stress*. London: Routledge and Kegan Paul.

Rawson, Claude (ed.). 2007. *The Cambridge Companion to Henry Fielding*. Cambridge: Cambridge University Press.

Redding, Cyrus. 1851. *A History and Description of Modern Wines*. 3rd ed. London: Bohn.

Reeve, Clara. 1785. *The Progress of Romance through Times, Countries, and Manners*. Colchester: W. Keymer.

Reynolds, Sir Joshua. 1975. *Discourses on Art*. Ed. Robert R. Wark. New Haven: Yale University Press.

Ribble. Fredrick G. 1981. "Aristotle and the 'Prudence' Theme of *Tom Jones*." *Eighteenth-Century Studies* 15: 26–47.

Richardson, Jonathan. 1971. *An Essay on the Theory of Painting*. 2nd ed. London, 1725. Rpt. Menston, Yorkshire: Scolar Press, 1971.

Richardson, Jonathan. 1972a. *An Essay on the Whole Art of Criticism as It Relates to Painting* in *Two Discourses 1719*. Menston, Yorkshire: Scolar Press.

Richardson, Jonathan. 1972b. *A Discourse on the Dignity, Certainty, Pleasure and Advantage, of the Science of a Connoisseur* in *Two Discourses 1719*. Menston, Yorkshire: Scolar Press.

Richardson, Samuel. 1971. *Pamela*. Ed. T.C. Duncan Eaves and Ben D. Kimpel. Boston: Houghton Mifflin.

Richardson, Samuel. 1972. *Sir Charles Grandison*. Ed. Jocelyn Harris. London: Oxford University Press.

Richardson, Samuel. 1985. *Clarissa*. Ed. Angus Ross. Harmondsworth: Penguin.

Rivers, Isabel (ed.). 1982. *Books and Their Readers in Eighteenth-Century England*. New York: St. Martin's.

Rizzo, Betty. 1994. *Companions without Vows: Relationships among Eighteenth-Century British Women*. Athens, GA: University of Georgia Press.

Roberts, David. 1989. *The Ladies: Female Patronage of Restoration Drama 1660–1700*. Oxford: Clarendon.

Rogers, Pat. 1979. *Henry Fielding: A Biography*. London: Paul Elek.

Rogers, Pat. 2007. "Fielding on society, crime, and the law." In Rawson 2007, 137–52.

Rogers, Pat. 2021. "Pope, Verrio and Hampton Court: The Stuart Monarch in *The Rape of the Lock* and *Windsor Forest*." In Cousins and Derrin 2021: 21–40.

Rompkey, Ronald. 1984. *Soame Jenyns*. Boston: Twayne.

Roper, Alan. 1965. *Dryden's Poetic Kingdoms*. London: Routledge and Kegan Paul.

Roper, Derek. 1978. *Reviewing before the* Edinburgh *1788–1802*. Newark: University of Delaware Press.

Rosbottom, Ronald C. 1974. *Marivaux's Novels: Theme and Function in Early Eighteenth-Century Narrative*. Rutherford, NJ: Fairleigh Dickinson University Press.

Ross, Shawna. 2020. *Charlotte Brontë at the Anthropocene*. New York: State University of New York Press.

Rothstein, Eric and Frances M. Kavenik. 1988. *The Designs of Carolean Comedy*. Carbondale: Southern Illinois University Press.

Rousseau, George S. 1982. "Science Books and Their Readers in the Eighteenth Century." In Rivers 1982: 197–255.

Rudé, George. 1971. *Hanoverian London 1714–1808*. London: Secker and Warburg.

Sabor, Peter and Betty A. Schellenberg (eds.). *Samuel Richardson in Context*. Cambridge: Cambridge University Press, 2017.

Sadleir, Michael. 1961. *Trollope: A Commentary*. London: Oxford University Press.

Saintsbury, George. 1933. *Notes on a Cellar-Book*. New York: Macmillan.

Sanders, Scott M. (2019–20). "Code Noir in Marivaux's Theatre." *Eighteenth-Century Fiction* 32 (2): 271–96.

Sarker, Sunil Kumar. 2007. *A Companion to E.M. Forster*. 3 vols. New Delhi: Atlantic.

Schmidgall, Gary. 1977. *Literature as Opera*. New York: Oxford University Press.

Schofield, Robert E. 1997. *The Enlightenment of Joseph Priestley: A Study of His Life and Work from 1733 to 1773*. University Park, PA: Pennsylvania University Press.

Scott, Nathan A. 1971. *The Wild Prayer of Longing: Poetry and the Sacred*. New Haven: Yale University Press.

Seward, Anna. 1974. *The Poetical Works*. New York: AMS.

Shenstone, William. 1802. *Essays on Men and Manners*. London: C. Cooke.

Shenstone, William. 1939. *The Letters of William Shenstone*. Ed. Duncan Mallam. Minneapolis: University of Minnesota Press.

Shepherd, Lynn. 2017. "The Visual Arts." In Sabor and Schellenberg 2017: 195–204.

Sherburn, George. 1959. "Fielding's Social Outlook." In Clifford 1959: 251–73.

Smail, Daniel Lord. 2008. *On Deep History and the Brain*. Berkeley: University of California Press.

Small, Helen. 2012. "Against Self-Interest: Trollope and Realism." *Essays in Criticism* 62 (4): 396– 416.

Smith, Adam. 1776. *An Inquiry into the Nature of the Causes of the Wealth of Nations*. 2 vols. London: W. Strahan and T. Cadell.

Smith, Adam. 1971. *Lectures on Rhetoric and Belles Lettres*. Ed. John M. Lothian. Carbondale: Southern Illinois University Press.

Smith, Dane Farnsworth and M.L. Lawhon. 1979. *Plays about the Theatre in England, 1737–1800: or, The Self-Conscious Stage from Foote to Sheridan*. Lewisburg, PA: Bucknell University Press.

Smollett, Tobias. 1967. *Humphry Clinker*. Ed. Angus Ross. Harmondsworth: Penguin.

Smollett, Tobias. 1981. *Travels through France and Italy*. Ed. Frank Felsenstein. Oxford: Oxford University Press.

Smollett, Tobias. 1983. *The Adventures of Peregrine Pickle*. Ed. James L. Clifford and rev. by Paul-Gabriel Boucé. Oxford: Oxford University Press.

Smollett, Tobias. 1988. *The Adventures of Ferdinand Count Fathom*. Ed. Jerry C. Beasley. Athens, GA: University of Georgia Press.

Soupel, Serge. 1982. "Science and Medicine and the Mid-Eighteenth-Century Novel: Literature and the Language of Science," *Literature and Science and Medicine*. Los Angeles: Clark Memorial Library: 1–43.

Spacks, Patricia Meyer. 1965. *John Gay*. New York: Twayne.

Stanhope, Philip Dormer, Earl of Chesterfield. *The Letters*. 1892. Ed. John Bradshaw. 3 vols. New York: Charles Scribner's.

Stanhope, Philip Dormer. 1929. *Lord Chesterfield's Letters to His Son and Others*. Ed. R.K. Root. London: J.M. Dent.

Stark, Ryan J. 2009. *Rhetoric, Science, and Magic in Seventeenth-Century England*. Washington, DC: Catholic University of America Press.

Staves, Susan. 1979. *Players' Scepters: Fictions of Authority in the Restoration*. Lincoln: University of Nebraska Press.

Steiner, Wendy. 1988. *Pictures of Romance: Form against Context in Painting and Literature*. Chicago: University of Chicago Press.

Stephen, Leslie and Sidney Smith (eds.). 1908. *Dictionary of National Biography*. London: Smith, Elder & Co. [*DNB*]

Stephens, John Calhoun (ed.). 1982. *The Guardian*. Lexington: The University Press of Kentucky.

Sterne, Laurence. 1940. *Tristram Shandy*. Ed. James A. Work. New York: Odyssey.

Sterne, Laurence. 1983. *The Life and Opinions of Tristram Shandy, Gentleman*. Ed. Ian Campbell Ross. Oxford: Clarendon.

Sterne, Laurence. 1984. *A Sentimental Journey through France and Italy by Mr. Yorick* with *The Journal to Eliza* and *A Political Romance*. Ed. Ian Jack. Oxford: Oxford University Press.

Stevenson, Randall. 2007. "Forster and Modernism." In Bradshaw 2007: 209–22.

Stewart, J. Douglas. 1974. "Pin-ups or Virtues? The Concept of the 'Beauties' in Late Stuart Portraiture," *English Portraits of the Seventeenth and Eighteenth Centuries*. Los Angeles: William Andrews Clark Memorial Library: 3–43.

Stone, Thomas. 1800. *Review of the Corrected Agricultural Survey of Lincolnshire*. London: George Cawthorn.

Stone, Wilfred. 1966. *The Cave and the Mountain: A Study of E.M. Forster*. Stanford: Stanford University Press.

Stoneman, Patsy. 2013. *Charlotte Brontë*. Tavistock, Devon: Northcote House.

Stovel, Bruce. 1996. "'The Sentient Target of Death': Jane Austen's Prayers." In McMaster and Stovel 1996: 192–205.

Sullivan, Alvin (ed.). 1983. *British Literary Magazines: The Augustan Age and the Age of Johnson, 1698-1788*. Westport, CT: Greenwood.

Sultzbach, Kelly Elizabeth. 2016. *Ecocriticism in the Modernist Imagination*. New York: Cambridge University Press. Online Publication.

Swann, George R. 1929. *Philosophical Parallelisms in Six English Novelists*. Philadelphia: University of Pennsylvania Dissertation.

Swift, Jonathan. 1960. *Gulliver's Travels and Other Writings*. Ed. Louis A. Landa. Boston: Houghton Mifflin.

Swift, Jonathan. 1963. *Gulliver's Travels and Selected Writings in Prose and Verse*. Ed. John Hayward. London: Nonesuch.

The Tate Gallery. 1987. *Manners & Morals: Hogarth and British Painting 1700-1760*. London.

Terry, R.C. 1977. *Anthony Trollope: The Artist in Hiding*. Totowa, NJ: Rowman.

Terry, R.C. 1987. *Trollope: Interviews and Recollections*. Basingstoke: Macmillan.

Thackeray. William Makepeace. 1963. *Vanity Fair*. Ed. Geoffrey and Kathleen Tillotson. Boston: Houghton Mifflin.

Thackeray, William Makepeace. 1980. *The Book of Snobs*. Woking: Gresham Press.

The Gentleman's Magazine. 1731–1922.

The London Magazine, or Gentleman's Monthly Intelligencer. 1732–1785.

Thomas, Keith. 1984. *Man and the Natural World: Changing Attitudes in England 1500–1800*. Harmondsworth: Penguin.

Thomson, George H. 1967. *The Fiction of E.M. Forster*. Detroit: Wayne State University Press.

Thompson, James. 1996. *Models of Value: Eighteenth-Century Political Economy and the Novel*. Durham, NC: Duke University Press.

Thornbury, Walter and Edward Walford. n.d. *Old and New London: A Narrative of Its History, Its People, and Its Places*. 8 vols. London: Cassell.

Thorslev, Peter L. 1984. *Romantic Contraries: Freedom versus Destiny*. New Haven: Yale University Press.

Thorslev, Peter L. 1989. "Dialectic and its Legacy." In Gallant 1989: 103–12.

Tillotson, Geoffrey (ed.). 1940. *The Rape of the Lock and Other Poems*. Vol. 2 of *The Twickenham Edition*, ed. John Butt. New Haven: Yale University Press.

Tillotson, Geoffrey, Paul Fussell, Marshall Waingrow and Brewster Rogerson (eds.). 1969. *Eighteenth-Century English Literature*. New York: Harcourt Brace Jovanovich.

Tillotson, Kathleen. 1961. *Novels of the Eighteen Forties*. Oxford: Clarendon Press.

Tinkler, John F. 1988. "Humanist History and the English Novel in the Eighteenth Century." *Studies in Philology* 85 (4): 510–37.

Towheed, Shafquat, Rosalind Crone, and Katie Halsey (eds.). 2011. *The History of Reading: A Reader*. London: Routledge.

Trickett, Rachel. 1967. *The Honest Muse*. Oxford: Clarendon Press.

Trilling, Lionel. 1943. *E.M. Forster*. New York: New Directions.

Tristram, Philippa. 1989. *Living Space in Fact and Fiction*. London: Routledge.

Trollope, Anthony. 1953. *An Autobiography*. Ed. Frederick Page. London: Oxford University Press.

Trollope, Anthony. 1980a. *Barchester Towers*. Ed. Michael Sadleir and Frederick Page with an introduction by James R. Kincaid. Oxford: Oxford University Press.

Trollope, Anthony. 1980b. *Doctor Thorne*. Ed. David Skilton. Oxford: Oxford University Press.

Trollope, Anthony. 1980c. *Framley Parsonage*. Ed. P.D. Edwards. Oxford: Oxford University Press.

Trollope, Anthony. 1980d. *The Last Chronicle of Barset*. Ed. Stephen Gill. Oxford: Oxford University Press.

Trollope, Anthony. 1980e. *The Small House at Allington*. Ed. James R. Kincaid. Oxford: Oxford University Press.

Trollope, Anthony. 1980f. *The Warden*. Ed. David Skilton. Oxford: Oxford University Press.

Trollope, Anthony. 1983. *The Letters of Anthony Trollope*. Ed. N. John Hall. 2 vols. Stanford: Stanford University Press.

Trollope, Frances. 1984. *Domestic Manners of the Americans*. London: Century.

Trowbridge, Hoyt. 1973. "Pope's *Eloisa* and the *Heroides* of Ovid." *Studies in Eighteenth-Century Culture* 3: 11–34.

Trowbridge, Hoyt. 1979. "White of Selbourne: The Ethos of Probabilism." In Backscheider 1979: 79–109.

Tull, Jethro. 1731. *The New Horse-Houghing Husbandry: Or, An Essay on the Principles of Tillage and Vegetation*. London: The Author.

Turner, Thomas. 1985. *The Diary of Thomas Turner 1754–1765*. Ed. David Vaisey. Oxford: Oxford University Press.

Veeser, H. Aram (ed.). 1989. *The New Historicism*. London: Routledge.

Van Til, Marian. 2007. *George Frideric Handel: A Music Lover's Guide to His Life, His Faith & the Development of Messiah and His Other Oratorios*. (Kenya: WordPower)

Waith, Eugene M. 1971. *Ideas of Greatness: Heroic Drama in England*. London: Routledge and Kegan Paul.

Wahl, C. W. "The Fear of Death" in Feifel 1965: 18–25.

Wall, Cynthia Sundberg. [2006] 2014. *The Prose of Things: Transformations of Description in the Eighteenth Century*. Chicago: University of Chicago Press.

Walls, Kathryn. 2021. "The Labours of the Passions in *The Rape of the Lock*." In Cousins and Derrin 2021: 137–152.

Walpole, Horace. 1837. *Correspondence. New Edition in three volumes*. London: Henry Colborn.

Warburton, William (ed.). 1751. *The Works of Alexander Pope*. 9 vols. London: J. & K. Knapton.

Warner, William B. 1979. *Reading "Clarissa": The Struggles of Interpretation*. New Haven: Yale University Press.

Weber, Hélène L. 1971. "E.M. Forster's Divine Comedy." *Renascence* 23: 98–110,

Weimann, Robert. 1974. "Past Significance and Present Meaning in Literary History." In Cohen 1974: 43–61.

Wendorf, Richard. 1981. *William Collins and Eighteenth-Century English Poetry*. Minneapolis: University of Minnesota Press.

Wendorf, Richard. 1983. "*Ut Pictura Biographia*: Biography and Portrait Painting as Sister Arts." In Wendorf 1983, 98–124.

Wendorf, Richard. 1990. *The Elements of Life: Biography and Portrait-Painting in Stuart and Georgian England*. Oxford: Clarendon.

Wendorf, Richard (ed.). 1983. *Articulate Images: The Sister Arts from Hogarth to Tennyson*. Minneapolis: University of Minnesota Press.

Wendt, Allan (ed.). 1965. *Samuel Johnson, A Journey to the Western Islands of Scotland, and James Boswell, The Journal of a Tour to the Hebrides with Samuel Johnson, LL.D.* Boston: Houghton Mifflin.

Wenner, Barbara Britton. 2006. *Prospect and Refuge in the Landscape of Jane Austen*. Aldershot: Ashgate.

West, John. 2018. *Dryden and Enthusiasm: Literature, Religion, and Politics in Restoration England*. Oxford: Oxford University Press.

White, Gilbert. 1949. *The Natural History of Selbourne*. Ed. R.M. Lockley. London: Dent.

Wilcox, John. 1939. *The Relation of Molière to Restoration Comedy*. New York: Columbia University Press.

Wilde, Alan. 1964. *Art and Order: A Study of E.M. Forster*. New York: New York University Press.

Williams, Kathleen. 1958. *Jonathan Swift and the Age of Compromise*. Lawrence: The University Press of Kansas.

Williams, Raymond. 1973. *The Country & the City*. London: Chatto and Windus.

Williamson, Tom. 1995. *Polite Landscapes: Gardens and Society in Eighteenth-Century England*. Stroud, Gloucestershire: Sutton Publishing.

Winborn, Colin. 2004. *The Literary Economy of Jane Austen and George Crabbe*. Aldershot: Ashgate.

Winn, James A. 1979. "Pope Plays the Rake: His Letters to Ladies and the Making of the *Eloisa*." In Erskine-Hill and Smith 1979: 89–118.

Winn, James Anderson. 1981. *Unsuspected Eloquence: A History of the Relations between Poetry and Music*. New Haven: Yale University Press.

Wood, Nigel (ed.). 2007. *She Stoops to Conquer and Other Comedies*. Oxford: Oxford University Press.

Woodforde, James. 1978. *The Diary of a Country Parson 1758–1802*. Ed. John Beresford. Oxford: Oxford University Press.

Wright, Andrew. 1975. "Anthony Trollope as a Reader." In *Two English Novelists*. Los Angeles: William Andrews Clark Memorial Library: 43–68.

Wright, Elizabeth. 1989. *Postmodern Brecht: A Re-Presentation*. London: Routledge.

Young, Arthur. 1770a. *A Course of Experimental Agriculture*. 2 vols. London: J. Dodsley.

Young, Arthur. 1770b. *Rural Oeconomy: Or, Essays on the Practical Parts of Husbandry*. London: T. Beckett.

Young, Arthur. 1793. *The Example of France, a Warning to Britain*. London: W. Richardson.

Young, Arthur (ed.). 1785. *Annals of Agriculture, and Other Useful Arts*. Vol. 4. London: The Editor.

Young, Edward. 1969. *Conjectures on Original Composition*. In Tillotson *et al* 1969: 871–89.

Younger, Wiliam. 1966. *Gods, Men, and Wine*. London: Joseph.

Zimbardo, Rose A. 1986. *A Mirror to Nature: Transformations in Drama and Aesthetics 1660-1732*. Lexington: University Press of Kentucky.

Zirker, Malvin R. 1966. *Fielding's Social Pamphlets*. Berkeley and Los Angeles: University of California Press.

Zwicker, Steven N. 1972. *Dryden's Political Poetry: The Typology of King and Nation*. Providence, RI: Brown University Press.

Zwicker, Steven N. 1984. *Politics and Language in Dryden's Poetry: The Art of Disguise*. Princeton, NJ: Princeton University Press.

Printed in the USA
CPSIA information can be obtained
at www.ICGtesting.com
CBHW080726120724
11410CB00014B/534

9 781039 187535